Staging a Comeback

Staging a Comeback

Broadway, Hollywood, and the
Disney Renaissance

PETER C. KUNZE

RUTGERS UNIVERSITY PRESS
NEW BRUNSWICK, CAMDEN, AND NEWARK, NEW JERSEY
LONDON AND OXFORD

Rutgers University Press is a department of Rutgers, The State University of New Jersey, one of the leading public research universities in the nation. By publishing worldwide, it furthers the University's mission of dedication to excellence in teaching, scholarship, research, and clinical care.

Library of Congress Cataloging-in-Publication Data

Names: Kunze, Peter C. (Peter Christopher), author.

Title: Staging a comeback : Broadway, Hollywood, and the Disney renaissance / Peter C. Kunze.

Description: New Brunswick : Rutgers University Press, [2023] | Includes bibliographical references and index.

Identifiers: LCCN 2022060835 | ISBN 9781978827813 (paperback) | ISBN 9781978827820 (hardcover) | ISBN 9781978827837 (epub) | ISBN 9781978827844 (pdf)

Subjects: LCSH: Musical films—United States—History and criticism. | Walt Disney Company. | Disney Theatrical Productions. | Animated films—United States—History and criticism. | Musicals—United States—History and criticism. | Musical theater—United States—History—20th century. | Stage adaptations—United States

Classification: LCC PN1995.9.M86 K86 2023 | DDC 384/.806579493—dc23/eng/20230522

LC record available at https://lccn.loc.gov/2022060835

A British Cataloging-in-Publication record for this book is available from the British Library.

References to internet websites (URLs) were accurate at the time of writing. Neither the author nor Rutgers University Press is responsible for URLs that may have expired or changed since the manuscript was prepared.

rutgersuniversitypress.org

For Mom and Dad
Thank you for letting me burst out into song.

Contents

Introduction   1

1   "Just Waiting for the Prince to Arrive": Broadway and Hollywood before the Disney Renaissance, 1982   23

2   "Sort of Like the Sopranos Took Over the Studio": Regime Change at Disney, 1983–1986   45

3   "Make the Audience Fall in Love with Ariel": Howard Ashman and Alan Menken, *The Little Mermaid*, and Disney, 1987–1989   68

4   "A Celebration of Certain Sensibilities": Howard Ashman and Alan Menken, *Beauty and the Beast*, and Disney, 1990–1991   92

5   "Like the Old-Fashioned Musicals Did": Robert Jess Roth, *Beauty and the Beast*, and Disney, 1992–1994   114

6   "I Don't Do Cute": Julie Taymor, *The Lion King*, and Disney, 1994–1998   136

Conclusion   159

Acknowledgments   171
Notes   175
Index   209

Staging a Comeback

Introduction

On February 3, 2020, Lin-Manuel Miranda tweeted a major announcement: the Walt Disney Company had acquired the worldwide distribution rights for the live capture of *Hamilton* in one of the costliest deals in Hollywood history. Disney's interest in *Hamilton* should come as no surprise to observers. The live capture would provide potentially sizable revenues during its initial theatrical run and subsequent release on the company's newly launched streaming service, Disney+. Furthermore, no media company has invested—and influenced—Broadway theatre more in recent decades than Disney has.[1] In 1981, Walt Disney Productions partnered with established stage producers Nelle Nugent and Elizabeth I. McCann, in the hopes that the theatrical workshops it was bankrolling might be developed into film projects. Walt Disney Theatrical Productions (now part of Disney Theatrical Group), the company's theatrical producing unit, has staged full-scale Broadway shows since 1994, mostly based on Disney's animated properties, including *Beauty and the Beast* (Gary Trousdale and Kirk Wise, 1991), *Aladdin* (John Musker and Ron Clements, 1992), *The Lion King* (Rob Minkoff and Roger Allers, 1994), and *Frozen* (Chris Buck and Jennifer Lee, 2013). Even Miranda himself has worked for Disney, composing music and lyrics for *Moana* (John Musker and Ron Clements, 2016) and then starring in *Mary Poppins Returns* (Rob Marshall, 2018). With *The Lion King* on Broadway as well as the *High School Musical* and *Frozen* franchises, Disney remains a powerful champion of the Broadway musical on stages, television sets, and film screens around the world. Yet this interest is far from a side project for the company. In fact, musicals helped to fuel Disney's "renaissance," bolster its diminished reputation, and reestablish its cultural influence both domestically and globally.

After years of poor creative decisions and decreased media production in the wake of its namesake's 1966 death, Walt Disney Productions desperately needed a renaissance. In the early 1980s, the studio produced a limited number of feature films and television programs. Indeed, the theme parks proved to be the company's major source of revenue during this period, especially after feature animation nearly ground to a halt following the dramatic 1979 exit of Don Bluth and a team of animators over leadership and quality concerns. Ron Miller, Walt's son-in-law and the company's president, publicly lamented the restrictions imposed on him by the company's family-friendly brand, but Disney's board, especially chairman and CEO Card Walker, insisted on maintaining the company's reputation for offense-free entertainment: "I know the marketplace is changing, but that doesn't mean we have to provide things we don't approve of."[2] In 1984, amid threats of a hostile takeover, Roy Disney and fellow board member Stanley Gold launched an effort to remove Miller and bring in new executive management: Michael Eisner from Paramount and Frank Wells from Warner Bros. Along with Jeffrey Katzenberg, Eisner's former right-hand man at Paramount, the men focused on what they knew best—live-action feature production, maintaining feature animation only at the insistence of Roy Disney. Katzenberg, in particular, insisted upon tight control over film production—especially film budgets—often favoring modestly priced comedies with affordable stars and directors who complied with Katzenberg's close oversight. What followed was an impressive decade of prosperity, including the flourishing of Touchstone Pictures, the establishment of Touchstone Television and Hollywood Pictures, and the acquisition of Miramax. In a period characterized by mergers, acquisitions, and hostile takeovers, Disney protected itself by focusing on fiscal conservatism, internal development, and strong, tight storytelling.

But while live-action filmmaking may have been what initially propelled the company forward, it was the rejuvenation of the animation division that ultimately energized contemporary Disney. The company's animated efforts since Walt Disney's death, including *Robin Hood* (Wolfgang Reitherman, 1973) and *Pete's Dragon* (Don Chaffey, 1977), had often faced a mixed reception due to what film critics sometimes saw as poor production values and weak storylines. But with the 1984 arrival of Disney's new executive team came a revised approach to feature animation production partly brought on by the hiring of talent from the theatre, including lyricist Howard Ashman and composer Alan Menken as well as managers and executives Maureen Donley, Kathleen Gavin, Peter Schneider, and Thomas Schumacher. Today, the Ashman-Menken musicals stand as highlights of this period that established Disney as a major film studio and initiated the company's transformation into a diversified entertainment conglomerate with global reach and influence. Miranda himself admits in the press release accompanying the 2020 Disney/ *Hamilton* deal, "I fell in love with musical theatre storytelling growing up with the legendary Howard Ashman–Alan Menken Disney collaborations."[3] This sentiment resonates with many contemporary musical theatre composers, including Benj Pasek, the lyricist for the stage musical *Dear Evan Hansen* and the film musical *The Greatest Showman* (Michael Gracey, 2017), who states, "It was our gateway drug for everything. The first movie that I ever saw in a theater was *The Little Mermaid*. A big part of why [musicals] are alive and well right now is because an entire generation grew up with their first stories being musicals and not even knowing that they were consuming musical theater."[4]

TABLE 1

DISNEY ANNUAL REVENUES, 1980–1995

Year	Theme Parks and Resorts	Filmed Entertainment	Consumer Products	Total Revenue
1980	$643,380,000	$171,965,000	$99,160,000	$914,505,000
1981	$691,811,000	$196,806,000	$116,423,000	$1,005,040,000
1982	$725,610,000	$202,102,000	$102,538,000	$1,030,250,000
1983	$1,031,202,000	$165,458,000	$110,697,000	$1,307,357,000
1984	$1,097,359,000	$244,552,000	$109,682,000	$1,655,977,000
1985	$1,257,517,000	$319,986,000	$122,572,000	$2,015,429,000
1986	$1,523,900,000	$511,700,000	$130,200,000	$2,470,900,000
1987	$1,834,200,000	$875,600,000	$167,000,000	$2,876,800,000
1988	$2,042,000,000	$1,149,200,000	$247,000,000	$3,438,200,000
1989	$2,595,400,000	$1,587,600,000	$411,300,000	$4,594,300,000
1990	$2,933,200,000	$2,250,300,000	$573,800,000	$5,757,300,000
1991	$2,794,300,000	$2,593,700,000	$724,000,000	$6,112,000,000
1992	$3,306,900,000	$3,115,200,000	$1,081,900,000	$7,504,000,000
1993	$3,440,700,000	$3,673,400,000	$1,415,100,000	$8,529,200,000
1994	$3,463,600,000	$4,793,300,000	$1,798,200,000	$10,055,100,000
1995	$3,959,800,000	$6,001,500,000	$2,150,800,000	$12,112,100,000

Source: Disney annual reports.

Howard Ashman and Alan Menken cowrote songs for only three Disney films: *The Little Mermaid*, *Beauty and the Beast*, and *Aladdin*.[5] Despite this limited output, the impact of these movies in generating revenue for Disney and enriching its brand remains undeniable. The trio reignited Disney's interest in the animated musical and in films about and for girls, in particular, which continues to this day with the recent success of the *Frozen* franchise. *Mermaid* was Disney's first princess fairy tale in thirty years, helping to reassert Disney's dominance in feature animation and relaunch the Disney princess films, which remain one of the world's most profitable media franchises.[6] *Beauty* catalyzed Disney's foray into theatrical production not only on Broadway but through professional sit-down and touring productions as well as licensed amateur, school, and regional productions. By the release of *Aladdin*, Disney's investment in consumer products had expanded to the point that the division offered over four thousand *Aladdin*-related merchandise items.[7] Based on its success, filmed entertainment surpassed the theme parks

Figure 1. Lyricist Howard Ashman, orchestrator Danny Troob, and composer Alan Menken supervise a recording session for *Beauty and the Beast* (1991). Credit: Author's screenshot.

as the company's profit center in 1993 for the first time in years. Collectively, these films reoriented the Disney Renaissance away from the live-action efforts of Touchstone and toward the previously moribund animation division. While historians too often treat *Mermaid* as the turning point, it more accurately represents a significant moment within a period of artistic development at Disney Animation, arguably beginning with *The Great Mouse Detective* (John Musker, Ron Clements, Dave Michener, and Burny Mattinson 1986), continuing through *Who Framed Roger Rabbit* (Robert Zemeckis, 1988), and peaking with the release of *The Lion King*. Subsequent animated releases achieved critical and commercial success, but none of them matched its box office performance and cultural impact.

The Renaissance also reaffirmed the company as a leader in media franchising as it strategically exploited its intellectual property across its divisions with theme park attractions, consumer products, films, television series and specials, and, of course, theatrical entertainment. In a period of considerable corporate growth, Disney avoided being acquired by becoming a global entertainment conglomerate in its own right.[8] This period marks the resurgence and expansions of business practices and storytelling strategies that inform much of contemporary media production, including the seeming omnipresence of remakes and reboots, franchise storytelling, and the tentpole mentality.

The animated features that drove the second phase of the Disney Renaissance resulted from a coordinated effort across a well-staffed creative team—most trained in animation, some in feature film production, others in theatrical production. But all of them were committed to a tradition of Disney animation many critics and audiences alike felt had lost its luster in recent years. As Charlie Fink, former head of story, observed in 2022, "All of us at the time did not think what we were doing had historic importance, which was part of the reasons the movies were so good.

It was that they were made out of humility and gratitude and respect."[9] Perhaps the most recognizable figures in that group were Ashman and Menken, who underscore the significant impact of theatrical talent at Disney during a crucial period of transition. While the spectacular British megamusical reigned on Broadway, Ashman and Menken—who never had a show together premiere on Broadway during Ashman's lifetime—brought the Golden Age–era integrated musicals of Richard Rodgers and Oscar Hammerstein II (*Oklahoma!, Carousel, South Pacific*) and Alan Jay Lerner and Frederick Loewe (*Brigadoon, My Fair Lady, Camelot*) to the Walt Disney Company (its name since 1986, previously Walt Disney Productions). As this book argues, their contributions provided the desperately needed expertise to revive Disney animation through musical theatre storytelling. However, despite Ashman and Menken's pivotal role in the corporation's rebirth, most popular and scholarly accounts have focused on and credited the executive leadership of Michael Eisner, Frank Wells, and Jeffrey Katzenberg.[10] This narrative sidelines and ignores the creative contributions of such people as Ashman and Menken—"micro-level" input that media industry scholars have long argued is vital to understanding the "macro" processes of corporate entertainment empires. *Staging a Comeback: Broadway, Hollywood, and the Disney Renaissance* historicizes Disney's hiring of musical theatre talent for the animation division as well as its adaptation of its animated musical properties for the stage. And it does so by reasserting the importance of producers, directors, screenwriters, songwriters, and animators who powered the Disney Renaissance, including several women and gay men who were crucial to saving an institution of American entertainment but often have been sidelined in subsequent accounts of the company's revitalization. Their collected, collaborative labor helped to sustain what has become one of the greatest second acts in the history of the U.S. entertainment industries.

For almost three decades now, the notion of a "Disney Renaissance" has circulated widely among fan communities, industry insiders, and even Disney itself. Disney fans and scholars alike generally demarcate the "renaissance" as the period from *The Little Mermaid* (1989) to *Tarzan* (Chris Buck and Kevin Lima, 1999), specifically grounding it in the animation division. An early application of "renaissance" appears in CEO Michael Eisner's 1986 letter to shareholders in which he calls his tenure's initial successes an "early indication of an enormous reawakening at Disney, a renaissance sure to occur when talented new people blend their fresh ideas with our company's traditional values."[11] Touchstone Films, a production company aimed at making adult-targeted entertainment that Walt Disney Productions launched just months before the new executive team's arrival, became the cornerstone of the new Disney, producing low-budget hit comedies *Splash* (Ron Howard, 1984), *Ruthless People* (Jim Abrahams, David Zucker, and Jerry Zucker, 1986), and *Down and Out in Beverly Hills* (Paul Mazursky, 1986) and, through the related television unit, *The Golden Girls*. The press began referring to a "Disney renaissance" as early as 1988, when *USA Today* used the term in an article reporting Eisner's impressive compensation.[12] By the early 1990s, however, it was clear that the renaissance—both commercially and creatively—was based not in live-action film-making but in *animated* feature production. James B. Stewart asserts that Disney knew an animation renaissance was underway soon after the songwriting team of Alan Menken and Howard Ashman won two Oscars for *The Little Mermaid* in March 1990.[13] In 1991, Eisner informed stockholders that *Beauty and the Beast* had salvaged a rather disappointing year for the company in other divisions,[14] and the cover of the 1992 annual report announced "The New Golden Age of Animation" and featured characters from the three Ashman-Menken musicals. Indeed, the Disney Renaissance was part of a larger renaissance in animation across film, television, even video games in the 1980s and 1990s, including Saturday morning cartoons, syndicated television animation, prime-time animation such as *The Simpsons*, and the films of Don Bluth.

The Disney Renaissance discourse deserves closer scrutiny for various reasons. First, it continues Disney's long tradition of crafting its own history—or, perhaps more appropriately, hagiography.[15] Beginning in 1954, the *Disneyland* television series allowed Walt Disney to manipulate his studio's history so as to brand and market Walt Disney Productions' creative efforts, specifically the films and theme park.[16] Disney's theatrical reissue of its animated features every seven years prop-agated the notion that its films were time-honored classics. By restricting access to its animated films in the "Disney Vault" and releasing them periodically on home video for a limited time only, the company actively fostered a legacy aura around these movies throughout the 1980s and 1990s. To this day, Disney uses its theme park attractions, coffee-table books, feature films, and documentaries to promote a romanticized interpretation of its past and reinforce the Disney magic. Second, Janet Wasko observes that Disney histories often conceal the company's operations in favor of glorifying its "genius" founder as well as its creative output.[17] Media historians, therefore, must navigate the Disney-produced historical account while situating the company's and its employees' efforts within larger corporate and industrial contexts.

Equally important, the Disney Renaissance discourse rhetorically positions the Michael Eisner era as one of rebirth while simultaneously casting the years after Walt's death as a veritable Dark Ages, both financially and creatively. To be fair, the managerial team of Michael Eisner, Frank Wells, and Jeffrey Katzenberg obviously were integral to the company's impressive comeback. But Walker's and Miller's administrations made decisions that would immensely benefit their successors, including the establishment of EPCOT, the Disney Channel, and Touch-stone Films. Team Disney built on these savvy investments by producing live-action comedies for adults that jump-started the company's domestic box office performance, while the blockbuster success of the animated films in the early 1990s reestablished the company as the leader in family entertainment. John Taylor, an early chronicler of company's tumultuous recovery, admitted the executives' incredible feat: "In a matter of months, Eisner and Wells had transformed Walt Disney Productions almost beyond recognition."[18] In *Prince of the Magic Kingdom:*

Michael Eisner and the Re-making of Disney (1991), Joe Flower proclaimed, "But whatever its future, Disney's rescue and turnaround, with Michael Eisner as its prince, is one of the great business bedtime stories."[19] Media scholars have mostly followed suit in acknowledging the executive leadership's transformational impact.[20] This narrative, whether written by Disney itself or by others, is tidy, self-aggrandizing—and incomplete.

Emphasizing the role of the executives in a Disney Renaissance ultimately centered in the animation division, journalists and scholars have omitted the contributions of creative personnel—most obviously the animators—in reha-bilitating Walt Disney Company. Of course, those operating in the highest offices at Disney made crucial business decisions and shaped that major renewal. But it was nurtured to no small degree by the creative and managerial laborers working across the company in above- and below-the-line positions.

Staging a Comeback argues that theatre, often perceived as a minor part of Dis-ney's corporate operations, nevertheless played an integral part in the animation renaissance during the late 1980s and early 1990s and therefore the company's rise to its current prominence.[21] Even though Disney executives attempted to turn the company around through live-action filmmaking, they realized by 1992 that ani-mation was generating far greater revenues at the box office, on home video, and through merchandising and licensing, laying the foundation for highly profitable entertainment franchises that continue to be a major profit center for the company. This book follows earlier scholarly histories of media convergence through deeper industrial contextualizing "to note relations among and between the various sites of information and entertainment."[22] In so doing, this cross-media history, in the words of Mark Williams, will "bring into relief significant but often overlooked visions and determinants of media history."[23] In this instance, the supposedly unmediated theatre played an energizing role in revitalizing the lagging media company.

Scholars have framed convergence from a range of critical vantages, including media, economic, technological, and industrial. But quite often, convergence is motivated and sustained by the labor of individuals moving between industries. Individual agency was central to early understandings of media convergence, such as Henry Jenkins's discussions of fandom in *Convergence Culture: Where Old and New Media Collide*, but the movement of media laborers across or among indus-tries also facilitates the aforementioned forms of convergence that scholars study more readily. Cari McDonnell argues that the film musical was developed in large part by individuals, both creative and executive, based in or contributing to other media industries. Therefore, to historicize the genre in an industrial context, scholars must acknowledge that film musicals are situated within "a web of rela-tionships among film, radio, recording, and music publishing."[24] Furthermore, as David Savran explains, the stage musical as a popular entertainment remains "first and foremost a product of the marketplace in which the aesthetic is always—and unpredictably—overdetermined by economic relations and interests."[25] The same thinking can be applied to the musical's filmic iteration. To understand the Disney Renaissance and the animated musicals that have come to define it, this book traces the creative significance of theatre on their production. Furthermore, it also historicizes the influence of the Hollywood film industry on the contemporary stage musical and Broadway as an entertainment industry.

If we follow Michele Hilmes in her assertion that convergence is the "very hall-mark of modern media,"[26] then such an approach to writing history is essential to understanding the revitalization of Disney during this period of diversification and conglomeration. Following Hilmes's lead, Jennifer Holt observes that media analy-sis "must view film, cable, and broadcast history as integral pieces of the same puzzle."[27] As entertainment conglomerates increase their investments and hold-ings in live entertainment, we must broaden our understanding of "media culture" to include theme parks, concerts, sports, and, of course, the commercial theatre. Media scholars might perceive theatre as unmediated by definition, but Philip Auslander demonstrates that live performance is, in fact, heavily mediatized.[28] For example, when someone goes to see *The Lion King* on Broadway, that experi-ence is likely mediated by their knowledge of the film version. Having an awareness of the show's narrative trajectory becomes particularly useful for comprehend-ing the more experimental aspects of Julie Taymor's innovative production. Con-temporary uses of microphones, speakers, and video projections further mediate live theatrical entertainment. Relatedly, Jonathan Burston explores how pro-duction practices from Hollywood have contributed to "cinematizing" the the-atre,[29] while work by Greg Giesekam and David Saltz, among others, examines the role of film, video, and new media in theatre and performance culture.[30] Partly inspired by digital culture, theatre and performance studies has reframed and theorized theatre as a medium in its own right.[31]

The defining distinction between film and theatre as media, which inspired foundational theoretical work by Vsevolod Pudovkin, Erwin Panofsky, André Bazin, and Susan Sontag, has become increasingly tenuous in an age of new media technologies and vertical integration.[32] Evidence suggests that film and theatre have informed how each other commercially operates since the very beginnings of the film industry,[33] as recent historical work has explored the narrative and industrial intersections of film and theatre.[34] This media and industrial convergence contin-ues in innovative and boundary-defying ways. Yet the history of Broadway and Hollywood, or the entertainment industries more generally, has been largely neglected since Robert McLaughlin's 1974 economic history.[35] (The few excep-tions include work by Jonathan Burston and Laura E. Felschow on Broadway and Hollywood as well as by Kelly Kessler on Broadway and U.S. television, in particu-lar.)[36] The mentioned research provides productive inroads for future scholarship, and the complex exchange between Hollywood and Broadway warrants critical attention to uncover one of the most important yet still underexamined interin-dustrial relationships in contemporary U.S. entertainment. This book traces one of the most important historical shifts for both film and theatre and Hollywood and

Broadway: the exchange of talent and narrative strategies from theatre to Disney filmmaking and later from Disney filmmaking back to theatre. By contextualizing this relationship in the larger history of Broadway and Hollywood, I build upon received accounts of Disney's relationship with Broadway while also charting significant artistic and economic developments in both industries that continue to shape twenty-first-century media culture. Understanding the Disney Renaissance in an interindustrial context also reveals a period of critical change for both Hollywood and Broadway, as both industries mobilized digital technologies, franchise storytelling, and a tentpole mentality to develop their current production practices and business operations.

———

Writing this form of industrial history requires navigating around various roadblocks. Like many Hollywood studios, Disney closely guards its corporate archives.[37] Scholars must either cooperate with Disney's strict guidelines or employ alternative approaches to understand its business operations. *Staging a Comeback* utilizes a range of methods and materials to narrate Disney's revitalization in the 1980s and 1990s and the company's developing role in both Hollywood and Broadway during this transitional period. This book is one of the first to make extensive use of the papers of lyricist and producer Howard Ashman, animator Don Bluth, journalist Bob Thomas, and screenwriter Linda Woolverton—all housed in publicly accessible archives beyond Disney's control. This is further enriched by trade and press coverage as well as published interviews with Disney personnel, which provide necessary perspectives on corporate decisions and creative labor. Discourse analysis on Disney-created materials, including press kits and annual shareholder reports, reveals a wealth of production and industrial information to understand how film and theatre production unfolded, how the entertainment industries both endured and changed, and how Disney responded in turn. Finally, new interviews and correspondence with a range of film and theatre workers, many of whom were directly involved, helps to address perceived gaps in published and archival materials. What hopefully becomes evident is a more complete account of the Disney Renaissance that also illustrates the complexity of Broadway and Hollywood's relationship in recent decades.

Disney's initial entrance, current position, and enduring effect on Broadway remain significant for the commercial theatre industry both domestically and globally, yet the extant discussions often reveal disciplinary limitations. Musical theatre scholars, for instance, rarely have contextualized Disney within a larger series of corporatized theatrical efforts at the time, led by Cameron Mackintosh, Andrew Lloyd Webber and the Really Useful Group, and Garth Drabinsky and Livent.[38] Media studies scholars who examine Disney's theatrical endeavors in their discussion and critique of the conglomerate's business activities often do not account for other media companies' efforts to move into the commercial theatre market before or during the same period, including Warner Theatre Productions, Universal Pictures (later Universal Theatrical Group), and, more recently, Sony (as Columbia

TABLE 2

BROADWAY ANNUAL PERFORMANCE, 1980–2000

Season	Gross	Attendance	New Productions
1980–1981	$197,000,000	11,010,000	64
1981–1982	$223,000,000	10,150,000	48
1982–1983	$209,000,000	8,400,000	53
1983–1984	$230,000,000	8,070,000	37
1984–1985	$209,000,000	7,250,000	39
1985–1986	$191,000,000	6,540,000	38
1986–1987	$208,000,000	7,050,000	48
1987–1988	$253,000,000	8,140,000	35
1988–1989	$262,000,000	7,950,000	36
1989–1990	$282,000,000	8,040,000	40
1990–1991	$267,000,000	7,310,000	29
1991–1992	$293,000,000	7,380,000	37
1992–1993	$328,000,000	7,860,000	34
1993–1994	$356,000,000	8,120,000	41
1994–1995	$406,000,000	9,040,000	34
1995–1996	$436,000,000	9,470,000	41
1996–1997	$499,000,000	10,570,000	34
1997–1998	$558,000,000	11,480,000	38
1998–1999	$588,000,000	11,670,000	33
1999–2000	$603,000,000	11,390,000	39

Source: The Broadway League.

Live Stage) and Annapurna Theatre. Warner's and Universal's efforts in the 1970s and 1980s, for example, were to develop properties for film production. In the 1990s, Disney inverted that formula by taking its film properties to the stage. Studying the Walt Disney Company through its film and theatre productions requires scholars to resist the ongoing critical tendency to treat Disney as exceptional. Disney succeeds and Disney fails, but it is always does so in relation to industry trends, which it alternately inspires, refines, or rejects.

Entertainment conglomerates' renewed interest in theatrical production in recent years stems not only from Disney's achievements on Broadway but from its success producing national and international tours as well as licensing regional, community, and school productions.[39] In studying Disney or media companies more generally, scholars must pay greater attention to the vital role of site-specific, live, and supposedly "unmediated" experiences in the corporate endeavors of the major entertainment conglomerates. Site-specific entertainment obviously has been important for Disney at least as far back as the opening of its first theme park in 1955. As Eric Smoodin reminds us, the construction of Disneyland "did not simply send [Walt Disney's] products—the films, for instance—out to the public. Instead, the public came to him, to one location."[40] These initiatives increase in a media age largely dependent on developing and maintaining entertainment franchises. And live performance—especially what Donald Crafton calls "performative branding"[41]—has become vital for entertainment conglomerates as they exploit these media franchises to their fullest potential. In so doing, such performances further the cultural afterlife of these properties while maximizing its ability to generate revenues in perpetuity. Perhaps more problematically, these licensed productions also introduce branded content into traditionally noncommercial spaces, such as community centers and schools. Theatre remains a vital extension of the franchising logics that define and dominate modern media production. A close study of the relationship between Disney and Broadway underscores the value of a cross-disciplinary, multimethod approach to convergence media history that aims to trace the origins and map the influence of this often underestimated facet of contemporary U.S. media culture.

———

As a historical study of the Disney Renaissance, *Staging a Comeback* highlights the network of stakeholders and decision makers, both executive and creative, who reinvigorated Disney during this important moment in its corporate history and in film history. The critical and commercial successes of media cultural products are rarely the result of visionary management or media creators alone but instead arise from the nuanced interactions among individuals across varying levels of authorial control—and even their audiences, real or imagined.

Studying feature animation foregrounds the complexities of film authorship that persist across all filmmaking. Each of Disney's animated features implicitly demonstrates the storytelling and stylistic contributions of animators, songwriters, performers, technicians, and executives, even though their individual input is subtly erased to brand the final product as a "Disney film." As Peter Schneider observed in 2019 about his time at Disney, "It's not a collective, but a collaboration—a collective means it's equal democratically but in a collaboration [it] is about how do you find the best idea for any particular moment and that is also a process of rejecting and to some extent allowing all the bad ideas to be expressed."[42] For instance, one of the most celebrated moments in Disney animation is the "Be Our Guest" sequence in *Beauty and the Beast*. In early drafts of the screenplay, the Enchanted Objects were supposed to sing this song to Maurice, Belle's father, upon his arrival at the castle. It was animator Bruce Woodside who suggested that it should be sung to Belle instead.[43] This casual suggestion, of course, reassigned the function of the song within the narrative and reshaped the final sequence. It also serves as a reminder that what we see on screen, whether live action or animated, is far more than the creative efforts of the screenwriter, the performer, and the director but rather represents a network of media workers with varying levels of influence and input. Film authorship, especially commercial film authorship, is not singular but plural—and networked, with varied and fluctuating levels of authority and control. As John Thornton Caldwell asserts, "Negotiated and collective authorship is an almost unavoidable and determining reality in contemporary film/television."[44] Reorganization in Disney animation in this time shifted authorial control away from the animators toward a complex network of contributors that also included theatrically trained talent serving as producers, composers, lyricists, and screenwriters.

Ashman was one of many talents that Disney placed under contract in the mid-1980s, when the company actively sought out inexpensive creative talent, often from theatre and television, but also established Hollywood directors and stars in a career slump. Years before Disney "invaded" the Great White Way with *Beauty and the Beast* in 1994, Disney hired theatrical talent—not just Ashman and Menken, but Maureen Donley, Kathleen Gavin, Pam Marsden, Peter Schneider, and Thomas Schumacher, all of whom took on managerial positions in the animation division. For his part, Schneider has admitted he restructured the division in a manner similar to repertory theatre: "You have a group of actors, animators in this case, who are cast correctly, and you have a director. And they are required to act within the frameworks of each of these pictures and that is very much like a resident theater company."[45] As Gavin, whom Schneider worked with at Chicago's St. Nicholas Theatre Company before he hired her as a manager for Disney animation, recounts, "If I'm proudest of anything, it's that we really gave people the opportunity to grow and the opportunity to do things they hadn't done before."[46] This management style converged with the Disney approach to animation, later taught at the Walt Disney–cofounded California Institute of the Arts (CalArts), in which animators understood what they did as a form of performance in its own right, which Donald Crafton has called *"embodied acting."*[47] And Howard Ashman, along with his songwriting partner, Alan Menken, renewed Disney's interest in the animated musical by applying the Broadway-honed tradition of the integrated musical to their Disney animated projects. Schumacher later observed that Ashman, in particular, "was able to cajole and educate Jeffrey into what makes great musical theater."[48] This unlikely union of animation and theatre—described by Donley in 2022 as a "weird, often uncomfortable mix of two cultures pretty much getting forced together"—cooperated to reinvent the production process and mode of storytelling behind Disney feature animation to align with live-action production while remaining artistically distinctive.[49]

Staging a Comeback follows media industry histories in its attention to below-the-line labor and its move away from "great man" narratives.[50] The temptation surely lies here to elevate Ashman as the visionary voice behind the Disney Renaissance. Cynthia Erb, Sean Griffin, and Sam Baltimore have written on Ashman's contributions to Disney, and I build upon their work to highlight his interactions with the larger creative team and contextualize the Disney Renaissance amid wide-scale industrial transformations in Hollywood and Broadway.[51] Michele Hilmes admits the "individual author approach" provides numerous benefits to historians, including a clear and limited focus, period, and narrative.[52] But by turning to the industry rather than the individual, one acknowledges "a concern for the creative forces of production behind the range of communicative texts and objects that comprise our field of analysis."[53] Thomas Schatz expresses similar concerns when he argues that auteur-focused approaches neglect industrial context, the collaborative nature of filmmaking, and the organization of labor throughout production.[54] Neither Hilmes nor Schatz wants to dispel with individual agency in creative production; rather, it remains central to the study of the media industries and the culture it produces. Schatz proposes a model of film industry analysis that considers style, authorship, and mode of production interchangeably.[55] Considering the available technologies and production practices alongside a network of creative, managerial, and executive personnel situates these films within both Disney's cumulative output as well as the standards and expectations that shaped Hollywood films during this pivotal period. It becomes clear upon closer examination that the distinctions between the creative, managerial, and executive workers become harder to parse out, as leaders like Jeffrey Katzenberg follow a creative executive approach exemplified by Irving Thalberg, David O. Selznick, and—of course—Walt Disney himself. Now in 2023, with talent regularly moving back and forth between Hollywood and Broadway under the aegis of the Walt Disney Company, one can more easily see the long-standing instability of the boundaries between film and theatre as storytelling media and as entertainment industries.

———

To explain the industrial exchange between Hollywood and Broadway, I focus on the way theatrical talent working at Disney innovated storytelling and narrative structure in animated musicals. While I cite research on Disney music, a musicological analysis of Menken's work is beyond the scope of my project.[56] This is also not a biography of Howard Ashman, though he is a worthy subject. Instead, I primarily draw upon the papers of Ashman to examine how the stories were structured and characters were developed in the films they worked on together. Political economists studying the media industries traditionally have focused on institutional and industrial structures, but I follow the lead of media industry scholars Michele Hilmes and Thomas Schatz to examine how texts reflect larger industrial trends and changes while also providing a way into how the industry itself works.[57] Furthermore, in her analysis of Miramax, Alisa Perren asserts that studying one division of a major media conglomerate allows scholars "to balance the 'top-down' concerns of political economy with the 'bottom-up' perspective of cultural studies."[58] In the process, she argues, scholars can redress the neglect of individual agency in industry practices and cultural production.

To demonstrate the contributions of theatrical talent as well as the exchange of production practices between industries, I turn to what I call "craft theory"—that is, the ways that artists understand, theorize, and explain what they do as creative laborers.[59] Traditional academic work theorizes media based on the completed text and using its own critical apparatus, but craft theory interprets creativity via craft as formulated and understood by the artists themselves. As John Thornton Caldwell reminds us, "Theorizing about the screen is far from confined to the academy."[60] In that spirit, "craft theory" is thinking through creative labor and textual inter- pretation via the concepts, practices, beliefs, and values that structure artistic praxis in film and across the entertainment industries. Creative laborers, like all artists, learn these principles in school, via apprenticeships or training programs, and through trial and error, and this acquired knowledge provides essential guidelines to follow or to consciously violate in the production of culture.

This is not theory determined by scholars from and for the close study of cultural products; it is fashioned through the very process of creation, its suc- cesses and failures, and it informs the day-to-day work that creative laborers undertake and the training of new generations of practitioners. We may under- stand craft theory through what Caldwell has called "*critical industrial practices*," a phrase that underscores the critical thinking behind creative labor.[61] "Craft the- ory" endows creative laborers with a degree of authority on set; this ready access to a body of technical knowledge allows them to have their say, earn respect, and garner power and control. Here I employ it to understand the nature of their cre- ative labor and interpret their cultural productions. Consequently, Ashman was not a singular creative genius inspired by some unexplainable force but rather a creative laborer who consciously worked within and through a well- established—and well-theorized—artistic tradition of musical theatre composi- tion. We can historicize and appreciate his work at Disney while also acknowledging its clear demonstration of craft.

Perhaps no concept within the craft theory of theatrical production has been more instrumental, contentious, yet enduring for musical theatre professionals than the "integrated musical." This supposed ideal imagines the musical, accord- ing to Broadway conductor Lehman Engel, as "a form which seeks to integrate drama, music, and dance, the qualities of all its elements must hang together; and what they must hang upon are the characters and action they have been created around."[62] Through his teaching and his writing (most notably, his 1972 book *Words with Music*), Engel theorized how the stage musical worked from a practitioner's point of view to offer "a set of viable principles that govern the working machin- ery."[63] Without these principles, Engel asserts, talent loses its utility and value. Understanding how a musical works provides both guidelines and restrictions to steer artists' practice and capitalize upon their abilities.

In over two hundred pages, Engel lays out the features, function, and defining characteristics of the U.S. stage musical. Its characters must be broad, recognizable, and sympathetic, as the musical generally leaves minimal time for complex charac- terization and development.[64] Speech and song are interdependent, and both are "integrated so as to share an equal importance with the other principal elements."[65] The songs, in turn, are written to the character and are "based on the communication of *feeling*, not of pure ideas."[66] Characters must be quickly introduced, then placed in an uncertain, but navigable, situation so that "we care to see them safely out of it."[67] A romance is at the center of the story, by necessity, though comedy is an indispensable component as well.[68] In combination, these various elements—song, drama, dance, and design combined with relatable characters, romance, and comedy—produce "the total effect."[69] Engel's almost dogmatic insistence upon these principles is explained through various exemplars, including *The King and I*, *My Fair Lady*, and *West Side Story*, as well as shows he designates as critical and commercial failures because of their deviations from these expectations.

Not only was he Howard Ashman's mentor, but Engel was also Alan Menken's instructor at the legendary BMI musical theatre workshop that now bears his name. Engel's influence here cannot be overstated: Ashman dedicated the published libretto of *Little Shop of Horrors* to Engel, while Menken asserts "it was when I joined the workshop that I really began to learn the craft of writing for the theater."[70] Although not an official workshop member, Ashman went on to espouse the integrated musical tradition during his brief tenure in the animation division at Disney. In April 1987, with *Mermaid* now in production, he called in the animators for an instructive talk on the history of the Broadway musical and the inner workings of the integrated musical, in particular.[71] Ashman's championing of this narrative form was so influential that Pixar animators subsequently tried to avoid it—and met resistance from studio consultants reviewing early drafts of their screenplays.[72] Ashman's time at Disney was tragically cut short by his 1991 death from AIDS-related complications, but even today, his lessons about the integrated musical remain evident in Disney's "live-action remakes" as well as recent animated features *Frozen*, *Moana*, and *Coco* (Lee Unkrich and Adrian Molina, 2017).

The "integrated musical," as indicated by Engel's use of "the total effect," appears to draw in part upon Richard Wagner's conceptualization of *Gesamtkunstwerk*—that is, the "total artwork"—in two 1849 essays, "Die Kunst und die Revolution" ("Art and Revolution") and "Das Kunstwerk der Zukunft" ("The Art-Work of the Future"). Wagner argues that the highest aesthetic achievement would be the successful integration of all the major artistic elements into one ultimate work of art. This synthesis was attainable in opera, perceived to be the superior art form: "The highest conjoint work of art is the *Drama*: it can only be at hand in all its *possible* fulness, when in it each *separate branch of art* is at hand in *its own utmost fulness*."[73] The ideal, however, has not gone unchallenged. Theodor Adorno, for example, criticized how it erased the labor of individual artists in the creative process.[74] Despite concerns like these, the idea of music and narrative cooperating for increased dramatic effect profoundly influenced film and theatre. Furthermore, as Bradley Rogers has noted, the association between integration and opera made it an appealing strategy for legitimating musical theatre as an art form since opera possesses a prestige that musical theatre, as a popular art, traditionally lacks.[75] Musical theatre artists employed the integration ideal in part to rescue the form from the popular perception of it as a frivolous entertainment and to reframe it as a serious artistic endeavor. Matthew Wilson Smith, in his study of *Gesamtkunstwerk* and its cultural afterlife, observes how the ideal is both artistic and political, rife with nationalist implications.[76] Furthermore, Andrea Most demonstrates that linking *Gesamtkunstwerk* and the emerging form of the Broadway musical allowed Jewish theatre artists to imagine the possibility of both empowerment and assimilation.[77] The musical, therefore, celebrates a national fantasy of community and belonging—one that is challenging to achieve in reality, but easy to market to audiences.[78]

As the integrated musical developed on Broadway, Walt Disney arguably contributed by integrating songs as storytelling devices into his animated fairy tales. Indeed, Disney strongly believed animators should have training in music to assist in animating character movement.[79] One can see in the films he produced a clear attempt to elevate animation as an art form through the use of music, most obviously through the incorporation of classical music in *Fantasia* (James Algar, Samuel Armstrong, Ford Beebe Jr., Norman Ferguson, David Hand, Jim Handley, T. Hee, Wilfred Jackson, Hamilton Luske, Bill Roberts, Paul Satterfield, and Ben Sharpsteen, 1940). Scholars have applied to this Wagnerian ideal to Disney before: Christopher Anderson to Walt Disney's development of the *Disneyland* series and Matthew Wilson Smith to Disneyland itself.[80] I extend this application by arguing the Disney Renaissance's revival of the animated musical offered integration and synergy at the textual level as well as across the company.

Walt Disney himself experimented with music in animated storytelling as early as *Steamboat Willie* (Walt Disney and Ub Iwerks, 1928), although the characters do not sing but whistle instead. Comments by animator Wilfred Jackson suggest that Walt Disney brought Hammerstein's interest in integrating music and storytelling to his work in animated shorts: "I do not believe there was much thought given to the music as one thing and the animation as another. I believe we conceived of them as elements which we were trying to fuse into a whole new thing that would be more than simply movement plus sound."[81] Similarly, *Show Boat* composer Jerome Kern reportedly stated in 1936, "Cartoonist Walt Disney has made the 20th century's only important contribution to music. Disney has made use of music as language. In the synchronization of humorous episodes with humorous music, he has unquestionably given us the outstanding contribution of our time."[82] Of course, we clearly see film animation adapt musical theatre conventions in *Snow White and the Seven Dwarfs* (David Hand, 1937), in which Snow White, the Prince, and the titular dwarves express themselves through song.[83] Although scholars of the stage and screen musical have taken the animated musical more seriously in recent years, the history of how the Disney animated musical coincides and converges with the rise of the integrated stage musical remains to be written.[84]

Scholars John Mueller and Geoffrey Block have offered generative outlines for understanding integration in the film and stage musical, respectively. Mueller proposes a useful taxonomy for assessing the relationship between the film's plot and its musical numbers, including (1) no connection between musical number and plot, (2) song furthers a theme or the "spirit" of the plot, (3) musical numbers "whose existence is relevant to the plot, but whose content is not," (4) musical numbers that enrich without advancing the plot, (5) musical numbers that move the plot forward despite the song's content, and (6) true integration.[85] Drawing on the work of Rodgers and Hammerstein, Block infers the following values behind stage musical integration: the song must emerge from the dialogue and further the storyline, revealing the character who sings it in the process; the dances also perform narrative labor by underscore the songs' meaning; and the orchestra similarly serves the plot through accompaniment and underscoring.[86] In short, the elements should cooperate to co-express the plot in a way that is (more or less) logical and seamless. As Engel insists, "For a musical show to succeed as an artistic entity (also, invariably, as a commercial one), all of its collaborative parts must work together."[87] Yet the degree of integration in any musical remains subject to debate. My interest here rests not so much on how well-integrated Disney animated musicals are but on the fact that Ashman and Menken understood what they were doing as applying the form's conventions to animation in order to produce integrated musicals. As Menken explains, "Your job is to enlist the audience in a journey that, first of all, has a dramatic tension to it, that can be driven through music and through song and through concept, but also more than the concept, the passionate desires of the characters earn being musicalized. And, of course, Disney has a great advantage in that you are dealing with highly charged fairy tales or stories with an exaggerated emotional profile to them—unabashedly. And how you support that is enormously important."[88] The integrated musical, as a craft theory honed among theatre professionals and reintroduced into Disney musicals by Ashman and Menken, reinforced an important creative, narrative, and industrial connection between Broadway and Hollywood that endures to this day.

In terms of the feature-length film musical, Mueller points to Fred Astaire's films in the 1930s as landmarks of an integrated musical tradition distinct from the musical revue.[89] *Oklahoma!*, the initial stage collaboration between Richard Rodgers and Oscar Hammerstein II, was celebrated as a turning point for its use of a distinctly U.S. musical idiom as well as Agnes de Mille's folk choreography. From *Oklahoma!* (1943) until at least Rodgers and Hammerstein's final show together, *The Sound of Music* (1959), the integrated musical experienced a Golden Age and dominated musical theatre storytelling as the exemplar to follow.[90] Scholars also have criticized the familiar narrative of *Oklahoma!*'s groundbreaking significance for its reductive understanding of musical theatre storytelling.[91] Rodgers himself admitted "everyone suddenly became 'integration'-conscious, as if the idea of welding together song, story and dance had never been thought of before."[92] Block offers the most detailed account of integration's introduction, development, and supersession by the concept musical. His historicization accounts for the importance of choreographer George Balanchine, choreographer Busby Berkeley, and composer Cole Porter, whose respective formal contributions have been traditionally underplayed in favor of Rodgers and Hammerstein.[93] Even artists have challenged this history, including Engel, who dates the form back at least as far as early operetta and John Gay's 1728 musical comedy *The Beggar's Opera*.[94] More recently, George C. Wolfe's

2016 metamusical *Shuffle Along, or, the Making of the Musical Sensation of 1921 and All That Followed* reasserted the role Black artists played in shaping the integrated musical through an examination of Eubie Blake, Noble Sissle, F. E. Miller, and Aubrey Lyles's 1921 show *Shuffle Along*. Despite these heavily debated histories, the integrated musical remains both an artistic model for creating musical theatre and a common evaluative heuristic for reviewing new productions.

Scholars have also debated the ultimate value of celebrating narrative and musical integration in film and stage musicals. In 1978, Margaret M. Knapp observed that theatre historians privileged integrated musicals, even though such shows represent only one part of the history of U.S. musical theatre.[95] In recent years, numerous musical theatre critics and scholars have followed Knapp's lead and thoroughly challenged the concept and valorization of the integrated musical.[96] For example, Scott McMillin insists "the crackle of difference," not integration, makes for an excellent stage musical.[97] He contends that the dramatic impact of the stage musical emerges not from the integration of the show's book and its musical numbers but from the deliberate juxtaposition—"the tension between two orders of time, one for the book and one for the numbers."[98] Although Rick Altman views integration as a well-intentioned link between theory and history, he nevertheless argues the model "champions a standard of realism which I believe to be antithetical to the spirit of the genre as a whole."[99] Since artifice is inherent to animation as a form and the musical as a genre, the forms converge more readily—and believably. For this reason, Menken noted in 1989 that Ashman felt "animation is one of the last bastions of musical theater."[100] In *Staging a Comeback*, the aforementioned scholars as well as practitioners Engel and Ashman are given equal footing for understanding the musical as a narrative form. Again, I am interested not in assessing how effectively integrated the Ashman-Menken musicals are but rather in how Ashman and Menken understood and explained what they were doing as theatrically trained craftspeople at Disney. As a result, the role that creative laborers played in reinvigorating Disney filmmaking and, by extension, the company as a whole becomes clearer and harder to ignore.

In historically contextualizing the Disney Renaissance, *Staging a Comeback* employs an alternative time frame—1982 to 1998—not so much to correct the periodization of the Disney Renaissance but to show how a longer timeline brings to the fore factors and forces that have been previously underestimated or neglected. In so doing, I reconfigure the role of executives Michael Eisner and Jeffrey Katzenberg as able collaborators and facilitators rather than the sole visionaries behind the company's transformation. Creative labor, so often obscured through skillful collaboration or through marketing and branding, is placed front and center to underscore the invaluable contributions of such workers in enabling corporate innovation and industrial convergence.

The first chapter focuses on 1982 as a veritable *annus mirabilis* during which four seemingly unrelated premieres—two animated films from Hollywood and two stage musicals near/on Broadway—laid the groundwork for the future of Disney. In the summer, Don Bluth's initial effort, *The Secret of NIMH*, posed the first serious challenge to Disney's dominance of feature animation in a generation. Unwilling to compromise its weakening stronghold, Disney moved up *Tron* (Steven Lisberger, 1982) to compete head-on with Bluth's film. Meanwhile, off Broadway and downtown, a musical version of the cult B-movie *The Little Shop of Horrors* (Roger Corman, 1960) with music by Alan Menken and lyrics by Howard Ashman transferred from the Off-Off-Broadway WPA Theatre to the Off-Broadway Orpheum Theatre. (Generally speaking, Off-Off-Broadway theaters can have up to 99 seats and Off-Broadway venues up to 499 seats; Broadway houses usually have 500 or more seats.) The show's producers now included Cameron Mackintosh and David Geffen, the latter of whom would introduce Ashman to Katzenberg in a few years when Disney was seeking fresh talent. *Little Shop* was not Mackintosh and Geffen's only triumph that year: in September, Andrew Lloyd Webber's *Cats* transferred from the West End of London and became a smash hit at the Winter Garden Theatre on Broadway. Although seemingly disparate, *The Secret of NIMH*, *Tron*, *Little Shop of Horrors*, and *Cats* collectively laid the foundation for Disney's comeback as the company recommitted itself to feature animation and musical theatre storytelling, explored computer animation, and pursued commercial theatrical production.

Chapter 2 considers Disney after *Tron* and up until the hiring of Howard Ashman in 1986 to examine how the animation division struggled through the first half of the 1980s, where Disney was at immediately before the arrival of Team Disney, and how they managed this increasingly convoluted situation. Katzenberg's attention was largely focused on live-action comedies, and similar to that aspect of the company, he enforced tight budgets and even tighter executive and managerial control on feature animation so that its modes of production more closely aligned with live-action filmmaking. He also hired employees who would respect his authority and be amenable to his creative demands and modest salaries, including theatre talent, such as Ashman and Menken. Far from seeing its potential upon their arrival, Eisner and Katzenberg were slow to realize animation's importance and profitability.

The next two chapters foreground *The Little Mermaid* and *Beauty and the Beast*, respectively, to more closely examine the trajectory of Ashman and Menken within the animation division. Chapter 3 examines their arrival at Disney, including the production and premiere of *The Little Mermaid*. This chapter traces the development of *Mermaid* as a musical and the collaboration between the animators and Ashman and Menken under Katzenberg's supervision. Together, they reenvisioned storytelling and production practices at Disney Animation not by proposing new approaches in line with contemporary Broadway theatrical production but by returning to the traditional model of integrated musical theatre storytelling promoted by Lehman Engel. Chapter 4 narrates how Disney expanded Ashman's creative control, in particular, on *Beauty and the Beast*. Reconceived from the ground up as an integrated musical, *Beauty* works to blend musical and dramatic modes to tell a fully realized story. The creators' narrative approach not only led to a commercial and critical success but compelled Disney's decision to produce a Broadway show, inspired by the business models developed by Mackintosh, Lloyd Webber, and Drabinsky.

With a special focus on the Broadway production of *Beauty and the Beast*, I detail Disney's business endeavors from 1991 to 1994 in chapter 5. By this time, Disney had fully realized that its renaissance was unfolding within animation, not live-action, filmmaking, where its successes were less unpredictable. Broadway offered yet another market to dominate, and Disney mostly used its own people to enter the industry with *Beauty* in 1994. Blending traditional integrated musical storytelling with the business practices developed by producers of the megamusical, Disney made a considerable—and controversial—impression on the commercial theatre industry.

The company continued to hone its approach to theatrical production on Broadway with the development and 1997 premiere of *The Lion King*, as I discuss in chapter 6. Learning the lessons from its initial effort on Broadway, Disney announced plans to lease and renovate the derelict New Amsterdam Theatre. The company also hired avant-garde director Julie Taymor to reconceive and stage *The Lion King* in the hopes it would curry favor among critics and popular audiences alike. The Broadway community embraced the final result, and Disney replicated the show and toured it worldwide. Bolstered by Taymor's vision and credibility, *The Lion King* affirmed Disney as a formidable presence on Broadway. The popularity of animated integrated musical and cel animated features slowly began to wane with film audiences, replaced by the digitally animated efforts of Pixar and DreamWorks.

The conclusion briefly examines the recent history of Disney, Broadway, and Hollywood, where evidence suggests the enduring legacy of Ashman's years at Disney remains relevant to the conglomerate's media culture. Of course, Disney does not simply get by on Broadway, it triumphs. *The Lion King* and *Aladdin* have been among the top grossing shows for years, joined by a stage adaptation of *Frozen* in 2018. Relatedly, *Beauty and the Beast* closed on Broadway in 2007, but the success of the live-action remake of the animated film in 2017 has laid the groundwork for a stage revival in the near future. It also continues in numerous regional and amateur productions. One area where Disney's brand has curiously expanded: licensing for community productions of shows, including one-hour stage versions of its tales for child performers under its Disney JR. label.[101] In fact, the Ashman-Menken musicals *The Little Mermaid* and *Beauty and the Beast* were respectively the ninth and fifth most frequently performed high school musicals in the United States in the 2021–2022 school year, while their 1982 show, *Little Shop of Horrors*, ranked seventh.[102]

———

Disney theatre has gone from being a creative and financial experiment to representing an important dimension of the company's franchising efforts. It allows Disney to exploit its creative property, promote its brand, and develop new talent for future collaboration on stage and screen. Along with Lin-Manuel Miranda, Disney has employed several members of a new generation of theatre talent—Kristen Anderson-Lopez, Robert Lopez, Benj Pasek, and Justin Paul—to write songs for its film division. Alan Menken, who has collaborated with many of them in his ongoing work at Disney, observes, "[Howard Ashman's] children are taking over the world, and they're wonderful."[103] Ironically, the dazzling musicals that Disney now produces on Broadway and the big screen could not be further from the intimate musicals that Ashman and Menken started out writing for Off-Off-Broadway productions in the 1970s. Yet Ashman's careful attention to complex characterization, clever and thematically revealing lyrics, and tight, structured plots continues to resonate throughout Disney's products, be it in its animated films, its theme park entertainment, or its Broadway stage shows. The Ashman and Menken influence synthesizes a nostalgic allegiance to the classical Disney animated musical and an artistic, intellectual, and professional investment in the Broadway integrated musical—a form that Disney has shrewdly capitalized upon in a manner characteristic of a diversified, globalized entertainment conglomerate.

This study of theatre talent at Disney and Disney on Broadway focuses predominantly on the musical because Broadway then and today privileges musicals over plays. In fact, new dramas and smaller musicals often are produced by nonprofit theaters, while commercial Broadway is dominated by long-running, large-scale musical productions.[104] Thomas Schumacher, the former animation producer who now leads Disney Theatrical Group, corroborates this observation: "We need to create shows that are franchisable and large enough to justify the level of support we have to give them on a continuing basis."[105] The crucial role that the integrated musical has played for Disney, both as a storytelling form and as an economic opportunity, underscores the equally vital role that theatre talent has played in the company's history over the past thirty years. And Disney's presence on Broadway has catalyzed the ongoing industrial shift toward large-scale musicals and event-style theatrical entertainment. While Disney's efforts on Broadway are its most visible theatrical effort, the theatre division is generating revenue from sit-down, touring, regional, and school productions of its shows around the world.

Hollywood and Broadway have a complex history of competition and cooperation that in an age of media conglomeration appears to be stronger than ever. Historicizing the Disney Renaissance allows for an in-depth examination of a crucial transitional period for this ongoing relationship. In a mainstream U.S. culture seemingly dominated by media franchising, theatre plays a crucial role in brand management, transmedia storytelling, and audience engagement for Disney. That process inspires a number of theoretical and methodological questions. How has creative labor in Hollywood and on Broadway driven change over the past four decades? How might animated film musicals be understood through the theatrical models that inspired its creators? How might theatre prompt a reexamination of the boundaries and concerns of media studies, especially as new media technologies proliferate and entertainment conglomerates continue to invest in live entertainment?

Staging a Comeback answers these concerns while narrating a crucial period whose influence continues to resonate at Disney, on Broadway, and across U.S. media culture. This book examines the significant part theatrical talent played in revitalizing Disney media entertainment as well as the impact of the company on theatre by situating this exchange amid the intersecting histories of Broadway and Hollywood. I carefully examine the movement of personnel, modes of storytelling, and production practices between the industries rather than writing a convergence media history that focuses exclusively on economic or technological convergence alone. In so doing, I show how the Disney Renaissance was a return to musical storytelling and to the "total merchandising" strategy, in which film provided characters and stories that could be ably exploited by the other divisions.[106] This important precedent to the transmedia storytelling of the conglomerate era finds renewed vitality in an age of media convergence that, in many ways, also marked a return to studio system-style organization and management at Disney.

Hollywood and Broadway may have a relationship as old as Hollywood itself, but understanding how they intersect in the late twentieth and early twenty-first centuries requires attention not only to corporate structures but to creative praxis, as media laborers facilitate this convergence as much as business deals or technological innovation. In so doing, the importance of not just the executives but the producers, directors, screenwriters, actors, and animators, among many others, to the formidable resurgence of Disney as a power player in Hollywood and across the entertainment industries in the 1980s and 1990s becomes clear. In this spirit, this book draws heavily upon their own words from published accounts and interviews as well as interviews I have recently conducted. *Staging a Comeback* attests to the vital contribution of live entertainment within the operations of "media" conglomerates. At the same time, however, it also demonstrates how the distinction between film and theatre remains tenuous in an age of media conglomeration and industrial convergence.

CHAPTER 1

"Just Waiting for the Prince to Arrive"

BROADWAY AND HOLLYWOOD BEFORE THE DISNEY RENAISSANCE, 1982

The Disney Renaissance has rarely been questioned in depth by scholars, though passing reference to it, of course, appears throughout film history, whether in discussions of the Walt Disney Company, contemporary Hollywood, or animation histories. Unsurprisingly, the periodization of the Disney Renaissance has varied considerably depending on the scholar's focus as well as the extent of the discussion. In his history of Disney feature animation, Chris Pallant identifies 1989 to 1999 as the Renaissance period, bookended by the release of *The Little Mermaid* and *Tarzan*.[1] Maureen Furniss, in her textbook *A New History of Animation*, follows a similar trajectory of 1989 to 1999—roughly the perceived change in Disney's attitude toward feature animation with *The Little Mermaid* to a reevaluation of 2D animation around the releases of *Tarzan* and *Toy Story 2* (John Lasseter, 1999).[2] Sam Baltimore does not offer a firm periodization, instead referring to the Disney Renaissance as "the 1980s–1990s run of musicals from a new generation of animators that reinvigorated the studio's animation division" and beginning with *Mermaid*.[3] These three examples are representative of a general acceptance of when the so-called Renaissance began, a narrative that has been untraced and unchallenged—and reinforced by Disney itself.

In part the issue with the received understanding of the Disney Renaissance is its overattention to one division: animation. A closer examination that focuses on Walt Disney Productions (later, the Walt Disney Company) demonstrates that the roots of the renaissance were not in animation at all but in live-action feature production as well as the theme park division. While *The Little Mermaid* makes for a convenient turning point for Disney animation, one can see in interviews with Disney personnel as well as trade and popular press coverage at the time that nearly every Disney animated film of the 1980s was being heralded by the studio, animators, executives, journalists, and/or film critics as a new day for the division. Centering animation within the Disney Renaissance arguably does not come until after

Beauty and the Beast, and a historicization of the period using press coverage, archival research, and interviews with the participants shows the emergence to be gradual, marked by a range of forces, setbacks, and unexpected developments. Writing a history of the Disney Renaissance that not only shows the continuity with the so-called Dark Ages created by the Renaissance discourse but takes a company-wide perspective in tracing the development readily complicates received understandings of Disney's turnaround, its leaders, and its motivations.

This study begins in 1982 not in an effort to argue that the Renaissance started seven years earlier but to demonstrate that it did not begin in 1989. My focus on 1982—and more specifically on four cultural productions, two in theatre and two in film—offers a window into the pre-Renaissance period while also situating what is to come amid developments, trends, discourses, logics, and production practices taking place and unfolding within two major commercial entertainment industries in the United States. A good deal of the thinking, creative work, and business strategies so often credited to the executives comprising "Team Disney" were common practices prior to their 1984 hiring. Rather than any kind of decisive break marked by new management, the arrival of Team Disney—and their strategic self-representation of their arrival—allowed the executives and the company to manufacture the renaissance narrative that so many scholars uncritically accept today.

While 1982 is a seemingly unexceptional year in the history of Disney, it does provide necessary context for the creative future of the company when studied from the vantage of film and theatrical convergence. In July 1982, former Disney animator Don Bluth released his first animated feature, *The Secret of NIMH*, since he and a group of animators dramatically resigned from the company in 1979. Backed by Aurora Productions, a company founded by former Disney executives, *NIMH* posed the first real threat in decades to Disney's dominance in feature animation. Not to be bested, Disney moved up the release date of its own latest effort, the video-game-inspired film *Tron*, so that the planned holiday release could instead compete head-on with Bluth's inaugural effort. Yet both were easily outperformed by Universal's summer blockbuster, *E.T. the Extra-Terrestrial* (Steven Spielberg, 1982), which went on to become Hollywood's highest grossing film to date.

At the end of the month, in New York City, a small musical based on *The Little Shop of Horrors* transferred from the WPA Theatre to a bigger venue, the Orpheum Theatre in the East Village. Produced by David Geffen, Cameron Mackintosh, and the Shubert Organization, *Little Shop* was a welcome throwback to the musicals of the 1940s and 1950s in terms of its form, but its music drew upon doo-wop and rock music to create a nostalgic smash with tongue-in-cheek black humor. The modest production would run for five years, making it still one of the longest and most profitable shows in Off-Broadway history. It also introduced many theatergoers and industry professionals to the work of composer Alan Menken and lyricist Howard Ashman, who also served as the WPA Theatre's artistic director. Meanwhile, the same producing team and Andrew Lloyd Webber's Really Useful Group were preparing a major production for Broadway: the transfer of Lloyd Webber's *Cats* from the West End in London, where it would take over the Winter

Garden Theatre for the next eighteen years. Unlike *Little Shop*, *Cats* defied a tight plot in favor of loosely connected songs, each employing a poem from T. S. Eliot's *Old Possum's Book of Practical Cats* (1939) to introduce a different feline character. Compared to the small, simple set of *Little Shop*, *Cats* was large-scale spectacle. Just as *Jaws* (Steven Spielberg, 1975) had helped bolster high-concept entertainment in Hollywood, *Cats* brought a similar mentality to the Broadway stage in the form of the "megamusical."[4] With a large set, a tuneful score, varying dance styles, big emotions, and a thin plot, *Cats* allegedly revolutionized what a musical could and should be, and the entertainment on and audience for Broadway supposedly changed forever in the process.[5] But as David Savran reminds us, "innovation in musical theatre is more likely to be revision than revolution."[6] Theatre critics and historians have often discussed the success of *Cats* with either ambivalence or derision, but in fact *Cats* was representative of various trends in commercial theatrical production at the time. The show typified then elevated a mode of production developing internationally long before its Broadway debut.

Seemingly, these four premieres were unrelated and of varying importance to their production companies and respective media, yet in the history of film and theatre convergence, they set the stage for what arguably remains one of the greatest comebacks in the history of the U.S. entertainment industries. In so doing, these productions vitally contributed to the future of Disney and the enduring relationship between film and theatre. In order to understand what Disney narratively does in *The Little Mermaid* and *Beauty and the Beast*, we need to think about what was happening in the film and theatre industries as well as how those trends in storytelling, modes of production, and industrial logic inform, converge, and operate within Disney's own cultural production. In 1982, we see that the roots of Disney's resurgence predate Eisner, Wells, and Katzenberg. While they may have steered the ship, the executive team benefited considerably from creative contributions, business decisions, and industrial shifts that forever changed U.S. film and theatre production and consumption during this period and, arguably, initiated our current media culture.

Despite its hallowed status as an U.S. cultural institution, Broadway has long operated at a loss, primarily salvaged through tax credits and write-offs. In 1938, George S. Kaufman and Moss Hart wrote an homage to their beloved Broadway titled *The Fabulous Invalid*—and the derisive nickname has remained ever since. A 1977 *New York Times* article reported as many as 80 percent of all Broadway productions fail to return backers' investments.[7] Relatedly, by the late 1960s, box office business began to decline, and within a few years many perceived the Times Square area as a den of iniquity, as theaters were deserted and subsequently converted into adult movie theaters. The presence of sex workers and sex shops increased exponentially, replacing restaurants and theatre craftspersons' workshops.[8] At the same time, New York City in general and Times Square in particular became a safe haven for the young as well as the marginalized. This tension between the interests of the city's most powerful and its most disenfranchised for control over Times Square's economics and culture would play out into the 1990s. Despite the elite's misgivings, economists William J. Baumol and Hilda Baumol found that the Broadway theater contributed nearly $250 million to the metropolitan and national economies during the 1974–1975 season alone, including both the industry's direct contributions as well as theatergoers' patronage of ancillary services, including taxis, parking, and restaurants.[9] Without a doubt, Broadway was indispensable to both the economy and the culture of the city, and it began to show promise again by the 1975–1976 season with numerous hit plays and theaters booked solid.

Although new and established plays received positive attention, the season truly belonged to musicals. *The Wiz*, an adaptation of *The Wizard of Oz* with R&B and soul music by Charlie Smalls and starring an all-Black cast, opened in January, followed by Bob Fosse's production of the John Kander and Fred Ebb musical *Chicago* that June. A month later, director/choreographer Michael Bennett's *A Chorus Line*, featuring music by Marvin Hamlisch and lyrics by Edward Kleban, opened at the Shubert Theatre, where it would make its home for the following fifteen years, becoming the longest running Broadway musical at the time. These shows demonstrated a marked departure from the traditional fare—bold, revisionist takes that pushed the Broadway musical to exhibit a greater diversity of talent (*The Wiz*) and to explore themes of violence, sexuality, and oppression (*A Chorus Line* and *Chicago*). Stacy Wolf observes that the major musicals of the 1970s, to which she adds *Company* and *Godspell*, experimented with tone and musical style and "exhibit[ed] the contradictory impulses that characterize the 1970s: an increased concern with one's self and growing engagement with social issues."[10] In particular, the Broadway musical was targeting younger audiences in ways it had not before, with shows by, about, and for young adults and featuring more rock, R&B, and jazz scores.

The increasing presence of rock music on Broadway also necessitated new technologies, as amplification became crucial with the introduction of electronic instruments into the orchestra. This development, in turn, required microphones to help actors project over the rock music in shows like *Hair*, *Godspell*, and the Andrew Lloyd Webber and Tim Rice import *Jesus Christ Superstar*. Microphones had begun to appear on the Broadway stage after World War II, but rock musicals as well as the casting of talent untrained in vocal projection increased the need for amplification.[11] Since many Broadway theaters dated back to the early twentieth century, they were not architecturally prepared for such acoustics without significant, costly retrofitting.

This electronic mediation prompted what we might call a "medium anxiety"—a growing nervousness even fear that a medium will be compromised or corrupted by technological innovation or formal experimentation adopted from another medium. Amplification was disparaged as a degradation of live theatre by actors, writers, and theatergoers alike. Harold C. Schonberg argued that it creates "generally awful" sound with "little to no feeling of directionality."[12] In 1986, playwright David Mamet opined that theatre "cannot be delivered conversationally and then amplified—that is not *drama*, that is *television*."[13] In an age of mediated sound, many felt that the theater lost the intimacy and immediacy that separated it from the cinema.[14] Of course, as Philip Auslander later demonstrated, the introduction of mediatization to the performing arts retroactively created the perception and virtue of liveness in the first place.[15]

Mediation was not the only issue plaguing Broadway's loyal customer base. As the box office grosses reached an impressive $70.8 million (from $57.4 million the year before), so too did ticket prices, which neared a startling $20 for the best seats in the house.[16] One reason for this surge rested in increasing production costs, especially with the returning popularity of spectacle in stage productions. Whereas *Hair*, *Company*, and *A Chorus Line* were fairly modest in their production design, several stage musicals of the late 1970s featured extravagant set pieces, costumes, and special effects. Harold Prince's direction of Stephen Sondheim and Hugh Wheeler's *Sweeney Todd* and then Andrew Lloyd Webber and Tim Rice's *Evita*, both in 1979, demonstrated his interest in both operatic-scale presentation and Brechtian aesthetics. Geoffrey Holder's production of *Timbuktu!*, a resetting of the earlier musical *Kismet* in imperial Mali, featured orange costumes and elaborate choreography. Holder himself proclaimed, "We have a world situation in which we need spectacle," and Bernard Jacobs, one of the heads of the Shubert Organization, a theater-owning outfit, concurred, "Spectacle is coming back—absolutely."[17] Some commentators connected this newfound optimism— and extravagance—to the zeitgeist of late 1970s America, but that soon took a turn (along with the economy). One of the biggest musicals of the 1979–1980 season, for example, was the nostalgic burlesque romp *Sugar Babies*, starring Mickey Rooney and Ann Miller. Broadway was treading cautiously, wary of large expenditures and risky new endeavors. Economists had long argued that entertainment is usually the last industry hit and the first to recover from economic downturns.[18] Although John Houseman argued that show business thrives in "bad times," bold innovation in U.S. theatre at the time seemed fairly limited, especially on the heavily commercialized Great White Way.[19] The lack of risk taking by producers as well as the flight of talent to other entertainment industries, however, posed their own problems.

Nevertheless, Hollywood demonstrated a renewed interest in Broadway as both a venue for developing and trying out new material and a division within a growing entertainment conglomerate. Under Dramatists Guild guidelines, companies that produced theatrical plays and musicals would have first refusal on film rights. Universal produced the 1978 musical *The Best Little Whorehouse in Texas* as well as *Nuts*, Tom Topor's play that was later acquired by Barbra Streisand's production company as a vehicle for the star. (*Nuts* initially premiered at the WPA Theatre.) Paramount funded a workshop of Maury Yeston's *Nine*, a musical adaptation of *8½* (Federico Fellini, 1963). They also bankrolled several successful stage productions, including the musical *My One and Only*, featuring Ira and George Gershwin music and starring Tommy Tune and Twiggy, and the original Broadway run of John Pielmeier's *Agnes of God* in 1982. Columbia backed perhaps the most unusual star vehicle: *Merlin*, an Arthurian musical featuring magician Doug

Henning. Warner Communications made the most extensive investment, hiring Broadway producer Claire Nichtern to head its theatrical division, Warner The-atre Productions. One of her earliest projects for WTP was a musical adaptation of Kurt Vonnegut's *God Bless You, Mr. Rosewater*, written by first-time collabora-tors Howard Ashman and Alan Menken. Although it had thrived in the intimate venue of the WPA Theatre, where Nichtern first saw it, it lost some of its charm when it hastily moved to a larger Off-Broadway house, the Entermedia Theater.[20] Nichtern continued to pursue creative properties with a spirited commitment to corporate synergy, telling the *New York Times* in 1982, "I want to option the play, sell the movie rights to Warner, the cable television rights to Warner-Amex, the music to Warner Bros. music publishing and Warner Bros. records, the toys to Knickerbocker and the games to Atari."[21] Under her supervision, Warner opened almost twenty new productions over the next three years, including *Crimes of the Heart*, *The Dresser*, and Kander and Ebb's musical adaptation of the MGM film *Woman of the Year* (George Stevens, 1942), with Lauren Bacall taking on the lead.

Rather than open a theatrical division, Disney decided in 1981 to partner with successful Broadway producers Elizabeth I. McCann and Nelle Nugent to develop some dramatic properties. Disney quickly worked to capitalize on this new cre-ative association by running a two-page announcement in *Daily Variety* on July 22, 1981, featuring graphics from McCann and Nugent's major stage productions, including *Amadeus* and *The Elephant Man*, underscored by "You can understand why we wanted to be part of this producing team's future." At the bottom of the advertisement, next to Disney's signature logo, a slogan—"Entertaining new ideas for the future"—played on the meaning of "entertaining" to signal that the com-pany was open to new projects and partnerships. The only production to make it to Broadway was *Total Abandon*, a Larry Atlas play about a father who brutally beats his toddler but then fights to have him taken off of life support. Disney financed the workshop at the Perry Street Theatre, but not the 1983 Broadway pro-duction. As Tom Wilhite, head of creative development for Disney, explained, "The material didn't seem right for Disney, but McCann and Nugent felt so strongly that we agreed at least to back a workshop."[22] Starring Richard Dreyfuss, it closed after seven previews and one performance. Nevertheless, this move clearly demonstrates that Disney's contemporary interest in Broadway theatrical production began not with its spectacular adaptations of its animated hits in the 1990s but with a more tentative venture a decade earlier into workshopping plays in the hopes they would eventually be filmed by the live-action division.

———

For a time in the late 1970s, Paramount chairman Barry Diller observed, "there was no way to lose money by making movies."[23] But the early 1980s were marred by a sharp downturn in box office grosses. Various factors were blamed for this decline, including an economic recession, increased marketing costs, rising inter-est rates (which would impact production costs), and anxiety following the breath-taking failure of *Heaven's Gate* (Michael Cimino, 1980).[24] Michael Eisner, president and COO at Paramount Pictures, decried the reckless spending and unbridled optimism of the time: "Our economic pattern is insanity, total out-and-out, unmitigated, predetermined insanity. This blind marching to the drum of Dr. Pangloss is an overriding death wish."[25] Studios had previously been able to produce low-cost films and have said costs covered by television licensing agreements and tax incentives, but the increasing production and marketing costs for high-concept blockbusters compromised their ability to maintain profitability. With escalating costs and risk, many studios sought coproduction partnerships to maximize on each other's strengths; Disney, for example, brought its skills in distribution and marketing to Paramount's strengths in story development.[26] Paramount nevertheless remained a market leader in 1980 through a diverse output, including *Airplane!* (Jim Abrahams, David Zucker, and Jerry Zucker, 1980), *Friday the 13th* (Sean S. Cunningham, 1980), and *Ordinary People* (Robert Redford, 1980). Despite this success, the studios were anxious, leading MGM/UA distribution executive Eddie Kalish to concede in late 1981, "This year, the most pervasive fact is that there's no film anyone can point to and say, 'This is the film to beat.'"[27]

As highly successful studios under the aegis of large multinational conglomerates, Paramount and Universal managed to navigate the crisis largely unscathed, while Columbia and 20th Century Fox became prime targets for corporate takeovers. Disney appeared to be remarkably stable: even though its film production division was regularly underperforming, it remained one of the most cash-rich studios due to the steady performance of its Anaheim and Orlando theme parks. As the tenth anniversary of Walt Disney World approached in 1981, plans were already underway for a Disneyland in Tokyo as well as a new park in Florida, EPCOT, a heavily modified version of Walt's dream of a planned community. EPCOT completely fell under Disney's aegis, and construction costs inched closer and closer to $1 billion. Tokyo Disneyland, on the other hand, would be primarily owned and operated by the Oriental Land Company. Disney took only a percentage of the gross, in part because Disney CEO Card Walker did not want to commit the company to covering Japanese pension requirements.[28]

Throughout the early 1980s, Disney strategically worked to assure its stockholders and the general public that the studio was preparing for a comeback. The twenty-seven-year-old executive Tom Wilhite made it clear to the press that "we're willing to talk to anybody. . . . At this moment this is a very open film company. We're looking for people with passion."[29] The front covers of the company's annual reports for 1981, 1982, and 1983 boasted upcoming amusement park attractions, while the introductory letters touted the promise that lay ahead for film and television production. But Wilhite's adaptability to contemporary industry trends placed him at odds with the conservative Walker, who remained intractable. Miller found himself caught in the middle: committed to protecting the Disney brand and legacy while keenly aware the film division was struggling amid social, cultural, and industrial changes. Indeed he found his compromise: the launch of a new production division titled Touchstone to handle more adult-oriented fare. If the company was going to survive, it would need to revitalize its film division, animation included.

Disney's television prospects seemed equally dismal, despite the report's customary optimism. NBC canceled *Disney's Wonderful World* on Sunday evenings amid tough competition from CBS's *60 Minutes*, but the show transitioned to CBS's Saturday night lineup. Various pilots were in the works, including *Gun Shy* and *Small & Frye*, but both premiered and fizzled out in 1983. The newly appointed head of television, William R. Yates, found himself, like Wilhite, butting heads with stubborn traditionalists in the boardroom and even in the audience: "We have to change, we have to grow and keep trying different things. It's not that we're going to do programs that won't be tasteful, but we've got to mature."[30] The problem plaguing both film and television, however, was the insularity of the studio, necessitating recruitment of promising young talent and building strong working relationships with other production companies and studios.

Despite the lackluster box office performance in 1981, buoyed only by inflation, the hope for a revitalized Hollywood came with the release of a series of blockbusters in the summer of 1982. In this highly profitable summer season, Paramount released *Star Trek II: The Wrath of Khan* (Nicholas Meyer, 1982); MGM/UA offered both *Rocky III* (Sylvester Stallone, 1982) and *Poltergeist* (Tobe Hooper, 1982); and Universal and 20th Century Fox co-distributed *Conan the Barbarian* (John Milius, 1982). Paramount's *An Officer and a Gentleman* (Taylor Hackford, 1982) was released in August and went on to blockbuster success. *E.T. the Extra-Terrestrial* emerged as the season's true victor, grossing an estimated $3.5 million daily for a time.[31] Three film musicals elicited very different critical and commercial responses: *Grease 2* (Patricia Birch, 1982) flopped amid dismal reviews; *Annie* (John Huston, 1982) failed to turn a significant profit due to sizeable production and advertising costs; and *The Best Little Whorehouse in Texas* (Colin Higgins, 1982) impressively grossed $69 million to become the year's tenth most successful release. The summer of 1982 revived the film studios, while also demonstrating the value of spectacular storylines, sizable budgets, and established franchises. Of course, not everyone reaped the benefits.

At the time of his death in 1966, Walt Disney was supervising the production of *The Jungle Book* (Wolfgang Reitherman, 1967), which went on to become the second highest grossing film of the year, behind *The Graduate* (Mike Nichols, 1967). Reitherman was one of Disney's "Nine Old Men," a group of animators who had worked on every Disney animated feature since *Snow White*. By the 1970s, they had begun to retire or pass away, and Walt had left no clear succession plan in place and unintentionally jeopardized the future of Disney animation. Through the 1970s, the studio worked to recruit animators, particularly from the California Institute of the Arts (CalArts), which Walt himself had helped cofound and fund. Production slowed down considerably during this time, in part because audience interest gradually waned as *The Aristocats* (Wolfgang Reitherman, 1970) and *Robin Hood* made noticeably less than their predecessors. Concerned for "a continuity of quality Disney animated films for another generation,"[32] Ron Miller put Eric Larson, another of the Nine Old Men, in charge of training a new crop of Disney animators. The company reportedly received over twenty thousand applications throughout the decade, but only a hundred fifty artists were deemed worthy of the training program.[33]

One of the leaders of this next generation of animators was Don Bluth. After his brief tenure at Disney in the late 1950s, when he assisted on *Sleeping Beauty* (Clyde Geronimi, 1959), Bluth had completed a mission trip in Argentina and started a theater in Culver City with his brother. He remained a great fan of Disney, though, and took the opportunity to return in 1971, where he worked on *Robin Hood* and *Winnie the Pooh and Tigger Too* (John Lounsbery, 1974). The next major animated feature out of Disney Animation was *The Rescuers* (John Lounsbery, Wolfgang Reitherman, and Art Stevens, 1977), featuring the voices of television stars Eva Gabor and Bob Newhart. Many critics saw promise in the film, and it even outperformed *Star Wars* (George Lucas, 1977) in Paris as well as West Germany, where it became the highest grossing film to date.[34] Unfortunately, it stumbled stateside.

Bluth went on to serve as animation director on *Pete's Dragon*, a mixture of hand-drawn animation and live-action filmmaking. Released only a few months after *The Rescuers*, *Pete's Dragon* was a modest success on par with *Robin Hood*. While the film was praised for its technological feats, critics blasted its two-hour running time (most animated features were less than ninety minutes long), lackluster musical numbers, and underdeveloped script.[35] Behind the scenes, tension was growing at the studio: some animators, led by Bluth, felt story and production values had waned over the past few years, much to the indifference of executives. The strong storylines and nuanced character development of classics such as *Pinocchio* (Ben Sharpsteen and Hamilton Luske, 1940) and *Bambi* (David Hand, 1942), Bluth's personal favorite of the Disney canon, had been forsaken in favor of broad characterization and episodic narratives. A schism increasingly developed between animators hired from CalArts and another group, more or less led by Bluth.

The resulting tension exacerbated an already troubled division. A Christmas-themed short, *The Small One* (Don Bluth, 1978), was originally planned as a directorial project for Larson and largely drawn by the younger animators, including Gary Goldman, John Musker, and John Pomeroy. Upper management soon reassigned the project to Bluth, a move some Larson loyalists saw as a sign of Bluth's ambitiousness and irreverence toward the old guard. Disappointed, Larson focused on continuing to develop the talent pool, reporting in July 1978 that Disney had found roughly forty-five of the seventy-five animation personnel necessary "to strengthen all the areas."[36] Disney had intended *The Black Cauldron* (Ted Berman and Richard Rich, 1985), an ambitious adaptation of Lloyd Alexander's *The Chronicles of Prydain* series, as the younger generation's *Snow White*.[37] It also would mark a return to the darker style of films like *Pinocchio*. Production was ultimately delayed while Disney prioritized *The Fox and the Hound* (Ted Berman, Richard Rich, and Art Stevens, 1981), an adaptation of Daniel P. Mannix's 1967 novel of an unlikely friendship. The former was a youth-oriented fantasy tale that was narratively in line with contemporary live-action filmmaking; the latter would be more recognizable Disney fare, with its emphasis on friendship and animal protagonists.

News of the mounting tension behind the scenes at Disney reached executives at Aurora Productions, a new production company established by former Disney executives Richard Irvine and James L. Stewart. They approached Bluth about striking out on his own, an offer the increasingly dissatisfied animator could not turn down. It became clear that the specter of Walt Disney hung over the studio, especially the animation division, and as a result, the studio remained reticent to take the necessary artistic risks, which, ironically, defied the approach Walt himself had embraced. On September 13, 1979, Bluth, along with Gary Goldman and John Pomeroy, walked into the office of their boss, Ed Hansen, resigned, and announced their intentions to open a competing production company. Eight other animators went with them, and several more followed in the coming weeks.

Of course, this mass departure of rising talent inspired anxiety and fury throughout the studio, especially as it was trying to revive its lagging animation division. Initially Ron Miller chastised Bluth's disloyalty, but diplomatically noted in the *New York Times*, "We develop the finest artists in the field of animation in the world. It's typical of artists to want to spread their wings."[38] (He later made the uncharacteristic move of publicly calling Bluth a "son of a bitch.")[39] Eric Larson was equally critical: "I think young people today"—Bluth left on his forty-second birthday—"lack a certain discipline. It's a big problem for them to become a cog in a team effort. But this place is so far ahead of any place else that I welcome competition. It's what we need."[40] Ed Hansen, head of animation, insisted, "We're still smiling";[41] years later, in 1984, he admitted, "My world collapsed on September 13, 1979."[42] Despite efforts to seem unperturbed, even self-congratulatory, executives and animators at Disney remained irate and worried about the future of feature animation at its hallowed home. Indeed, a former Disney executive reportedly told Bluth years later, "We met daily about how to get rid of you, because you were on our turf."[43]

Some commentators, including Pamela G. Hollie of the *New York Times*, faulted Disney's commercial-driven focus on theme parks and live-action films as the motivating reason behind the waning quality of Disney animation and, by extension, the departure of the Bluth group.[44] She claimed their defection not only would delay *The Fox and the Hound*, but "more fundamentally, it has dashed the studio's efforts to rebuild the Disney animation department to its past glory."[45] The shift in focus was somewhat understandable, from a business perspective. The theme park provided a steady revenue stream and the live-action films were relatively inexpensive to produce; feature animation, on the other hand, required up to four years to develop, draw, and film, with no promise of financial return. The earlier animated films—often called the "annuities" within the company—proved profitable during reissue, so the need for new films from the animation division was not as pressing. But now Disney had work to do. As the heir apparent departed with a crop of its young talent, the drive to succeed seemed more urgent than ever before.

Bluth felt confident he could deliver his first feature film within two and a half years and the $7 million budget he had been allotted. The new animation studio, named Don Bluth Productions, also found supplemental work, such as animating a two-minute sequence for *Xanadu* (Robert Greenwald, 1980). By the time the film was released, Bluth and company—roughly forty-three personnel—were hard at work on their first feature film, an adaptation of Robert C. O'Brien's novel for children, *Mrs. Frisby and the Rats of NIMH*.

In 1981, Disney finally released *The Fox and the Hound* after five years in production. The film grossed over $39 million, placing it just behind *Reds* (Warren Beatty, 1981) and far behind Steven Spielberg's *Raiders of the Lost Ark*, the top film of the year with over $200 million in domestic gross alone. Ron Miller, now president of Walt Disney Studios, assured the press and the public that change was coming, but Bluth had noted that the higher-ups, especially Miller, lacked the drive and the backbone to venture into new territory, both thematically and artistically. In reality, the Disney brand, long associated with G-rated entertainment, could go only so far, even as film became increasingly edgier in its representation of sexuality and violence. Miller publicly lamented the state of Disney filmmaking in general: "They'll have to blindfold and gag me before I'll let them do anything more than a soft P.G. . . . Sure, I'm a hypocrite. I let my children see everything—R's and P.G.'s—the lot. But I have a responsibility to this company. One racy picture could do incredible damage to a name built up over 55 years."[46] David Ehrman, a young executive story editor at Disney, advocated for a broader, more modern, more daring film product at Disney. "We're considered a kid's studio," he candidly remarked, "and that isn't enough. I want the Disney image to stand for fantasy and adventure, as it always has, but also for some updated drama as well."[47] Among the new projects were a live-action adaptation of S. E. Hinton's young adult novel *Tex* (Tim Hunter, 1982) and the partially computer-animated movie *Tron*.

Coincidentally, executive Tom Wilhite's rhetoric at this time aligned with many of Bluth's critiques years earlier, though he obviously drew no such parallel: "We want to follow the philosophy of Disney himself, who was always interested in progress and change. Perhaps change hasn't occurred as often as it should here, but we feel we're moving in the right direction with the kinds of pictures we have in production now—pictures that are different from what other people are doing and that involve new artists. We're discovering the essence of what made this studio what it is: change, chance, risk-taking, escapes, innovation, upbeat films."[48] Surely Bluth was chagrined to read of this young executive championing risk-taking and innovation, even at the expense of an overbearing loyalty to tradition. He had lamented Disney's narrow-mindedness during his time there, especially the deference to a misguided notion of what Walt would have done. Bluth saw himself as carrying on the Disney tradition of *Bambi* in his careful attention to renderings of character, backgrounds, and the more challenging artistic elements of landscape, such as water and wind. While Wilhite faulted Bluth for his obsession with early Disney feature animation, the latter attempted to dissuade the perception among industry professionals, critics, and audiences that he was mimicking his key influence and former boss: "There will be no 'second Disney.' It's wonderful that his success could occur, and he could show all that animation can be. Unfortunately, his legacy has been left to those who could chop it up and sell it in the meat market. But he didn't tell all the stories. We want to understand how he told stories and then go from here."[49] Bluth may have been a traditionalist, but it proved to be a necessary catalyst for a new age of U.S. animation.

Don Bluth Productions completed *The Secret of NIMH* on budget in May 1982, and MGM/UA released the film that July. The press kit proudly proclaimed, "The Second Age of Animation is here."[50] Furthermore, the filmmakers prided themselves on their homage to classical animation, including their investment in costly, time-consuming techniques to heighten the film's quality, including multiplane shots, close attention to shadows and reflections, and the "orchestration of color" (including the use of over 600 colors, 500 of which were created by the studio).[51] Clearly, Don Bluth Productions (in conjunction with MGM/UA) used its press materials to goad its former colleagues at Walt Disney Studios. Bluth told *Variety*, "We'll worry them into reformation, with our competition a useful impetus for Disney Studios to make improvements."[52] While the likes of Miller, Hansen, and Larson saw Bluth as a troublemaker and defector, he obviously positioned himself as the champion, even savior, of classical cel animation. As he told interviewers at the time, "With Don Bluth Productions, I hoped to start a second age of animation."[53] If animation was going to captivate audiences, Bluth believed, it would need to return to its classical roots.[54] Crafting a fiercely contrasting world of light and dark, good and evil, and courage and cowardice, *The Secret of NIMH* aims to provide the entertaining but also the morally elevating experience of the early Disney animated features.

Aurora Productions and distributor MGM/UA pursued a rigorous marketing campaign for the film. "We want to outdo Disney in marketing a G-rated family film," Aurora president Richard Irvine told the *New York Times*. "We needed to be sure enough money was there to compete head-to-head with Disney."[55] In addition to brief stage shows in department stores nationwide featuring actors costumed as the lead characters, *NIMH* merchandise included an ice cream flavor, cups, puzzles, books, clothing, toys, and school supplies.

Critics, however, were not impressed with the film. Sheila Benson, writing for the *Los Angeles Times*, commended the technique but felt the story itself fell flat.[56] Nevertheless, she saw promise: "What *NIMH* proves amply is that Bluth's idealistic young company has both technique and heart for the painstaking, expensive work of fully detailed animation."[57] Roger Ebert of the *Chicago Sun-Times* similarly praised the animation but lamented, "It is not quite such a success on the emotional level, however, because it has so many characters and involves them in so many different problems that there's nobody for the kids in the audience to strongly identify with."[58] Vincent Canby of the *New York Times* was no less forgiving, finding the characters well-drawn, yet the story lacking and the characters unworthy of an audience's sympathies. While the animation delighted, he admitted that the characters rarely resonated in the same way that they did in early Disney features.[59]

Ultimately, Canby laid the blame on the weak storyline by Bluth, Goldman, Pomeroy, and Will Finn—a particularly damning critique when one considers Bluth had charged Disney with weak storytelling.

Audiences apparently agreed with the critics, and *NIMH* unimpressively grossed less than $15 million domestically. The news must have hit Bluth particularly hard. When he had gone for financing, potential backers told him only Walt Disney had ever made a profit doing feature animation.[60] They were right then, and they were still right. Bluth had to look to additional avenues for animation, eventually pursuing video game animation (including *Dragon's Lair*) before finding support from Disney's biggest competition: Steven Spielberg. A lifelong fan of animation, Spielberg saw potential in feature animation as a direct competitor to the studio whose name was synonymous with the artform. Together, both men not only directly challenged Disney's supposed stronghold on feature animation but also woke the resting beast, spurring the struggling company to reinvest in what it perceived to be its birthright.

———

Even though *Tron* proved to be a commercial and critical failure upon its initial release in July 1982, the film nevertheless warrants attention for several reasons. In the mad rush to capitalize on the profitable youth market, especially the rising popularity of video games, the major media companies employed various strategies to exploit the increasing interest in this new medium and foster synergies across their divisions. Ultimately, Disney's approach to license its own creative properties for gaming rather than become directly involved in the design, development, and manufacturing of software and hardware was a cautious, wise decision. The company's efforts in animation and special effects, however, reveal the larger, often ignored, industrial and aesthetic intersections between cel and digital animation, visual effects technologies, and digital game design.[61] *Tron* features Disney's earliest foray into computer animation, which it would use judiciously over the next decade, including the Big Ben sequence of *The Great Mouse Detective* and the finale of *The Little Mermaid*.

One might date the beginning of *Tron* to Warner's 1976 purchase of Atari—and its debt—for a reported $28 million, emphasizing the company's desire to hold a stake in the creation of not only video game software but hardware as well.[62] This approach was the first major effort by an entertainment conglomerate with a Hollywood film studio to enter the video game industry. By 1981, Americans were spending an estimated $9 billion a year on video games.[63] This figure represented nearly three times the domestic box office revenues for the film industry that year, the first time video games eclipsed movies.[64] The failure of RCA's home video game console in 1977 compelled many to steer clear of hardware, so the film studios met the threat of video games in two ways: developing games for the existing hardware (Atari, Intellivision, Odyssey) or licensing their film properties to video game manufacturers. Since the best-selling home video games were based on arcade games, industry insiders figured games based on films would equally benefit from the

presold audience that follows a major feature film release. Lucasfilm signed a contract with Atari to develop new games. Paramount's Michael Eisner argued that
video games would follow films as a "replacement business": every few weeks,
arcades would need new games, and media companies could easily facilitate
that consumer desire.[65] Studios pursued efforts to capitalize with fervor, with
20th Century Fox even announcing plans for a video game based on the work-
place comedy *9 to 5* (Colin Higgins, 1980), which was eventually scrapped before
release. Other surefire winners failed to garner an audience. Atari, for example,
paid $25 million to create an *E.T. the Extra-Terrestrial* video game, which was
produced in less than six weeks and went on to become one of the most notorious
failures in video game history. For its own part, Disney decided to stick to licensing content to video games, arguing that it was too late for them to enter the design
and development end of the video game industry.[66] With the massive losses it had
suffered at the box office in recent years as well as the considerable expenditure
for EPCOT (estimated over $1 billion), the company was hardly in the position to
make such a bold venture into a new media industry. Disney ultimately offered a
fourth strategy: bring the culture and aesthetics of video games to the screen.
Carly Kocurek argues *Tron* and subsequent films including *WarGames* (John Badham, 1983) and *Joysticks* (Greydon Clark, 1983) were deliberate attempts to "cash
in on the games' existing visibility," and a closer look at the production history
around *Tron* reveals it was also a strategic effort to revitalize the Disney brand and,
for Lisberger, to push animation into new territory.[67]

To many observers, Disney's theatrical audience was gone, especially with the
rise of home media technologies, including the VCR and the home gaming console (and, much earlier, the television).[68] By the late 1970s, audiences had shifted
considerably so that nearly three-fourths of the moviegoing public were between
the ages of eighteen and thirty-five.[69] Tom Wilhite argued that films like *Star Wars*
and *Close Encounters of the Third Kind* (Steven Spielberg, 1977) were exactly the
kind of effects-heavy films Disney made in its heyday and should be making now.[70]
In order to revitalize the company, Disney would need films that were both narratively and technically innovative—traits ably demonstrated by video gaming.
Unlike the children who were heart of Disney's earlier audience, *Tron* targeted both
personal computer users as well as arcade patrons, particularly teenagers.[71]

For the creative team behind *Tron*, however, the appeal of video gaming came
after the fact. The film's director and co-screenwriter, Steven Lisberger, had initially started in cel animation. His company produced a television special, *Animalympics*, to correspond with the 1980 Olympics, but the Atari game *Pong* inspired
him to experiment in animating with light. Video gaming, after all, was animated
by lit pixels, so in it Lisberger found a conceit for his film: set it inside a computer
mainframe where the characters were "programs." As he later told the *Globe and
Mail*, "I knew Disney needed a shake-up at the castle. Sleeping Beauty was just waiting for the prince to arrive."[72] Intrigued by reports of *Tron's* development, Xerox
PARC researcher Alan Kay eventually convinced Lisberger that the film would
need to use computer technology as well as cel animation and visual effects.

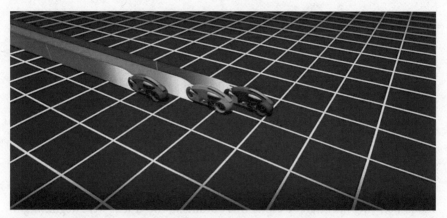

Figure 2. The light cycle sequence from *Tron* demonstrates the company's developing interest in computer animation. Credit: Author's screenshot.

Much of what appears to be computer animation is a combination of computer-generated imagery, live-action shots, and cel animation. Lisberger and his special effects team benefited enormously from working at Disney, where animation staff and technology, including animation stands and optical printers, could assist in creating the imagery and shots he wanted for the film. Ironically, though *Tron* aimed to show the inherent creative potential that computers possessed, technologies at the time could not achieve the desired effects and required composites in the tradition of cel animation. Bill Kroyer, who worked on computer animation choreography for *Tron*, observed, "Now we are able to apply all the things that the Disney animators have learned over fifty years—that we have inherited from their experience—and show that the entertainment principles that they struggled to learn can be applied to the totally different computer medium. And we feel especially great about the fact that we're doing it at Disney, and that Disney is the first to benefit."[73] Disney did benefit from these forays into computer animation, but it also made such an endeavor possible through the artistic techniques that it had honed over the years in feature cel animation. One problem persisted nevertheless: story. Even Bruce Boxleitner, who played both Alan Bradley and Tron, struggled to explain the film's plot: "I really feel uncomfortable talking about this film. . . . It's kind of hard to explain [my character]. It's real complicated."[74]

Boxleitner was not the only one baffled by *Tron*. Previous to its release, Disney made the unusual move of screening the film for Wall Street analysts to build enthusiasm for the film and confidence in the company. To Disney's dismay, the analysts found the film confusing, and many analysts advised their clients to sell off their Disney stock.[75] Film critics were not much kinder: David Sterritt of the *Christian Science Monitor* observed, "It would be futile to describe the story, which is totally wrapped up in the flashy visual style, and probably too weak to stand up any other way."[76] In the *Los Angeles Times*, Sheila Benson deemed *Tron* a "stick-figure story" that sacrificed character, story, action, and humor for revolutionary visual effects.[77]

Disney had anticipated *Tron* could generate $400 million at the box office and in related merchandise.[78] It fared well in its first two weeks of release, but the profits soon dropped in light of the blockbuster success of *Poltergeist*, *Star Trek II: The Wrath of Khan*, and *E.T.* Card Walker insisted the film would find its audience by word of mouth and refused to increase the marketing budget.[79] Instead, it failed to build momentum, forcing the company to write off the bulk of its hefty production costs. Yet it succeeded, unsurprisingly, in the place where the world of *Tron* was perhaps best suited to do so: as a video game—with nearly eight hundred units shipped to arcades across the country by the first week of the month.[80]

By November 1982, six of the seven major media companies in the United States had an investment in the video game industry, but only Warner had ventured into manufacturing hardware. Despite this optimism, the cracks were beginning to show, and the industry faced trouble. For one, video game design became increasingly complex, marking an end to the era of the one-person design team as technology and artistry required more labor and expertise.[81] Another reason was that the demand simply did not meet the number of games developed and the units produced. By November 1983 the market was glutted, with estimated losses of $1.5 billion across the industry.[82]

Martin Picard argues that the commercial failure of *Tron* inspired Hollywood to avoid computer-generated imagery for nearly a decade, but this conclusion does not hold for all studios.[83] Disney and Pixar, then the Graphics Group of Lucasfilm, experimented with computer animation to differing levels of enthusiasm. In the wake of *Tron*, Tom Wilhite acknowledged computer technology had promise, but it was not yet at a point where it could contribute effectively to classically animated Disney features. Disney tested out digital animation over time, gradually introducing computer-generated imagery into feature animation on *The Black Cauldron*. *Tron* remains an important marker in computer animation at Disney and in the industry. Although Disney would use it to varying degrees in subsequent years, digital animation's dominance of the industry by the early 2000s served as another signal that the Disney Renaissance period may have concluded. But Disney would need more than technological feats to win back its audience: it would need skilled storytellers. It found them not only in Hollywood but on (or near) Broadway, where artists working in the integrated musical tradition demonstrated the necessary dramatic acumen to help reignite the Disney magic.

––––––––

Little Shop of Horrors, with music by Alan Menken and book and lyrics by Howard Ashman, debuted at the WPA Theatre in May 1982. The two creators were introduced to each other by composer Maury Yeston while Howard was directing an early workshop of Yeston's *Nine*. Yeston and Menken were alumni of Lehman Engel's influential BMI musical theatre workshop in New York City, and while not an official member, Ashman occasionally made use of the workshop and considered Engel to be a mentor. The famed incubator for musical theatre talent offered rigorous training in integrated musical theatre storytelling. Menken, a skilled musician trained in piano and violin with a degree in musicology from New York University, enrolled as a composer. One year younger than Menken, Ashman also had had a Jewish upbringing, but in Baltimore, where he was active in theatre and an avid fan of Disney films. His education took him to Boston University, Goddard College, and Indiana University. He headed to New York after graduate school and joined the WPA Theatre, serving as its artistic director from 1977 until 1982. Although *God Bless You, Mr. Rosewater* had stumbled after its Off-Broadway transfer, it nevertheless helped them to hone the "cynical sensibility" that made their next effort such a success.[84]

With *Little Shop of Horrors*, Ashman turned his attention to the B-movie canon of independent producer Roger Corman. Using films as the basis for musical theatre was not unprecedented: *Make a Wish*, a 1951 Broadway musical by Hugh Martin and Preston Sturges, adapted the latter's screenplay for *The Good Fairy* (William Wyler, 1935),[85] and *Silk Stockings*, with music by Cole Porter, was based on *Ninotchka* (Ernst Lubitsch, 1939). Even Ashman's artistic role model, Stephen Sondheim, had found inspiration in cinema for a stage musical when he (and librettist Hugh Wheeler and director Harold Prince) adapted Ingmar Bergman's *Smiles of a Summer Night* (1955) into *A Little Night Music* in 1973. But Broadway's most lucrative successes in the early 1980s had been revues and glitzy spectacles, including *Sugar Babies* and *42nd Street*. With their Off-Off-Broadway *Little Shop*, Ashman and Menken nostalgically re-created the 1960s city life and its distinctive blend of doo-wop, R&B, and rock, including Phil Spector's "Wall of Sound."[86]

Little Shop of Horrors is fairly restrained as far as musicals go: it features minimal dancing, a small cast, and a score of pop pastiche songs. While loyal to the tradition of the integrated musical, it did not aim to be the blockbuster *Cats* would be months later. In fact, Audrey, its heroine, was partly based on Judy Holliday's performance as Ella Peterson in the 1956 Broadway musical *Bells Are Ringing*.[87] Ashman and Menken initially tried to give it a traditional Broadway-style musical score, but they did not find the show's sound until they reimagined the project as "the dark side of *Grease*."[88] In his history of *Little Shop*, Adam Abraham also notes the influence of *Damn Yankees*, *Sweeney Todd*, even the Muppets on the development of the show.[89] Ultimately, *Little Shop* embraces a modest scale and sardonic sense of humor that gives a Bronx cheer to the spectacular musicals appearing in Midtown. In an interview with Ira Weitzman, Ashman noted,

> I just think you have to be honest about what Broadway is. If I work on Broadway, I would like to work on a Broadway show. What I would *not* like to do is try to torture one of my innocent, unpretentious little musicals into Broadway scale. I think that's an enormous mistake whenever it's done. . . . I just think you need to very honest and above board about what Broadway is and what it requires and the kind of story—the kind of experience—that is appropriate to that medium. It's a *different* medium. It's film and television. It's a whole different kettle of fish.[90]

Although he praised Lloyd Webber's talent for crossover success, Ashman understood that his own work was intentionally—necessarily—small in scale, an

Figure 3. Howard Ashman poses with Audrey II. Credit: © Peter Monsees–USA Today Network.

approach distinctive from recent Broadway fare. Ashman saw himself in the integrated musical tradition of Rodgers and Hammerstein and Stephen Sondheim, who preferred telling stories through music, not spectacle. As his partner Bill Lauch observes, "He really admired Michael Bennett—he thought his direction was amazing, especially *Dreamgirls*—and he wanted to write lyrics as good as Stephen Sondheim, who he thought was a genius."[91] The strength of *Little Shop of Horrors* therefore lies in its strong characters, tight plotting, and comically dark tone. Although its content was bold and innovative, its form was traditional, even old-fashioned—yet it was a hit nevertheless.

There is, of course, one caveat to this discussion: Audrey II. The deep-voiced monster at the heart of the musical is a giant plant, a villainous puppet initially voiced off stage by actor Ron Taylor and manipulated by puppeteer Martin P. Robinson. A murderous houseplant hardly evokes the traditional stage villain, and its absurdity underscored the playfulness of the musical. As Ashman told the *Los Angeles Times*, "It's sort of fun-scary—the way certain rides are at Disneyland."[92] Yet not all critics got the joke. Walter Kerr of the *New York Times* viewed Audrey II as evidence that "the stage takes to aping its much younger and less sophisticated brother," film.[93] He warned that stage effects should be used minimally: "Beware, however, the evening that depends on them for its life's blood."[94] Kerr went on to connect such gimmicks to the early film experiments of Georges Méliès: "Its vogue vanished quickly and suddenly and has resurfaced rarely, briefly."[95] Yet again, theatre and its stakeholders expressed "medium anxiety" out of concern that their beloved art form was being undermined by filmic techniques, including spectacle.

But *Little Shop* found its champions. Mel Gussow, also of the *New York Times*, celebrated it as "a rarefied idea for a musical comedy . . . a show for horticulturists, horror-culturists, sci-fi fans and anyone with a taste for the outrageous."[96] Its reputation grew among New Yorkers, eventually earning the attention of major players in the Broadway theatre. The Shubert Organization, along with David Geffen and Cameron Mackintosh (all of whom would be involved with the arrival of *Cats* months later), took great interest in moving it to the Orpheum Theatre, where it could accommodate roughly three hundred attendees, in July 1982. The show's success in the East Village continued, and it would run for five years and eventually became Off-Broadway's most profitable musical to date.[97] Ashman and Menken had done something few composers had accomplished of late: a successful new U.S. musical. Their triumph amid a seeming creative drought captured the attention of not only Broadway but also Hollywood.

———

No show was blamed for changes in Broadway theatrical production, however, as much as Andrew Lloyd Webber's *Cats*. On the surface, the show had the makings of a Broadway hit: it had catchy melodies, a range of dance styles, and a gorgeous eleven o'clock number—a dramatic ballad sung at the climax of the show—that had already received considerable airplay in the United Kingdom, where the show originated. As a work of contemporary musical theatre, *Cats* was surprising in its loose plotting. The musical was originally devised in 1977, when Lloyd Webber, after a falling out with Tim Rice, sought a new project that would afford him some degree of creative independence. Years earlier, he had found a copy of *Old Possum's Book of Practical Cats*, a book of children's verse by T. S. Eliot that he had enjoyed as a child, in a bookshop. Lloyd Webber realized that the poems had a musical quality that betrayed Eliot's love of popular music and music hall entertainment. Furthermore, Eliot was long deceased, seemingly offering Lloyd Webber a silent partner and a relative degree of independence in this production compared to his earlier work with Rice.

Of course, such an easy working relationship was not immediately guaranteed. Years earlier, Walt Disney had approached T. S. Eliot about adapting *Practical Cats* into an animated film, but according to his wife, Valerie, he declined because he did not want his mischievous cats "to be pussycats or turned into cartoon cats."[98] When Eliot died in 1965, the rights to his work had fallen to his young widow, Valerie Eliot. First secretary, then wife, and finally faithful editor and executrix of his estate, she remained protective over her husband's literary legacy. Seeking her blessing and the rights to the book, Lloyd Webber prepared some melodies and invited Mrs. Eliot and his friends to his estate in Sydmonton to hear a preview of his work in progress. She approved of his efforts, even providing him with poems not included in the original collection. The most significant of these uncollected poems chronicles Grizabella, the dejected "Glamour Cat" whom the other cats scorn.

Eliot allegedly found the poem too depressing for a children's book,[99] but Griz-abella becomes the emotional core of *Cats* through her show-stopping perfor-mance of "Memory."[100] Lloyd Webber assured Valerie Eliot that he would avoid a Disney treatment of the book, insisting he had Hot Gossip, a popular—and provocative—British dance troupe of the time, in mind. To Lloyd Webber's amuse-ment, she was delighted: "Yes, yes, I think Tom would've liked that!"[101] With her approval, Lloyd Webber could proceed with relative autonomy in writing *Cats*. Consequently, the show has no discernible plot but rather follows a pageant-like format, featuring a range of song (music hall, jazz, operetta) and dance (tap, jazz, ballet) numbers accompanied by pantomimed action. While the Eliot estate did not meddle in the creation of *Cats*, its restriction undeniably had a signifi-cant impact on the final product in that *Cats* is more accurately a music hall revue or a dance musical than a traditional integrated musical.

Despite the accolades from Tony voters, Broadway critics and denizens were less than thrilled with the final result. Theatre traditionalists saw it as a dumbing down of the stage, departing from the intellectual stimulation that they believed was the traditional charge of serious drama. Robert Brustein wryly observed in the *New Republic*, "British theater skills have hitherto been essentially verbal and techni-cal, but they have never been so totally mechanical. This spectacle could have been manufactured by Disneyworld [*sic*], using autodynamation instead of actors; I per-ceived no sign of flesh-and-blood behavior beneath the glitter and flash."[102] Lloyd Webber's peers have been no less critical. Stephen Sondheim later observed, "Where there's no substance, it gets boring. . . . I remember going to *Cats* and wondering why they just didn't stack five million dollars on the stage."[103] Sondheim's derision refers to the show's $4.5 million budget, far exceeding anything Broadway had seen up to that point in 1982. Within five years, the average cost of staging a new Broad-way musical was $5 million.

Following years of dance musicals and various stage spectacles, *Cats* on Broad-way, under the direction of Trevor Nunn, typified rather than originated a new theatrical experience—the high-concept musical. Even as a stage show, *Cats* worked perfectly into Justin Wyatt's explanation of high concept as "a striking, easily reducible narrative which also offers a high degree of marketability."[104] Plot was all but irrelevant; *Cats* was an immersive event to be experienced and cher-ished, as indicated by its "Now and Forever" ad campaign, featuring nothing more than two yellow cat eyes with dancers as pupils. Indeed few theatergoers knew exactly what they would see when they went to *Cats*, in part because, at the time, the concept of anthropomorphic cats was curious, if not downright ludi-crous, for many. While Broadway musicals had always included dance numbers, the foregrounding of dance here was integral, and the musical's appeal lay in both the variety of dance styles as well as the amount of dancing the musical showcased. *Cats*, as choreographer Gillian Lynne explained to *Newsweek*, was "really England's first dance musical," distinct from the U.S. dance musical tra-dition with its roots in jazz.[105] The music featured Lloyd Webber's trademark melodies, catchy tunes that would follow theatergoers out the door and have been described by conductor Lorin Maazel as Lloyd Webber's "great talent—I would say genius."[106]

Style triumphed over the storyline, but audiences obviously did not seem to mind. Two populations have predominantly composed Broadway audiences: local residents of the New York City metro area and tourists who occasionally see shows while visiting. Steven Adler reports that from 1980 to 2000, the percentage of Broadway audiences made up of residents within and around the city dropped from around 60 to 44 percent.[107] Recognizable, accessible, and sensational, *Cats* appealed to this surging demographic of tourist-attendees, and indeed there was good money to be found there; in fact, ticket prices for *Cats* were the highest on Broadway, and its presale was the most successful in Broadway history to date. Writing for the *New York Times*, drama critic Frank Rich declared, "Whatever the other failings and excesses, even banalities, of *Cats*, it believes in purely theatrical magic, and on that faith it unquestionably delivers."[108] While Rich agreed the show charmed audiences, he lamented "that this ambitious show [didn't] lift the audience—or, for that matter, the modern musical—up to the sublime heaviside layer."[109]

Rich's aesthetic concerns ultimately lost out to the audience's desire for family-friendly spectacle. The 1980s was an age of crowd-pleasing blockbusters on the screen, and *Cats* popularized that spirit—and market logic—on the Broadway stage. Even though Lloyd Webber faced harsh dismissals from drama critics stateside, in part because he dared to triumph in what many perceived to be a distinctly U.S. art form. Mainstream audiences flocked to his spectacular shows, and he and Cameron Mackintosh seemed to mechanically reproduce on stages around the world. With greater emphasis on the production design, shows no longer depended on star talent to sell tickets, and budgets were reoriented away from famous performers toward increased expenditure for special effects. In the process, Lloyd Webber and Mackintosh paved the way for a family-friendly theatre that offered its diverse audiences an easily accessible and spectacular event.[110] As Maureen Donley, who worked on the *Cats* U.S. national tour, observes, "you were going to see what Trevor and Andrew had cooked up . . . the unifying thing was spectacle—a really big show."[111] But it also inspired an "audience anxiety"—that is, a concern over what audiences were being targeted and which traditional stakeholders were being sidelined. Mackintosh and Lloyd Webber appeared to be unfazed by the tastes of New York's cultural elite. Furthermore, the starless spectacle could easily replace cast members and be effortlessly replicated for touring and sit-down productions around the world—a globalized "live" entertainment produced in a fashion not unlike the most efficient of Hollywood studios.[112]

Looking back at Hollywood and Broadway in 1982, these four premieres seem relatively unrelated. After all, *The Secret of NIMH* and *Tron* were commercial and critical failures, Off-Broadway *Little Shops of Horror* thrived, and *Cats* proved to be a worldwide phenomenon, despite critical ambivalence. Nevertheless, they remain important milestones for where Disney and (arguably) the film and theatre industries would creatively venture. Classical animation would gradually make a long-awaited return, while computer animation would slowly integrate itself into the animation process before becoming a celebrated art form in its own right. *Cats* popularized an emerging mode of theatrical production, serving as a template for the widely replicated, large-scale spectacles to come. But it was *Little Shop of Horrors* playing downtown, a modest but memorable contribution to the musical theatre canon, that would signal the roots of Disney Renaissance may lie not so much in brilliant executives but in talented storytellers who could craft polished narratives to appeal—and sell tickets—across generations of audiences.

CHAPTER 2

"Sort of Like the Sopranos Took Over the Studio"

REGIME CHANGE AT DISNEY, 1983–1986

The arrival of Michael Eisner and Frank Wells (and, soon after, Jeffrey Katzenberg) came in the wake of a dramatic, yet ultimately unsuccessful, attempt by corporate raiders to seize control of the struggling Walt Disney Productions. In June 1984, the company paid Saul Steinberg a reported $325.5 million (including $28 million for "expenses") for his 4.2 million shares, effectively defusing the threat posed by the famed financier, who ended up making a healthy profit of $14.25 on each share.[1] The resulting chaos allowed Roy E. Disney, who was supported by the Bass family, to push out Ron Miller, the current CEO and husband to Roy's cousin, Diane. The board subsequently hired Michael Eisner from Paramount and Frank Wells from Warner Bros. Eisner assumed the chairman's role, while Wells accepted the presidency; shortly thereafter, they hired Jeffrey Katzenberg, a promising young executive also being considered by former Paramount chairman Barry Diller to join him at Fox, to head up film and television production at Disney. Subsequently, the company allegedly began a comeback that represents one of the most impressive feats in modern U.S. business history.

Even at the time this turmoil garnered considerable media attention, leading to bold claims of how the three men were the company's much-needed saviors. The *New York Times*, in particular, covered the new regime closely and positively. Aljean Harmetz observed that Disney hoped Eisner would "wake Sleeping Beauty."[2] Eisner, for his own part, encouraged this growing legend. Upon being hired, he told another *New York Times* reporter, Thomas C. Hayes, "It sounds corny, but there are few companies in this country tha[t] deserve to be protected. We can do more here than just manage some other people's store. We can help maintain it."[3] A month later Eisner told Harmetz, "People here are dying for leadership. They've [been] dying to get to work."[4] As the public face of the new leadership team, Eisner strategically worked to foster the impression of a new era at Disney.

The hiring of Eisner, Katzenberg, and Wells has been perceived by journalists, industry observers, and scholars alike as a crucial turning point in Disney history.[5]

Under their leadership and in Reagan's America of corporate prosperity and wide-scale inflation, Disney went from $1.65 billion in revenues in 1984 to $5.8 billion in 1989 and to $10 billion by 1994. The problem, however, is that such histories reinforce Eisner's legacy while marginalizing, even erasing, the contribution of the creative workers. Even Eisner admitted in a 1989 letter to stockholders, "We have our corporate health and we continually take its pulse. Only a lack of continued creativity and nerve can impede us as we move into the 90's."[6] Eisner's observation reveals that Disney's viability rested on the strength of these very producers, directors, screenwriters, actors, and animators. Too often, however, their labor has been sidelined in press coverage at the time and subsequent accounts, including James B. Stewart's *DisneyWar* (2005) and Eisner's own *Work in Progress: Risking Failure, Surviving Success* (1998). Understanding Team Disney's impact on the company has to be done not through a focus on executive leadership alone but with close attention to the contributions of creative individuals—some of whom had to routinely push back again Eisner and Katzenberg's suggestions—to lead the company from below. This chapter not only complicates the valorization of Team Disney's transformational leadership but elevates and analyzes their working relationships with creative laborers and managers to produce the cultural products that propelled the turnaround. From this perspective, it becomes increasingly clear that, despite the power imbalance, the distinction between "creative" and "executive" labor was effectively blurred via film workers' leadership and executives' hands-on approach to media production.

———

In October 1982, CEO and board chairman Card Walker announced his intention to retire following the launch of the Disney Channel and the opening of Tokyo Disneyland. At that time, Ron Miller, the current president, presumably would ascend to Walker's position and guide the company forward. With EPCOT behind them, Miller anticipated great success for the Disney Channel, which he personally considered to be the "most rewarding project we have going."[7] He also developed a new film and television subsidiary, headed by Richard Berger, a 20th Century Fox executive with fifteen years of experience. Berger's position bore similarity to that of Wilhite, who now answered to him. It also left Berger reassessing Disney's strategy to date, which had led to remarkably few film releases: in 1983, for example, Paramount, 20th Century Fox, and Warner Bros. had all released fifteen to twenty films; Disney delivered just eight, including three animated rereleases. Following the withdrawal of its Sunday night television series, Disney also had no network television presence in the United States. Berger's strategy was to increase film production in part to minimize risk, telling the *Los Angeles Times* in April 1983, "We want a body of films to come out that will take the emphasis off one individual film."[8] The preceding years had demonstrated how Disney had staked a great deal of hope in a relatively small number of film projects, leading to considerable disappointments and an overreliance on the theme park divisions to maintain revenues. The company was able to stay afloat through the theme parks, but the concentration in one sector placed a heavy burden on the division, especially when Disney possessed a formidable library and cast of characters. Licensing offered revenues, including *Walt Disney's Magic Kingdom on Ice*, a traveling ice show produced by Feld Productions that featured upward of seventy-five performers, one hundred Disney songs, and three hundred costumes.[9] But Disney also could be producing more in-house to effectively capitalize upon its properties rather than merely supervising outside efforts.

Disney needed to more effectively diversify its investments and maximize synergy across those divisions, and the Disney Channel seemed to be a promising avenue to pursue. Within six months it was boasting upward of 350,000 subscribers, to become one of the most successful launches in cable television history at that point.[10] Part of this success lay in the contemporary television landscape. The Federal Communications Commission, under the leadership of Mark Fowler, advocated for a marketplace approach rather than aggressive regulation of children's television.[11] Consequently, activists and commentators regularly lamented the domination of children's television by programming promoting toys, cereal, and related merchandising. As his show *Captain Kangaroo* was moved to an early morning time slot or discontinued altogether in some markets, Bob Keeshan decried the FCC's laissez-faire approach: "Frankly, I think the needs of our nation's children are just too important to be left to the networks and their profit motives, or to Mark Fowler's market concept."[12] The Disney Channel offered an alternative with sixteen hours of family entertainment a day—for a monthly premium ($7.95 to $12.95, depending on the cable provider).[13] While it was not alone in catering to young audiences—Nickelodeon was up and running and PBS offered over thirty hours of children's programming every week—it did offer the Disney brand, and by December the channel had surpassed 600,000 subscribers. Combined with the early success of EPCOT, now considered "the nation's most heavily trafficked vacation resort,"[14] industry analysts were suggesting Disney might be on track to fully realize its potential.

But there was shake-up at the company, too. In November 1983, Tom Wilhite, the ambitious young vice president, resigned his post due in part to ongoing tension with Richard Berger. To his mind, the company essentially had two heads of production now, which was untenable for a studio of its size. Wilhite also expressed dissatisfaction with Berger's reform of compensation, creating a conflict between those who were already at Disney and those hired from the outside.[15] Despite his ongoing defense of *Tron*, both it and *Something Wicked This Way Comes* (Jack Clayton, 1983) had been costly missteps that had shaken executive confidence in Wilhite's judgment.

On February 24, 1984, Disney ran an advertisement in *Daily Variety* announcing Touchstone Films. The embellished rhetoric attempted to establish Touchstone as a sign of the company's coming-of-age with a keen awareness of contemporary audiences and their interests while also protecting the family-friendly Disney name. "All across America, moviegoers want mature entertainment," it declared.[16] "They want quality. They want standards." Touchstone, Disney insisted, would deliver contemporary quality entertainment. In effect, the advertisement signals a break with Disney's earlier feature efforts, not only in animation but even Wilhite's idealistic attempts to modernize the film division through direct appeals to younger adult audiences. (In fact, *Never Cry Wolf* [Carroll Ballard, 1983] had been the company's most successful live-action release to date.) Miller and company seemed to be announcing a renaissance of their own. But trouble lay ahead, not only for the company but for the team positioning themselves as its stewards.

———

Rumors had often circulated in the business world that Walt Disney Productions was a prime target for a corporate takeover. Although it admittedly released few films since Walt's death, Disney was perhaps the only Hollywood studio to bankroll its film output rather than depending on outside financiers. In January 1984, the *Wall Street Journal* noted the company's relatively low debt as well as its considerable assets, including the recently opened EPCOT, which offered the possibility for even more cash flow in the coming years.[17]

On March 9, 1984, *Splash* premiered—and Roy E. Disney, Walt's nephew and the head of the losing side of a family showdown that had resulted in Ron Miller's installation as company leader, unexpectedly resigned from the board. Stanley Gold, Roy's lawyer and confidante, later conceded doing so effectively put a "for sale" sign on the company, and while Roy prepared a leveraged buyout, an anonymous investor began to accumulate shares of the company.[18] Over the next three weeks, said investor bought over two million shares while Roy himself raised his stakes in the company to 2.7 percent.[19] On March 29, financier Saul Steinberg revealed himself to be the investor, having purchased the shares via his company, Reliance Financial Services. Steinberg claimed he planned to be a passive investor, but Walt Disney Productions understandably remained suspicious of his motivations. With a production unit, extensive film library, and sizable real estate holdings, Disney was an attractive acquisition that Steinberg could easily dismantle and sell off.

Over the month of April, his stake continued to rise to over 9 percent, and Steinberg declined an offer from chairman Ray Watson to sit down and discuss his intentions. The company continued to fare well across its divisions, as Disney Channel surpassed 900,000 subscribers, *Splash* took in over $50 million at the box office, and Miller celebrated EPCOT's "terrific" reception by the general public.[20] In the boardroom, the executives strategized how to handle the impending threat from Steinberg. Years earlier, the company's stockholders had approved a plan that required 80 percent approval for a change in ownership, so Steinberg was likely seeking allies in his efforts, perhaps even Roy Disney. By May, Disney announced plans to acquire a real estate development company, the Arvida Corporation, through stocks, which would add almost $200 million in debt to the company and increase the overall number of shares. It also would add Disney-friendly investors to the board. Roy publicly criticized the move as potentially "dilutive and wasteful of corporate assets,"[21] while Steinberg claimed the move forced him to become a more active investor than he originally said that he intended to be. He sought permission from the SEC to pursue a 49.9 percent stake in the company. Steinberg announced plans for a proxy contest, which Wall Street perceived as a sign that Steinberg was unable to garner support for his planned takeover. Steinberg also unsuccessfully sued to prevent Disney from acquiring Arvida. Disney soon after announced plans to purchase Gibson Greetings for a surprising $310 million in stock, effectively watering down Steinberg's ownership in company stock from over 12 percent to less than 10 percent.[22] Furthermore, concerns grew among stockholders that the purchase price for an unexceptional greeting card company was inflated.

Steinberg eventually found partners such as MGM owner Kirk Kerkorian, who put up $75 million in the hopes he would be able to purchase the film division upon takeover. Within days, business journalists reported Disney had made an offer in excess of $300 million to buy back Steinberg's over four million shares and cover his related business expenses. The agreement constituted a "greenmail" deal, in which a company buys back its own stock at a premium to defuse a potential hostile takeover. Disney investors and Wall Street analysts were alternately surprised and angered by the maneuver, perceiving it as a sign of weakness on the company's part as Steinberg stood to make upward of $60 million on the settlement. In the aftermath, each share's value sank by over $15. Roy E. Disney rejoined the board, along with allies Stanley Gold and Peter Dailey, while the company removed both Card Walker and Donn Tatum from the executive committee.

But Disney was not in the clear yet. Prominent Disney investor Irwin Jacobs decried the ongoing plans to acquire Gibson Greetings, calling upon the company to either cancel the acquisition or put it to a vote. Watson soon announced the deal, in fact, would be canceled, prompting one analyst to lament, "This company is going to continue to be very, very vulnerable to threats from the outside."[23] The costly Gibson deal, in particular, struck many as a poor management decision. Rumors began to circulate throughout the industry that Disney would ask for Miller's resignation. Despite a spokesperson's firm public denial of such plans, a September 7 board meeting officially brought an end to Miller's tenure.

Since the motion picture unit was the most troubled and most promising, a seasoned film executive seemed to be Miller's likely successor. A list of contenders quickly emerged: Dennis Stanfill of 20th Century Fox, Frank Wells of Warner Bros., and former Columbia executive Alan J. Hirschfield. Michael Eisner, the president of Paramount Pictures and whom Ron Miller had initially tried to hire for Richard Berger's position, was also among the leading candidates to replace Miller. Although the board had supported Stanfill, Roy favored the Eisner and Wells team, with Eisner handling creative matters and Wells supervising corporate affairs. Both Eisner and Wells publicly downplayed their interest, though they ultimately accepted the offer. "This is going to be a full-service entertainment company, with a regular stream of products," Eisner declared.[24]

Eisner's vision for Disney was not only diversified but synergistic. Paramount had developed a successful strategy of modest budgets for respectable films, and one of Eisner's first hires was his faithful head of production, Jeffrey Katzenberg.

At Disney, the strategy for the film division was clearly focused on producing live-action films for a mature audience. In television, Eisner wanted the company back on network television immediately. He had cut his teeth overseeing Saturday morning cartoons as well as the hits *Laverne & Shirley* and *Happy Days*. Comedy, in both film and television, would be central to Disney's recovery not only because of Eisner's past success with it but because he and Katzenberg perceived it as a noticeable gap among current releases. Within a year, Touchstone was working on *Down and Out in Beverly Hills* (1986), a Paul Mazursky–directed remake of Jean Renoir's comedy of manners *Boudu Saved from Drowning* (1932), while Touchstone's television division was producing its second series—and first hit—*The Golden Girls* with the team behind *Soap*, Susan Harris, Paul Junger Witt, and Tony Thomas. The animation division, the symbolic heart of the company, was hardly the priority—an impression among the animators that was cemented by their relocation from the Burbank studio lot to trailers in Glendale. In fact, it may have been closed altogether without the intervention of Roy Disney. Seeking to appease the very man who had put them in their current positions, Eisner and Katzenberg continued feature animation production and installed Roy himself as the supervisor. The Renaissance today may be synonymous with family-friendly feature animation, but at the outset the production of live-action comedies for adults was seen as the most efficient way back to relevance and vitality.

———

The 1982–1983 Broadway season was marred by a significant drop in attendance, nearly 30 percent lower than just two years earlier.[25] *Cats*, the British spectacle from Andrew Lloyd Webber, proved to be the season's only smash success, with top tickets priced at $45. But the vitality of U.S. theatre was precarious. Joseph Papp, leader of the nonprofit Off-Broadway Public Theater, noted, "What has happened historically is that Broadway has shown it cannot initiate dramatic works because they're too costly and the potential revenue is small compared to a musical. Broadway has abdicated that role."[26] Consequently, the Great White Way became dependent on regional, Off-Broadway, and London theatre to nurture original works for transfer. This new arrangement posed both a financial and an artistic crisis throughout the 1980s. Particularly in the nonprofit sector, theaters shaped their season around producing works that were transferable to Broadway—not unlike a similar crisis on Broadway in the 1930s, in which shows were often staged not just for the New York audience but in the hopes of being optioned by the Hollywood studios.[27] This commercial focus dissuaded many theaters from developing the daring, innovative, often anticommercial work that had justified their very creation in the first place.[28] An economic downtown, decreased tourism, and the flight of theatre talent to Hollywood for more lucrative paydays further compounded Broadway's woes.

Despite a bleak outlook for Broadway theatre, *Little Shop of Horrors* continued to entertain audiences at the Orpheum Theatre in the East Village. A delighted Ashman told his hometown newspaper, the *Sun*, "Plants and I don't get along. I've done so much for them, and they're so ungrateful."[29] Playing two miles from the Great White Way, *Little Shop* was celebrated for its intimate, fresh, and effective musical theatre storytelling in the Broadway tradition. Frank Rich, one of its major cheerleaders, lauded the show for "spread[ing] simple delight in the way a *Pajama Game* or *Bells Are Ringing* once did uptown."[30] The small scale and strong integrated storytelling of *Little Shop* made it a perfect fit for the Orpheum. Despite producing one of the most original and successful new U.S. musicals of the 1980s, Ashman and Menken were not hard at work together on their follow-up effort. The costly and competitive world of musical theatre made getting a show on stage harder and harder. With so few new shows premiering on Broadway, emerging talent rarely had the opportunity to try—and try again. Stephen Sondheim, perhaps the most influential living composer in musical theatre, lamented in 1985, "My goodness, what's wrong with the theatre is that shows are *so* expensive to put on that young writers don't get a chance to try their stuff out in public. That's the only way you can learn. By getting it on and writing another one and getting it on and writing another one and getting it on—that's how everybody in the world of art through 4,000 years has gotten good. By getting it on, writing it down, painting it, hanging it up."[31] Composers and lyricists alike found themselves in multiple partnerships as they worked to finish something viable for the stage. Even Sondheim was working with a new collaborator, James Lapine, on a stage musical about the artistic process, *Sunday in the Park with George*, at the Off-Broadway Playwrights Horizons. As Alan Menken noted in 1986, "It's such a barren landscape. You have to work on more than one at a time; no one has the luxury of sitting back and waiting."[32] In the years after *Little Shop*, Menken, for instance, was working with *Dreamgirls* lyricist Tom Eyen on an ultimately unproduced musical about the Rockettes, *Kicks*. Ashman would alternate between two projects: a screenplay for the film version of *Little Shop of Horrors* as well as the book and lyrics for Marvin Hamlisch's new musical, *Smile*. As Ashman later told the *New York Times*, "Today it takes three or four years to get a show on. It makes you feel that you only have a limited amount of time. If you're lucky, you may be able to do only a few shows in your whole life. In order to stretch and learn and stay healthy, you want to work with more than one person. That's why there's more wife-swapping going on."[33] Surviving in the New York theatre often meant working with a variety of collaborators on a range of projects. With a larger paycheck and greater chance of seeing your work produced, theatre talent found more fruitful opportunities in film and television.

David Geffen, a producer behind both *Cats* and *Little Shop of Horrors*, hired Ashman to do the screenplay for *Little Shop of Horrors*. The film would be produced by the Geffen Company and distributed by Warner Bros., a partnership that had already yielded Robert Towne's *Personal Best* (1982). Ashman largely stayed faithful to his stage version, including the dark ending in which Audrey II consumes both his namesake and his caretaker. Geffen, well-known for his keen insight into popular tastes, felt the ending would not work on screen, and he encouraged Ashman to offer a happy ending that left Seymour and Audrey together, both romantically and physically. Ashman rebuffed the idea: *Little Shop* was a Faustian tale, and he strongly believed an uplifting ending for a character who had fed his enemies to a flesh-hungry houseplant would leave the film on "morally shaky ground."[34] In the stage show, Audrey sings "Somewhere That's Green" to express her aspirations, but of course that "green" place ends up being (inside) Audrey II. Revising the ending would alter the stakes of Seymour's wager with the devil. The original ending stayed for now, while the Geffen Company pursued directors. A short list included a who's who of emerging directorial talent: Ron Howard, Jonathan Demme, and John Hughes, for instance.[35] There was even a playful suggestion of Jim Henson, with Kermit the Frog as Seymour and Miss Piggy as his beloved Audrey. Martin Scorsese was attached to the project for some time, and John Landis entered negotiations with the Geffen Company, which broke down because his team felt the opposing side was too aggressive.[36] Frank Oz came aboard to direct, imagining a small-scale film production to capture the intimacy and artifice of the original stage show. But ironically, the film would be shot in one of the biggest soundstages at Pinewood Studios in London.

The film retains Ellen Greene, the original Audrey, but casts Rick Moranis as Seymour, Vincent Gardenia as Mr. Mushnik, and Steve Martin as Orin the sadistic dentist. Audrey II was brought to life by puppeteer Martin P. Robinson and voiced by Four Tops front man Levi Stubbs because, in the words of Frank Oz, he wanted the part to be "street, black, edgy and tough."[37] Cringeworthy comment aside, Stubbs's rich bass-baritone brought Menken's pop-pastiche score to life while also giving Ashman and Menken the opportunity to work on new songs. "Mean Green Mother from Outer Space," a rousing number Stubbs sings when Seymour becomes increasingly reluctant to satiate Audrey II's culinary desires, later became Ashman and Menken's first Oscar-nominated song. Their competition included "Somewhere Out There" from *An American Tail* (Don Bluth, 1986), but both songs lost out to "Take My Breath Away" from *Top Gun* (Tony Scott, 1986). Despite that outcome, both *Little Shop of Horrors* and *An American Tail* suggested a new life for the film musical, returning to the more integrated model popularized by Broadway artists rather than the diffuse form of the 1980s high-concept dance musicals such *Flashdance* (Adrian Lyne, 1983) and *Footloose* (Herbert Ross, 1984). *Little Shop* was originally intended for a summer release, but it hit a roadblock in previews. Test audiences loved the quirky comic musical—until its bleak ending. Geffen had been right, at least according to this group of viewers, and the musical went back into production to offer a new ending. The revision delayed the film until December 1986, making it an ironic counterpoint to the lighthearted fare traditionally offered around the holidays. But the reception from critics was remarkably positive. Rita Kempley of the *Washington Post* deemed it "destined to become a classic of camp comedy,"[38] while the *New York Times*'s Janet Maslin praised its "right mixture of playfulness, tunefulness and blood lust."[39] Julie Salamon, writing in the *Wall Street Journal*, mused, "The cheeriest Christmas picture by far is *Little Shop of Horrors*," with special admiration for the "sly, campy lyrics."[40] (Ashman rejected the camp readings of *Little Shop* because it lacked a "nasty edge.")[41] The often

Figure 4. The film version of *Little Shop of Horrors* alludes to the first animated musical, *Snow White and the Seven Dwarfs*, as Audrey (Ellen Greene) sings her "I want" song, "Somewhere That's Green." Credit: Author's screenshot.

acerbic Pauline Kael celebrated the film's "jivey, senseless fun" in the *New Yorker*, singling out Ellen Greene in particular for praise: "Ellen Greene seems to have created the sexpot-waif Audrey out of some dreamy dementia," deeming her "a weird little wow."[42] The critics' enthusiasm did not match the audience's initially, and the film grossed a modest $38.7 million on a budget exceeding $22 million. *Little Shop* eventually found an adoring audience, however, in an increasingly popular format: home video.

———

From the moment of its arrival, Team Disney, especially Michael Eisner, positioned themselves as saviors of a great brand with a formidable legacy. Much like Steven Lisberger had in 1982, Eisner mused he was the prince to wake Sleeping Beauty, a narrative that journalists, business analysts, and industry chroniclers have largely run with ever since.[43] Their first stockholder meeting in early 1985 reportedly included a brief animated video featuring Saul Steinberg as a wolf—and Eisner and Frank Wells as the courageous cavalry officers here to defend the company against attack.[44] Yet much of what Eisner and company did was a continuation of what Ron Miller had already been doing with his focus on EPCOT, the Disney Channel, and feature film production. Eisner himself admitted at the beginning of his tenure, "Ron Miller had the right idea. I think it's unfortunate that he may not have had the time to exercise it completely."[45] While it is true that the broad plans may have been similar, the details of the execution may have taken a very different direction. Therefore, the specifics of the Disney Renaissance cannot be understood merely at the level of the executives because the logics and strategies of Miller and Eisner in the grand scheme of things were quite similar. Turning attention to the creative personnel not only reveals the complex network of industry figures necessary to run Disney but offers a more accurate and nuanced account that understands creative talent as major engines powering the company's comeback.

Similar to Miller's, Eisner's early efforts were largely grounded in feature production. Wilhite had appealed to young talent, in particular, with mixed results. Eisner hired Jeffrey Katzenberg away from Paramount, and under Katzenberg's supervision film production increased exponentially so that Disney had reportedly initiated a hundred new projects by the end of 1985.[46] Many of these films would be broad comedies for adults operating under the "no snow, no rural" dictum Eisner instituted at Paramount.[47] Rather than pursuing major stars, as Warner Bros. was doing, Disney focused instead on promising new talents (as Wilhite had) and, quite interestingly, proven talent who had hit a career slump. It was a strategy similar to one Walt himself had used in the 1950s and 1960s, hiring actors like Fred MacMurray and Maureen O'Hara for live-action comedies such as *The Shaggy Dog* (Charles Barton, 1959), *The Absent-Minded Professor* (Robert Stevenson, 1961), and *The Parent Trap* (David Swift, 1961). Directors John G. Avildsen and Paul Mazursky as well as actors Richard Dreyfuss and Bette Midler, for example, were signed to contracts similar to the studio system. The pay was hardly lucrative, but the talent rarely had the standing to refuse. Midler later observed with her trademark self-effacement, "My career was in the sewer. Why shouldn't I trust them?"[48] Katzenberg maintained a reputation as a micromanager, reading scripts, monitoring budgets, and making decisions with a swiftness that garnered him respect around Hollywood. Disney may not have paid well, but it was a fast decision maker. And Katzenberg was especially good at maintaining contact with talent, allegedly making six hundred phone calls every week.[49] In short, Katzenberg played the part with a youthful gusto—an engaged, eagle-eyed creative executive ready to take credit for his efforts.

The animation division, however, did not appear to be a priority during his early days at Disney. Coming from Paramount, Katzenberg felt live-action feature production was the way forward in contemporary Hollywood. Animation seemed like dated children's entertainment—not to mention how time-consuming and costly the production process could be. But Roy Disney, who had essentially ushered in Eisner and Wells (and therefore Katzenberg), was a tireless champion of animation. To his mind, it may not have made the most money—indeed, the films often failed to make back their exorbitant production and marketing costs on initial release—but they did feed the other divisions via theme park attractions, television content, and now home video. In 1985, Roy told the *Financial Times*, "Disney lost track of what their basic business was over the past seven or eight years—films. From the films flows everything else. That was why we were able to create Disneyland."[50] To placate Roy, Eisner installed him as the head of animation.

Neither Katzenberg nor Eisner had much confidence in feature animation's potential at first. Katzenberg therefore ran it much like he had run live-action production at Paramount. As he told the *New York Times*, his goal was "to bring to the process of making animated films my knowledge and experience with live-action movies."[51] To the shock of the animators, he insisted on a screenplay.[52] As Roger Allers later explained, animators used storyboards to work out and tweak the plot as necessary.[53] But in contemporary Hollywood, a screenplay served as "a financial prospectus, a detailed investment opportunity, and a corporate proposal," giving a studio a sense of the structure, trajectory, cost, and profit potential of a film project.[54] Katzenberg also committed a veritable sacrilege for many animators by editing the feature animation. Animators insisted it could not—and should not—be done, but Katzenberg ignored their concerns, streamlining narratives while also expending hours and hours of animation labor (and thus thousands and thousands of dollars). Katzenberg's underlings had even suggested outsourcing the animation overseas or shutting it down all together. Joe Hale, producer of *The Black Cauldron*, perceived it as an unwelcome and unexpected attempt by Katzenberg to assert his authority over animation, later remarking, "We were not prepared for this Eisner/Katzenberg team. It was sort of like the Sopranos took over the Studio."[55] Katzenberg would keep feature animation running, but in a way that he felt was more logistically and financially manageable. With Roy's approval, he installed Peter Schneider, who had served as company manager for *Little Shop of Horrors*, worked in the Chicago theatre, and, more recently, served as associate director of the Olympic Arts Festival, to supervise animation. Under his leadership, he helped to reorganize animation to run more like the repertory theatre company he had run in Chicago.

The Black Cauldron—a prolonged and costly project—was allowed to proceed because it was nearing completion, but Eisner and Katzenberg required the animation division to pitch to them *Basil of Baker Street*, even though it was already underway. The film had stagnated while its producer, Ron Miller, dealt with Steinberg; his eventual dismissal did little to get the film back on track. After reviewing the completed artwork, Eisner and Katzenberg greenlit the film (again), in part because they knew Steven Spielberg was producing *Young Sherlock Holmes* (Barry Levinson, 1985) for Paramount and hoped *Basil* might benefit from the film's success. They had conditions, however: *Basil* must be completed in half the time, on half the budget. *Young Sherlock Holmes* later struggled at the box office, prompting Katzenberg to change the film's title—much to the animators' embarrassment—to *The Great Mouse Detective* to distance it from Spielberg's flop. One animator, Ed Gombert, circulated a fake memo claiming to rebrand classic Disney films with new, easier-to-understand titles: *Seven Little Men Help a Girl*, *The Wonderful Elephant Who Could Really Fly*, *Two Dogs Fall in Love*, *A Fox and Hound Are Friends*, and *Robin Hood with Animals*.[56] The animation team got a good laugh in their satirical act of resistance, but the higher-ups were less pleased by the playful irreverence characteristic of the division. Furthermore, the abrupt title change upended licensing deals and left a noticeable dearth of merchandise, much to management's embarrassment.

Still, animation was hardly at the forefront of the executives' minds. *The Black Cauldron*, now the most expensive animated film produced to date, was finally

released in the summer of 1985. It was not even the most successful animated feature out that year, as *The Care Bears Movie* (Arna Selznick, 1985), a feature-length
adaptation of the inexpensively animated TV series, grossed more money while
playing in fewer theaters. Disney explained it away as the result of poor performance across the board in Hollywood, even though *Back to the Future* (Robert
Zemeckis, 1985), *Rambo: First Blood Part II* (George P. Cosmatos, 1985), and *Rocky IV*
(Sylvester Stallone, 1985) all surpassed $100 million domestically that same year.
Even *Pinocchio* had performed respectably during its rerelease the previous Christmas, while *Fantasia*, complete with a digitally remastered soundtrack, had earned
$8 million. In addition, Disney Channel subscribers now eclipsed two million
households.

The executives may have been unsure of how best to proceed with animation,
but they certainly saw hope for it in home video. Richard Frank, the newly appointed
Disney Studios president, noted that the new management had sat down within
the first week to figure out the safest and most effective way to exploit the company's past animated features.[57] Under Miller's tenure, the company had cautiously
released the animated films it considered to be of lesser quality, such as *Dumbo*
(Ben Sharpsteen, 1941), *Alice in Wonderland* (Clyde Geronimi, Wilfred Jackson, and
Hamilton Luske, 1951), and *Robin Hood*, along with compilation videos of cartoon shoots. The crown jewels so to speak—*Snow White*, *Bambi*, *Cinderella* (Clyde
Geronimi, Wilfred Jackson, and Hamilton Luske, 1950)—would not even air on
the Disney Channel out of fear home viewers would record it on their VCRs. (Disney had been the co-plaintiff [with Universal] in a prolonged and ultimately unsuccessful lawsuit against VCR manufacturers to prevent what it saw as encouraging
copyright violations.) Furthermore, these films continued to perform well upon
rerelease: in 1983, for example, rereleases of *Snow White*, *The Sword in the Stone*
(Wolfgang Reitherman, 1963), and *The Rescuers* had outperformed Disney's live-
action effort, *Something Wicked This Way Comes*. Eisner's team tested out a new
strategy: it released *Pinocchio* for a period of time at $79.95. The price would
appeal to the rental market as well as parents willing to make the investment for a
video sure to be watched over and over again. Disney operated a "vault" strategy,
making a video available for a limited period of time before withdrawing it from
circulation for several years. As Don Hahn later observed, "Home video was a
chance to print money—such a lucrative business."[58]

But the success of feature animation on home video posed a problem: a finite
amount of content. As Frederick Wasser contends, "The challenge was to avoid
exhausting the old library of classic animation and to build further. Katzenberg
decided to make new Disney classics to replenish the old ones."[59] The first animated
film initiated and greenlit under Katzenberg was *Oliver & Company* (George Scribner, 1988). The film occupies a curious spot in Disney history. Some scholars have
suggested it may represent the beginning of the Disney Renaissance, not only for
its solid box office performance but also for the participation of lyricist Howard
Ashman.[60] (Ashman worked on the film briefly, cowriting the lyrics on the opening song, "Once Upon a Time in New York City.") Eisner later claimed the film

was "the first clear evidence that animation had the potential to become a highly profitable business once again."[61] While *Oliver* shows traces of what the major Renaissance films would do in its use of musical numbers and emphasis on friendship, it clearly has a looser narrative structure and "sketchier" animation aesthetic (similar to *101 Dalmatians* [Wolfgang Reitherman, Clyde Geronimi, and Hamilton Luske, 1961]) compared to subsequent animated features. But the film helped to build confidence in the animation division while developing animators' skill sets.[62]

Not released until 1988, *Oliver & Company* should be understood as a transitional film in Disney history, blending Disney animation with Paramount-honed high-concept storytelling, therefore revealing the mandates imposed by Eisner and Katzenberg. "High-concept" films have a clear, easily relayed premise that can be ably exploited in marketing and promotion. In his foundational study, Justin Wyatt traces it back to Barry Diller, who favored film projects that could be clearly and succinctly explained in thirty-second television advertisements.[63] For his part, Katzenberg credits high concept to Eisner, a Diller protégé who promoted the ideal while all three were working at Paramount Pictures.[64] One also might link it to the spectacular genre films of 1970s and 1980s, described by Stephen Prince as "the popcorn movies of Spielberg and Lucas were aimed at what thereafter became Hollywood's sacred demographic—teens and older children. The breathless narrative pacing of these films, top-heavy with climax after climax, seemed to equate cinema entirely with the provision of spectacle. The iconic emotion in Spielberg's films of this period is awe—close-ups of stunned characters, staring slack-jawed at visions that overwhelm them, exactly as the films aimed to do with their audience."[65]

Journalists at the time noted that high concept's most prominent proponents often came to film from television—not just Diller and Eisner, but also Robert Daly (Warner Bros.), Frank Price (Universal), and Jeff Sagansky (Tri-Star).[66] Although many of these executives saw themselves in the creative executive tradition of Irving Thalberg, David O. Selznick, and, of course, Walt Disney, they were also committed to the bottom line. Their close attention to budgets and returns prompted director Peter Bogdanovich to lament, "It seems to me that a lot of us blew it in the '70s.... If the directors aren't responsible for the money, then the producers are going to take over, as they have."[67] Indeed, Katzenberg, often compared to Thalberg for his youth and success, saw himself moving away from the package deal model and returning to the practices of the classical Hollywood studios: "Warner Bros., by design, is in the megastar business: Goldie Hawn, Chevy Chase, Clint Eastwood. Paramount is in the annuity business—Paramount has created what Frank Mancuso [Paramount's chairman] would call 'tent-pole' assets, like *Star Trek IV*. We're a new version of the old studio system. We do believe in an enlightened golden handcuff. Basically, we're in the business of home-growing talent in every area."[68] *Oliver & Company*, not only in its loosely plotted storyline but in its use of star talent, ably captures Katzenberg's plan in action.

The premise for *Oliver & Company*—a loose adaptation of Charles Dickens's *Oliver Twist* recast with cats and dogs—was pitched by Pete Young during one of Eisner and Katzenberg's *Gong Show*–like meetings. The animation employees were required to prepare several ideas to quickly pitch to the executives: a gong was a rejection, but promising projects would be advanced to development. (At the same meeting, animator Ron Clements pitched *The Little Mermaid*, and Eisner himself suggested a sequel to *The Rescuers*.) The rapid-fire proposal, rejection, and approval process instituted here captures the high-concept approach at the preproduction level: was the idea understandable and appealing enough to garner attention in a brief, concise pitch? In interviews and even Eisner's memoirs, the idea for *Oliver & Company* was often credited not to Young, an experienced member of the story development team, but to Katzenberg himself—that is, the executive who pushed it forward rather than the employee who suggested and developed it.[69] With its easily distilled premise, *Oliver & Company* represented a fusion of traditional Disney animation and the Paramount-honed high-concept approach. It should come as no surprise that this attempt to marry tradition and innovation frustrated workers in the animation division. Pete Young, for instance, felt torn as he tried to satisfy not only Roy Disney's but also Eisner and Katzenberg's varying expectations.[70] Roy, for instance, proposed a plotline about kidnapping a prized panda—an idea Eisner and Katzenberg scrapped upon review because they found it confusing.[71]

Patrick C. Fleming praises *Oliver* as "the first animated musical produced under Eisner and Katzenberg" and because of the contribution of Howard Ashman to the title song, "a crucial turning point for the Walt Disney Company."[72] Yet the film clearly does not operate in the integrated musical tradition (nor does it try to) that Ashman advocated for so passionately.[73] *Oliver & Company* features five musical numbers, which are cumulatively credited to eleven different songwriters. "What was interesting about *Oliver*, of course," the film's production manager Kathleen Gavin recalls, "is that all of the songs were written by different people, so you did not have the benefit cohesive style of music."[74] The emphasis on musical numbers written for and performed by pop stars speaks to high concept's synergistic emphasis on marketing and promotion. As David Geffen, one of the producers of *Top Gun*, observed in 1986, "One of the reasons *Top Gun* has hung in there for so long is because the music was so effective. And it doesn't hurt to have a radio station saying *Top Gun* eight times a day."[75] (Katzenberg had passed on *Top Gun* when he was at Paramount; it was the first project greenlit by Mancuso after Katzenberg's departure and the biggest hit of 1986.) Eisner undoubtedly imagined similar possibilities for *Oliver & Company*. This pop music approach represents the musical of the 1980s: a disintegrated form in which musical numbers would be sung by recognizable names rather than by the characters, exemplified by *Flashdance*, *Footloose*, and *Dirty Dancing* (Emile Ardolino, 1987).

Although Marc Napolitano assesses *Oliver & Company*'s score as "serv[ing] ornamental purposes as opposed to storytelling purposes,"[76] Disney never really claimed *Oliver & Company* to be a musical. The theatrical poster features Oliver and Dodger on a piano above the city (a subtle cue, perhaps, to the "Piano Man" singer's starring role); the theatrical trailer places greater emphasis on the film as an action-adventure film with musical numbers rather than a film musical. One can hardly deny Napolitano's claim that the songs serve to "showcase[e] the musical talents of the celebrity voice-cast,"[77] which includes Billy Joel and Bette Midler, who surprisingly had not sung in any of her previous film projects for Disney. The pop-style songs serve more narrative purpose than Napolitano acknowledges, yet *Oliver* does not adhere to an integrated film musical structure wherein songs are distributed and balanced throughout the plot to hold up and move the story forward; in fact, the five musical numbers are performed within the first half of the movie, leaving the action-adventure sequences to carry the rest of the film. Therefore, the film's blend of musical, action-adventure, and buddy comedy appears to be indicative not only of high-concept storytelling but of a complex negotiation of the new executives and the established animation team. It also ably represents a period of Disney animation when several stakeholders—animators, story developers, managers, and executives—struggled to redefine the Disney animation aesthetic to operate within standard practices of 1980s Hollywood live-action feature production.

Whereas attention and investment in theme parks, feature production, and home video continued initiatives by Miller's regime, Team Disney was distinct in its attention to and investment in television. Disney had largely withdrawn from television then amid lagging ratings so they could focus on EPCOT, but Eisner promised Disney would be back on network television in no time. Eisner wanted Disney to be present in the Saturday morning programming block, where he had built his career at ABC, but he had to navigate the costs of Disney full animation against the potential revenues. Saturday morning was dominated by incredibly lucrative cartoon series linked to merchandise, but nearly all of these shows employed cost-saving limited animation techniques. Don Bluth, for example, often derided these shows for commercial crassness and lack of artistry, and they were repeatedly lambasted by advocates for children's television who wanted more educational programming and less targeted advertising. Despite his initial hesitation over Saturday morning cartoons' lower production values, Eisner ultimately greenlit two series that employed limited animation techniques, *The Adventures of the Gummi Bears* and *The Wuzzles*.

Syndication, in particular, proved to be a vastly underutilized opportunity for Disney, and Eisner and Katzenberg vigorously pursued it. They achieved early success syndicating *At the Movies*, featuring Chicago film critics Gene Siskel and Roger Ebert. *DuckTales* was conceived as an animated afternoon series for syndication. But Disney was also keenly aware that a successful prime-time series, later sold into syndication, could yield millions in revenue for years to come. The company's emphasis on comedies in film production carried over to television, and Touchstone Television's second series and first sitcom, *The Golden Girls*, emerged as the most promising new show of fall 1985.

The concept itself came not from Disney but from NBC: Warren Littlefield and Brandon Tartikoff had been delighted by a sketch that Selma Diamond and Doris Roberts had performed while introducing *Miami Vice* at the NBC showcase, in which they bickered over whether or not the show's title was *Miami Nice*. During a meeting with Tony Thomas and Paul Junger Witt, the producers behind *Soap*, Little-field asked them if they were interested in a sitcom about older women in Miami. The details hereafter get muddy: Littlefield claims he wanted them to try to get Susan Harris, whereas Tony Thomas claims Paul Junger Witt knew the perfect writer for the show: Witt's wife, Susan Harris.[78] Harris was arguably the finest comedy writer in television at the time, having written on *All in the Family*, *The Partridge Family*, and *Maude* (including the two-part reproductive rights episode "Maude's Dilemma") before creating *Soap* and *Benson*. The series cast sitcom veterans Bea Arthur, Rue McClanahan, and Betty White alongside Estelle Getty, a stage actress who had gar-nered critical acclaim in Harvey Fierstein's *Torch Song Trilogy*. But NBC would only cover $200,000 of the $320,000 production costs, so Witt-Thomas-Harris sought out a partner to finance the remainder. Disney therefore coproduced and distributed the show via Touchstone Television, uncharacteristically accepting only one-third the profits and surrendering creative oversight in exchange for being in business with Susan Harris and a network presence.[79] It paid off handsomely: *Golden Girls* became its first hit, tying with *Dynasty* at seventh in the ratings. It went on to win the Prime-time Emmy Award for Outstanding Comedy Series in its first year, defeating ratings powerhouses *Cheers* and *The Cosby Show*. Despite the major success on its sopho-more effort, Touchstone Television struggled to repeat it in prime time—that is, until Susan Harris developed a spinoff, *Empty Nest*.

Meanwhile, the entrance of Steven Spielberg into the feature animation market through his collaboration with Don Bluth on *An American Tail* not only increased competition but also underscored Disney animation's struggles in recent years—and its need to right the course. *An American Tail* clearly exhibits Spielberg's touch. The protagonist, Fievel, was named after Spielberg's grandfather, who was a Russian Jewish immigrant. Despite Bluth's penchant for the menacing evil of early Disney animation, *An American Tail* is noticeably toned down, in part because Spielberg, now a young father, was, according to Bluth, "very insistent that his son, Max, could watch this without repercussions."[80] The film features the rich, dark tones produced through the use of the six-hundred-color palette developed for Bluth's earlier work, and one cannot help but draw comparison yet again to the mettlesome yet well-meaning mice of *Cinderella* or even the painful devasta-tion of parental separation of *Bambi* (although Bambi's mother dies, whereas Fievel and his family are reunited). Explaining *An American Tail*'s debt to classi-cal animation, Gary Goldman observed, "many people—particularly younger people who have not seen the classics—believe that what they see on television will be what they will see in the theaters. We hope to change that perception, not only for now, but for future productions in the industry."[81] Following a lead forged in part by Lucas and Spielberg, Bluth and company attempted an animated spectacle to underscore the fundamental difference between the theatergoing and home-viewing experiences.

An American Tail strategically employs aspects of the Disney film that were lacking in animation over the previous two decades. For one, it clearly owes a debt to the musical and early Disney animation, as the mice break out into the joyous "There Are No Cats in America" or, more memorably, Fievel and his sister Tanya's long-distance duet of the Oscar-nominated song "Somewhere Out There." While the musical numbers are not as tightly integrated into the plot as in subsequent Disney animated musicals, the songs are vital contributors to both the narrative development as well as the emotional impact of the film. Furthermore, "Somewhere Out There" is repeated over the end credits, this time performed by pop stars Linda Ronstadt and James Ingram. This use of a romantic ballad was evocative of high-concept filmmaking, and it set the stage for a new era of pop hits coming out of animated feature films. Peaking at number two on the *Billboard* Top 40 chart, the version performed by Ronstadt and Ingram proved an effective promotional device for the film.

Bluth's latest effort quickly found supporters, including Eleanor Ringel of the *Atlanta Journal and Constitution*, who praised the film's artistic superiority to television cartoons: "*An American Tail* celebrates the rich diversity of our melting-pot heritage; it doesn't insult kids (or adults) with fifth-rate Saturday-morning non-animation; and it gives us some wonderfully memorable characters that weren't already sitting on the Toys R Us shelves, waiting for a feature-length plug to stimulate sales."[82] Unfortunately, most critics were no more taken with *An American Tail* than with *The Secret of NIMH*. Vincent Canby of the *New York Times* faulted the film's troublesome politics, including its lighthearted representation of a pogrom and damning conclusion, in which cats are gleefully deported to Hong Kong.[83] The title of Charles Solomon's review in the *Los Angeles Times* sarcastically notes that the film "lavishly disappoints," observing that "rarely has so much animated opulence been wasted on such a thin, badly told story."[84] Yet again, Bluth, the great champion of stories rich in emotional complexity that fostered audience identification, was faulted for a feeble screenplay. For all his adorableness, Fievel is a fairly weak character who is often overshadowed by the more amusing supporting cast. (*Oliver & Company* would face similar criticisms.) While critics praised the animation, it was often undercut by the unsatisfying ending, which some felt featured three back-to-back climaxes. Harry McCracken, writing for *Cinefantastique*, opines, "*An American Tail* manages to be a better film than such ramshackle underpinnings suggest largely because of Bluth's insistence on high production values."[85] In critics' eyes, Bluth's efforts were noble and the artistic results satisfying, yet the foundational elements of his art form—its characters, its plot, its emotional resonance—remained hollow.

Yet audiences were warming up to animated features again. Months earlier, in July 1986, Disney had released *The Great Mouse Detective*, which grossed a staggering million dollars per day in its first five days.[86] Roger Ebert optimistically declared, "For a long time, I was down on the full-length animated efforts of Disney and others, because they didn't seem to reflect the same sense of magic and wonderment that the original animated classics always had. Who, for example, could ever equate *101 Dalmatians* with *Snow White and the Seven Dwarfs*? But now, maybe thanks to computers, animated movies are beginning to sparkle again."[87]

Disney Animation seemed to be rebounding artistically, even though the film ultimately grossed only $25 million. Released in November 1986 by Universal Pictures, though, *An American Tail* beat *The Great Mouse Detective*, easily becoming the highest-grossing animated film of the year, while partnerships with Sears and McDonald's drew additional revenue. Spielberg and Bluth announced their next collaboration—a dinosaur film, later titled *The Land Before Time* (Don Bluth, 1988)—but this time another entertainment titan, George Lucas, was on board. The success of the Spielberg-Bluth venture, combined with Bluth's ongoing antagonism toward both Disney and Saturday morning cartoons, demonstrates that the Disney Renaissance was part of a much larger surge in animation production across film, television, and video games.

In 1986, Team Disney also revived the Sunday night television series as ABC's *The Disney Sunday Movie* with plans to produce several original movies as well as broadcast films from its library, as Walt himself had done. The company searched for an appropriate host before settling on Michael Eisner—on the condition he lose some weight and improve his wardrobe. Eisner's duties as the host of the series presented him directly to the U.S. public much the same way it had for Walt years earlier. It was a parallel Eisner did not seem to mind; in fact, he actively fostered it. Throughout the late 1980s, Eisner promoted his efforts to turn the company around with profiles in several prominent venues. Katzenberg, Eisner's subordinate, also seemed to be in on the game—often in the same venues. Aljean Harmetz wrote a 1985 profile of Eisner in the *New York Times* titled "The Man Reanimating Disney"; three years later, the title of her profile of Jeffrey Katzenberg posed the question "Who Makes Disney Run?" Rarely has executive leadership been covered in so much depth, not only revealing tensions between the two of the leaders helming Disney but inspiring ire from the very man who had helped install them, Roy E. Disney. With his thin mustache, propensity for sweaters over ties, and unassuming folksy manner, Roy fashioned himself in a manner not unlike his uncle.[88] He certainly favored the creative side of the business, while proving himself to be a savvy investor and boardroom strategist. Although he did not oppose the occasional interview or profile of his own efforts, he appeared uneasy, at times flummoxed, by the egoism and showmanship of Eisner and Katzenberg. Yet in many ways, whether it was hyping their latest projects or slyly taking credit for the company's achievements (especially on film), all three men seemed to be more or less taking their cues from the company namesake.

Although he was far more humble, Frank Wells's efforts during this time cannot be downplayed. He negotiated and supervised the reopening of the Chinese market to Disney, including the broadcast of Disney cartoons on national television. He took a special interest in theme parks, encouraging the company to pursue television advertisements that resulted in a noticeable bump in attendance. He also actively sought new financing opportunities to expand feature production while minimizing risk, leading to the founding of Silver Screen Partners II to raise almost $200 million (via limited partnerships) to fund twelve to fourteen film projects. While the majority of these new films would be produced under the

Touchstone banner, 25 percent of the money was set aside for animated family films. The resulting films—*Down and Out in Beverly Hills, The Great Mouse Detective, Ruthless People*—demonstrated renewed vigor at Disney, especially in live-action production under Touchstone. In particular, they demonstrated the benefit of investing in proven talents, such as Abrahams, Dreyfuss, Mazursky, Midler, and the Zucker Brothers. In October 1986, Silver Screen Partners raised another $300 million to produce eighteen new films in the wake of Touchstone's recent triumphs. These partnerships demonstrated a change not only in Disney's feature production but in its financial management. It also introduced a new contributor into filmmaking at Disney. While the partners had no direct influence on individual films, the funding specified the types of projects to be made and added a noteworthy stakeholder to the production process.

Although many commentators have praised Team Disney's transformation of the company during this period, the break was hardly as clean or abrupt as many would have it. The political and economic climate of Reagan's America was also clearly favorable to Disney, leading one *New York Times* columnist to boast that 1984 was a great year for capitalism: "The spirit of capitalism, stirred by a conservative Administration in the White House, spread across the land."[89]

It is mere conjecture to suggest whether or not Miller could have been equally successful; some analysts at the time said he did not have the vision or ambition of Eisner. As David Kline asserted in the *Globe and Mail*, "A revolution was needed, and Ronald Miller offered only reforms."[90] Furthermore, the focus on television, aggressive expansion of home video, investment in adult-oriented comedies, and financial restructuring were clearly innovations that Team Disney piloted. It should come as little surprise then that the stockholders approved a renaming in early 1986, transforming Walt Disney Productions into the Walt Disney Company. Yet a key factor in Team Disney's myriad successes was undeniably its ability to attract talent on screen and off—and put them under contract. By focusing on proven talent who had faced setback or had thrived in another industry (most obviously here, theatre), Team Disney created a brain trust of sorts that provided the creative energy that drove management decisions in the years ahead. Eisner clearly understood this fact to be true, despite his willingness to tout his and the company's achievements in the press. As he told the *New York Times* early in his tenure, "The major asset of any film company is not the library but what walks home at night."[91]

––––––

The critical success of the film version of *Little Shop of Horrors* was in complete opposition to the reception of Ashman's concurrent stage effort, *Smile*. Based on a 1976 Michael Ritchie film, *Smile* was originally a project for composer Marvin Hamlisch and lyricist Carolyn Leigh. They were a formidable team: Leigh had written the lyrics for the Broadway hits *Peter Pan* and *Little Me*, while Hamlisch had been one of the most successful composers of the 1970s, winning Oscars for *The Sting* (George Roy Hill, 1973) and *The Way We Were* (Sydney Pollack, 1973) and a

Tony Award for the score of *A Chorus Line*. Following Leigh's 1983 death, Ashman expressed interest as lyricist, book writer, and director—but only if they would start over with a new book and lyrics.[92] While the *Little Shop* film adaptation moved into production in London, Ashman focused on *Smile* in New York, though he had an open invitation to visit the set.[93] His recruitment to *Smile* helped to secure $400,000 for a workshop performance from the powerful Shubert Organization. But troubles arose as Hamlisch and Ashman found it difficult working together, perhaps because of Hamlisch's monumental success versus Ashman's growing reputation. Hamlisch also took issue with the seemingly relentless fundraising required to put on a Broadway show in the 1980s, as he publicly admitted in several interviews: "It was terribly hard. I don't know if I want to do that again."[94] Ashman and Hamlisch struggled to balance *Smile*'s mix of satire and sentimentality, and a mixed reception to a backer's audition prompted the Shubert Organization to decline investing in the Broadway run.[95] In November 1986, Ashman observed, "*Little Shop* would never have been produced had I not had my own theater. In order to reach the public, it had to get past the New York theater establishment. And if that establishment had had its way, it also would have roadblocked *Smile*."[96]

Furthermore, the audience for Broadway was not necessarily the same audience as for Off-Broadway. The metropolitan crowds that had sustained Broadway through its Golden Age in the 1940s and 1950s were being increasingly replaced by tourists. The success of *Cats* was not just because of its spectacular dancing or family-friendly subject matter but also a result of its tuneful score. Early in his career, Andrew Lloyd Webber and then-partner Tim Rice found an alternate way to the stage: they produced concept albums of *Jesus Christ Superstar* and *Evita*, which helped secure the funding for a full theatrical production. In fact, in London "Memory" was a hit song on the radio before *Cats* even premiered. The interest of David Geffen, the show's producer, in musicals was intimately connected to producing the cast albums—and for *Cats*, he produced not only one for both the London and New York casts but also a single-disc highlights album and a double album of the entire show. While popular audiences embraced this new model of musical, it earned the ongoing derision of drama critics; Clive Barnes of the *Sunday Times* dismissed shows like *Cats* as "nothing more than an excuse for theatre."[97] With little to no dialogue, *Cats* is a combination of catchy songs, energetic dancing, and pantomime—a form that would play particularly well to foreign audiences who may not have the necessary command of the English language to closely follow an intricately plotted narrative. Broadway's audience in the 1980s was both ageing and changing. Ashman publicly derided Broadway, now populated by an audience that was older and/or from out of town, as "a tourist attraction and a museum."[98] In turn, Broadway theatergoers did not express much fondness for *Smile*.

Critics were not much kinder to the show when it finally opened on Broadway at the Lunt-Fontanne Theatre in November 1986. Frank Rich of the *New York Times* felt *Smile* was "schizoid in tone, dramatically diffuse and undistinguished in such crucial areas as music, dance, and humor."[99] He praised Ashman's lyrics but derided

Hamlisch's music. Writing for the *Atlanta Journal and Constitution*, Linda Sherbert felt the show was "too often as vapid as the beauty pageants it intends to satirize."[100] Richard Hummler of *Variety* offered measured praise—"sufficiently entertaining and expertly packaged"—but did single out Ashman's direction for praise in his first Broadway effort.[101] Several critics made comparison to both creators' previous efforts, but not necessarily in a positive manner, linking the hopeful number "Disneyland," sung by Jodi Benson, to "Somewhere's That Green" in *Little Shop* and "At the Ballet" in *A Chorus Line*. Word of mouth did not build, and the economics of Broadway were not in *Smile*'s favor. With over fifteen hundred seats, the Lunt-Fontanne Theatre was one of Broadway's larger venues, and the show's operating costs required weekly grosses of $250,000. Amid these financial pressures, the show eventually closed in January 1987 after the holiday season, having only played forty-eight performances. *Smile* was a casualty of a new Broadway: one preoccupied with spectacle, British imports, and minimal creative and financial risk.

The end of 1986 proved turbulent for Ashman: the critical success of the *Little Shop* film, the critical lambasting of *Smile*, and the varying commercial failures of both. His uncomfortable experience on *Smile*—both in working with Hamlisch and in navigating the Broadway theatre scene—unsurprisingly dissuaded Ashman from diving into another theatrical effort. But he was hardly soured from writing. At the behest of his best friend, David Geffen, Jeffrey Katzenberg had approached the promising young lyricist in April 1986 about coming to work for the Walt Disney Company. Following their meeting, Katzenberg offered Ashman his pick of prospective projects to "co-conspire" on with Disney, including *The Little Mermaid*, a sequel to *Mary Poppins* (Robert Stevenson, 1964), a *Sesame Street*–like show for the Disney Channel, as well as several live-action projects, including *Holiday Blues* (later made by TriStar as *Mixed Nuts* [Nora Ephron, 1994]) as well as *Straight Talk* (Barnet Kellman, 1992), developed for Bette Midler but ultimately produced with Dolly Parton.[102] Ashman chose *The Little Mermaid* because, to his mind, animation was the remaining stronghold of the Broadway-style musical in filmmaking. Katzenberg and Roy Disney had previously approached Andrew Lloyd Webber to write songs for *Mermaid*, but he was preoccupied with *Phantom of the Opera*.[103] For Ashman, though, *Mermaid* had the potential to be more than a movie with songs; it could be an integrated musical. In a Hollywood where *Annie* had floundered under production and marketing costs and where dance musicals with pop soundtracks had proven popular and profitable, Ashman saw the integrated musical tradition—in which songs were narrative information advancing the plot and characterization—in jeopardy. His interest, in part, was in exploiting animation's artifice to create worlds where characters bursting out into song was not old-fashioned or ridiculous but natural and pleasurable. As Don Hahn observes, the integrated musical "was a lost art—or at least a losing art, and Howard was able to articulate what it was about musical theatre was unique and why it was so good for storytelling."[104] Ashman typified exactly what Disney needed: promising (but affordable) talent, committed to effective, time-honored storytelling.

In May 1986, Ron Clements and John Musker met with Ashman at the Helmsley Palace Hotel in New York City to discuss *The Little Mermaid*. Ashman was particularly concerned with characterization, posing questions with the intention of fleshing out the characters' personalities and backstory.[105] It was at this meeting that Ashman began to introduce the key tenets of the integrated musical. Rather than "passive and general" musical numbers, Ashman advocated for "active and specific" songs that would serve to "move the narrative forward."[106] Clements and Musker wanted to start underwater, introducing the world of the mer-people, but Ashman advocated beginning with a sea shanty that would showcase the human world before moving underwater to establish the tensions between Triton (at this point "the Sea King") and Ursula ("the Sea Witch"). Although Ashman felt the song could be challenging, he asserted that it would establish the tensions both between the mer-people and the humans as well as the Sea King and the Sea Witch while also carrying out "a lot of exposition . . . quickly and entertainingly." Curiously, Ashman worried that this approach was more "theatrical" and "stylized" than Musker and Clements may have wanted. As Musker later explained, "Ron and I felt that songs should advance the story, but Howard's ways of doing that were revelatory. He liked his songs to have information and to carry essential plot material. To take the key story beats and though the use of music to underline them and drive them home."[107] In short, Ashman was making *The Little Mermaid* into an integrated musical, and with it came certain storytelling conventions that would shift the narrative away from the more ornamental approach employed in *Oliver & Company*.

Ashman then recommended a central conflict similar to Blake and Alexis Carrington on *Dynasty*, by which Ursula "is plotting to overthrow the Sea King and gain power."[108] By framing this tension using the famed sibling rivalry between the Carringtons, Ashman called upon the heightened emotions characteristic of the soap opera to increase the film's dramatic excitement. The witch's backstory needed to be simple and streamlined: she wants power and is simply "biding her time, waiting for the right moment to make her move." Ultimately, they realized that the Sea Witch uses Ariel in her attempt to achieve power, and Ursula's death must bring peace to both worlds.

A major concern at this meeting was Ariel's main song, which she sings for the first time in her grotto and later reprises after rescuing Prince Eric from the shipwreck. Ashman told Clements and Musker that the song, unbeknownst to them, followed the "classical 'stage musical' structure." This ballad for Ariel would establish her desire and then clarify her mission to achieve it in the classic "I want" song formula. Ashman assured the animators that the "I want" song not only is essential for motivating the protagonist and therefore the plot but also establishes the affective bond between the viewer and the protagonist necessary to create an emotionally satisfying narrative. If the audience comprehends what the protagonist wants from this song, they not only understand what is motivating her decisions and actions but also root for her to succeed in her pursuit.

Similarly, Sebastian's spirited defense of underwater life, "Under the Sea," was also discussed. Howard reimagined Sebastian the crab as "a Rastafarian, Geoffrey Holder type," a noted Broadway performer from Trinidad known for his rich bass voice. While Clements and Musker wanted it to be a "fun, upbeat song," Ashman clearly planned to elevate it to a traditional Broadway showstopper—a moment of pure narrative excess. Musker and Clements returned to California to flesh out and revise the screenplay, now a requisite starting point for Disney feature animation. Ashman would soon join them, along with an old friend: composer Alan Menken. Although he never took to living in California, Ashman would commute back and forth from New York. At Disney, he found not only an outlet for his talent but a much-needed respite from the artistic and economic pressures that he felt were obstructing his success on Broadway. The recruitment of Ashman and Menken, much like the hiring of Peter Schneider the previous year, infused Disney with theatrically trained talent, adept in the area where animation was the weakest: narrative. Together with the executives, managers, and animators, Ashman and Menken started Disney on a new path forward for animation storytelling—a path that, in many ways, returned the division to the conventions first employed in *Snow White*.

CHAPTER 3

"Make the Audience Fall in Love with Ariel"

HOWARD ASHMAN AND ALAN MENKEN, *THE LITTLE MERMAID*, AND DISNEY, 1987–1989

The closure of *Smile*, Howard Ashman's sole effort on Broadway during his lifetime, prompted the thirty-six-year-old director/lyricist to distance himself from the theatre. His partner Bill Lauch recalls Ashman's ambivalence about the increasing dominance of the British megamusical: "It was so much about spectacle and that wasn't the kind of musical theatre he had great interest in doing. For him to try following in the vein of *Starlight Express* or *Cats* was just like *eeecck!* Why bother?!"[1] Broadway was changing, and the opportunities for artists like Ashman were dwindling precipitously. Instead, Ashman focused on his new project for the Walt Disney Company, a musical adaptation of *The Little Mermaid*. Ashman was familiar with the story as well as with Hans Christian Andersen's oeuvre more broadly: his master's thesis at Indiana University had been a children's theatre adaptation of "The Snow Queen." (Disney Animation later adapted the same story—to monumental success—as *Frozen*.) Howard enjoyed the creative control that Disney would provide, but he did not know how to compose music. He needed Alan Menken. "Howard brought the dramatic intelligence, and I brought the schmaltz," Menken later mused.[2] Menken had been balancing several projects as well, but it seemed serendipitous because with a newborn daughter at home, he found himself recently immersed in Disney videotapes. The company not only offered the collaborators a chance to reunite—it offered them a chance to definitely get their "show" on.

This chapter examines *The Little Mermaid* as Ashman and Menken staging a Broadway-style integrated musical within an animated feature. Indeed, *The Little Mermaid* demonstrates the legacies of theatrical presentation in the film musical, akin to what Jane Feuer identified as the genre's tendency to draw attention to its own artifice.[3] It also represents a return to an older mode of musical theatre storytelling detached from recent developments in Hollywood and Broadway. Many film musicals of the 1980s utilize a looser narrative form in which musical numbers are danced to, but not sung, by the characters. While the film musical was

68

disintegrating, however, the Broadway musical was "hyperintegrating." Broadway seemingly doubled down on the sung-through megamusicals imported from the West End, while Hollywood saw a return of more adult-oriented fare as well as media franchises. *The Little Mermaid* was somewhat old-fashioned in its approach and yet right at home in feature animation with its dependence on the integrated musical, complete with a love story, "I want" song, and love ballad. That *The Little Mermaid* was released during the holiday season following the reign of *Batman* (Tim Burton, 1989) over the summer box office also should not be ignored. But Disney found its wellspring of franchise revenues not in gritty comic book heroes as Warner Bros. had—though they did try—but rather in strong-minded princesses more likely to demonstrate compassion than engage in combat. In so doing, Disney ended up striking their own path, revitalizing animation, musicals, and princess culture in the process. While critics have challenged this reinvestment in patriarchal fairy tale narratives with heterosexual romance plots, these stories also privileged young girls as an important audience for the company while centering headstrong, independent young women in major media franchises.

Despite a stock market crash in 1987, the box office remained surprisingly strong, returning some of the highest grosses in Hollywood history. Paramount and Disney were the primary beneficiaries of this upswing, whereas Warner Bros., 20th Century Fox, MGM, and others found mixed success due to a range of factors, including poor management and box office flops. In 1987 alone, over 575 films were made and released, the highest number in years. It also marked the return of an older audience to theaters, as roughly half the year's thirty top-earning films at the box office targeted adults rather than the youth audience who had ruled the box office during the heyday of spectacular genre films.[4] Even Steven Spielberg's seemingly invincible Amblin struggled with the underwhelming commercial response to *Harry and the Hendersons* (William Dear, 1987), *Innerspace* (Joe Dante, 1987), and *Empire of the Sun* (Steven Spielberg, 1987). Bolstered by increased film output, the number of movie screens in North America neared twenty-three thousand—the most in decades—and the Toronto-based Cineplex Odeon, with Garth Drabinsky at the helm, owned the greatest share.[5]

The domestic box office, yet again, belonged to Paramount, whose major successes—*Beverly Hills Cop II* (Tony Scott, 1987), *Fatal Attraction* (Adrian Lyne, 1987), and *The Untouchables* (Brian De Palma, 1987)—demonstrated its ongoing dependence on stars, sequels, sex, and sophistication. Encouraged by both renovated and brand-new theaters, older adults increased their moviegoing, and the studios obliged to the point that films often did poorly not so much for their quality as for the considerable influx of releases targeting more mature audience members. Independent producers and distributors, including Cannon Films, Cinecom, and even Vestron, proved themselves to be potential competition. The high-concept filmmaking championed by the likes of Spielberg and Lucas and embraced by young audiences was yielding to "low-concept" fare—except at

Paramount, Warner Bros., and Disney.[6] The importance of mature audiences and high-concept storytelling remains evident in Disney's three most successful releases of 1987, which were not rereleases of animated classics but Touchstone projects: *Three Men and a Baby* (Leonard Nimoy, 1987), *Stakeout* (John Badham, 1987), and *Outrageous Fortune* (Arthur Hiller, 1987). In these adult-oriented films, several Disney live-action strategies are at work: a focus on film comedy, an emphasis on hiring film actors in a career slump or television stars, an investment in promising young writers. *Three Men and a Baby*, Disney's biggest hit of the year, was also the latest in a string of French-film remakes that began with *Down and Out in Beverly Hills* (1986) and continued with *Three Fugitives* (Francis Veber, 1989) and *Paradise* (Mary Agnes Donoghue, 1991), all of which curiously coincided with Disney's developing plans for a theme park near Paris.

Americans' interest in home video increased during this period, and by the end of 1987 Americans had purchased sixty-five million video cassettes and rented two billion more.[7] At last, Hollywood appeared to accept home video as "an immutable fact of life."[8] Few studios were as well-positioned to tap this market as Disney was, and its strategic release of cartoon shorts compilations and its back catalog of animated classics led to its domination of best-sellers lists. Disney had thirty-six titles available on video cassette, and although it did not theatrically release a new animated film in 1987, Disney's *Oliver & Company* would be the first film in a proposed plan to produce one animated feature each year. The plan was incredibly ambitious, and to pull off *The Little Mermaid* eventually required 150,000 cels, an animation staff exceeding four hundred people—and three years.[9] To maintain their ambition, Disney would have to manage multiple feature animation projects simultaneously.

In his 1987 letter to stockholders, Michael Eisner gushed that he found it challenging to write his annual letter to them "without sounding too cocky, too confident and certainly too proud!"[10] The company's revenues were nearing $3 billion annually, with filmed entertainment experiencing a 153 percent increase in operating income, and the merchandising division alone boasting more than three thousand licensees manufacturing over fourteen thousand products in over fifty countries.[11] Not all decisions, of course, were prudent: waffling between Spain and France for its next park, Disney settled on the latter in large part because of Eisner's personal preference. Spain's temperate climate would have provided a more accommodating locale, but the country lacked the necessary infrastructure, and Eisner sought the cultural capital that came with building a Disneyland satellite so close to central Paris.[12] (Admittedly, France was Disney's strongest foreign market.)[13] The decision would prove a troublesome one.

While Disney decided to divest its interests in real estate in 1987 when it sold off Arvida for $400 million, it did open three Disney Stores, which allowed them to sell theme park tickets, home videos, and other merchandise while also promoting the most recent film and television productions. By the end of the 1980s, there would be forty retail locations with plans for one hundred by 1992. Furthermore, Disney forged a partnership with McDonald's for toys related to Disney releases;

in 1988, for example, children could collect toys related to the highly popular television series *DuckTales* as well as the reissue of *Bambi*. As Douglas Gomery later observed, "Paramount, Warner Bros., Universal, Fox, Disney, and Sony-Columbia, all with vertically integrated operations, made possible initially by lax enforcement by the Federal Trade Commission (FTC) and Federal Communications Commission (FCC) in compliance with President Ronald Reagan's policies of deregulation. These six companies controlled almost 80 percent of the movie business in the United States and approximately half the market around the world."[14] Under Reagan appointee Mark Fowler, the FCC continued to pursue deregulation, allowing Disney to expand its holdings in television to include the purchase of the local CBS station in Los Angeles, KHJ-TV (later KCAL), for over $300 million.

The 1987 annual report was the first one released under Eisner's tenure to lead off the discussion of the company's success in filmed entertainment by focusing on animation. It was not, however, a new release that earned such attention, but rather the reissue of *Snow White*, which took in a reported $46 million. The impressive gross led Jeffrey Katzenberg to brag that the 1937 film was "the most popular movie seen in movie theaters, ever."[15] Despite its surprisingly strong performance, *Snow White* alone probably did little to inspire much confidence in upcoming feature animation. As Katzenberg noted, echoing Roy's earlier sentiment, "Usually the animated films don't (hit home runs), but they are the foundation of our company. They're our heritage and it is a good, reasonably profitable business for us to be in."[16] *Video* magazine placed a more positive spin on the situation: "Disney's classic children's fare is familiar to parents in the nostalgic glow of matinee memories and boasts animation that's still considered state of the art."[17] With sales exceeding seven million units, nearly half of which were *Lady and the Tramp* (Hamilton Luske, Clyde Geronimi, and Wilfred Jackson, 1955), home video proved to be the steadiest stream of revenue from Disney animation.

Industry analysts predicted the increase in releases and box office returns would continue into 1988, although only about 20 percent of the films would turn a meaningful profit.[18] Disney, less than five years after the arrival of Team Disney, claimed the highest share in an incredibly competitive (and glutted) market due to continuing revenues from *Three Men and a Baby*; the exceptional performance of a 1987 holiday release, *Good Morning, Vietnam* (Barry Levinson, 1987); and the year's biggest success, *Who Framed Roger Rabbit*. Paramount also performed well, thanks to *Coming to America* (John Landis, 1988) and *Crocodile Dundee II* (John Cornell, 1988), while *Big* (Penny Marshall, 1988) and *Die Hard* (John McTiernan, 1988) gave 20th Century Fox two spots in the top ten. Warner Bros., on the other hand, struggled mightily, with only one film—*Beetlejuice* (Tim Burton, 1988)—in the top twenty-five highest grossing films of the year.

The significance of *Who Framed Roger Rabbit* for the future of animation and of Disney was considerable. "Achieving that ever-difficult integration of art and technology, it epitomizes the glories of traditional methods of special effects compositing at the onset of a digital future," Stephen Prince contends.[19] Unlike many earlier Disney films, *Roger Rabbit* was a coproduction with another studio—in this case, Steven Spielberg's Amblin Entertainment. Disney had held the rights to Gary K. Wolf's novel *Who Censored Roger Rabbit?* since soon after its 1981 publication, but according to director Robert Zemeckis, "They just didn't have the energy to pull together a movie this massive."[20] Fresh from the blockbuster success of *Back to the Future*, Zemeckis wanted to revisit the project. Animation was supervised by British animator Richard Williams in London rather than by the Disney animators in exile in Glendale. Set just outside of Toontown, *Roger Rabbit* features cameos by scores of famous cartoon characters, many of whom are not Disney intellectual property, including Betty Boop, Bugs Bunny, Daffy Duck, and Woody Woodpecker. The live-action Eddie Valiant (Bob Hoskins) attempts to track down the true killer of Marvin Acme (Stubby Kaye), leading him on a madcap chase in and out of Toontown and eventually to a confrontation with the murderous Judge Doom (Christopher Lloyd). Fast-paced, anarchic, and ripe with innuendo, *Roger Rabbit* stands out as an adult-oriented film with some appeal for children—inverting Disney's usual formula—and made over $150 million domestically. Michael Eisner held up *Roger Rabbit* as a source of pride not only because it fared better overseas but because of its considerable franchising potential. The costly *Roger Rabbit* demonstrated the value in investing in animation as well as the sizable international audience for such films.

On the back of *Who Framed Roger Rabbit*, Michael Eisner declared, "I wish 1988 would never end, because it has been one of those perfect years for all of us."[21] In addition to *Roger Rabbit*, the success of *Three Man and a Baby*, *The Golden Girls*, home video, and *Good Morning, Vietnam* pushed film and television entertainment's revenues over $1 billion for the first time. The future looked optimistic: the Bette Midler vehicle *Beaches* (Garry Marshall, 1988) would premiere near Christmas 1988, while the attractions division was set to open Disney-MGM Studios (later, Disney's Hollywood Studios), Typhoon Lagoon, and Pleasure Island by summer 1989.

The 1988 report even made mention of *The Little Mermaid*, boasting, "The coming year holds ever more promise for Disney animation."[22] Alongside the profuse excitement following *Roger Rabbit* in Eisner's introductory letter, this statement appears rather nonplussed, again demonstrating the modest expectations of feature animation. The worldwide gross of $53 million for *Oliver & Company* closely edged out Don Bluth's latest feature, *The Land Before Time*, which made $48 million, but animated features were expensive and laborious. If these new films were ever going to garner the respect not only of the general public but of the executives, they would have to hold their own against the live-action releases generating $100 million returns. They would also have to go to greater lengths to innovate the form, much like *Roger Rabbit* had.

The following year, Warner Bros.'s luck changed with another Tim Burton film, *Batman*, a summer blockbuster that went on to gross over $250 million in domestic release. Just as Claire Nichtern had predicted Broadway plays and musicals could be effectively exploited across Warner's media investments in the entertainment industries, Eileen Meehan notes that "with sequels in the planning, *Batman* promises to feed WCI's interests in comics, books, albums, sheet music, film production, music videos, MTV Networks, film distribution, theaters, and home video cassettes for quite sometime."[23] Its formidable performance was accompanied by the release of a successful sequel, *Lethal Weapon 2* (Richard Donner, 1989), which effectively secured Warner Bros.'s spot at the top of the box office. Paramount's strategy of sequels and stars served them well: *Indiana Jones and the Last Crusade* (Steven Spielberg, 1989), *Harlem Nights* (Eddie Murphy, 1989), and *Star Trek V: The Final Frontier* (William Shatner, 1989). 20th Century Fox installed a new chairman, Joe Roth, and struggled in light of the underwhelming performance of *The Abyss* (James Cameron, 1989). Disney continued to show strong returns with a family comedy (*Honey, I Shrunk the Kids* [Joe Johnston, 1989]), a boarding school melodrama from the producing team behind *The Golden Girls* (*Dead Poets Society* [Peter Weir, 1989]), and *Turner & Hooch* (Roger Spottiswoode, 1989), a vehicle for young star Tom Hanks. But the structure and organization of the film industry was changing rapidly: Time Inc. acquired Warner Bros., while Columbia became part of Sony. Sony tapped *Batman* producers Peter Guber and Jon Peters to run Columbia, and studios began assembling major stars, big budgets, high-concept storylines, and familiar creative properties in the hopes of lucrative returns. As Thomas Schatz argues, making movies in the early 1990s required studios to be "not only well-financed and productive, but also diversified and well-coordinated."[24] *Batman*'s success signaled a new day in Hollywood, doubling down on franchises and blockbusters—a strategy in direct opposition to tight budgets and minimal risks at Disney (and at Touchstone, in particular).

Consequently, Disney moved away from its reserved approach with a planned adaptation of *Dick Tracy* (1990), directed by and starring Warren Beatty, in the hopes of having a *Batman*-like triumph. Meanwhile, the animation division finished its follow-up to *Oliver & Company*. A return not only to the princess narrative but also to the integrated musical tradition, *The Little Mermaid* would offer the kinds of success and opportunity the company sought in the elaborate but ill-fated *Dick Tracy*. But it was also a major risk. As animator Tom Sito explains, "When they did *Mermaid*, the conventional wisdom was a female lead can't carry one of these movies. It has to be a male lead. And it was a big deal that Ariel is the focus, is the actual star."[25] Disney clearly needed time to realize the error of its thinking about protagonists, audiences, and feature animation. In its list of 1989 triumphs, the return of feature animation was listed at #6, far behind the company's ambitious expansion of the theme parks.[26] Eisner notes, perhaps with some amusement, "Maybe this should have been first on the list of accomplishments. Certainly Roy Disney would place it as our most important achievement."[27]

Through the late 1980s, Broadway box office grosses steadily increased—with an especially large jump in revenues from the 1986–1987 to the 1987–1988 season, fueled in large part by the domination of British megamusicals. In the months following *Smile*'s closure, both *Starlight Express* and *Les Misérables* transferred from the West

End in time for the latter to win that season's Tony Award for Best Musical. Meanwhile, *Starlight Express*, a musical about trains performed on roller skates, received derisive comparisons to Disney on Ice and theme park entertainment.[28] The creative team did not necessarily take offense to this charge; Trevor Nunn, in fact, observed in the *Wall Street Journal*, "This is quite deliberately based on the same, basic, unspoken contract as Disneyland. That is: 'Here is my money; hit me with the experience.'"[29] But the success of *Starlight Express* was a mere symptom of ongoing problems on the Great White Way, including a dearth of original material, escalating costs to stage a new production, and negligible support from the city government for the industry.[30] While journalists and scholars alike have drawn a throughline from the British megamusical to the Disney stage musical, Lloyd Webber, Mackintosh, Nunn, and the like clearly took their cues from Disney in a complicated exchange that has gone largely unacknowledged by theatre historians.

Amid this anxiety and hardship, British talent thrived on Broadway, both on stage and behind the scenes. Playwrights Christopher Hampton and Willy Russell, actors Glenda Jackson and Pauline Collins, and, of course, Andrew Lloyd Webber and Cameron Mackintosh found critical and commercial success on Broadway in a period of creative stagnancy domestically. This perceived domination prompted a derisive backlash from U.S. talent and critics, inflected by both nationalism and elitism. Theatre director Des McAnuff, writing in *American Theatre* magazine, dismissed contemporary Broadway theatre as dreck for the lowest common denominator: "The main fare on Broadway is the Las Vegas-style musical with gads of spectacle aimed at a tourist audience that visits the theatre the way tourists visit theme parks."[31] Lloyd Webber, in particular, incurred derision from both sides of the Atlantic: Frank Rich of the *New York Times* blasted him as "a canny, melodic pastiche artist" who "can't yet be compared seriously with Broadway's best of any period," while British critic Clive Barnes argued in the *Times* that the *Cats* composer was "not cut out to be Broadway's saviour."[32] The sheer hostility toward Lloyd Webber was characteristic of an Anglophobia that resonated in press coverage of Broadway during the period. In fact, Lloyd Webber became the personification of various trends that frustrated and enraged Broadway denizens, including spectacle, amplification, and populist sentimentality. Cameron Mackintosh, the British producer behind many of these high-concept stage musicals, dismissed the criticism as naïve and ahistorical: "I'm convinced that the so-called megamusical has been happening every few years ever since musicals became musicals."[33] Indeed, across Mackintosh's productions, one sees the legacies of Florenz Ziegfeld and Billy Rose, popular showmen who offered as much for the eye as for the ear.

The sharpest observers understood Lloyd Webber and Mackintosh were hardly to blame compared to a lack of industry support for innovative creators and producers. While there were some major U.S. plays from emerging playwrights, including August Wilson's *Fences*, David Henry Hwang's *M. Butterfly*, and Wendy Wasserstein's *The Heidi Chronicles*, these impressive efforts were few and far between compared to the Broadway of only two or three decades earlier. This absence was due in part to the ongoing AIDS crisis, and the performing arts community was hit particularly hard. Director and choreographer Michael Bennett and original *Cats* cast members Reed Jones and Tim Scott were but three of many talents struck down in their prime. To add insult to injury, not only was the federal government ignoring the needs of AIDS patients, but performing arts organizations found it increasingly difficult to secure health insurance for their artists amid alleged fears of AIDS-related expenses.[34] Theatre talent, particularly beyond Broadway, addressed AIDS in their work, including Larry Kramer's *The Normal Heart*, Harvey Fierstein's *Safe Sex*, and Robert Chesley's *Jerker*. (William M. Hoffman's 1985 play *As Is* is generally understood to be the first play on Broadway to represent the AIDS crisis.) The devastating impact on Broadway theatre, both its artists and its audiences, remains incalculable—and was too often unaddressed in Broadway press of the time. Hollywood unsurprisingly remained reticent to tackle AIDS head-on, but some argued that the increase in safe sex and decline in promiscuous sexual behavior on screen was a direct result of AIDS concerns (and fears).[35] Film historian Vito Russo, for example, observed, "One would say that Hollywood's alleged sense of moral values has altered in response to the AIDS crisis. Films like *Fatal Attraction* and *Someone to Watch Over Me* [Ridley Scott, 1987] are metaphors for AIDS, about the dangers of promiscuity, about a return to family values, responses to the existence of AIDS. *Fatal Attraction* is a sort of AIDS horror movie, what can happen if you cheat on your wife once."[36] Amid this fear and anxiety both in the entertainment industries and across the country, Howard Ashman learned that he was HIV-positive in March 1988. He would conceal this devastating secret from his colleagues—even Alan Menken—for almost two years.

Carole Shorenstein Hays, a San Francisco theatre owner who produced the Broadway run of *Fences*, echoed another familiar concern of New York drama critics: "The problem with Broadway is there are no bold producers; they are tempered by the economics of the theater."[37] The era of colorful impresarios had folded amid high costs and low risks, leaving Hollywood money and British megamusicals to fill the void. This absence placed an even greater dependence on regional theaters (sometimes referred to as "resident theaters") to develop new work and artists for Broadway. Established in the 1960s, such theaters were intended as incubators for drama across the country, producing some of the boldest, most innovative work. But the financial incentives possible in a successful transfer to Broadway had tempted many artistic directors to develop more commercially minded projects. Robert Brustein of the American Repertory Theatre lamented the practice as almost vampiric: "The problem is that Broadway's future seems to depend at present on the progressive destabilization of the resident theater movement in this country and possibly abroad."[38] The tendency had already plagued the British stage, where commercial ventures by Trevor Nunn from the Royal Shakespeare Company and Peter Hall of the National Theatre prompted their resignations. Nunn, the director behind *Cats* and *Starlight Express*, earned millions for these projects, which he initially directed while on leave from the RSC. (Nunn's production of *Les Misérables* was done with the RSC.) Not only did these raise audience expectations, but their popularity (along with that of the musicals *Chess*, *Me and My Girl*, and *Phantom*) accounted for a substantial portion of Broadway's $253 million gross in the 1987–1988 season.[39]

Despite almost persistent vitriol toward West End transfers, they were clearly symptomatic of larger industrial changes. Only five years after Sondheim criticized the production costs of *Cats*, his latest effort, *Into the Woods*, cost $4.5 million to mount. A playful revision of established fairy tales blended with an original story, *Into the Woods* faced mixed reviews—but solid box office returns. Sondheim later noted that the musical partly depends upon and plays with "the audience's collective memory of Disney fairy tales."[40] And like those animated fairy tale movies, the stage show has coincidentally proven itself to be quite an annuity for its creators.[41] Its major competition at the Tony Awards that year was Lloyd Webber's latest, *Phantom of the Opera*, which had been received more positively than his previous endeavors. To be fair, Mimi Kramer of the *New Yorker* linked it to "the age of the mindless, nonverbal musical,"[42] and the *New York Times*' Frank Rich criticized the show, in part, for its failures to achieve the ideal set out by the integrated musical tradition:

> The melodies don't find shape as theater songs that might touch us by giving voice to the feelings or actions of specific characters. Instead, we get numbing, interchangeable pseudo-Hammersteinisms like "Say you'll love me every waking moment" or "Think of me, think of me fondly, when we say goodbye." With the exception of "Music of the Night"—which seems to express from its author's gut a desperate longing for acceptance—Mr. Lloyd Webber has again written a score so generic that most of the songs could be reordered and redistributed among the characters (indeed, among other Lloyd Webber musicals) without altering the show's story or meaning.[43]

In writing generically rather than to the character singing the song, Lloyd Webber (allegedly) had violated one of the key principles of songwriting for the integrated musical—a value espoused not only in the writings of Lehman Engel but in the implied criteria by which New York theatre critics evaluated Broadway musicals. Yet many critics found something to praise in this Lloyd Webber effort, whether it was his romantic melodies, production values, or impressive collaborators. *Phantom*, for instance, was directed by Harold Prince, perhaps the most celebrated living U.S. director of Broadway musicals and, in the words of Foster Hirsch, "a true pioneer, the *auteur* of the modernist concept musical who has expanded a genre's thematic and theatrical possibilities."[44] Prince had directed Lloyd Webber's *Evita* years earlier, but his direction of *Phantom* lent the production artistic credibility and homegrown distinction. According to David Richards, writing in the *Washington Post*, "Unlike *Cats* or *Starlight Express*, Lloyd Webber's other reigning Broadway hits, *Phantom* does not make a frontal attack on the spectator. Granted, the spectacle is abundant and the sleights of stagecraft are astonishing."[45] *Phantom* proved to be a theatrical phenomenon—a blockbuster in the new mode of musical theatre production. Its residency in the Majestic

Theatre would last over thirty years, eventually eclipsing *Cats* to become Broadway's longest-running show.

The success of *Phantom* reveals a change in the primary audience for Broadway, as tourists readily paid high ticket prices for the biggest hits. Efforts to offer the next popular hit encouraged risk-averse New York theatre producers to stick to musicals (*Me and My Girl* and *Jerome Robbins' Broadway*), productions with big names (Madonna in David Mamet's *Speed-the-Plow*; Steve Martin and Robin Williams in *Waiting for Godot*), and revivals (Patti LuPone in *Anything Goes*; Tyne Daly in *Gypsy*). New shows either soared or crashed, with minimal success to be found in between. Elizabeth I. McCann, who eight years earlier had partnered with Disney, asserted, "Broadway *often* makes the assumption that audiences are dumb. In point of fact, the audience waits to be challenged."[46] Artistic aspirations aside, producers lamented that staging theatre on Broadway was further complicated by union contracts and production costs. Advances in digital technology could standardize and facilitate theatrical productions, but trained, unionized talent would still be necessary to keep the shows running. Huge hits often necessitated huge operating costs: *Phantom* cost around $400,000 a week, *Les Misérables* $300,000.[47]

But there were some intriguing exceptions to the high-concept megamusicals during this time, too. *City of Angels*, a metatheatrical musical comedy drawing from film noir, opened in late 1989 to mixed reviews but a rave by Frank Rich, making it one of the most popular U.S. musicals in years. *Largely New York* opened the same year. Running just over an hour and featuring minimal dialogue, the show combined elements of hip-hop culture, including rapping and break dancing, with other performance art forms such as pantomime. Conceived by and starring clown Bill Irwin, *Largely New York* blended an aesthetic that was minimalist and contemporary, eclectic and inclusive. Reviewing for the *New Yorker*, Mimi Kramer wrote, "In the tradition of the movie-musical, *Largely New York* offers a fictional resolution for the problems that beset the real world."[48] The show was produced not only by Kenneth Feld, the licensee behind the Disney ice shows, but also by Disney itself. The company would serve only as a backer in this instance, but *Largely New York* remains its premier (albeit little known) theatrical production on Broadway—five years before *Beauty and the Beast* sparked controversy and broke box office records.

———

In the eighteen months that elapsed following the meeting with Ashman in New York, the directors of *The Little Mermaid* developed the initial script—a first for Disney Animation. An initial pass by Pulitzer Prize–winning playwright Michael Cristofer was rejected as too dark, so Musker and Clements lobbied to take over.[49] The idea of farming out this labor to an outsider who did not have a long-term investment in the animation division remained suspect, even sacrilegious, for many Disney animators.

Ashman, too, was an outsider—the first, in fact, to serve as executive producer on a Disney animated film without any previous animation experience.[50] "He

Figure 5. In "Part of Your World," Ariel sings about what she wants: not Prince Eric, but to be human. Credit: Author's screenshot.

absolutely respected what they did and was in awe of it," Howard's sister, Sarah Ashman Gillespie, recalls.[51] Furthermore, his knowledge of the integrated musical endowed him with an artistic authority and an enthusiasm for Disney animation that endeared him to the animators. Ashman's papers at the Library of Congress include notes on the integrated musical that demonstrate his understanding of and investment in this influential craft theory. Around the same time that he gave his integrated musical lecture to the animators, Ashman visited Indiana University to deliver the Collins Lectures and attend a campus production of *Little Shop*. One of his lectures surveyed the narrative function of music for theatre and film, providing students with a primer on the integrated musical as well as Ashman's own theoretical musings on film as a medium for musical theatre storytelling. Ashman admits that film as a medium faces a challenge in carrying the songs that further the narrative, but the integrated musical, invested as it is in songs as storytelling devices, is better prepared to do so. Because of its stylization and admitted artifice, animation "offers complete freedom" that allows the audience to disregard reality (and realism) and suspend its disbelief.[52] In this spirit, Ashman emphatically notes, "ANIMATION MAY BE ONE OF THE LAST PLACES WHERE WE'LL CONTINUE TO BUY THE USE OF MUSIC IN A NARRATIVE FORMAT."[53]

Ashman subsequently works through each song in *The Little Mermaid* (then in development), revealing how each song serves the character and/or the plot. Much like "Somewhere That's Green" in *Little Shop*, "Part of Your World" provides Ariel the opportunity to deliver the "classic girl's inner monologue" that both establishes what she wants and underscores that plot point for the audience by singing it aloud. (Ashman jokingly referred to it as "Somewhere That's Wet.") It also separates Ariel from her princess predecessors in that she is clearly a more active protagonist: rather than waiting and hoping for a better life, she is an agent of change. As

Amy M. Davis observes, "Ariel actively seeks adventure and works hard to achieve goals she has set for herself, rather than simply responding to the crises with which she is presented."[54] Roberta Trites, for instance, characterizes Ariel's search as for a romantic partner when in actuality she is seeking new knowledge, community, and embodiment.[55] Indeed, Laura Sells notes that Ariel "yearns for subjecthood and for the ability to participate in public (human) life."[56] So while "Part of Your World" is often treated as a love song, Ariel wants not the prince but rather entry to his world—to be human. Therefore, Eric is not the ends but the means. In fact, he is only the first human she has ever seen in person, underscoring her attraction to him as convenient rather than destined.

Making Sebastian "a Rasta crab" enables Ashman and Menken to update the sound of the film musical while also legitimating the singing of "Under the Sea" and "Kiss the Girl" in a Calypso style. (As Ashman reportedly told Musker, "Never go white when you can go Black.")[57] These songs also help to underscore and visualize the crises within the text: first, Ariel's desire to go to the human world; later, the need for Prince Eric to kiss Ariel and free her from the contract. "Poor Unfortunate Souls," here described as "URSULA'S SONG," reinforces the central conflict while raising the stakes; therefore, Ursula singing the "sales pitch" of Ariel's voice in exchange for a human form underscores the drama of the scene while intensifying the pleasure it elicits. The opening vamp of "Poor Unfortunate Souls" tips its hat to the music of Kurt Weill, and the pacing underscores Ursula's sinister movement. Taken together, the six songs Ashman and Menken wrote for *Mermaid* function, as Ashman told the animation team in the lunchtime lecture similar to the one he delivered in Indiana, as "tentpoles" holding up the narrative.[58] The musical numbers are strategically placed throughout the film, supporting the plot structure without overwhelming the film narrative. Animated musicals generally contain five or six songs over eighty minutes, whereas the traditional integrated musical score on stage can include three or four times as many musical numbers. The stylization of animation endows the integrated *animated* musical with artistic license to be eclectic, excessive, and fanciful.

As Ashman demonstrates in his lecture notes, *The Little Mermaid* functions as a stage musical in the integrated musical tradition. He gave a similar lecture to Disney animators around the same time, and excerpts can be seen in Don Hahn's documentary, *Waking Sleeping Beauty*. In one moment, Ashman explains the "I want" song as a narrative device: "In almost every musical ever written, there's a place, usually the third song of the evening—sometimes it's the second, sometimes it's the fourth. The leading lady usually sits down on something—a tree stump in *Brigadoon*, under the pillars of Covent Garden in *My Fair Lady*, or a trash can in *Little Shop of Horrors*—but the leading lady sits down on something and sings about what she wants in life. And the audience falls in love with her and then roots for her to get it for the rest of the night."[59] In *Little Mermaid*, Ashman and Menken invoke this convention through "Part of Your World," and in doing so they reintegrated the Disney musical after years of the looser model evident in *The Great Mouse Detective* and *Oliver & Company*. For Ashman, music was another mode of

narrative information: not only did the songs facilitate exposition, plot development, and characterization, but without them the plot would have noticeable gaps.
The Great Mouse Detective and *Oliver & Company* had used music as well, but their
function was more ornamental than plot-driven. Ashman and Menken's songs for
Mermaid, however, are crucial to storytelling and structure in their deliberate positioning at key plot points. The animation could accentuate that information, but
Ashman also understood that sometimes the lyrics contained more information
that viewers could reasonably grasp. Upon rewatching, however, they could pick
up even more of those details. By chance, *The Little Mermaid* would become the
first Disney animated feature to be released on home video not long after its initial
theatrical run. Roy Disney, Ron Clements, and John Musker resisted the decision,
but the executive team saw great profit potential in the move. What was less obvious at the time was that animated musicals were an ideal genre for home video
because the music and animation would encourage children to view them over and
over again, whereas adults could more fully appreciate the structure and detail in
the films and their songs by rewinding or rewatching.

But Ashman was not the only non-animator shaping *The Little Mermaid*. Katzenberg was a very hands-on producer, strongly invested in the reinvention of the
animation studio's product. In January 1988, his first set of notes identifies four "elements" to the story—in descending order, Ariel, King, Eric, and Ursula. Like Ashman, Katzenberg wanted the opening to be situated in the human world and then
to move under the sea to Ariel and the mer-people. Furthermore, Katzenberg
observes, this film is much "more of a musical than *Cinderella/Pinocchio*."[60]

Key to the revision of the Disney musical is reenvisioning the friendship between
the protagonist and her animal companions. In *Snow White*, the animals help, but
they do not talk nor have distinctive personalities. With *Pinocchio*, the animal companions begin to not only talk but also serve as moral guides. Similarly, in *Bambi*
and *Cinderella*, the animal companions have distinctive personalities, serving as
characters to be adored (Thumper and Flower in *Bambi*) or laughed with (the mice
in *Cinderella*). Katzenberg wants Flounder, Ariel's loyal fishy companion, to be
"a magical character" in this tradition, though he fears the relationship between
Flounder, Scuttle (the seagull), and Sebastian does not yet cohere in the way it needs
to for the film to work.[61] The characters, Katzenberg contends, need a major revision: Scuttle's demeanor echoes the Wizard of Oz, while Sebastian is "too strong
and self-assured." Katzenberg argues that for the latter character to work he must
be a befuddled member of the King's court—highly likeable but unable to properly manage affairs.

In the same vein, Katzenberg fears the prince fails to satisfy the expectations
the audience will have of him. He is described as "white bread," when what he needs
to be is both "heroic" and charismatic. Katzenberg suggests the team model Prince
Eric on Tom Cruise, the handsome young star of the Touchstone-produced *The
Color of Money* (Martin Scorsese, 1986) who was currently starring in another
Touchstone film, *Cocktail* (Roger Donaldson, 1988). Ariel, on the other hand, needs
to be more like Daryl Hannah, star of Touchstone's first major success, *Splash*,

but right now she does not work vocally.[62] Clearly, the characters are in place—including a later-jettisoned timid merman, Harold, who may or may not be Ariel's brother—but the personalities do not quite work, or, at the very least, do not sufficiently interact with each other in the necessary way for Katzenberg to be placated.

Within two weeks, the animators screen initial reels for Katzenberg's consideration, and again he feels the characters are not quite where they needed to be: the mermaids need to be vain, while the King—now named Triton after Poseidon's son—needs to be less paternal and instead more royal in his vocal performance.[63] Sebastian, on the other hand, must be more panicked. Katzenberg's suggestions establish a tension between Ariel's nonchalance, even flightiness, and Sebastian's self-interested concern and pragmatism. He wants her to be more conscientious, more obedient, and perhaps less solipsistic. These differing personalities and worldviews foster dramatic tension as well as comedy, as the latter becomes increasingly flustered in his unsuccessful efforts to control the whimsical princess.

As executive producer, Howard Ashman worked with Albert Tavares, casting director on *Little Shop* Off-Broadway, to bring in the right voice actors to act and sing. Unsurprisingly, they advocated for, called upon, and selected theatrically trained talent. Embarrassed by the earlier closure of *Smile*, he invited the cast to try out for *Mermaid*. For Ursula, Clements and Musker's initial choice was Bea Arthur, an accomplished stage actress with roles in the original Broadway casts of *Fiddler on the Roof* and *Mame*, for which she won a Tony Award. Arthur had built her national reputation, however, as a sitcom star, first in *Maude* and then in the Touchstone Television's *The Golden Girls*. Arthur's agent was not interested, allegedly because she was appalled that her client would play a witch. Ashman, on the other hand, wanted Joan Collins for the part, but producer Aaron Spelling refused to allow her even to audition. The search continued, with Musker and Clements favoring *Facts of Life* star Charlotte Rae and Ashman championing Elaine Stritch, the Broadway veteran known for her curmudgeonly demeanor and raspy voice. Rae, unfortunately, could not perform "Poor Unfortunate Souls" as Ashman wrote it, so Stritch became the frontrunner. John Musker admits that she gave a "loopy, eccentric reading," and Ursula was set—or so they thought.[64]

To Ashman's frustration, Stritch refused to take his direction, singing "Poor Unfortunate Souls" as she thought it should be done. (Coincidentally, she irritated Susan Harris while auditioning for Dorothy on *The Golden Girls* by changing the lines—and similarly lost the role.)[65] As an established stage actress, Stritch was accustomed to being given latitude to craft her own interpretation of the role. Ashman, as both lyricist and producer, was less accommodating to such notions. Ultimately, he fired her, revealing the demands of film versus theatrical production as well as the way Ashman had to adjust to the production culture of his new medium—not just film, but animation.

The role went to Pat Carroll, an accomplished stage actress perhaps best known for her role as Bunny Halper in Danny Thomas's sitcom, *The Danny Thomas Show*. Unlike Stritch, Carroll was amenable to Ashman's direction, later admitting that she "stole" his "very sardonic, raunchy, low down approach" to the role.[66] The character's tendency to speak with dramatic affect and exaggerated gesture led Carroll to further round out her character with the sliminess of a used-car salesman and the "kind of arrogance" one finds in a "has-been Shakespearean actress."[67] Taken together, Ashman and Carroll were able to craft a performance that captured the character's complex allure.

As the creative team discussed behind the scenes, the character is a wicked seductress with grace who, despite her evil nature and Rubenesque figure, still—in the words of animator Will Finn—"thinks she's Ava Gardner."[68] Despite early efforts to draw the character in the vein of Joan Collins, the eventual design was inspired by drag performer Divine, best known for his performances in the films of John Waters. Ursula stands in a long tradition of Disney villains whose exaggerated femininity—sensual, temperamental, glamorous—lends itself to drag as an art form. In that spirit, Carroll's performance captures not only the theatrical nature of the character but the performance style that musical theatre necessitates.

Ariel, on the other hand, needed to be an actress who could come across as an adolescent. Jodi Benson, who had sung "Disneyland" in the ill-fated *Smile*, was selected for Ariel. For the next twenty years, the Disney princess would be performed with a Broadway-style vocal (as opposed to the operatic style of earlier and the pop vocal of later princesses).[69] As a stage actress, Benson was able to bring the needed singing talent, but admitted she struggled with emoting vocally since she could not rely on the benefits of her gestures and body language to convey character. Glen Keane, lead animator of Ariel, based his designs on his wife and on Benson. Sherri Stoner, an actress hired to come in and pose as Ariel, even swimming around a large pool, was also crucial to capturing Ariel's facial expressions and choreography. Having trained in improvisation at the Groundlings, Stoner helped work out Ariel's movement under Keane's direction. The use of live-action actresses as models dated back to the earliest Disney features, when dancer Marge Belcher, who would later achieve Broadway fame alongside her husband Gower Champion, posed as Snow White and Dopey for animators. In their efforts to recapture the spirit and aesthetics of classical animation, Disney animators on *Mermaid* also relied on long-established practices, even using the multiplane camera—crucial for creating the illusion of depth in animation—after years in "retirement."[70]

Much like Jiminy Cricket in *Pinocchio*, Sebastian functions as an adviser whose relationship with the main character remains essential to the film's narration. In fact, his gradual conversion from loyal courtier to Ariel's accomplice reinforces the audience's rallying behind Ariel and Eric while also moving the plot forward. Unlike the protagonist and her love interest, though, Sebastian has *two* big musical numbers: the showstopping "Under the Sea" and the romantic ballad "Kiss the Girl." Samuel E. Wright, another stage actor who had been nominated for a Tony for his work in *The Tap Dance Kid* before going on to play Dizzy Gillespie in *Bird* (Clint Eastwood, 1988), was hired to play him. Early conceptions of Sebastian imagined a Geoffrey Holder type, and Wright later noted that he had lived with

Trinidadians in college, so he was familiar with the necessary accent for the role.[71] As with Benson, Wright's performance in the recording studio informed his character's appearance, right down to the bags under his eyes. Broadway became a point of reference in casting Scuttle, in particular. As the authoritative yet consistently misguided seagull, Scuttle was often discussed in terms of Rex Harrison's famed performance in *My Fair Lady* (George Cukor, 1964). Katzenberg emphasized the comical character "needs to be professorial. Henry Higginish. Very animated in his lecturing."[72] The role eventually went to comedian Buddy Hackett, who played the character with an endearingly self-assured (yet goofy) affect.

Katzenberg devotes much of his attention at this time to the vocal performance of the characters. He recommends that Scuttle sound more like Walter Matthau than Elmer Fudd, whereas Sebastian should have a sterner, yet smooth, even "suave" cadence similar to Harry Belafonte or Frank Sinatra. He did, however, praise the relationship between Ariel and Flounder, while also suggesting more choreography is necessary to make Ariel's movement more "evocative."[73]

But Katzenberg was not the only critic whom Clements and Musker were answering to behind the scenes. President of feature animation Peter Schneider, producer and lyricist Howard Ashman, and even two of the "Nine Old Men," Frank Thomas and Ollie Johnston, offered regular feedback regarding the story, characterization, artwork, music, and vocal performance. In a February 1988 memo, Clements and Musker identify six persisting weaknesses in the plot:

1. The opening, (first twenty pages), seemed slow in getting going and a little unfocused.
2. The character of Flounder seemed undefined and the character of Scuttle was not as funny and entertaining as he needs to be.
3. The relationship between Triton and Ariel was not as real, (easy for the audience to identify with), as we wanted it to be.
4. The character of Prince Eric seemed vague and wimpy.
5. Ariel seems too passive once she gets on land. She loses some of her spunk.
6. The climax dragged, was hard to follow, and was not as satisfying as it should be.[74]

These pressing concerns, while succinct and focused, reveal fundamental structural issues with the text at nearly all levels. They also demonstrate, however, how Disney actively worked to revive its animation division in large part through a focus on story, which Don Bluth had charged was faltering in the animated features that he had worked on at Disney following the namesake's death. Bluth had publicly stated that Disney animation needed a visionary leader to provide guidance and direction. In *The Little Mermaid*, we begin to see that such leadership came not from Katzenberg or even Ashman but from the relationship—alternately respectful and contentious—between these two figures as well as the network of creative laborers who surrounded them.

Clements and Musker, in the meantime, offered various strategies for rectifying what ailed *The Little Mermaid*. Concerns over budget, running time, and artistry motivated them to keep the film's length under control. The costly, labor-intensive nature of feature animation compels screenwriters to deliver tight storylines, maximizing dramatic and aesthetic impact within a brief time frame, usually seventy to ninety minutes. *The Little Mermaid* had four intersecting conflicts to balance and resolve: Ariel's insolence toward Triton, Triton's feud with Ursula, Ursula's assault on Ariel, and Ariel's affections for Prince Eric. On top of these narrative threads, the trio of Scuttle, Sebastian, and Flounder needed to both underscore the dramatic tension and provide comic relief for the audience primarily composed of children.

Even with these facts in mind, one cannot help but notice how memos and other studio correspondence become battlegrounds of power, creative and otherwise, behind the scenes. While Clements and Musker yield on certain matters, they also seem firm in others, as demonstrated by the rhetorical repetition in their defense of Flounder: "To reiterate on paper some things we've said before, basically we like Flounder. We like him being a cute, tubby fish. We like him being a kid. We like using his timidity and awkwardness to contrast with Ariel's bold exuberance. We like him being honest, good natured and innocent to contrast with Sebastian's grand dignity and Scuttle's overbearing abrasiveness. We like him being ernest [*sic*] and loyal to Ariel throughout."[75] While they concede the character could be stronger, their firm insistence on his virtues reveals a network of power dynamics at work as various interests wield authorial control: Katzenberg and Schneider as executives, Musker and Ashman as executive producers (and also Ashman as lyricist), Thomas and Johnston as experienced animators and storytellers themselves.

Furthermore, this clear albeit respectful tension uncovers a fundamental shift in both the hierarchies and protocols at Disney following the arrival of the Eisner/ Wells regime. True, Katzenberg was two and a half years into his tenure by this point, but the notes from story meetings versus the memos from Clements and Musker demonstrate Katzenberg's seemingly autocratic management style that nevertheless allows for a certain level of dissension from his subordinates. Clements and Musker, however, appear to resist in a very measured manner: pushing back is often couched in acknowledging the criticisms and admitting the shortcomings, though they are not beyond dismissing, certain executive feedback. For example, while they agree with Ashman that Ariel should realize the potential devastation she almost caused in her pursuit of Eric, they also insist that Triton should detest humans as "dangerous barbarians," thereby setting up his own epiphany before allowing Ariel to live as she pleases by becoming human.[76] This resistance, in part, is eased by the diversity of voices offering their take, be they executive, creative, or in between.

Ursula continued to be a source of ongoing frustration between the creative and executive teams. Initial feedback found her, ironically enough, to be too cartoonish: "Huge jowls, huge lips, high cheekbones, pointed head" with a sizeable "chest, bordering on bad taste."[77] The character, animated by a team led by Ruben Aquino, was hardly a model for moderation.[78] Initial notes on "Poor Souls" (later "Poor

Unfortunate Souls") found Ursula "overacting in singing/meanness and nastiness/needs seductiveness/too shrill/doesn't work for story." Katzenberg wanted her to be a "seductress," but concluded that "everything we do now with her is completely disgusting and unlikable."[79] The character herself must be both monstrous and appealing, evil and electrifying, sensual and grotesque. Furthermore, her title song, "Poor Unfortunate Souls," requires a singer who can essentially ham it up, sliding up and down the scales while also operating in several registers. Katzenberg found Ashman's rendition to be endearing, but Carroll's version had "too many edges."[80] Roy Disney suggested making Flotsam and Jetsam as "evil as possible" to exhibit their boss's wickedness, leaving Ursula to be "more seductive."[81] The meeting participants concluded that Pat Carroll would have to rerecord her part.

In May 1988, the creative team had identified a series of problems that needed the most attention: the design of Ariel and Eric, the relationship between humor and emotion, and characterization.[82] As production ramped up, meetings between the executives, producers, directors, and animators took place regularly, even weekly as necessary. The discussions—and debates—that ensue lay bare the complex networks of power behind media authorship, especially within animation, where characterization develops among producers, directors, screenwriters, voice actors, animators, and, in this case, lyricists.

Since Ariel and Eric are the focus of the narrative, a great amount of attention was paid to their relationship. To facilitate this crucial romance, the creative workers turned to Broadway musicals. For example, during one of their earliest encounters, the suggestion was made to consult the "Maria" scene from *West Side Story*, in which Tony recounts his first meeting with his new love interest as he walks home.[83] The physical appearance and personalities of these characters were also closely attended to by the creative team, who sought a necessary balance to make the characters both believable and relatable. Concerns over Eric's muscular physique prompted revision, as executives felt he was "too beefy" and "jaw too strong."[84] Tom Cruise was again offered as an exemplar for the ideal masculinity here, especially his performance in *Risky Business* (Paul Brickman, 1983). To this end, the character needs to be charming and handsome, underscored by his boyish grin and the conspicuous presence of his bare chest.

Similarly, Ariel's charm and beauty were a primary concern. The animators spent substantial time debating her hair color, for instance. While Disney princesses since Cinderella had often been blonde, red hair would both set Ariel apart and look better aesthetically during scenes where she swam through shadows. As a mermaid, Ariel would also be more "exposed" than previous princesses. The animators found inspiration in Fred Moore's drawings of mermaids for *Peter Pan* (Clyde Geronimi, Wilfred Jackson, and Hamilton Luske, 1953) for artistic inspiration. Moore's renderings featured women who wore clamshells over their breasts—and little else. The animators followed suit, adding a thin strip to explain how the shell brassiere was held in place. Undoubtedly, this design appears to have satisfied Katzenberg, who consistently pushed animators to make Ariel more physically appealing.

"Spontaneity and spark" were also crucially missing, Glen Keane lamented, while Katzenberg contended that the protagonist lacked proper definition.[85] Increased emphasis was placed on her eyes while also thinning her face. Howard Ashman curtly directed the animators, "Your job is to make the audience fall in love with Ariel," a responsibility, no doubt, that he felt he shared with them as the lyricist behind "Part of Your World."[86] The creative team also needed to make her more endearing, leading Katzenberg to propose actress Elisabeth Shue, star of Touchstone's *Adventures in Babysitting* (Chris Columbus, 1987), as a prototype for what they needed Ariel to exhibit: "Embraceable, huggable, appealing, attractive. WARMTH."[87] To increase the audience's empathy, more emphasis was placed on her reaction to Eric's engagement to Ursula in disguise. In their opinions, the animation could be over the top, as it was impossible "to be too saccharine here" as Ariel feels Eric slipping away.[88] Katzenberg went so far as to advocate excessive bawling, verging on a nervous breakdown. Ariel's complete devastation would not only heighten the comedy of the animals' subsequent attack and the drama of Eric's battle with Ursula but also solidify the audience's support for Ariel to triumph in the end. After all, as the emotional core of the film, Ariel's relatability was indispensable not only to the story but to the film's commercial success.

As Katzenberg told the animators in preparing *The Little Mermaid*, *Oliver & Company* had failed to deliver emotion, the key element of classic Disney features.[89] It was a comedic story with a bit of emotion thrown in, but *The Little Mermaid* needed to be an emotional story with a bit of humor. While the romantic couple would obviously handle the emotional element, the secondary characters of Sebastian, Scuttle, and Flounder helped to facilitate the text's humor. In fact, Sebastian's humorous reaction and eventual disruption of Ariel's heartfelt "Part of Your World" was intended, in part, to maintain the interest of young children. The French chef Louis's "Les Poissons" may appear to be a comic diversion, but Gary Trousdale asserts that it reveals how the world that enchants Ariel terrifies Sebastian.[90] (He also notes that he merely illustrated the lyrics, demonstrating how Ashman's authorship works both sonically and visually.) In addition to her troubled relationship with her father and Sebastian's emotional arc, *The Little Mermaid* succeeds where critics felt *Oliver* had faltered. Despite concern that *Mermaid* would not perform as well as *Oliver* because it was "a girl's movie,"[91] the film eventually doubled *Oliver*'s box office returns.

As *The Little Mermaid* neared completion, Katzenberg showed an early cut to children to gauge their response. When one child reportedly became distracted searching for his popcorn during the "Part of Your World" scene, Katzenberg took it as a sign that the song bored children and initiated efforts to cut it.[92] Protests sprang up across the creative team, including John Musker and Ron Clements, Howard Ashman, and Glen Keane. After much lobbying from all sides, Keane was able to convince Katzenberg to leave it in the film. Working up until seemingly the last moments, the animators finished the film in time for its release date, the week before Thanksgiving 1989. As the "I want" song, "Part of Your World" was a crucial element for structuring the film as an animated musical. In maintaining the structural integrity of the generic formula, *The Little Mermaid* was the first con-certed attempt at an integrated musical from Disney animation in over twenty years—and one of its biggest successes to date. As animator Andreas Deja later reflected, "I was very pleased with the new form of musical. It was the first one that looked like a cohesive story."[93] Critics noticed that after years of struggling, Disney was rediscovering its magic for animated storytelling, and its source was the theatrically honed craft theory of the integrated musical.

———

Yet again, Disney found itself—not unintentionally—up against the newest feature from its prodigal son, Don Bluth. In 1982, *Tron* had outperformed *The Secret of NIMH* $33 million to $14 million, but *Tron* was considerably more expensive. *An American Tail*, produced by Steven Spielberg and loosely based on his own family history, grossed an impressive $47 million worldwide, easily besting *The Great Mouse Detective*'s $25 million. Two years later, *The Land Before Time* had a strong opening, but it was eventually edged out by *Oliver & Company* worldwide. Confident in its latest endeavor, Disney representatives welcomed the showdown, noting that Bluth had not impaired the company's commercial success in the past.[94] Massive nationwide marketing campaigns, including toys, clothing, books, and other branded merchandise, accompanied both films. Nearly 3,800 Wendy's franchises featured toys from Bluth's *All Dogs Go to Heaven* (Don Bluth, 1989), while McDonald's 8,100 restaurants carried *The Little Mermaid* figures.[95] Macy's built Little Mermaid Sea Palace Outposts with exclusive T-shirts, toys, sweaters, and rain gear. Early birds could win tickets to free screenings of the film, while select stores offered children the chance to "meet" Max, Prince Eric's (animated) dog, in real life. Supermarkets even held contests in which children could competitively color images of the film's major characters. This synergy between the films and the consumer products division underscores the franchising strategy underway at the new Disney as well as the increasing emphasis on children as consumers and as major influences on their parents' purchasing decisions. Even still, Disney was embarrassingly unprepared for the consumer demand for *Mermaid* merchandise—a mistake it would not make again.

In marketing *The Little Mermaid*, at least three distinct theatrical posters were produced. The first shows Ariel looking off-frame while Prince Eric stares longingly. Triton, surprisingly terrifying and patriarchal, looks down, balanced on the other side by a grimacing Ursula. While the poster makes clear this is an animated film, it remains unclear that it is a musical. In fact, the castle, treasure, and sea creatures seem to highlight the action/adventure aspects. The second poster shows Ariel, in profile, reaching toward the light on the surface. It alludes to "Part of Your World" but, more clearly, the aspiring, active characterization of Ariel, a future princess. Similarly, the third poster features Ariel on a rock, staring skyward, while the moon backlights her. The theatrical trailer opens with Ariel vocalizing, highlighting that the film is both an adaptation of a classic story and a new entry into the Disney canon of animated classics. The trailer uses "Part of

Your World" and "Under the Sea," eventually boasting the new characters and "seven magical new songs." But the montage features the film's various genre claims: its comedy, its "fantastic adventure," even its thrilling moments when Ursula cackles at the duped Ariel. The musical is but one of many genres at work here in this self-described "very special entertainment event."

Both *Mermaids* and *All Dogs* were released on November 17, 1989, and though they were bested by the new Eddie Murphy / Richard Pryor comedy *Harlem Nights*, their premieres were nevertheless promising. *All Dogs Go to Heaven* opened to $4.7 million in roughly sixteen hundred theaters and after a slight bump during the Thanksgiving holiday slowly tapered off during the subsequent five weekends. *The Little Mermaid*, on the other hand, opened in around one thousand theaters during the same weekend but grossed over $6 million. Although it never hit number one at the box office, it performed solidly through November and received clear pops around Christmas and Valentine's Day. In fact, the latter reveals the film's unexpected popularity with couples. Duncan Marjoribanks, lead animator on Sebastian, noted, "You could see as the songs were coming in that they were really making strong tentpoles for the story. And Ashman was more than you know just writing the lyrics; he was writing the libretto for the movie, which is kind of a new thing. And they were really combining you know two art forms: one, musical theatre, which was average age [of] the viewer was 60 years old, and cartoons, the average age of the viewer was 6. Somehow or the other, they put them together and they made a movie that teenagers were going on for dates."[96] Of equal importance, *The Little Mermaid* triumphed over *All Dogs Go to Heaven* among the critics. Reviews of *All Dogs* were clearly divided, as several critics chided the faulty plotting and modest animation. *Mermaid*, on the other hand, was largely celebrated as the long-awaited return to form for Disney feature animation. In the *Chicago Tribune*, Dave Kehr did not rank the film as "a transcendent masterpiece of the Disney canon," but he did see it as evidence that "the Disney magic isn't lost after all."[97] Roger Ebert, whose top-rated review show with Gene Siskel was syndicated through Disney's Buena Vista, expressed similar enthusiasm in the *Chicago Sun-Times*. While the popular impression was that feature animation was kid's stuff, Ebert asserted such films could have wide appeal as long as the story rose above the typical "dim-witted" fare. "*The Little Mermaid*," Ebert concluded, "has music and laughter and visual delight for everyone."[98]

Despite this effusive praise, few critics lauded the film to the extent Janet Maslin did in the *New York Times*. Not only did she call *The Little Mermaid* "the best animated Disney film in at least 30 years," but a few days later she wrote an article on Disney's slow rebound in which she complimented the film's cross-generational appeal that still managed to focus on its young audience. "The single most brilliant stroke," she insisted, "is the inclusion of a Broadway-caliber score."[99] In her initial review, she had similarly observed, "Any Broadway musical would be lucky to include a single number this good." As if this compliment to Ashman and Menken were not welcome enough, to have it appear in New York City's paper of record must have further underscored the honor for the theatrically trained talent. In fact, Bernice Cohen, director of musical theatre activities at ASCAP, drew attention again to the line in her letter of congratulations to Ashman, adding, "Isn't it wonderful to know you will be immortal?"[100]

Unsurprisingly, nearly every critic, even those who gave the film a tepid review, praised the songwriting team of Ashman and Menken. Michael Wilmington of the *Los Angeles Times* concluded a somewhat mixed review with the concession that the songs (along with Carroll's and Wright's performances) would ensure the film's success.[101] In the *Boston Globe*, Jay Carr admits, "Just as I was about to write off the songs by Howard Ashman and Alan Menken as generic hack work, a couple of them emerged with real freshness and flair."[102] Hal Hinson shared a comparable sentiment in his review for the *Washington Post*; though he found the film to be "accomplished but uninspiring," overall, he admitted, "a couple of the musical numbers . . . are genuine winners."[103]

The executives at Disney shared the critics' enthusiasm for Ashman's essential efforts toward turning around animation. A grateful Roy Disney wrote to say, "Remember one more thing: The best is yet to come!"[104] In an introductory letter to Academy voters regarding *The Little Mermaid*, Katzenberg lauded Ashman and Menken for their "remarkable job in creating music for the film that is in the best tradition of the Disney animated classics."[105] ("Under the Sea" would go on to win the Oscar for Best Original Song—the first Disney song to win since "Chim Chim Cher-ee" from *Mary Poppins* twenty-five years earlier.) Even Eisner sent Ashman a handwritten note proclaiming, "You have put the stamp on the new Disney. You have created with *The Little Mermaid* what history will mark as our turn around!"[106] With the note dated November 17, 1989, the day the film was released, Eisner is obviously overstating the case to flatter his contracted talent, but later accounts, including Eisner's own memoir, would position *Mermaid* as the turning point of the so-called Disney Renaissance. In *Work in Progress*, Eisner writes, "The most important creative decision we made on *The Little Mermaid* was to work with the lyricist Howard Ashman and his composing partner Alan Menken. . . . It was then that the true renaissance of Disney animation began to take shape."[107] The renaissance was not restricted to animation alone and in fact shaped efforts across the company—in the theme parks, in merchandising and licensing, and on Broadway—for years to come. With *Mermaid*, Disney continued to explore possibilities in animation, though the company's revitalization efforts still primarily rested in live-action Touchstone film and television projects rather than animated features. This fact is made all the more surprising in light of *Mermaid* becoming the highest grossing animated film (in initial release) to date by January 1990.[108]

Perhaps the most validating compliments, though, came from Ashman's fellow artists, especially members of the Broadway community. Songwriter Cynthia Weil gushed that Ashman's lyrics "move the story forward, illuminate the characters and they're funny, fresh, clever and touching at the same time. . . . you are an artist and I really love your work."[109] Producers Lynne Meadow and Lawrence Gordon (the latter of whom produced *Smile*) sent congratulations, while Jack Viertel, creative director for Jujamcyn Theatres, mused, "You've managed to be a producer-lyricist-auteur and the results are just dazzling. The disastrous thing about all of this, of course, is the possibility that it will make it all that much harder to keep you working in the theatre, but that's a problem I simply have to solve for myself by coming up with the right project. . . . you've brought first-rate everything back to animated film, and that's no mean feat."[110] While Menken maintained a presence in the theatre community with various projects in development, including a musical adaptation of *The Honeymooners*, Ashman was firmly committed to Disney. In addition to the progress he was making on *Beauty and the Beast*, he had pitched *Aladdin* and conducted interviews with Tina Turner to adapt her memoir, *I, Tina* to screen (later reconceived as *What's Love Got to Do with It?* [Brian Gibson, 1993]). With relative creative freedom and the respect of his coworkers and bosses, Ashman seemed quite comfortable at his new home, where it became increasingly clear that his contributions were indispensable to the new life in Disney feature animation.

———

Despite Michael Eisner's laudatory remarks to Howard Ashman in 1989 and in his memoir nine years later, the reality is that Disney did not, in fact, view the release of *The Little Mermaid* as a turning point for the Walt Disney Company beyond the animation division. The film was the third highest grossing Disney release of 1989, easily outdone by two summer releases, *Honey, I Shrunk the Kids* and *Dead Poets Society*. Yet again, the theme park division remained the most profitable sector of the growing conglomerate, dwarfing filmed entertainment by over $1 billion. To drive home this point, in a list of Disney's major accomplishments in 1989, Eisner placed the resurgence of feature animation at number six of nine, behind the successful openings of Disney-MGM Studios, Splash Mountain, Typhoon Lagoon, and Pleasure Island; the initial stock offering for Euro Disneyland; and the aforementioned live-action blockbusters. Unbeknownst to the company or himself, Ashman may have been facilitating an animation renaissance, but he was still just another talent among many at the company in the late 1980s. Within filmed entertainment, live-action filmmaking and television production (and, as of 1989, the syndication of *The Golden Girls*) proved more profitable and less labor-intensive.

While this modest reception made sense at the time, it obviously seems shortsighted in retrospect. The industry-wide impact is now clear: *The Little Mermaid* furthered Hollywood's serious reconsideration of feature animation and musicals in the early 1990s. For example, 20th Century Fox distributed the Australian American animated film *FernGully: The Last Rainforest* (Bill Kroyer, 1992). Although it had left animation behind decades earlier, Paramount reentered the market by aiming for an older demographic with edgier fare: the hybrid animation film *Cool World* (Ralph Bakshi, 1992) and a comedy based on the stand-up of the late Robin Harris, *Bébé's Kids* (Bruce W. Smith, 1992). Similarly, several studios and production companies—Universal Pictures, Amblin, Castle Rock—greenlit film musicals, broadly defined. Most of these projects would languish in development hell, but some were eventually produced, including 20th Century Fox's *For the Boys* (Mark

Rydell, 1991) and Disney's *Newsies* (Kenny Ortega, 1992). None of these films, however, matched the commercial success or critical respect that Disney animated musicals garnered during this period.

The Little Mermaid furthered the company's promise of fulfilling Walt Disney's goal to produce an animated feature annually and provided the necessary momentum to proceed with *Beauty and the Beast* as a musical. This decision, of course, not only granted Ashman greater authority in the development and production of the next film but also intensified the ongoing (but generative) power struggle between himself, Katzenberg, and the animators. Yet regardless of their creative differences, the writing was on the wall at Disney animation: musicals make money.

CHAPTER 4

"A Celebration of Certain Sensibilities"

HOWARD ASHMAN AND ALAN MENKEN, *BEAUTY AND THE BEAST*, AND DISNEY, 1990–1991

In order to maintain its ambitious production schedule of a new animated feature every year, Disney already had begun work on *Beauty and the Beast* before the November 1989 premiere of *The Little Mermaid*. Unlike with *Mermaid*, however, the creative team behind *Beauty and the Beast* discarded initial plans, and by December 1989 the film was reconceived as an animated musical. Ashman, working alongside composer Alan Menken and the recently hired screenwriter Linda Woolverton, structured the film similarly to Richard Rodgers and Oscar Hammerstein II's *The King and I*. As Menken explained, "In approaching the animated musicals, we did everything as if we were writing a stage show."[1] Together, they were not only returning Disney to its early days producing musicals but also, unbeknownst to them at the time, laying the foundations for the company's ambitious move to the Broadway stage in the years that followed.

This chapter examines how Disney produced *Beauty and the Beast* during a crucial period of transition both at the company and in the film industry more broadly. With *Beauty and the Beast*, Disney doubled down on the integrated musical espoused by Howard Ashman, despite its divergence from the most popular modes of musical theatre storytelling on Broadway or in Hollywood at the time. The Broadway megamusical appeared to be in decline, whereas studio efforts at the film musical struggled in nearly all attempts. With the exception of *Pretty Woman* (Garry Marshall, 1990), Disney's film division also stumbled in 1990 after years of live-action successes. But *Beauty and the Beast*—with its emphasis on story over star power or special effects—typified what Katzenberg called for across film production at Disney in the wake of the disappointing box office performance of *Dick Tracy*. *Beauty* not only provided the media franchise that *Dick Tracy* failed to initiate but also earned the company its first nomination for the Academy Award for Best Picture since *Mary Poppins*.[2]

To fully understand and appreciate this achievement, this chapter situates Ashman's contributions amid the labor-intensive, collaborative, bicoastal production process required by feature animation while also contextualizing *Beauty and the Beast* in the industrial moment from which it emerged. Anxious about the high expenditures of blockbuster filmmaking, the company realized the safer investment to be found in the modest, well-worn traditions of feature animation and musical theatre storytelling. Much of the critical work on *Beauty and the Beast* connects the film to earlier adaptations of the fairy tale, especially Jean Cocteau's 1946 film *La Belle et la Bête*.[3] Indeed the 1991 Disney version does borrow from Cocteau's film, including the Enchanted Objects and the male rival for Belle's affections (Avenant in *La Belle*, but here Gaston). Yet the structure and the mode of storytelling reveal an indebtedness less to Jeanne-Marie Leprince de Beaumont's fairy tale or Cocteau's arthouse classic than to Rodgers and Hammerstein's *The King and I*. Notes in Ashman's papers reveal that he modeled the Beast after Yul Brynner, the star who created the part of the titular king on stage and won an Academy Award for the role in the 1956 film version by 20th Century Fox, directed by Walter Lang.[4] Although she states that Ashman also encouraged her to watch *My Fair Lady*, Linda Woolverton recalls that *The King and I* was the primary template he wanted her to use in drafting the screenplay.[5] Combined with Menken's music, Ashman continued to promote the craft theory of the integrated musical and facilitated what Michael Eisner would call in 1992 "the resurgence and reinvention of Disney animation."[6] Disney's allegiance to the integrated musical varies in subsequent animated releases, including *Aladdin* and *The Lion King*, but its deployment here effectively demonstrates Disney's debt to the form (and the craft theory behind it) in helping the company expand into the theatre industry—including Broadway and the West End as well as touring, regional, and amateur productions—soon thereafter.

——————

After almost two decades of struggling, Disney finally could compete head-to-head again with the major film studios. The production company itself had never been a chief power player in feature production during the classical Hollywood era. As Disney's holiday release, *The Little Mermaid* had achieved the most successful opening weekend for an animated film and was the highest grossing animated film to that point. Meanwhile, Disney's daring decision to greenlight *Dick Tracy* speaks to both its increasing confidence in its ability to produce successful live-action films and the volatility underlying an otherwise exciting year within the film industry. Joe Roth left independent production to take over Fox, while Australian businessmen Christopher Skase and Rupert Murdoch unsuccessfully battled it out for MGM. But the newly formed Time Warner quickly emerged as the exemplar for other entertainment conglomerates to follow throughout the 1990s.[7] Disney echoed Warner Bros.'s interest in diversification, synergy, and franchise storytelling. Under the leadership of Eisner, however, the company predominantly built and developed these divisions from the ground up rather than expanding through the acquisition of existing media companies.

Disney's renewed success in feature animation underscores its efforts to expand its investments and revenues across the media industries. In 1990, Disney had launched a second record company, Hollywood Records, led by Peter Paterno, who had represented Metallica and Guns N' Roses. Estimates suggested that the recording industry, fueled by the successful introduction of the compact disc in the 1980s, brought in over $23 billion annually among just six global distributors.[8] Eisner and his team of executives felt the record companies available for sale were considerably overpriced, so Disney started its own to release pop music (as opposed to Walt Disney Records, which had focused on soundtracks and children's music). In 1990 Disney also founded Hyperion Books, a new division specializing in nonfiction titles with ambitions of publishing around fifty books annually. On television, Disney found success with syndicated cartoons on weekday afternoons in addition to the highly competitive Saturday morning programming block, and *TaleSpin* and *Chip 'n Dale: Rescue Rangers* soon ranked among the highest rated shows in children's television. The parks division announced plans to expand the Florida and California locations while building new parks in Japan and France. In his role as Disney's biggest cheerleader, Eisner declared the 1990s the "Disney Decade"—and with it came an elaborate rollout of development plans across nearly every division.[9]

The film entertainment division exhibited similar confidence in 1990, going so far as to ban exhibitors from airing commercials before any Disney films, including those produced by Touchstone and the recently launched Hollywood Pictures. Disney also began courting Jerry Bruckheimer and Don Simpson, the powerhouse producing team behind *Beverly Hills Cop* (Martin Brest, 1984) and *Top Gun*, after their departure from Paramount, and the company hired Dawn Steel following her ouster as the head of Columbia. That June, film critic Roger Ebert deemed Disney's summer blockbuster *Dick Tracy* "a sweeter, more optimistic movie, [that] outdoes even *Batman* in the visual departments,"[10] and the film went on to gross nearly $104 million domestically and another $59 million abroad. Its considerable production and marketing budgets, including an all-star cast and original songs by Stephen Sondheim, ultimately impeded Disney from netting significant profits, a stinging lesson in blockbuster economics.[11] In August 1990, the company boasted that nearly one-third of U.S. theaters were showing a Disney film, and a high-profile deal with Japanese investors allowed Disney to replace its relationship with Silver Screen Partners in favor of the newly formed partnership Touchwood Pacific Partners I. This symbiotic partnership protected Disney from major financial losses while boosting its reputation for innovative film financing.

During the time, however, the animation division suffered a major blow. While *The Little Mermaid* and the syndicated cartoons were undeniable successes, *The Rescuers Down Under* (Hendel Butoy and Mike Gabriel, 1990) failed to resonate with audiences despite its technological feats and picturesque landscapes. Directors Hendel Butoy and Mike Gabriel heavily promoted the film's strong characters, realist aesthetic, and epic vistas—inspired by no less than *Lawrence of Arabia* (David Lean, 1962).[12] In spite of its dependence on computer animation (including the Pixar-codeveloped Computer Assisted Production System [CAPS]) for such visual effects, Butoy minimized digital technology's contribution out of fear it would distract from the animators' creative labor: "it's not a computer picture. Technology is getting better and better and new things are tried, but it's the artists who created the film."[13] Throughout the press, Disney downplayed the use of CAPS even though computer animation had been used as early as *The Black Cauldron*. While several critics praised *The Rescuers Down Under* for a bold vision in the spirit of George Lucas and Steven Spielberg, they also lamented the glaring absence of Broadway-style musical numbers similar to *Mermaid*.[14] Grossing a disappointing $27 million, *The Rescuers Down Under* joined *Mr. Destiny* (James Orr, 1990), *Spaced Invaders* (Patrick Read Johnson, 1990), and *Where the Heart Is* (John Boorman, 1990) as prominent Disney failures in 1990 and revealed that despite the promise on the horizon, the Walt Disney Company was far from infallible. The smash success of the Cinderella story *Pretty Woman* after these setbacks further emboldened Disney, proving its winning strategy of a strong story, a rising star (Julia Roberts), and a solid director (Marshall) who could accept executive feedback rather than demanding complete creative control.

This moment of reckoning at Disney Studios fueled Jeffrey Katzenberg's decision to pen a notorious 1991 memo titled "The World Is Changing: Some Thoughts on Our Business." Allegedly written while he was on vacation in Hawaii and intended for private distribution among Disney's film and television executives, the memo quickly circulated throughout the industry—as did rumors that Katzenberg himself had leaked it.[15] *Daily Variety* published the twenty-eight-page memo in its entirety in its January 31 issue under the title "Katzenberg's Bottom Line Strategy for Disney." In particular, Katzenberg voiced concern for an industry threatened by "a tidal wave of runaway costs and mindless competition."[16] Financial analysts had long argued that entertainment stands among the last industries affected by economic downturns, while also being one of the first to rebound. Katzenberg challenges this conclusion, warning that soaring production costs had compromised Disney's ability to generate substantial revenues. Furthermore, the increasing popularity of video rentals was undermining films' profit potential during theatrical release. Disney would have to make concessions to not only survive but thrive during the recession.

Katzenberg's memo articulates several common anxieties in the industry, but no point raised more ire than his discussion of movie stars and their compensation. The rampant pursuit of big-name directors, actors, and screenwriters had led to inflated salaries, yet the final product had not significantly improved. Katzenberg pointed to *Dick Tracy* as a textbook example of this problem because its high production and marketing costs had undermined its box office grosses. Katzenberg mused that when Warren Beatty or Barry Levinson pitch their next film projects to Disney, "we must hear what they have to say, allow ourselves to get very excited over what will likely be a spectacular film event, then slap ourselves a few times, throw cold water on our faces and soberly conclude that it's not a project we should choose to get involved in."[17] Katzenberg instead advocated for a focus on talent and story as a way to ensure the future health of the company. While *The*

Rescuers Down Under had had excellent animation, he argued, it lacked emotionally resonant storytelling and a dynamic protagonist. *The Little Mermaid*, on the other hand, offered "enchantment" while also including the requisite "sympathetic protagonist who goes through some transforming experience with which the audience can relate."[18] These observations are the only mentions of animation in the memo, suggesting Disney had not yet fully realized the central role feature animation might play in its future.

Ultimately, Katzenberg's solutions promoted strategies that Disney had doubled down on in recent years: compelling stories, affordable talent, and tightly managed budgets. Like Walt Disney, he advocates making films that (in Katzenberg's words) appealed to "the kid that exists in each and every one of us."[19] Resist the temptation to make decisions based on test audiences and hire talent who are on the rise, are on the wane, or are open to taking creative risks. Finally, and perhaps most romantically, the moviegoing experience is unique, and films should reflect that sense of exceptionality.

The responses to Katzenberg's memo were mixed, erring often on the side of derision. Although Eisner eventually expressed admiration for the diagnosis and prescription by his sergeant at arms, he disagreed with his wording.[20] Others found it to be an accurate, albeit obvious and sentimental, assessment. Shawna Kidman recently observed that Katzenberg's "somewhat reactionary and perhaps even naïve" concerns attempted to resist "an emerging paradigm that favored big films with big built-in expectations and big opportunities across a whole conglomerate."[21] Disney had been resisting this very logic for years with its modestly budgeted comedies produced under the Touchstone label. Katzenberg consequently played down the memo's intentions or effect: "I don't want to be a spokesman for the industry. I have enough to do here [at Disney]."[22] Yet it was reminiscent of a similar memo Eisner had issued years earlier when he was at Paramount. Whether one reads it as Katzenberg's positioning himself alongside other creative executives like Disney and Eisner or taking undue credit for the company's success, the memo remains an influential critique of the blockbuster mentality of the early 1990s and an early gesture toward the requisite sobering up from the intoxication of high concept, high costs, and high risk needed at that point. Of course, by the 2010s such scale and expenditures would prove the safer bet yet again,[23] but it would require a careful diversification of investments, synergy among properties, and understanding of audiences (especially fandoms).

Although Katzenberg's admonitions may have seemed pretentious or unoriginal, they accurately forecast how to navigate the tempestuous film industry of the early 1990s. At the time, global conglomerates seeking to expand their media investments gradually acquired Hollywood studios: Columbia by Sony in 1989 and MGM by Pathé and Universal by Matsushita in 1990. But making movies proved to be a volatile business. Paramount made the surprising move to scale back feature production, while MGM struggled to get its footing. Despite the impressive performance of *Robin Hood: Prince of Thieves* (Kevin Reynolds, 1991), Warner Bros. could not duplicate the monumental success of *Batman*. Mark Canton, its executive vice president for worldwide movie production, observed in January 1991 that "the swing of any one movie among the top-five market share studios could have made that studio number one";[24] he resigned from Warner Bros. later that year. *Variety*, unsurprisingly, titled its assessment of the film industry's 1991 performance "Welcome to Reality, Hollywood."[25]

Disney fared this turmoil comparatively well, but not without some noticeable bruises. Eisner noted that up to that point nearly three out of every four Disney films released under Katzenberg had earned a profit—a remarkable achievement, but hardly one that could be easily maintained.[26] Disney had made some impressive strides in other divisions on the global market: Disney ended its deal with Warner Bros. International and began an international distribution arm, Disney television programming expanded aggressively across the newly available Eastern European markets, and Eisner visited the Soviet Union to discuss copyright laws and a possible EPCOT pavilion. Stateside, Disney premiered the animated series *Darkwing Duck* in the afternoons and the sitcom *Home Improvement* in prime time; both were hits with their target audiences. The company acquired *Discover* magazine and launched the Disney Vacation Club. But the economic recession negatively affected the theme parks division, leading the company to raise ticket prices to a new high of $33.[27] Once champions of the revitalized Disney, Wall Street advisers and investors became increasingly skeptical of the company's livelihood and financial promise.

Undeniably, Disney's performance in 1991 dealt a significant blow to the executives' confidence after years of hubris fueled in large part by government deregulation, economic prosperity, and creative talent. Eisner's letter to investors reveals an uncharacteristic humility balanced with a hopeful harbinger at the end of the year:

> It is amazing how a single creative act can change everything. I know *Snow White* did it for Walt. Well, *Beauty and the Beast* is doing it for us. It has reconfirmed that your company still has it! It is that simple, because *Beauty and the Beast* is one of the great movies of all time (he said shamelessly). And it will be around forever. And the products coming out of *Beauty* will be around forever. And the rides emanating from *Beauty and the Beast* will be around forever. And someday the home video of *Beauty and the Beast* will sell twenty million cassettes worldwide the way *Fantasia* is now doing.[28]

Positioning himself not unlike Walt, Eisner admits, perhaps for the first time publicly, that animation rather than live action represents an important future for the company. Prosperity will be staked not just in filmmaking but in cross-media promotion: narrative extensions, merchandising, and product licensing. This "single creative act," of course, resulted from complex collaboration among many contributors, including (but not limited to) animators, executives, screenwriter Linda Woolverton, directors Gary Trousdale and Kirk Wise, producer Don Hahn, composer Alan Menken, and lyricist-producer Howard Ashman. Integrating Disney animation with Broadway-style musical theatre storytelling, the team cemented a model for future Disney animated features and provided the impetus for decades of franchising that would reinforce the company's financial viability and cultural influence.

––––––

The years 1990 and 1991—or, perhaps more accurately, the 1989–1990 and 1990–1991 Broadway seasons—marked a transitional period on Broadway. In fact, one might accurately call it a reversal of fortune, as U.S. plays had particularly strong showings and British musicals began to stumble. In recent years, the premiere of a U.S.-created Broadway musical generally inspired cautious optimism about the future of the form, especially if it meant a move away from the global megamusical as a mode of production. Nevertheless, as one industry observer remarked in March 1990, "Stephen Sondheim's work excepted, the Broadway musical has been a disaster for the better part of two decades."[29] Even Lloyd Webber struggled with his latest show, *Aspects of Love*, which premiered in April 1990. Based on a little-known novel by David Garnett, the musical seemed to resist the scale and accessibility of his earlier fare in its tangled web of relationships and desire. But drama critics were unconvinced by the more modest and intimate effort. Perpetual Lloyd Webber detractor Frank Rich noted that the "earnest but bizarre career decision" demonstrated "a naked Sondheim envy,"[30] while in the *Washington Post*, David Richards contended "in their reckless pursuit of the libido's demands, [Lloyd Webber's] characters are really behaving no differently than the trains that pushed and shoved and elbowed one another off the track in *Starlight Express*."[31] Lloyd Webber's attempt to appeal to a mature audience faltered. Although it ran for almost a year, the high investment costs made *Aspects of Love* the biggest Broadway flop to date, losing an estimated $8 to $9 million.[32]

While Lloyd Webber stumbled, two U.S. musicals fared remarkably well: *Grand Hotel* and *City of Angels*. The former was based on the 1929 Vicki Baum novel, which had also been the basis for a 1932 MGM film starring John Barrymore, Lionel Barrymore, Joan Crawford, and Greta Garbo. With music and lyrics by Robert Wright, George Forrest, and Maury Yeston and a book by Luther Davis, the stage version was helmed by Tommy Tune, whose direction and choreography won him another two Tony Awards. Michael Jeter won a Tony Award for his turn in the Lionel Barrymore role Otto Kringelein. The show played for over two years in part through its use of high-profile replacements, including Cyd Charisse. *City of Angels* did not run as long but proved to be a bigger critical success, even besting *Grand Hotel* for the Tony Award for Best Musical. The show, blending comedy and film noir, employs a split screen effect, in which the film-in-the-musical is in black-and-white and the real world of the filmmakers is in color. *City of Angels* featured a book by *M*A*S*H* producer Larry Gelbart, music by Cy Coleman, and lyrics by David Zippel. Despite the promise therein, however, neither show seemed destined for the musical theatre canon. Revisiting the shows after major cast replacements, Frank Rich deemed both as "transitional" in nature: "If the American musical is now poised to rally for another era of international glory, it can make good on that promise only by transcending the sum of both these shows' better theatrical parts."[33]

The play, on the other hand, was undergoing a bit of a revival. To be sure, British plays were still imported to critical acclaim, including Peter Shaffer's comedy *Lettice and Lovage*. But major works, often incubated in resident theaters, showed promise for the U.S. theatre's future on Broadway, including Craig Lucas's *Prelude to a Kiss*, Aaron Sorkin's *A Few Good Men*, and August Wilson's *The Piano Lesson*. The following season saw the import of William Nicholson's *Shadowlands*, based on the life of C. S. Lewis, but the major successes included John Guare's *Six Degrees of Separation* and Neil Simon's autobiographical dramedy *Lost in Yonkers*, which swept the Drama Desk, Tony Award, and Pulitzer Prize for Drama.

The U.S. musical continued to inspire optimism among critics and audiences alike during the 1990–1991 Broadway season. *The Will Rogers Follies*, directed by Tommy Tune, was created by a team of Broadway veterans, including composer Cy Coleman, lyricists Betty Comden and Adolph Green, and book writer Peter Stone. Based on the life of the famed humorist, the show was a nostalgic piece of Americana in the tradition of the Ziegfeld Follies—and a welcome departure from the solemnity of the British megamusicals. Another success that season was *The Secret Garden*, an adaptation of Frances Hodgson Burnett's classic novel for children, with music by Lucy Stone and lyrics and book by Marsha Norman. Based on a novel by Rosa Guy, *Once on This Island* was a musical retelling of Hans Christian Andersen's "The Little Mermaid" set in the Caribbean. The show introduced a major new creative team to Broadway, Lynn Ahrens and Stephen Flaherty, who sent the cast album to Disney. The company expressed interest, placing the two under contract. They worked on an ultimately unproduced film musical about whales titled *Song of the Sea*. Broadway talent continued to move into Disney, yet Disney remained hesitant to pursue the notoriously volatile world of Broadway.

But the buzz around Broadway during the 1990–1991 season was the impending import of *Miss Saigon*, the latest megamusical effort from Claude-Michel Schönberg and Alain Boublil. Actors' Equity, the stage actors' union, had initially blocked producer Cameron Mackintosh's plans to have Welsh actor Jonathan Pryce reprise his role as the Engineer, a hustler of French and Vietnamese ancestry, in part because of protests by Asian American actors. Mackintosh threatened to cancel the whole production, forcing the union to relent soon after. B. D. Wong, who had won a Tony Award for *M. Butterfly* and protested Pryce's casting, later recounted, "It was profoundly sad. I remember feeling so misunderstood."[34] Furthermore, attempts to prevent Lea Salonga, the Filipina actress who created Kim in the West End, from re-creating the role on Broadway were lost in arbitration.

The show, a loose adaptation of Giacomo Puccini's *Madama Butterfly*, employed all the pyrotechnics of the megamusical, including a film montage and, most notoriously, a helicopter that descended during the dramatic fall of Saigon. The spectacle and the melodrama worked yet again, even winning approval from critics who had been underwhelmed by previous British imports. As Cameron Mackintosh claimed, "If there is one thing that connects these shows that I have stumbled on, it's that the subject matter is universal and crosses every language barrier."[35] Of course, Asian and Asian American activists criticized the show's stereotypical characters, casting practices, and treatment of the Vietnam War.[36] Despite this backlash, the show's presales were the highest in Broadway history at over $30 million two months before it even opened—and the show had the highest top-tier ticket prices on Broadway as well, at $100. *Miss Saigon* would run for ten years, but despite blockbuster box office returns from the beginning, critics and commentators still predicted the decline of the British megamusical. Lloyd Webber was years away from finishing his ambitious adaptation of *Sunset Boulevard* (Billy Wilder, 1950), and the lack of product combined with the dismal performance of *Aspects of Love* left a noticeable gap in the musical theatre marketplace. Mackintosh and Lloyd Webber had refined a highly effective and incredibly lucrative strategy for commercial theatrical production on a global scale. Would their approach fizzle out, or would a new competitor enter the fray?

The authorial control behind animated features is complex, networked, and fluid. While producers (Walt Disney) or directors (Hayao Miyazaki) occasionally receive credit for hand-drawn animated films, one would be hard-pressed to fairly and accurately determine the so-called auteur behind most works of contemporary feature animation.[37] Indeed, animation's time-consuming, labor-intensive production process has often vexed any effort to discuss it through auteurist criticism. The available production materials for *Beauty and the Beast* lay bare the knotty negotiations of power and creativity behind authoring animated films. Throughout the production of *Beauty*, Ashman received medical treatment for HIV in New York; consequently, Disney occasionally dispatched a production team to the Residence Inn in Fishkill, New York, to meet with Ashman so that he could live at his home upstate. So authorship was not only shared among a team of creators but split between units working in California and in New York.[38]

Walt Disney himself had planned an adaptation of *Beauty and the Beast*, but the company did not earnestly pursue it until the late 1980s. Katzenberg did not include the project in his overview of possible Disney projects he presented to Ashman in 1986, but within two years *Beauty* was underway with a screenplay by James Douglas Cox. The earliest drafts were nonmusical, and British animators Richard and Jill Purdum were hired to head the project based on the recommendation of Richard Williams, the director of animation on *Who Framed Roger Rabbit*. Shortly thereafter, Disney sent a team of its animators to London to begin work.

Richard Purdum and producer Don Hahn presented the preliminary story reel to Katzenberg in Orlando, where the company had opened a satellite animation studio on the backlot of the Disney-MGM Studios theme park in 1989. This version borrows from the original story and the Cocteau film: Maurice is a merchant who loses his wealth when his ships are lost at sea; Belle requests a rose that sets the story in motion; Cocteau's aristocratic Avenant is here the equally vain Gaston. They also added a domineering aunt and a younger sister, both of whom do not appear in subsequent versions of the story. Although they do not sing and dance, the Enchanted Objects were another feature borrowed from Cocteau, and the reel concludes before the arrival of the Beast. Katzenberg disliked the Purdums' approach—it was pretty, but dull—and offered Ashman and Menken the opportunity to come aboard and compose the songs for the film. But unlike *Mermaid*, in which Ashman and Menken wrote the songs after the story development had been in progress, *Beauty* provided an opportunity to start over and redesign the film from the very beginning as a musical.

In November 1989, a lengthy meeting took place to lay down the foundations of the story. Although the notes from this meeting are detailed, it remains unclear who was present besides Ashman and who was speaking at any given time in the discussion. Yet this lack of clarity seems appropriate since efforts to isolate animation authors often prove difficult, if not downright impossible. Inspiration, conception, and execution come from a range of sources who have varying degrees of power and influence over the project. From the outset, the attendees agreed that the true beast was the aggressive male suitor (here unnamed, though called "Gaston" in the early drafts). Belle (here "Beauty") and her father are outsiders within the community, even though the film portrays their core values as superior to the townspeople's. Efforts to complicate the Disney princess surface within these early conversations, as Belle is neither pure nor essentially good, but funny, intelligent, and mature—"not an airhead gone goo-goo eyed."[39] Belle builds upon Ariel: fiercely independent, sometimes stubborn, always proactive. As one attendee says, "So she's not just sitting around having the world happen to her." Snow White hopes her prince will come someday; Belle needs no rescuer. Critics and scholars alike later criticized Belle as a regressive and sexist depiction of modern femininity, but the creators conscientiously attempted a character with increased agency and an assertive demeanor in their hopes of updating the Disney princess template.

Linda Woolverton, the screenwriter for *Beauty and the Beast*, shared these ambitions to modernize the Disney princess. Katzenberg expected animation to use a screenplay, not storyboards, for the plot, and he hired her to work on subsequent drafts of *Beauty* after Cox's exit. She held an MFA in children's theatre, had run her own children's theatre company, and had written for Saturday morning television. Initially, she had scripted an unproduced screenplay for a Winnie-the-Pooh feature before Katzenberg assigned her to *Beauty*. Woolverton and others working on *Beauty* wanted Belle to be intellectual, proactive, and perceptive, rather than a sexual object. Yet Woolverton still faced opposition at Disney animation, and she found herself often at odds with her collaborators while also learning how to write an animated musical.[40] Coming from the world of children's theatre, Woolverton was understandably protective over her work. Yet, as Charlie Fink explains, "The tricky part of these animation scripts and credit in animated movies is that whatever gets written is completely rewritten by the story team with the active participation of the producers and the directors."[41] Although Woolverton was not the only woman in Disney animation at the time, it remained very much a boys' club. One of the directors, she claimed, avoided eye contact with her.[42] Producer Don Hahn, on the other hand, observed that Woolverton "at times could be combative."[43]

But Woolverton had Katzenberg's support, and she ultimately found an ally in Ashman, who, as both lyricist and producer, shared her ideological ambitions but was able to mediate between her and the animation division. Although Woolverton believed Ashman would have rather written the script himself if he physically could have, he nevertheless taught her about writing musicals and encouraged her to stick up for herself in her interactions with the animators and management.[44] From these arguments emerged the model for the modern Disney princess: strong-willed, independent, self-reliant, caring, and romantic.[45] But they were not inspired by Snow White and Cinderella alone or even Cocteau's take on Belle. Time and again, Ashman pointed to *The King and I* as the model for Woolverton to follow, and upon closer examination, one can see greater parallels to Anna than to early Disney princesses.

The King and I, Richard Rodgers and Oscar Hammerstein II's 1951 masterpiece, remains one of the hallmarks of the Golden Age of Broadway musical theatre. Based upon Margaret Landon's popular 1944 novel *Anna and the King of Siam* (itself based on Leonowens's published accounts), the show takes place in the early 1860s as the British governess Anna Leonowens arrives in Bangkok to teach the King of Siam's children.[46] Although he imagines himself to be an enlightened ruler dedicated to modernizing (and Westernizing) his country, the King appears to be irascible, headstrong, and boorish. He finds a worthy adversary in Anna, who demands the residence promised to her in their agreement. Ultimately, as Lehman Engel observes, "The audience's strongest wish is to see both of them helped, and each of them in this situation is the only one who has the power to help the other."[47] The King craves the admiration of a visiting British delegation and the Western world, while Anna wants the King to respect her autonomy by permitting her to live in a home of her own. The tense (yet eroticized) relationship between the title characters as well as the tightly plotted narrative arc clearly lays the groundwork for *Beauty and the Beast*. Indeed, both musicals embrace a narrative technique that Rick Altman recognizes in the screwball comedy: "a couple who attract us not so much by their romantic attachment but rather by the masking of their attraction for each other behind an antagonistic front."[48] *The King and I* stages the tension between female and male, West and East, civilized and (as Anna says) "barbarian." Laura Donalson argues that Anna's passion to "liberate," in fact, reinforces imperialism,[49] and Caren Kaplan similarly contends that film representations of Anna Leonowens have escalated the tension "between an enlightened Western civilization that emphasizes fair play and chivalrous 'respect' for women and a sinister, despotic culture that operates through deceit and the ill-treatment of women."[50] In invoking *The King and I* as a model, *Beauty and the Beast* opens itself to readings of race and empire, especially as the domesticated Beast transforms into not only a human being but a white prince.

Quite problematically, both Anna and Belle are prisoners within the King's palace and the Beast's castle, respectively. This predicament provides the dramatic conflict for both narratives and compels interactions through which their relationships can evolve. Like Anna and the King of Siam, social conventions prevent Beauty and the Beast from acknowledging their attraction and being together, though both ultimately concede when faced with the possible death of the male lead. (The King dies; the Beast does not.) The subtle erotic tension between the principals remained a focus throughout the production of *Beauty and the Beast*, as the creative team navigated the commercial investment in making the characters attracted to one another while minimizing any suggestion of sexuality. *The King and I* is a strong character study, and its romance plot is subtle, if not completely implied. *The King and I*'s chasteness compared to *Guys and Dolls* or *West Side Story* translated well into family-friendly animation, though the creators and executives behind *Beauty and the Beast* repeatedly denied the film was primarily children's entertainment. Menken, for example, explains, "The general idea will be you're writing it for kids. No, we are not. I mean, we are writing it for the child in us as well as the adult in us. It's a cultural homage. It's a celebration of certain sensibilities. And it's using them in unexpected ways."[51] At the time, Katzenberg told reporters, "This movie is made for adults and about adults."[52] Two years earlier, Katzenberg had been surprised to learn that *The Little Mermaid* had fared particularly well with couples. Consequently, he needed the romance for the older audience but the innocence of a children's film for the family audience. The subtle nature of Anna and the King's relationship also was necessary because of the heightened sensitivity toward interracial romances in 1950s America, so it would prove a useful model for navigating a truly unnatural pairing: a woman and a beast.

The songs Ashman and Menken wrote for *Beauty and the Beast* effectively work toward both character and plot development. In that November 1989 production meeting, Howard Ashman had proposed ten possibilities for songs, including a song between Belle and the other girls in town ("Silly Virgin Song"), a song for Maurice ("World Out There"), a song for Belle to her father that the Beast could later sing to Belle ("Hurry Home"), a song for the Objects to sing to Maurice ("Be My Guest"), and a song about Gaston's machismo ("Gaston's Song"). One proposed number, "Shall we dance," in which Belle would teach the Beast how to dance, shares its name with a song from *The King and I*, in which Anna teaches the polka to the King. The decision to have the couple polka dance, rather than a more refined (and feminine) waltz, implies a desire to juxtapose Anna's sophistication and the King's machismo.[53] Of course, the dance never escalates beyond that, but the emotional implications are hard to deny. The love theme, "Beauty and the Beast," operates in much the same way. The songs in *Beauty and the Beast* are more than narrative adornments; they underscore the relationships, the high stakes, and the turning points of the story. Most importantly, as Ashman's mentor Lehman Engel observed, the score should "characterize the singers, further the plot, and in themselves help to form a coherent unity."[54] In following suit, Ashman's efforts directly address the element that many critics charged Disney animation with lacking: strong, emotionally resonant storytelling.

"Be My Guest" (later "Be Our Guest"), much like "Getting to Know You" in *The King and I*, underscores the relationship between the female lead and the supporting characters: Anna and the children in *The King and I*, and Belle and the Objects in *Beauty and the Beast*. Not only does it establish goodwill among the characters, it sets the tone for their working relationship. "Something Wonderful," sung by the Lady Thiang to Anna in defense of the King's as-yet-unseen charm, functions somewhat similarly to "Something There," in which Belle and the Beast (in his only song) begin to see something more in each other. Most importantly, "Beauty and the Beast" confirms any inkling of an emerging romance, much like the "Shall We Dance" sequence in *The King and I*. While Anna and the King sing "Shall We Dance," Belle and the Beast's romantic relationship is confirmed by a love song sung not by them, but by Mrs. Potts. That dramaturgical decision, of course, links the film to its predecessor, *The Little Mermaid*, where Sebastian performs the love ballad instead of the lead couple.

Within a week of the initial story meeting between Ashman and the creative team, the characters started to take form and discussions over casting commenced. Don Hahn pitched Richard Purdum various actors to serve as models for characters' personalities as well as possible voice actors. While he imagined that an unknown ingenue would portray Belle, he suggested Mandy Patinkin for the role of the Beast. Patinkin's performance as Inigo Montoya in *The Princess Bride* (Rob Reiner, 1987) cemented his fame, but he first made a name for himself on Broadway playing charismatic, yet volatile, young men, originating the roles of Che in *Evita* and Georges Seurat in *Sunday in the Park with George*. The remaining recommendations came not from Broadway but from Hollywood and included Arnold Schwarzenegger for Gaston, Paul Reubens (Pee-wee Herman) as Gaston's "adoring sidekick" (later Lefou, French for "the fool"), Betty White for the Teapot, Robin Williams for the Candelabra, and Julia Child for the Kitchen Pots, a character who was eliminated in subsequent drafts.[55] For Belle, though, Ashman wanted Paige O'Hara, whom he admired from her performance as Ellie in the 1988 studio cast recording of *Show Boat*.[56] While Hahn's list favors Hollywood talent, Ashman's preference for Broadway talent demonstrates the need for actors who could act *and* sing—ideally, without requiring star salaries.

By the middle of December 1989, Linda Woolverton had revised the story outline with suggested placements for Ashman and Menken's songs. Reviewing the marginalia of such documents, alongside memos and screenplay drafts, reveals the complex authorship and negotiations taking place as *Beauty and the Beast* began to take shape. Ashman, for instance, rejected the idea of the Beast learning to read, while Eisner championed the suggestion that Belle should offer to take her father's place in the Beast's jail.[57] The songs combined Ashman's skill for storytelling with Menken's genius for pastiche. By the latter's own admission, the music over the prologue takes inspiration from Camille Saint-Saëns's *The Carnival of the Animals*, "Belle" borrows from Jerry Bock, Sheldon Harnick, and Joe Masteroff's *She Loves Me*'s "Good Morning, Good Day," and the beer hall revelry of "Gaston" owes a debt to composer Sigmund Romberg (presumably "The Drinking Song" from *The Student Prince*). That February, Ashman and Menken met with the rest of the creative team to discuss how "Be Our Guest" would work in the narrative. From its inception, Ashman and Menken had intended the song as

a Broadway-style showstopper with a chorus line of dancing forks and a spectacular staircase reminiscent of the Ziegfeld Follies. As Menken later explained, Ashman "wondered what it would be like if we did a Jerry Herman number but set in
a French music hall and if it sounded like *Hello, Dolly!* but went over the top and
was a little ridiculous."[58] The melody is fairly simple, Menken explains, so that
the lyrics can rest upon it.[59] But the animators wondered if the Beast would be
aware of what was happening in the dining room, or would this moment be a private one between Belle and the Objects? Story notes ultimately reveal the latter
prevailed, and the team imagined the sequence akin to an Esther Williams
movie.[60] This discussion speaks to the centrality of the musical numbers as well
as the conception of the project squarely within the tradition of film musical.

Animation was underway by March 1990, and creative decisions remained a
source of ongoing discussion and debate among the animators, executives, producers, and other creative team members. The team alternately drew from Broadway musicals and earlier Disney films for inspiration. Much to the animators'
confusion, Howard Ashman held up the boastful military leader Miles Gloriosus
from *A Funny Thing Happened on the Way to the Forum* as the model for Gaston.
In a scene developed by Brenda Chapman, Belle dresses the Beast's wounds; the
discussion of the scene found the creative team referring to how Anna handles
the King: nurturing, but firm and assertive. When Belle refuses to join the Beast
for dinner, the exasperated Beast turns to the Enchanted Objects and points to
the door: a comic gesture that some saw as an allusion to Jackie Gleason in *The
Honeymooners*, others as an homage to Yul Brynner as the King. Director Kirk
Wise observed that the pirates in *Peter Pan* served as prototypes for Gaston's
drinking buddies, while Maurice's relationship with Belle reflects, in part, Triton
and Ariel's bond in *The Little Mermaid*. Ashman and Menken offered up "Belle"
as an ambitious opening number in a jaunty style more common to operettas
than film musicals. It would function as the "I want" song, an integrated musical
standard that lays out the protagonist's motivations and ambitions. *Beauty and
the Beast* starts with this song, and it makes clear that Belle's dreams are bigger
than her village can offer. The lyrics of "Belle" are the first words Belle expresses,
and they lay out the problems she faces as well as her dreams. Ashman and Menken feared it was too long, but Disney loved it. Yet disagreements over the lyrics
still arose: Roy Disney felt Belle's patronizing dismissal of "this provincial life"
might alienate middle America, a criticism Katzenberg swiftly dismissed: "Well,
she wants more."[61] Although contributions came from entry-level opinions up
through Eisner, it remains clear that Katzenberg wielded the most creative
authority and final say on the project.

But Katzenberg did concede that Belle was "the most difficult challenge of any
character that we have done here in a long time."[62] Animators struggled with her
movement and her physicality, turning to ballet for inspiration and attempting to
give her a familiar, down-to-earth appearance. Central to the problem of creating
a complex, endearing protagonist was the tension between Disney's realistic aesthetic and the appeal of using a more "cartoon-like" style: Belle would not have

Ariel's large, innocent eyes, and Gaston animator Andreas Deja wrestled with making the villain—described by Katzenberg as a "real full-of-shit schmuck"[63]—an exaggerated caricature or a genuine menace. As he later said, "I tried to retain the whole range of expressions—the sarcasm, the broadness and the expressiveness—that the handsome leading man seldom gets to show."[64] Ultimately the animators emphasized Belle's natural beauty and Gaston's amusing arrogance.

Katzenberg opened an August 1990 meeting in Burbank by congratulating the team: "Well, you have a movie."[65] But creative disagreement persisted in spite of the difference, especially between Katzenberg and Ashman. Katzenberg believed the theme of the film was "don't judge a book by its cover," but the team argued that Ashman (who was back in New York) saw the film as what it means to be human—the same theme Ashman believed to be at the center of *The Little Mermaid*. In fact, for Ashman, *Beauty and the Beast* was the Beast's story, despite Woolverton's emphasis on Belle and the animators' insistence on the couple as dual protagonists. (Later critics have discussed the film as Ashman's subtle examination of the AIDS crisis and how society treated the afflicted, but no evidence presently exists to verify this claim.)[66] Furthermore, Katzenberg clearly did not understand the integrated musical when he complained that the lyrics too often did the storytelling. Katzenberg laments, "It's said in a song, but a song is not emotional. And it's not cognitive—it doesn't, it's never going to drive home the same thing as coming in on an intimate moment in which someone tells you how they feel. A song, especially, is a suspension of disbelief—it's a magical, bigger-than-life moment. We have got to make sure that the people moments in this are really, really, really strong. And they're not—they're substituted by musical moments."[67] For Katzenberg, using the songs to underscore—rather than dramatize—the central tension of the narrative should be the goal. Key moments should be spoken rather than sung, he contends, but the music could then recapitulate these sentiments already expressed in dialogue. The end result here would be "driving home emotional and dramatic dilemmas with a sledgehammer," and by "wear[ing] its sentimentality on its sleeve," a film could resonate with audiences and generate substantial returns. (To prove this point, he reported that *The Little Mermaid* was the most viewed home video of all time.) Ashman, on the other hand, believed the songs took over telling the story when emotions intensified. Had he been present, he undoubtedly would have defended the time-honored craft theory to his misguided boss. In an interview with Ira Weitzman years earlier, Ashman explained how the musical book and the songs should work together:

> The book for a musical is more than the words that connect the songs. The book is the structure, and there is no such thing as a "bookless musical" except maybe *Dancin'* but the structure is libretto. The book hasn't disappeared—people talk about the book disappearing. No—that's not true at all. The songs simply in contemporary musicals are fulfilling the function of scenes. We're singing more of the plot material, we're singing more of the action in the forward thrust. And the action can be imagistic or can be naturalistic, depending on the material,

just as in a play. Depending on what you're trying to do. I like to tell stories. Narrative interests me. And I do love construction. It's a puzzle.[68]

Their different interpretations reveal the competing nature of their authority: as an executive and successful production chief, Katzenberg easily could assert his authority over Ashman as his subordinate, but Ashman's command of the Broadway idiom made him invaluable to Katzenberg and Disney. Since Ashman's illness kept him out of the room (he received a cassette recording of this meeting later), he could not defend his efforts in the moment. Yet in viewing the film, one sees that Ashman's, not Katzenberg's, approach to musical theatre storytelling prevailed.

Katzenberg believed the task at hand remained creating an emotionally satisfying story: "We should be crying. I want to cry. I want this movie to make me cry. Not yet."[69] After meeting with Katzenberg, Woolverton revised the screenplay to address persistent problems, particularly the Beast. Agreeing that the theme is "don't judge a book by its cover," she stated that the prologue would show that doing just the opposite triggered the Beast's transformation, a suggestion with which Katzenberg unsurprisingly agreed.[70] Greater effort also was needed to show the Beast's development from monster back to man, which, in turn, allows the audience to identify with both Belle and the Beast. Woolverton suggested that Belle use the Wardrobe as a sounding board for her own anxieties: "We can feel her pain at being locked in this castle and losing everything she's ever dreamed of."[71] As a confidante and cheerleader of sorts, Lumiere served much the same role for the Beast. The Objects function as comic relief and as interlocutors for the protagonists to express inner monologues that would be out of place in a film but would work in a stage production. Finally, Woolverton stressed that the audience needed a stronger understanding of what Belle sees in the Beast, to which the screenwriter added that he listens, makes her laugh, treats her kindly, and provides the romance she is seeking. As Belle begins to see "beneath the beastly exterior," so, too, would the audience.[72] If Belle is the audience's point of identification, then the film charts Belle and the audience's developing affection for the Beast.

As the film entered nearly a year in production, the creative team worked to tighten up the narrative while removing ambiguous or unseemly aspects of the plot. To avoid any sense of impropriety, Belle—not the Beast—suggests that she should replace her father in a castle jail cell. Initially a boisterous, even obnoxious, character, the Wardrobe was toned down, and in turn, her role was significantly reduced. Katzenberg, increasingly confident in the film's progress, exclaims, "We're finally making the same movie."[73]

On November 8, 1990, the animation division screened *Beauty and the Beast* for Eisner, who echoed the ongoing apprehension about the Beast's characterization. In particular, Robby Benson's performance as the Beast did not adequately capture the necessary nuances of the character. Overall, the Beast needed to be more developed, Eisner argued, and he offered two ways to proceed with the character. In the first approach, the Beast would be similar to Barry Diller, Eisner and

Figure 6. The "Beauty and the Beast" scene demonstrates the influence of "Shall We Dance" from *The King and I* as well as ongoing developments in computer animation in rendering the ballroom. Credit: Author's screenshot.

Katzenberg's former boss at Paramount, who can be stubborn but, over time, begins to reveal his lighter side through his interactions with Belle. Eisner also cited the relationship between Eliza Doolittle and the stuffy Professor Henry Higgins in the Broadway musical *My Fair Lady* as a useful antecedent for this dynamic.[74] The other model, Eisner contended, should be *The Elephant Man*, a play (and, later, a 1980 David Lynch film) about Joseph Merrick's struggles for social acceptance in nineteenth-century England. The Beast is so ashamed of his physical appearance that he hesitates to talk to Belle. Katzenberg offered a compromise: Belle must choose between Gaston and the Beast, raising the question of whether or not the Beauty in the title is Belle (literally, "beautiful" in French) or Gaston, the more traditionally handsome of her suitors.

Watching the film in light of Eisner's notes, it becomes clear the November 8 screening may have been a formality for the creative team since so few of his suggestions were actually implemented. For example, he recommended moving "Be Our Guest" to Belle's first meal with the Beast, rather than her late-night encounter with the Objects after refusing to join the Beast for dinner earlier than evening. Eisner also did not think the audience needed to know how the Beast became cursed. In his opinion, "Belle" dragged on and created the impression that the film was a stage musical, which he insisted it was not.[75] In light of Eisner's concerns, Woolverton did revise the scene in which Belle offers herself to replace her father, while also emphasizing that Belle would return during the confrontation between Gaston and the Beast so that the latter regains the will to fight back.[76] Overall, though, Eisner's vision conflicted with the creative team's (even Katzenberg's) intentions, and Katzenberg simplified Eisner's criticism to "Un-bore Michael"—that is, keep him interested—in subsequent meetings to keep production moving while placating his boss.[77] The lip service paid to Eisner demonstrated that though creativity was collaborative, it was also hierarchized. One's power could vary, even fluctuate, changing the final product as a result. Eisner obviously outranked Katzenberg, but the latter garnered more creative influence over the film through his close supervision to the production process. While giving notes implicitly stages the struggle for authorial control in contemporary media production, how a creative laborer—or in this case lower-ranked executive—responds to feedback from above demonstrates the nuance necessary to navigate personal expression and executive oversight.[78]

In mid-November, Katzenberg called a meeting with the belief that the filmmakers desperately needed to address several matters immediately, including the Beast, his romance with Belle, the placement of the songs, and the handling of emotions.[79] Despite the urgency in his tone, these issues had persisted for much of the film's production. To him, *Beauty and the Beast* most closely resembled *Pinocchio* in terms of aesthetics, and he sought solutions based on that film. Katzenberg encouraged the team to take greater advantage of scope, color palate, and camerawork. (He also warned against "Marty Scorsese flourishes," which he felt would violate the willing suspension of disbelief with their blatant self-awareness.)[80] He worried that they would need to ask Ashman and Menken to write a song for the Beast. One suggestion was to rewrite "Human Again" for the Beast instead of the Objects, while animator Roger Allers suggested a musical number similar to the "Tonight, Tonight" in Leonard Bernstein and Stephen Sondheim's *West Side Story*, in which various characters alternately sing their varied responses regarding the impending rumble between the gangs.[81] The Beast's role was expanded because Katzenberg insisted that, despite Eisner's protests, the prologue was necessary and the audience should see the Beast. Woolverton finished a new prologue—less stuffy, more succinct—in the following days that won Katzenberg's approval, and this version appears in the final film.[82]

Ashman eventually was able to view a cut of the film in New York, and Katzenberg reported that although Ashman was disappointed with some of the changes, he nevertheless agreed that they needed to be made. Ashman sent along notes for improving the film, particularly to enhance the Objects' role while also maintaining the storylines of Gaston, Lefou, and Maurice during the love montage between Beauty and the Beast. It was never quite clear how long this story took place, so Ashman's comments reminded the filmmakers to focus on balancing the various plots more carefully. Ashman promised to work on the montage song, eventually titled "Something There," while also polishing "Be Our Guest" so it worked better with Belle as the audience. Ashman's lyrics, therefore, would improve the film's pacing and the character arcs that so desperately needed improvement. "Something There," for instance, allows the Beast to sing and articulate his growing affections for Belle. This addition, in turn, encouraged the audience to empathize with him. Katzenberg remained unsatisfied with the Beast, the Objects, and even Lefou, though he was pleased with Gaston and Belle.

As Christmas 1990 approached, Katzenberg, management, and the animators continued to finetune the film. His recommendations varied from small suggestions, such as Belle rolling her eyes when she sings "his little wife" during the reprise of "Belle," to depicting the Beast as turned away during the prologue so that his stance conveys his inner turmoil rather than his face. The animation for the songs particularly troubled Katzenberg, as if it was not yet capturing the spirit of the lyrics. A month earlier, he encouraged animators to let "Be Our Guest" really soar, since it is the "most burlesque number in the film."[83] Now, he found inadequacies in each of the musical numbers: he disliked Lumiere's lead-in to "Be Our Guest," felt Gaston's chest should be "less sensual" when he rips open his shirt during his song, and suggested the layouts for "Something There" needed to channel cinematographer Vittorio Storaro (of *Apocalypse Now* [Francis Ford Coppola, 1979] fame) and the landscapes in *Doctor Zhivago* (David Lean, 1965).[84] Perhaps most troubling for the team, he was still dissatisfied with Robby Benson's vocal performance. In December he felt it was flat and emotionless, while a month later he claimed the bargaining scene was infused with a disconcerting eroticism.[85] In addition to tweaking it further, the animators would have to work on how they animated the latter scene to capture the desired propriety. They had a musical, but now they needed a film.

Amid all this turmoil, they were also losing an important collaborator. In the early months of 1991, Ashman became increasingly weak as his health declined. Eventually, he was rendered unable to see or speak. Around this time, Disney previewed an unfinished version of *Beauty and the Beast* in New York City to build excitement and a possible Oscar nomination for Best Picture. After the screening, Katzenberg, Peter Schneider, and David Geffen visited Ashman at St. Vincent's Hospital, the best equipped medical facility on the East Coast for treating patients with AIDS. They gushed at the warm reception it had received. Geffen, Katzenberg later recounted, "told Howard he was a man who inspired people to believe in magical things, that he had to believe, that maybe it wasn't over, that he should never give up."[86]

On March 14, 1991, Ashman passed away in New York City. He was forty years old. Ashman never saw the final version of *Beauty and the Beast*, yet it remains the clearest example of his (and the integrated musical's) artistic impact on contemporary Disney feature animation. As Lin-Manuel Miranda asserted, "So many musicals have tried to chase that formula—the sidekicks, the bad guys. But *Beauty and the Beast* did it at its pinnacle. It's the best it's ever been done."[87]

In early fall 1991, nearly two months prior to its nationwide release, *Beauty and the Beast* was screened at the New York Film Festival. This decision was uncharacteristic for two important reasons. For one, the film was presented as about 60 percent complete;[88] it was, in fact, further along but was manipulated to appear less finished.[89] Furthermore, film festivals generally do not screen works in progress, especially not Disney animated features. Disney decided to try it out because of the increased interest in animation following *Who Framed Roger Rabbit*, but the decision also reveals the company's efforts to legitimate feature animation as an art form. Showing *Beauty* at a major film festival clearly reinforced animation's cultural value as cinema. In an interview with the *New York Times*, Don Hahn made the case for animation being as artful as live-action cinema by connecting animators' work to actors': "Whether you're Dustin Hoffman or an animator, if you're doing a scene from *Beauty and the Beast* when two characters fall in love you have to find the exact expressions that convey that feeling. Animators are closet actors. They spend hours in [front] of the mirror trying to solve these problems."[90] Disney was satisfying its founder's dream of producing an animated film every year. The company also seemed to share Walt's desire for two forms of validation from his Hollywood peers: respect as a film artist and a Best Picture Oscar.[91] Disney was both reviving feature animation and elevating its prestige within the industry.

The marketing efforts for *Beauty and the Beast* included one theatrical poster that features Belle's arms outstretched while donning an apron and pinafore, not unlike Maria in *The Sound of Music* (Robert Wise, 1965). (A shot of Belle walking uphill during the reprise of "Belle" clearly pays homage to the Oscar-winning film musical.) The Enchanted Objects line the foreground, smiling and arms open. In the distance stands the Beast's castle, while in the clouds overhead the gruff Beast looks back disapprovingly. Another poster shows the title characters dancing in silhouette, a cascading tagline declaring, "The most beautiful love story ever told." Even here, the film positions itself as a classic perhaps even aimed toward adults rather than a lighthearted children's cartoon. The theatrical trailer similarly emphasizes it as the thirtieth animated film and a classic story. "Something There" functions as the underscore, emphasizing the film's investments in comedy, musical, adventure, and romance. It bolsters the inclusion, too, of "six new songs from the Academy Award–winning composer and lyricist of *The Little Mermaid*," the sole acknowledged (though unnamed) members of the creative team. Finally, it encourages the audience to come enjoy "the fun, the magic, and the music of an entertainment event you'll never forget" before ending on "Be Our Guest."

A holiday release like *The Little Mermaid*, *Beauty and the Beast* opened right before Thanksgiving 1991. The film's primary competition was Paramount's reboot of *The Addams Family* (Barry Sonnenfeld, 1991) and Universal's animated sequel *An American Tail: Fievel Goes West* (Phil Nibbelink and Simon Wells, 1991). *The Addams Family* took the top spot, but *Beauty* outperformed *Fievel Goes West* ($9.6 million to $3.4 million, respectively) despite playing in seven hundred fewer theaters. U.S. audiences had reaffirmed Disney as the leader in feature animation.

The majority of critics were impressed by Disney's latest effort. Roger Ebert proclaimed the film is "as good as any Disney animated feature ever made."[92] "Close to seamless," Richard Corliss wrote in his review for *Time*, concluding, "The voluptuousness of visual detail offers proof, if any more were needed after *The Little Mermaid*, that the Disney studio has relocated the pure magic of the *Pinocchio-Dumbo* years."[93] Even Hal Hinson of the *Washington Post*, who had skewered *The*

Little Mermaid two years earlier, declared that *Beauty* was a "near-masterpiece that draws on the sublime traditions of the past while remaining completely in sync with the sensibility of its time" and "a giant step forward for Disney's animation unit."[94] Jeff Strickler of the *Star-Tribune* reviewed the film positively but observed that the Beast's voice "sounds slightly mechanically enhanced a la Darth Vader."[95] Janet Maslin noticed the Beast's modified voice but conceded that Benson's performance was "so convincing that it eradicates all memory of his mild manner."[96]

These criticisms were often tempered by praise for Belle, whom Jay Carr lauded as "a thoroughly modern young woman."[97] In fact, the centrality of Belle and her headstrong independence prompted one critic to call *Beauty and the Beast* "classic in style, yet most contemporary—almost feminist—in substance."[98] The compliment speaks not so much to Katzenberg's micromanagement as to the production team's modern take on the Disney princess. They attempted to move beyond the perceived naïveté and objectification of Ariel to offer a female lead who was neither lovesick nor hypersexualized. It was a promising step forward, but not far enough for some critics, both then and now.[99]

Numerous reviewers commended Ashman and Menken for their exemplary application of the Broadway idiom to *Beauty and the Beast*. For example, several reviews allude to the skillful integration of music and lyrics with the storyline: "The production numbers are terrific and help advance the plot while serving up first-rate entertainment."[100] Theatre critic Thomas O'Connor praised the film as an antidote to the megamusicals that had "plagued" Broadway in recent years: "If you love Broadway-style musicals, you have surely seen plenty of chandeliers crashing, spandex-clad cats scampering and bloody barricades falling in the past decade. But, save for that minority of musical-theater fans who savor the more rarefied airs of Stephen Sondheim or William Finn. Broadway has not been particularly tuneful in years. . . . The vivacious score for *Beauty and the Beast* . . . puts Broadway's puny output to shame."[101] Deriding *Phantom of the Opera, Cats,* and *Les Misérables,* O'Connor then elevates Ashman and Menken's work through flattering comparisons to the rhythms of Leonard Bernstein, the magnetism of Frederick Loewe, and the liveliness of Jerry Herman. Writing for the *Atlanta Journal and Constitution,* Eleanor Ringel declared, "To put it bluntly, there aren't songs on Broadway this good," singling out musical performances by Broadway veterans Jerry Orbach and Angela Lansbury.[102] As had happened with *The Little Mermaid,* critics highlighted the musical numbers, prompting theatre journalist Jesse White to suggest mournfully, "Will Broadway win them back, or have we lost a generation of talent to Tinseltown?"[103]

The most influential member of *Beauty*'s laudatory chorus was Frank Rich. When Menken discussed his preference for Hollywood over Broadway shortly after the release of *Beauty*—"The atmosphere in New York is too dangerous. So much rests on the opinion of too few critics"[104]—he was undoubtedly pointing a finger at Rich and the *New York Times.* Yet on his radio broadcast and in a subsequent article, Rich summed up the Broadway season by stating, "The best Broadway musical score of 1991 was that written by Alan Menken and Howard Ashman for the

Disney animated movie *Beauty and the Beast*."[105] This evaluation slammed the quality of Broadway musicals in 1991 while endorsing Disney musicals as Broadway-quality fare. Rich was not the first person to make this observation, but when he spoke, people listened. And according to Disney, the comment sparked its serious interest in pursuing theatrical production.[106]

———

More than any other film, *Beauty and the Beast* demonstrates theatre talent's contribution to Disney's renewed commercial and critical success. The production team dedicated the film "To our friend, Howard, who gave a mermaid her voice and a beast his soul, we will be forever grateful." The reception of the film, which later included the first Best Picture Oscar nomination for an animated feature, testifies to the power of bringing together the various artistic elements—music, lyrics, dramatic scenes, and, of course, animation—into one coherent narrative. For years, critics from within and outside of Disney had chastised its films' flimsy storylines, but the company found its answer in theatre through Ashman's dramaturgical labor and Menken's melodious scores.

But the film industry was changing, leading studios to aggressively pursue properties that would avail themselves to franchising, licensing, and cross-promotion. Companies merged with or acquired one another, while media technologies converged. So, too, did the entertainment industries as they found themselves increasingly at the mercy of multinational conglomerates. As a cinematic exemplar of Broadway integrated musical theatre storytelling, *Beauty and the Beast* provided Disney with the necessary inroad to the commercial theatre industry. A major obstacle, of course, would be how the company would enter the world of Broadway without one of its leading creators.

CHAPTER 5

"Like the Old-Fashioned Musicals Did"

ROBERT JESS ROTH, *BEAUTY AND THE BEAST*, AND DISNEY, 1992–1994

Michael Eisner's explanation of how Disney made its way to Broadway differs from others' accounts. In December 1991, Frank Rich of the *New York Times* opined that the finest Broadway score of the year actually was not on Broadway but in *Beauty and the Beast*. In his memoir, Eisner claimed Rich's remarks inspired Disney's move: "It was clear that Rich meant this partly as a backhanded slap at Broadway's current musicals, but he was also acknowledging the power of *Beauty*'s score. His comment encouraged us to think more seriously about adapting the movie to the stage."[1] Eisner's account conveniently absolves Disney of culpability, crediting the company's decision to Broadway's premier tastemaker.

The reality is that Disney had flirted with the idea for years. Bob McTyre, an executive who would leave attractions to help lead Disney's theatrical division, told the *Los Angeles Times*, "The idea of doing theater is not a new one for Disney, . . . there have been many people, including myself, who prior to this wanted to motivate the company to go into the theater business. But the company never felt it was right before."[2] He noted the company had produced shows at Radio City Music Hall, the touring production of *Disney's Symphonic Fantasy*, and *Fantasmic!* every night in the parks.[3] Similarly, Matthew Wilson Smith has argued that Walt Disney's investments in theme parks were, in fact, his "grandest experiment in theatrical totality," while more recently, theatre and performance studies scholars have turned their attention to the theme parks as a performance space.[4] Alan Menken himself had presented Disney with the idea several times, but the company consistently declined to move into the notoriously challenging (and often unprofitable) business.[5] As McTyre recollects, Eisner was ready to pursue a Broadway production of *Beauty* before the film was released.[6]

Robert Jess Roth, who worked in the theme park division, also wanted Disney to pursue theatre, and he began pitching the idea to Eisner and Katzenberg in 1990. Eisner initially declined but encouraged Roth to pitch the idea again in the future.

By 1991, Eisner was on board and charged Roth with determining which Disney property was best suited to be its "premiere Broadway production." After some research, Roth selected *Mary Poppins*.[7] The release of *Beauty* soon after made the ideal candidate clear, and the show was in the works shortly thereafter.[8] Theatrically trained theme park personnel—Roth, scenic designer Stan Meyer, and choreographer Matt West—took the lead on the project, but the business model was inspired in large part by the British megamusical. Roth explains, "Was I inspired storytelling-wise and staging-wise by those shows? No. Was I inspired by how they rolled the shows out around the world? Well, yeah, that's what I pitched to Michael and Jeffrey back in 1990: 'Hey, *Phantom* just passed $1 billion. *Star Wars* hasn't grossed $1 billion.'"[9] As Hollywood in the early 1990s proved itself to be as temperamental as ever, Broadway theatrical production afforded Disney a new avenue to diversify its entertainment investments and reinforce its financial stability.

Transferring *Beauty and the Beast* to the Broadway stage was not only a commercial triumph for the Walt Disney Company but an artistic triumph for the U.S. musical, especially the integrated form that dominated Broadway's Golden Age. Drama critics dismissed Disney's arrival with suspicion and condescension, deeming its efforts little more than theme park entertainment. While several members of the production team were from the company's theme park division, including director Roth and scenic designer Meyer, they had come to theme parks from the world of theatre. *Beauty and the Beast*, therefore, draws on traditions of entertainment production in theatre, film, and theme parks. Although it is not sung through, its use of spectacle, heavily branded marketing strategy, and easily reproducible staging aligned it with the British megamusical, at least from an economic and production point of view. But even on Broadway, Belle was more indebted to Anna Leonowens and Eliza Doolittle than to Eponine (of *Les Misérables*) or Christine Daaé (of *Phantom*). The unlikely, perhaps uneasy mix of the integrated musical, theme park entertainment, and the British megamusical made *Beauty and the Beast* both familiar and strange. Despite a mix of critical ambivalence and derision from theatre industry insiders and local residents, it founds its audience—and became one of the longest running shows to date.[10]

The 1991 holiday season failed to provide the robust box office that the studios had hoped for, due in large part to the coming economic downturn. National Amusements chairman Sumner Redstone lamented, "Things just aren't that good, and the business is not recession-resistant."[11] By 1992, it was clear ticket sales were declining as admissions slipped below $5 billion, and Hollywood had to reevaluate its strategy of big budgets and serious, adult-oriented fare.[12] Movie budgets declined slightly to $26.1 million. But the greatest cuts were needed in marketing and advertising, and few studios were willing to risk scaling back on promotional expenses.[13]

The blockbuster success of *Beauty and the Beast* helped protect Disney from the unfolding economic turmoil. CEO Michael Eisner more fully realized the possibilities available for the company in animation. In his letter to shareholders, he boasted, "Your company has nothing less than the most talented, inventive, creative, original, resourceful and brilliant people working in animation."[14] This praise, of course, was also a not-so-subtle pat on his own back, as Eisner firmly believed his role called on him to find, hire, and cultivate such talent.

But Howard Ashman, one of the most influential of those hires, was now gone. On March 30, 1992, Ashman posthumously won an Academy Award for Best Original Song for "Beauty and the Beast." Although he contributed lyrics to only five films, Ashman received seven Best Original Song nominations between 1986 and 1992. Accepting the award on his behalf, his partner Bill Lauch delivered a heartfelt plea for compassion:

> Howard and I shared a home and a life together, and I am very happy and very proud to accept this for him. But it is bittersweet. This is the first Academy Award given to someone we've lost to AIDS. In working on *Beauty and the Beast*, Howard faced incredible personal challenges, but always gave his best, and what made that possible was an atmosphere of understanding, love, and support. That's something everyone facing AIDS not only needs, but deserves. There's an inscription at Howard's grave in Baltimore. It reads, "Oh that he had one more song to sing." We'll never hear that song, but I am deeply grateful for this tribute you've given to what he left behind. For Howard, I thank you.[15]

Ashman's final project, *Aladdin*, premiered eight months later, but in a significantly altered version from the one he had pitched years earlier. Although he had completed work on the film before *Beauty*, subsequent revisions to *Aladdin*'s storyline, including the removal of the title character's mother, necessitated new songs. Disney turned to British lyricist Tim Rice, who had collaborated with Andrew Lloyd Webber on the stage musicals *Jesus Christ Superstar* and *Evita*, to write lyrics with Menken. The film's signature song, "A Whole New World," continued the tradition of the love ballad that Ashman and Menken had brought back to Disney, although here the lovers perform the song rather than it being delivered by a supporting character in the wings.

Aladdin did have something that was rather unexpected for a Disney film and a musical: the use of major star talent in Robin Williams. The celebrated comedian, known for his manic delivery, had turned to more dramatic roles in recent years, including Oscar-nominated performances in *Dead Poets Society* and *The Fisher King* (Terry Gilliam, 1991). As the Genie in *Aladdin*, however, he returned to the quirky, digressive style that had made him a successful stand-up comedian. He often ad-libbed for long periods of time, leaving filmmakers to decide how to incorporate his trademark polyvocality, rich in allusions to a range of pop culture figures, from Ed Sullivan to Groucho Marx and William F. Buckley Jr. While Williams brought the film an invaluable vitality, his performance disrupted the integration of narrative and musical elements that define the Broadway musical theatre. One wonders if Ashman would have granted him such creative license since the story effectively pauses to allow for Williams's gleeful improvisations, leaving the title character to marvel at his sidekick's virtuosity. Nevertheless, Williams found a suitable partner in animation, an art form that could accommodate his associative, highly allusive approach through rapid metamorphoses of the Genie. Critics and fans alike welcomed his brand of revelry, and he received a special Golden Globe for his voice acting. The film itself eclipsed the success of the earlier animated features to become, by far, the most profitable release of 1992.

Although *Aladdin* dominated the global box office, Warner Bros., bolstered by two sequels, *Batman Returns* (Tim Burton, 1992) and *Lethal Weapon 3* (Richard Donner, 1992), reigned over Disney domestically. Nevertheless, the companies had a considerable lead over their competition: Warner Bros. took a 19.8 percent share and Disney had 19.4 percent, easily outpacing 20th Century Fox (14.2 percent), Columbia (12.5 percent), and Universal (11.7 percent).[16] As Roy Disney had long insisted, animation was always the symbolic foundation of Disney; by 1992, it began to emerge as the heart of its business operations. Not only were *Mermaid*, *Beauty*, and *Aladdin* well-received across various demographics, but unlike the live-action comedies, they proved to have a considerable cultural afterlife on home video, in licensing, and at the theme parks. *Beauty and the Beast* reaffirmed for Disney the value not only of musical theatre storytelling but of media franchises. Indeed, by the time *Aladdin* was released in 1992, the company was fully prepared to continue the "experience" of the film with books, music, television programming, video games, toys, and other merchandising. By the end of 1993, *Aladdin* had inspired thousands of Disney-manufactured or -licensed products.[17] While film was certainly a profitable division, it could connect to other industries where the profits could prove to be even more exorbitant. Nevertheless, these highly profitable franchises usually emerge from a film initially, and the need to remain invested in developing such properties within the feature division was abundantly clear to the financial viability of Disney moving forward.

In the 1992 annual report, Eisner also began to historicize this period in his opening letter. He curiously positioned *Who Framed Roger Rabbit* at the outset, followed by *Oliver & Company*, *The Little Mermaid*, and *The Rescuers Down Under*. Over time, however, *Oliver* and *Rescuers* have fallen to the wayside, while *Mermaid*, *Beauty*, *Aladdin*, and *The Lion King* have become the focus of a great deal of Disney's self-congratulations and fans' embrace of this period's films. Part of that legacy was cemented through video sales, where the video of *Beauty* had sold over twenty million units to become the company's best-selling video to date, surpassing the previous record holder, *Fantasia*.[18] But animation was not the only division that was thriving, as the studio took second place at the box office in large part due to the success of low-budget comedies such as *Father of the Bride* (Charles Shyer, 1991), *Encino Man* (Les Mayfield, 1992), and *Sister Act* (Emile Ardolino, 1992). Hollywood Pictures' psychological thriller *The Hand That Rocks the Cradle* (Curtis Hanson, 1992) rounded out the top releases from Buena Vista. Katzenberg's formula, cemented by his notorious memo, was working for the time being: tell high-concept stories, tightly manage the budgets, avoid top stars and directors (and therefore big egos), and give priority to family-friendly fare with broad appeal.

While Universal was scaling back production costs nearly 25 percent,[19] Disney aimed to increase its output with the June 1993 acquisition of Miramax. This move, as Alisa Perren has observed, doubled Disney's film library and "provid[ed] the conglomerate with heightened prestige and adult-oriented material at a relatively low cost."[20]

Despite the upcoming series finale of *The Golden Girls*, television continued to be a highly profitable sector for Disney. *Home Improvement*, a sitcom starring stand-up comedian Tim Allen, proved to be the most popular new show of the 1991–1992 season, while syndicated cartoons like *Darkwing Duck, Goof Troop*, and *Bonkers!* dominated after-school and Saturday morning television schedules. Cable subscriptions declined nationally, yet Disney managed to raise its own subscriber base for the Disney Channel to almost seven million households.[21] Globally, the fall of the Soviet Union and the thaw of Eastern Europe fueled Disney's expansion into Bulgaria, the Czech Republic, Hungary, Poland, and Russia.

The crown jewel for Eisner, however, continued to be Euro Disneyland, which opened in April 1992. The reception was mixed to say the least. Clearing nearly five thousand acres of sugar beet fields to develop the park, Disney's final effort was nearly "one-fifth the size of Paris itself."[22] Disney did not adjust its policies to reflect the cultural expectations of its host country, refusing, for example, to sell wine in the park. (This rule was later revised.) While Eisner clearly had seen the endeavor as a prestigious addition to the attractions division, French theatre director Ariane Mnouchkine dismissed Euro Disneyland as evidence of an impending "cultural Chernobyl."[23] But as Sabrina Mittermeier has argued, the concerns of the elites did not accurately represent the response to Euro Disneyland, nor did they capture some of its legitimate shortcomings related to intended audience and significant differences between U.S. and French culture.[24] The future of Euro Disneyland initially appeared uncertain despite Disney's public optimism.

If any sector warranted hope and optimism, it was feature animation, and the spirit of synergy energized other divisions. Disney became keenly aware that audiences wanted to continue the experience they had in movie theaters, and the Consumer Products division worked overtime to provide it. As the 1993 annual report touted, "People didn't just want to *see* the movie [*Aladdin*]. They wanted to read it, wear it, listen to it and play with it . . . and Disney's many operating units made those things happen."[25] Throughout the 1990s, Disney came to realize that the income generated after the movie, not directly from it, proved more long-lasting and substantial. Treating its animated films as creative properties, the company sought new markets to exploit as it continued to diversify. It found a new home in an unlikely place: Midtown Manhattan.

In the past, prominent playwrights brought their shows directly to Broadway, but rising costs and changing demographics meant that many emerging and established playwrights continued to develop and open their latest plays in resident, Off-Broadway, or Off-Off-Broadway theaters. Funding from the Ford Foundation and, later, the National Endowment for the Arts catalyzed this transition through-out the 1960s, making venues outside of New York City increasingly vital to the future of U.S. theatre. With few exceptions, Broadway appeared to be increasingly inhospitable to the play as a dramatic form unless it possessed financial promise. Echoing Brustein's earlier sentiment, Mark Taper Forum artistic director Gordon Davidson noted in 1994, "Broadway has become, rather than the generator, the receiver of material."[26]

This period also saw the rise of the "flop 'hit,'" a term coined by Frank Rich in 1998 to refer to shows that play to full or nearly full audiences for months, even years, yet fail to return on their initial investment because of high operating costs.[27] Rich notes that the 1981 musical *Woman of the Year*, starring Lauren Bacall, was an early example, but the most prominent examples came in the 1990s with *The Will Rogers Follies*, *Sunset Boulevard*, and *Victor/Victoria*. Even though it won the 1989 Tony Award for Best Musical, *Jerome Robbins's Broadway*, a revue of the choreographer's most iconic musical numbers, played over six hundred perfor-mances without returning its investment, due in large part to its cast of sixty-two and its complicated strategy for paying out royalties.[28] Furthermore, spectacular effects, highly paid stars, and unions were all blamed for preventing shows from generating profits for their investors, demonstrating the "perilously inflated, if not completely absurd, state of Broadway economics."[29] But Alex Witchel of the *New York Times* reported on one show that managed to succeed in this climate: *Black and Blue*. Perhaps not easily recognized today, it ran for over eight hun-dred performances and generated a profit. Since the show was a revue featuring blues and jazz songs, tap dance, and skits, it developed a following among tourists who may not have had the command of English necessary to follow more dialogue-driven shows.[30] Furthermore, an appearance on the 1989 Tony Awards broadcast and a successful school discount program kept the show afloat through its impres-sive tenure.

In the early 1990s, Broadway began a gradually rebound, despite the prevalence of the flop hit. Thirty-eight shows opened in the 1991–1992 season, and media com-panies continued to invest in new productions, such as Polygram's stake in *Jelly's Last Jam*, a biographical musical about jazz musician Jelly Roll Morton. Ticket prices rose to an average of $39.71, and attendance of 7.4 million people brought the box office gross to a new high of $292 million.[31] In addition to successful reviv-als of *Guys and Dolls* and *The Most Happy Fella*, *Crazy for You*, a jukebox musical featuring songs by Ira and George Gershwin and starring *The Little Mermaid*'s Jodi Benson, placed the U.S. musical front and center on Broadway. Frank Rich boldly declared in the *New York Times*, "When future historians try to find the exact moment at which Broadway finally rose up to grab the musical back from the Brit-ish, they just may conclude that the revolution began last night. The shot was fired at the Shubert Theater, where a riotously entertaining show called *Crazy for You* uncorked the American musical's classic blend of music, laughter, dancing, senti-ment and showmanship with a freshness and confidence rarely seen during the *Cats* decade."[32] In retrospect, Rich's proclamation regarding the state of the U.S.

musical may have been premature. With the abysmal failure of Lloyd Webber's *Aspects of Love* and Mackintosh's turn toward revues and revivals, it should come as little surprise that theatre critic Matt Wolf asserted in 1993 that "the days of the British musical behemoth are pretty much over."[33] Nevertheless, Jeffrey Katzenberg knew the truth: "There are 37 performances of an Andrew Lloyd Webber musical every day."[34] Lloyd Webber's newer shows may have been struggling, but his approach to sit-down and touring productions worldwide clearly remained highly profitable.

A new theatrical force seemed to be building strength—not in Europe, but in Canada. A portmanteau of "Live Entertainment," Livent was initially the theatrical production division of the Toronto-based exhibitor Cineplex Odeon. It was spun off by Garth Drabinsky, who became the high-profile producer behind Kander and Ebb's musical adaptation of *Kiss of the Spider Woman* and a lavish revival of Jerome Kern and Oscar Hammerstein II's *Show Boat*. Described by theatre critic John Lahr as "a nineties theatre-production company structured like a thirties film studio,"[35] Livent was doing exactly what drama critics had called for: an ambitious, visionary producer identifying and nurturing new dramatic work. Livent also was a publicly traded company, effectively making any shareholder a Broadway producer. Livent's corporate structure reportedly permitted Drabinsky to pump seemingly endless amounts of money into any given production at his discretion. (Traditional Broadway producers raised money for single productions, so they could not use one show's funds to bolster a different production.) In short, Drabinsky and Lloyd Webber's Really Useful Group formally incorporated Broadway producing. In so doing, they proved to Broadway (and, presumably, Disney) that well-funded corporations could produce critically acclaimed new musicals while turning a profit.

Beyond Broadway, another entertainment company, was modeling the profitability of well-maintained touring companies. *Walt Disney's World on Ice* began in 1981 as the brainchild of Kenneth Feld, the owner of the largest live-entertainment company in the world. Feld's family had established themselves as the producer of Ringling Brothers and Barnum & Bailey circus, but in 1978 his acquisition of two ice shows inspired him to consider ways to liven up the concept. Initially, he wanted a segment with Disney characters, which the company rejected, though it warmed up to the idea of an entire show devoted to Disney characters. The ice shows were not produced, but licensed, by Disney. Feld kept the prices relatively low, $8.00 to $10.00 in 1987 and $11.50 to $25.00 in 1994, in his efforts to be "the Wal-Mart of the entertainment business."[36] And like Wal-Mart, Feld sold much more than tickets, including food and drinks, T-shirts, stuffed animals, and toys.

The elaborate *Beauty and the Beast* ice show featured dialogue and songs that the film's cast, Paige O'Hara, Robby Benson, Angela Lansbury, Jerry Orbach, and David Ogden Stiers, recorded specifically for the tour.[37] At a price of $6 million, the ice show cost Feld Productions about half as much as the eventual Broadway production by Disney. It included not only forty-six skaters (eighteen male, twenty-eight female) but fourteen separate scenes. Its tour was planned for eight years:

three in the United States, in which it would cover eighty-three cities, followed by five more abroad (largely in Europe and in the Pacific).[38] The production included 178 costumes, 205 props, and 8,000 lights. Although the show was largely disregarded by critics as frivolous, Lawrence Van Gelder of the *New York Times* relented, "Maybe it helps to be a child to be thoroughly enchanted by this show, but grownups needn't be ashamed to be captivated by the immense skill that underlies this entertainment."[39] The shows were wildly successful: twelve performance in Minneapolis in the Target Center set records with 115,000 attendees,[40] and the production company generated annual revenues exceeding $250 million by 1990.[41] Furthermore, they were often running around the world: three productions in the United States, another in Europe, and a fifth company touring the Pacific.[42] Therefore, Feld Productions ice shows demonstrated how live shows employing Disney properties could be replicated and toured globally to sizable profits. The extent to which the company studied and employed this model, however, remains unclear.

One thing is evident: New York City wanted to be in business with Disney on an ongoing basis. For some time, architect Robert A. M. Stern and philanthropist Marian Sulzberger Heiskell had attempted to convince Eisner that Disney could play a central role in the revitalization of 42nd Street.[43] Heiskell, in particular, was influential in the city politics not only as the chairperson of the New 42nd Street but also as a member of the Sulzberger family, who published the *New York Times*. (In fact, the newspaper's headquarters sits a block off of 42nd Street, at 41st Street and Eighth Avenue.) Eisner initially resisted their persuasive efforts, especially since the highly regulated urban environs of New York City starkly contrasted with the relative autonomy Disney enjoyed in Anaheim and Orlando. Broadway was simply too unpredictable for the risk-averse Disney. As Eisner conceded, "If you produce a movie, it can open in as many as three or four thousand theaters across the country. Even if it performs poorly, it has other lives on video, cable, network television, and overseas. By contrast, if you produce a full-scale Broadway musical— at a cost not all that much less than a midrange movie—it can close in a single night, forever."[44] Despite his own efforts to push the brand globally, Eisner understood Disney on Broadway would reinforce the company as quintessential U.S. entertainment. Disney was a tough negotiator, and Eisner realized he had New York under his thumb. The city certainly needed him more than he needed it, affording him a bargaining power that laid the groundwork for considerable demands. As the premier family brand, Disney would be the perfect ambassador for the future of New York City and the ambitions of its newly elected mayor, Rudy Giuliani.[45]

The move was certainly a bold one on Disney's part. After all, Euro Disneyland had hardly been the smash success that Eisner had hoped for. Critics lambasted Disney's efforts in Paris, but Disney was being welcomed with open arms in New York City by both government officials and nonprofit representatives. Disney would be a veritable savior—the name needed to jumpstart lagging renovation efforts. In 1992, Gap had successfully opened a store at 42nd Street and Seventh Avenue, but the popular clothing store had not inspired similar confidence in major entertainment companies.[46] Disney could serve as a beacon of what was to come. Furthermore, as a Manhattan-raised and liberal-arts-college-educated person, Eisner saw the potential for raising the brand's cultural legitimacy through a Broadway presence. If Paris could not give him the respectability he sought for Disney, perhaps New York could?

Disney quickly realized that the New York theatre scene was dominated by three theater owners: Jujamcyn, Nederlander, and Shubert. Any show it would produce on Broadway would entail substantial rent to one of them. *Beauty and the Beast*, for example, premiered at the Palace Theatre, partly owned by the Nederlander Organization. A long-term commitment on Broadway would require Disney's own house. During a meeting between Eisner and Stern in summer 1993, the topic of 42nd Street came up again, and Stern, along with Cora Cahan, president of the New 42nd Street, decided to take Eisner to the New Amsterdam. Completed in 1903, the theater was the first major Art Nouveau building in the United States. Home for many years to the Ziegfeld Follies, it stood ten stories tall with a rooftop garden. Following a Walter Huston–led production of *Othello* in 1937, the theater transitioned to become a second-run movie house, eventually closing in 1982. In the following decade, the derelict building fell into disrepair: plaster fell from the walls, renovation plans were abandoned because of its corroded infrastructure, and a growing hole in the roof caused the theater to be covered in water damage, bird droppings, and animal carcasses.[47] Eisner nevertheless understood the potential in restoring the building, one of the largest and most ornate houses on Broadway. Disney would not shoulder the burden alone, of course, and extensive assistance from the city (which owned the theater and leased it out to New 42nd Street) and the state would be necessary. The City of New York would retain ownership and, in exchange, offer Disney a favorable long-term lease.

While some New Yorkers remember Times Square of the 1970s and 1980s with great affection, the district nevertheless plagued leaders at the city and state levels. Once the undisputed center of U.S. entertainment, it eventually gave way to sex shops, adult movie theaters, and sex work. (The New Amsterdam reportedly was the only theater on 42nd Street that did not become an adult movie theater.)[48] Annual arrests for prostitution in Times Square peaked at nearly twenty thousand in the early seventies,[49] while many of the decadent theaters of Broadway's Golden Age now screened adult films, fell into disrepair, or were razed. Times Square was also a safe haven for the marginalized, including gay, lesbian, and transgender communities. In 2013, film critic B. Ruby Rich painted the New York City of this time as a veritable utopia:

> The city was ours. Property values were low, apartments had rent control, clubs were everywhere, and the streets were locations of congregation, invention, and celebration. New York City wasn't yet the post-Giuliani, Bloomberg-forever, Disneyland-Vegas tourist attraction of today, trademarked and policed to protect the visitors and tourism industry. It was still a place of diversity, where people of color lived their lives in vibrant communities with intact cultures. Young people could still move to New York City after or instead of high school or college

and invent an identity, an art, a life. Times Square was still a bustling center of excitement, with sex work, "adult" movies, a variety of sins on sale, ways to make money for those down on their luck. The benign economics and easy density enabled the continuation and even growth of a widespread community united by issues, sexualities, politics, aesthetics.[50]

Rich's comments underscore how the revitalization of Times Square was the result of both an ambitious corporation and a government-led crackdown on the district and its marginalized communities. Related to this point, Samuel R. Delany observed, "The Times Square renovation is not just about real estate and economics, however unpleasant its ramifications have been on that front. Because it has involved the major restructuring of the legal code relating to sex, and because it has been a first step not just toward the moving, but toward the obliteration of certain businesses and social practices, it has functioned as a massive and destructive intervention in the social fabric of a noncriminal group in the city—an intervention I for one deeply resent."[51] While the crime rate certainly alarmed both citizens and government officials, the area also served as home for various disenfranchised communities, many of whom were unjustly targeted under the new Republican mayor's aggressive law-and-order agenda.

Boosted by his reputation as a fierce prosecutor undaunted by organized crime, Giuliani had initially ran for mayor in 1989 on a platform that emphasized the need to "clean up this city, clean up its streets, [and] clean up its criminals."[52] Giuliani was not as well-versed in the issues as his opponents, so he appealed directly to voters: "The great civil rights struggle of the 1990's is creating in this city a reasonable degree of safety for its citizens."[53] His Democratic opponent, Manhattan borough president David Dinkins, was seen as a leader who could mend raising racial tensions in the city, a central issue for voters that election. Facilitated in part by inadequate fundraising and poor leadership in the Giuliani campaign, Dinkins prevailed with 50.4 percent of the vote to become the city's first African American mayor.[54]

Dinkins proved no more effective, however, than his beleaguered predecessor, Ed Koch, and conservative commentators framed the city's ongoing woes as a moral failure. *Commentary* editor in chief Norman Podhoretz insisted the city needed to "stop tolerating the intolerable," while *Firing Line* host William F. Buckley Jr. chided "bad citizens."[55] The focus of their criticisms—the unhoused, young criminals, single-parent households—reinforced the conservative belief that New York needed aggressive moral leadership, rather than the supposedly lenient approach offered by Democrats. Giuliani returned in the 1993 election with much the same message, but fueled by the economic downturn, voters' priorities had largely shifted to crime and jobs. "What we have to do in this city," Giuliani espoused, "is expect ever-increasing standards of behavior."[56] This strategy, outlined in *New York* magazine three years earlier, reads like a playbook for neoliberal policy, emphasizing privatization and "restructuring" of healthcare and education.[57] Unimpressed with Dinkins's progress, New Yorkers elected Giuliani, who brought with him a firm hand and a moralizing vision for the future of New York City.

While Giuliani took over the mayor's office, the governorship was held by Mario Cuomo, a liberal Democrat who had famously delivered an impassioned speech distilling those ideals at the 1984 Democratic National Convention, where he declared, "We believe we must be the family of America, recognizing that at the heart of the matter we are bound one to another."[58] Cuomo's avowed compassion was diametrically opposed to Giuliani's firm discipline, but both men shared an Italian Catholic ancestry that united them in their belief in moral leadership. Perhaps these values motivated the city and state's decision to collaborate by loaning Disney over $20 million in low-interest loans, whereas Disney would put up $8 million of its own money.[59] Disney would hire an architect to handle the renovation, while the city would have approval over any modifications to ensure preservation of the original building. In February 1994, Eisner, Cuomo, and Giuliani held a joint press conference to announce Disney's intentions to lease and restore the New Amsterdam, making it the second major renovation on 42nd Street. (The New Victory Theater, committed to producing children's theatre, was already under construction across the street and would open at the end of 1995.) Cuomo welcomed the collaboration as a move in the right direction: "The partnership among Disney, the city, and the state can save an historic theater and help restore this area to its former glory."[60] Giuliani claimed Disney's efforts might just save Broadway, a sentiment many agreed with begrudgingly. For his part, Eisner framed Disney's intentions as an altruistic effort to return to a sense of community: "As important a development as the information superhighway will be, we believe that there is a growing desire for people to interact socially at live events in theaters, sports arenas, and theme parks."[61]

Of course, the planned renovation was not met with universal acclaim. While cultural critics decried the theme park takeover of 42nd Street, Broadway theater owners lashed out at the city and state governments for making low-interest loans available to Disney, even though they had been seeking such public assistance for years. They publicly criticized the initiative until similar concessions were made for them as well. But generous public financial assistance was not the only problem the Broadway community had with Disney. Many producers felt they would be unable to compete with Disney's seemingly endless resources.[62] Producers have to raise money for each show individually, but corporate producers such as Disney could pull from their company well as needed to fund any project. Stewart Lane, a Broadway producer who co-owned the Palace Theatre, where *Beauty* premiered, admitted, "I do think the single producer will become a dinosaur. He already is."[63] (Disney's Bob McTyre responded in turn, "We're a publicly traded corporation, and we have strict financial controls. To try and marry those with a business where people kind of run it out of their pocket is quite an interesting prospect.")[64] During this period, the single producers were increasingly replaced with large production teams, ranging from corporate executives to generous investors.

The names above the title on Broadway advertisements grew to comic proportions, as extensive funding became necessary to stage an original show on the Great White Way. But this problem was in the works long before Disney arrived, fueled by a range of factors, including royalty agreements, union fees, city taxes, and elaborate theatrical production technologies. Furthermore, only the nonprofit institutions, such as the Roundabout Theatre Company, seemingly could manage to produce a new show annually. Despite their reservations, Broadway producers remained hopeful that Disney's reputation as a notoriously tough negotiator would help them gain concessions from their favorite scapegoat for Broadway's economic woes: the unions.

The reality is that the critiques of Disney, both popular and academic, were largely incomplete. While Disney was charged with cheapening what theatre represented and sanitizing Times Square, it also could be seen as a complicit figurehead providing cover for several interest groups. For example, the nonprofits leading the revitalization wanted a safer, more vibrant place for New Yorkers and tourists alike. "I'm not sure you'll ever get people from Fifth Avenue penthouses on 42d Street," Rebecca Robertson, head of the Times Square Redevelopment Project, conceded. "It's always been a place for the masses, and I think it should stay that way."[65] Disney was only capitalizing on something that Broadway producers had learned years earlier: the audience for Broadway shows was now out-of-towners, not New Yorkers.[66] Broadway producer Tom Viertel observed, "We cater to a tourist audience now that is ever-renewing, which is why something like six or seven of the seventy or so shows that have ever run a thousand performances in Broadway history are all running right now."[67] Not only were Broadway shows increasingly advertising outside of the United States, but shows such as *Beauty and the Beast* did not necessarily require audiences to speak English to understand the plot or enjoy the music.[68] This attention to spectacle was hardly new; in fact, Steve Nelson traces it back to Ziegfeld himself, who did for burlesque what Walt Disney did for the carnival—that is, made a mass culture experience into a middle-class entertainment.[69] In so doing, Disney was not so much destroying Broadway as returning it to its roots, continuing the legacy revitalized by *Cats*.

Disney entered Broadway at an opportune moment not only for the company but for Broadway. The company actively pursued franchising animated properties by developing extensive product lines and extending the narratives into television, direct-to-video releases, and video games. Broadway had honed the megamusical formula, but its preeminent proponents, Cameron Mackintosh and Andrew Lloyd Webber, had faltered by the early 1990s. Drabinsky's model, however, seemingly demonstrated that corporate financing and tightly managed productions could yield prestige and profits. Finally, Feld Productions achieved profitability with streamlined productions that starred familiar characters and toured on a global circuit. Therefore, Disney's entry into Broadway was not on a whim following an offhand remark by its preeminent critic but a strategic attempt to exploit its intellectual property, capitalize upon contemporary storytelling practices, legitimate its cultural products, and strengthen its standing as a diversified entertainment conglomerate.

———

The production of such a Broadway show, of course, would have to be done the Disney way. On projects such as *Roger Rabbit*, the company had learned a tough lesson on collaborating with other studios, and a move into Broadway could spell another disastrous clash. After all, Broadway itself operated under strict union rules, hierarchies of creative power, and its own production practices. No Hollywood studio had maintained a long-lasting, visible presence on Broadway, often because of creative differences stemming from the different protocols governing the respective industries.[70] If Disney were going to do this, it would do it on its own terms and with its own people. Eisner corroborated this idea in his memoir, reportedly telling Katzenberg, "We must do the show without partners, so that we can retain creative control, and we have to use as much of our own talent as possible."[71] But since Disney did not have a long-standing, formalized theatrical division, it turned to the division most prepared to stage live entertainment: theme parks. As Stan Meyer explains, "Everybody I know who has worked in the theme park has had theatre training."[72] By Eisner's estimation, Disney produced more live theatre every day than anyone else around the world because of the daily shows in its theme parks,[73] and Katzenberg told the press that live theatre is "a natural extension of what we already do."[74] Nevertheless, the decision to adapt *Beauty* with theme park personnel concerned Menken, though he eventually conceded that it would work.[75]

To the surprise of some in the Broadway community, Disney's choice of director for the project was Robert Jess Roth. An alumnus of the Mason Gross School of the Arts at Rutgers University, Roth had interned under Ira Weitzman at Playwrights Horizons during the time Sondheim and Lapine were fine-tuning *Sunday in the Park with George*. He also had worked as an assistant under some of the leading theatre directors in the United States, including Gerald Gutierrez, Thommie Walsh, and Jack Hofsiss. As a freelance director, Roth staged half-hour musicals for Disneyland, including an adaptation of *Dick Tracy*. "People can judge it for being at a theme park," Roth admits, "but it also had this score by Sondheim."[76] As Bob McTyre, the head of Disney Theatrical Productions, explained, "*Beauty* is not just a Disney-checkbook production. It's a *Disney* production."[77] Regardless of how many hours of singing and dancing Disney entertainers did on a daily basis, only Broadway could bestow the essential prestige the company sought for its theatrical ventures.

The hiring of such a young director prompted charges that Disney was really in control. Roth himself told *New York* magazine, "Everyone has an opinion, from my mother to Eisner. But I have control; that's not a question."[78] Roth, working with scenic designer Stan Meyer and costume designer Ann Hould-Ward, had developed the formal pitch for *Beauty and the Beast*. He delivered it to the board in Aspen in the hopes they would allow him to keep developing it; instead, they greenlit the project outright.[79] Roth would be working with quite a lineup, including the film's composer, Menken, and its screenwriter, Linda Woolverton. Stepping in for Ashman would be Tim Rice, Lloyd Webber's former collaborator. The formidable team worked on the show for over two years, often via fax machines, since Roth worked from New York City, Menken in Upstate New York, Woolverton in Los Angeles, and Rice in London. While Menken assured the press that Disney had left "Broadway pretty much to the people who know Broadway,"[80] an unnamed source declared to the *New York Times* that "none of [the executives] had any idea what Broadway entails."[81]

Since the rise of megamusicals in the 1980s, critics had often derided spectacular productions as nothing more than theme park attractions. David Richards observed, "Nobody should be surprised that it brings to mind a theme-park entertainment raised to the power of 10."[82] Greg Evans of *Variety* proclaimed that Disney had brought "the concept of a corporate umbrella to Broadway."[83] The charges, however, were not wholly fair—or true: Hollywood has long had a presence on Broadway as investor, producer, even talent poacher. As the lyricist of *Jesus Christ Superstar*, *Evita*, and *Chess*, Rice brought over twenty years of experience on Broadway and in the West End. While the show marked Menken's first official production on Broadway, he had studied musical theatre composition under Lehman Engel, and his *Little Shop of Horrors* had been one of the longest running shows in Off-Broadway history. Furthermore, orchestrator Danny Troob, musical director Michael Kosarin, company manager Kim Sellon, lighting designer Natasha Katz, sound designer T. Richard Fitzgerald, and costume designer Ann Hould-Ward were all well-established theatre professionals with Broadway experience. Roth had first observed Hould-Ward's work on *Sunday* at Playwrights Horizons, where she designed a mechanical dress for the female lead to step out of, before she went on to further success with another fairy tale musical, *Into the Woods*. "We were able to do a ton of experimentation and trials that would not normally be within budget constraints of a show," she recalls.[84] Scenic designer Stan Meyer, another New York–based artist who had worked with Roth in the Disney theme parks, conceded, "The pay isn't very good, but the Disney company has given us the chance of a lifetime, and you work your ass off to do it."[85]

Initially, the creative team had a mixed reaction about staging *Beauty and the Beast*. Roth himself was unsure how he would handle Lumiere, Cogsworth, Mrs. Potts, and company.[86] In the twenty-minute version at Disneyland, these characters were portrayed by actors in foam suits who danced while the soundtrack played; this approach would not fly in a Broadway house, where the show would run for over two hours and cost upward of forty-five dollars a seat. Rice thought the task "impossible, because the movie was so good."[87] Woolverton was equally concerned at the outset, exclaiming "*Yikes*" at the proposition.[88] She, too, conceded, since fleshing the show out for Broadway would allow her to develop characters and scenes that had to be pared down for animation. Looking back, she acknowledges the rewarding artistic opportunity that the theatre afforded her. Hollywood privileges directors while treating writers as easily replaceable, but the theatre reveres writers and the text itself.[89]

Adapting *Beauty and the Beast* for Broadway afforded the creative team the opportunity to return to what had been cut in the film version. British megamusicals had dominated the Broadway stage, but Roth very much saw the show as a return to the Broadway musicals of the 1950s: "I wasn't going to update it and make it sung-through. It's going to have book scenes and musical numbers, like the old-fashioned musicals did. That's what Howard's idea was."[90] As book writer, Woolverton worked to enrich the relationships between the characters, and Menken and Rice did the same through the new songs. "Doing *Beauty and the Beast* as a Broadway show allowed us to cover emotional territory that was only touched on in the movie," Menken explained as the time.[91] Maurice sings "No Matter What" to Belle, for example, which not only develops his characterization beyond a scatterbrained old man but also expands on the father-daughter relationship. The song "Me" further accentuated Gaston's ridiculousness, as he sings of his greatness to a disinterested Belle. While the film gives Belle only one solo, the stage version allowed her more stage time, and the songwriters wrote "Home" for her to sing while imprisoned in the Beast's castle. In the second act, Menken and Rice comically musicalize the sinister plot by Gaston, Lefou, and the asylum warden Monsieur D'Arque to institutionalize Maurice in "Maison Des Lunes." Most notably, "Human Again," a song that Menken and Ashman had originally written for the Objects to sing in the film, was restored to the score after Menken figured out how to integrate it into the plot.

Considerable work had to be done on the Beast, both narratively and visually. Roth wanted a more mature Beast, who bared his chest "to create animal magnetism on stage."[92] The filmmakers had struggled to find opportunities for him to sing, and as a result his characterization was not as strong in the film as Belle's was. On Broadway, however, the character would need more development in order for the lengthy show to work. To add to the Beast's emotional complexity, Menken and Rice wrote "If I Can't Love Her" for the Beast to sing after he frees Belle and realizes he may never be freed himself. Rebecca-Anne Do Rozario notes that, in effect, "The theatrical performance actually shifts to Beast's tragic predicament."[93] In making this move, the stage version aligns more closely with Ashman's vision of the Beast as protagonist compared to that of his colleagues in animation, some of whom privately objected to the film's adaptation as a stage musical.

Perhaps the greatest challenge rested in live actors performing animated characters. While Belle was obviously an easy character to adapt for the stage, the Beast and the Enchanted Objects posed a range of concerns, including mobility, credibility, and audibility. In addition to a hefty costume that would simulate a hump, the Beast would have heavy makeup on his face that initially took hours to apply. The fangs and jowls were mounted on the outside of the actor's mouth, and makeup preparation was eventually scaled back to less than two hours. Moving away from the foam costumes worn in the Disneyland show, the faces of the actors playing the objects would need to be visible for live performance. An illusionist was hired to devise a cart for Chip, the young boy who becomes a teacup. Furthermore, the Enchantress would have to throw a fire ball, Lumiere would require propane-fueled

Figure 7. According to director Robert Jess Roth, he went back to Busby Berkeley, not Andrew Lloyd Webber, when staging elaborate production numbers such as "Be Our Guest." Credit: Joan Marcus.

flames from both arms, Cogsworth needed a swinging pendulum across his midsection, and Mrs. Potts would have to produce steam from her left arm. Consequently, the design team managed to produce flameproof costumes, while Actors' Equity required Disney to compensate several actors with hazard pay.[94]

Since a Broadway show obviously employs live actors, the costumes were crucial for establishing whom each actor's animated counterpart was. According to costume designer Ann Hould-Ward, "They need to be introduced in the clothes worn in the animation, but after the first appearance, you can go on to other clothes that might be in the characters' closets."[95] Therefore, Susan Egan made her stage entrance wearing a blue pinafore dress and white blouse, as Belle does during her opening number in the film. Similarly, as Gaston, Burke Moses wore a belted vest and brown pants. (It was red in the film, with gold lapels, but on Broadway the vest was gold.) While the characters' outfits in the animated film were obviously simply in design, Hould-Ward and her team took the opportunity to make the costumes far more intricate in real life by researching in depth the period of the original tale. With tulle and beading, Belle's signature yellow dress in the ballroom scene weighed over forty pounds.[96]

Fortunately for the production, its lead actor was already familiar with elaborate makeup and costuming. Terrence Mann was a Broadway veteran who had originated the role of the Mick Jagger–like Rum Tum Tugger in *Cats*. A Tony Award nominee for his portrayal of Javert in the original Broadway production of *Les Misérables*, he was perhaps the most well-known stage performer in the show.

Burke Moses first appeared on Broadway two seasons earlier when he replaced Peter Gallagher as Sky Masterson in the hit revival of *Guys and Dolls*, and Susan Egan, Heath Lamberts (Cogsworth), and Kenny Raskin (Lefou) were making their Broadway debuts. Gary Beach (Lumiere) and Beth Fowler (Mrs. Potts) were seasoned pros: Beach in *1776* and *Annie*, Fowler in *A Little Night Music* and the revival of *Sweeney Todd*. In fact, the most famous cast member was Tom Bosley, best known as Mr. Cunningham on *Happy Days*, though he had won a Tony Award years earlier as the title character in the 1959 musical *Fiorello!* The casting of *Beauty and the Beast* reveals the economics of the blockbuster megamusical: cast solid performers—not major stars—who can service the story and the spectacle, but can easily be replaced. While established recording artists Debbie Gibson and Toni Braxton would eventually play Belle on Broadway, the show easily survived for over five thousand performances with up-and-coming actresses. Just as Lloyd Webber was the true star of his megamusicals, Disney—its stories, its music, its stagecraft—would be the major draw here.

Prior to its Broadway run, *Beauty and the Beast* held out-of-town tryouts in December 1993 in Houston, where the show was part of the nonprofit series Theatre Under the Stars. Premiering at the three-thousand-seat Music Hall, the show had an opportunity to gauge audience response before the costly move to the Great White Way the following April. Union fees, city taxes, and general running costs had long ago encouraged shows to do a test run in relatively nearby cities, such as New Haven, Connecticut. The Houston tryout provided Disney with the time to make the necessary adjustments before previews—and the critics' exacting judgments—in New York City.

The reception was predictably mixed among the critics who reviewed the show in Houston. Many critics seemed unable to evaluate the show on its own terms, considering how well-regarded the film had been. A reviewer for the *Austin American-Statesman* dismissed the show as "a colorful but ordinary stage musical—neither as magical nor as moving as the original."[97] Following the critical tendency to elide the megamusical with theme park entertainment, the reviewer added that Disney's arrival in the wake of Andrew Lloyd Webber was inevitable, though they conceded the tight storytelling and tuneful score of *Beauty and the Beast* "ma[de] it inherently more stageworthy than the aforementioned theater rides."[98] Jerome Weeks, reporting for *Variety*, accepted the show as Disney's attempt to seek legitimation on Broadway with a family-friendly musical: "At one end, Ann Hould-Ward's costumes and Stan Meyer's set give the show plenty of magical gloom and glitter. At the other, *Beauty and the Beast* gets close to a big-budget kiddie show with its overdone glitz and effects."[99] Furthermore, the emotion was lacking in key scenes, so Woolverton rewrote them prior to the Broadway transfer.[100] Disney was prepared for many of these charges, but it did not have to worry: audiences loved it, and the show regularly received standing ovations. Much like the Andrew Lloyd Webber shows that preceded it, *Beauty and the Beast* appeared to be "critic-proof"—not only because the reviews did little to sidetrack ticket sales, but presumably because the target audiences probably were not reading such reviews in the first place.[101]

_____

It appears highly unlikely that Disney anticipated that its show would be well-received. Michael David, cofounder of Dodger Productions, which served as general manager on *Beauty and the Beast*, even warned Disney, "This is a world that needs targets."[102] News of the company's plans for the New Amsterdam Theatre brought charges that it would turn 42nd Street into a theme park. (In fact, Disney initially planned to close off 42nd Street as a Downtown Disney–like venue, but city officials quashed the proposal because it would cause traffic nightmares for the nearby Lincoln Tunnel.)[103] Nevertheless, Eisner maintained a positive public face about the possibility of negative reviews: "I would be devastatedly surprised, but it would only increase my resolve."[104] After all, Disney had already put millions of dollars into the show, and its lease of the New Amsterdam committed the company to spending upward of $30 million, with $4 million a year in city taxes alone. Disney shored up its bet through partnerships with Bloomingdale's, which opened a Belle-themed shop in its store, and American Express, which underwrote a behind-the-scenes documentary for the Disney Channel.[105] "We're steamrolling ahead," he insisted[106]—an apt metaphor for many of his detractors.

The Broadway poster, curiously enough, does not represent the title Beauty. Instead, much like the iconic images of the megamusical marketing, it is a mere outline of the Beast's silhouette in white against a black background, set off by the red of his shedding rose. Broadway producers started buying television advertising spots in the 1970s, and while Disney did too, its commercial was remarkably simple. It begins with Cogsworth saying, "It's time for . . . ," finished by Lumiere saying, "something special." Then, "Be Our Guest" plays over a video montage of the stagings of songs adapted from the film—"Gaston," "Be Our Guest," and "Beauty and the Beast." The commercial is less a pitch than a reminder of what the audience can anticipate.

Much of the negative criticism directed toward the production took issue implicitly with the fact that the show was family-friendly. While children may have been an often overlooked demographic on Broadway, the reality is that the industry needed them. While a good portion of ticket buyers were in their thirties and forties, the audience was getting older. Family-friendly shows would not only increase ticket sales exponentially but foster new generations of theatergoers. Bob McTyre noted, "If those people see the show and enjoy it, it's our belief that they'll then go and see something else. This property will build audiences and have a positive impact on theater for years to come."[107] Jane Alexander, chairperson of the National Endowment for the Arts, expressed similar sentiments: "We must create an entirely new audience for theatre from the ground up and give young people the experience of the finest as well as the school curriculum."[108] Unsurprisingly, Alexander had an ally in *Beauty and the Beast* director Robert Jess Roth, who had grown up attending Broadway shows. "If there's going to be a Broadway 25 years from now, there has to be an audience for it. If not, we're going to go the way of the Hollywood musical, an extinct form," he said shortly after the premiere of *Beauty*.[109] Disney animated features were trying to revive the genre, though to be fair, only Disney had fared well in producing such musicals. Furthermore, the shows could tour well. Booking agency executive Jeffrey Seller hypothesized that "if Cincinnati is a one-week town for [*The Who's*] *Tommy*, I think it could easily be a three-week town for *Beauty and the Beast*."[110] (Seller himself would go on to produce two smash hits: *Rent* and *Hamilton*.) As Disney was keenly aware, Broadway was the necessary starting point for its future plans for theatrical productions in New York, across the country, and around the world. While Disney on Broadway appeared localized to Manhattan, it was and remains an extensive corporate endeavor with global reach.

But New York critics found themselves in a bit of a dilemma. On the one hand, they reveled in taking potshots at Disney, fearing that the company would sanitize the Broadway district and infantilize its theatre. Edwin Wilson of the *Wall Street Journal* decried it as "the moment when theme-park glitz and expertise intersected with traditional show business."[111] But on the other hand, Times Square could be a dangerous, rundown place, populated by drug dealers, muggers, and sex workers—especially from the perspective of the privileged readership to whom these drama critics often wrote. Many glamorous theaters of the Golden Age of Broadway had long gone derelict. Disney may have been sanitary and family-friendly, but special interest groups felt it better than the crime and vice that ran rampant in the theatre district. One critic even admitted hesitancy to disparage *Beauty and the Beast* because he did not want to jeopardize Disney's plans to lead New York's economic revival.[112] "All told," David Patrick Stearns wrote in *USA Today*, "Disney could be a much-needed vitamin B-12 shot for the New York theater scene for years to come."[113]

This critical hesitation, of course, did not deter everyone. David Richards, writing for the *New York Times*, dismissed the show's spectacle and pandering to tourist audiences: "You don't watch it, you gape at it, knowing that nothing in Dubuque comes close."[114] Similarly, *New York*'s acerbic drama critic John Simon mused, "*B & B* bored the pants off me. But only the show; some of the special effects are first rate."[115] Attacks on the show's spectacle, especially the elaborate "Be Our Guest" scene with pyrotechnic champagne bottles and high-kicking cutlery, seem misplaced when one considers its theatrical precedents. Several critics linked it to the lavish production numbers of choreographer Busby Berkeley or impresarios Billy Rose and Florenz Ziegfeld.[116] Besides, damning critiques were rather pointless, as Thomas R. King noted, because *Beauty and the Beast* was intended for "the kind of folks who don't read reviews but love shows like *Cats*."[117] Eisner agreed: "We're dealing in a very sophisticated market, and some people are looking for things that this *Beauty and the Beast* was not ever meant to be."[118] To his mind, Broadway theatrical production expanded the company's branding, but it also expanded Broadway's potential audiences.

While the critics at the major papers were often the most derogatory, many the-atre critics offered mixed reviews of the show. Jeremy Gerard of *Variety* took issue with the show's direction, choreography, sets, and length, but he praised the per-formances of its stars, singling out Burke Moses as Gaston.[119] In the *New Yorker*, John Lahr conceded that "at its best, Disney's *Beauty and the Beast* has a few moments of solid-gold theatrical amazement."[120] Both Frank Scheck of the *Chris-tian Science Monitor* and Robert Feldberg of the *Record* gave the show largely pos-itive reviews, with the latter proclaiming the show "a real Broadway musical, not a blown-up Disneyland stage show."[121] Unsurprisingly, the one area where most critics, even David Richards, agreed was the strength of its score. Several did take issue with Rice's lyrics for the new songs, apparently in agreement with Janet Maslin's sentiment that Ashman's "barbed, mischievous style was a far cry from the middle-of-the-road Broadwayisms that now pad the show."[122] But writing months later, Charles Marowitz feared Disney's lasting impact on theatre itself: "The essence of theatre is dissent, contention, criticism, and controversy, the very qualities Disney abominates and surgically removes from all its products. Imag-ine a Broadway dominated by the simplistic, mendacious, sanitized works that the Disney factory is committed to turning out. It would be a theater as bogus as a theme-park, as artificial as a cartoon, as tendentious as a fairy-tale, the very antith-esis of what vital and dangerous theater ought to be."[123] Theatre that did not enrich the mind and the soul of the viewer, Marowitz implied, stood on par with the allegedly cheap thrills of theme park rides.

Yet the reservations, even indignation, of theatre critics did little to diminish popular interest in the show, and despite the late start, it was on track to become the hit of the season.[124] By the end of May, it was head-to-head with *Phantom of the Opera* and bringing in over $700,000 a week.[125] Disney had won over the most important critics of all, the mainstream audience, but there was another battle on the horizon. The Tony Awards, the highest honor within the Broadway commu-nity, would be announced shortly. If Disney received a respectable number of nom-inations, it might be a good sign that it had won over the industry. If not, it might suggest that it would have a difficult working relationship with the industry in the years ahead.

———

By all accounts, the 1993–1994 Broadway season was underwhelming. Several land-mark plays had opened—Tony Kushner's *Angels in America: Perestroika*, Robert Schenkkan's *The Kentucky Cycle*, and Anna Deavere Smith's *Twilight: Los Ange-les, 1992*—but none were box-office hits. The biggest critical successes before *Beauty* opened were revivals of Broadway shows like *Carousel* and *Damn Yankees*, but the box office was still dominated by the megamusicals *Phantom*, *Miss Saigon*, and (to a lesser extent) *Les Misérables*. The announcement of the Tony Award nominations was actually delayed because nominators petitioned to nominate only three pro-ductions (as opposed to the required four) in three categories: Best Musical, Best Original Score, and Best Book.[126] *Cyrano*, a costly Dutch musical based on Edmond

Rostand's *Cyrano de Bergerac*, had notoriously flopped, as had the disastrous sequel, *The Best Little Whorehouse Goes Public*. Although Stephen Sondheim stood "like a solitary colossus, pitilessly overlooking the arid landscape that is the modern musical theater,"[127] his latest show with James Lapine, *Passion*, divided critics and failed to gain an audience beyond faithful theatergoers. The now-closed *A Grand Night for Singing* was a Rodgers and Hammerstein revue, so it had no book. The governing board denied two of the three requests for exception, and the nominations were released: *Passion* received ten, while *Beauty* garnered a respectable nine.

For many commentators, the showdown between *Passion* and *Beauty* symbolized a battle over the soul of Broadway. At $4.5 million, *Passion* had cost about one-third as much as its competitor.[128] But many audience members found *Passion* inaccessible: its protagonist was ugly (by design), manipulative, and unlikeable, and its source material was an obscure Italian arthouse film, *Passione d'amore* (Ettore Scola, 1981). Stephen Sondheim reigned as the musical theatre's foremost artist, but his last two Broadway shows, *Sunday in the Park with George* and *Into the Woods*, had lost out at the Tony Awards to more mainstream fare: *La Cage aux Folles* and *Phantom of the Opera*, respectively. (*Sunday*, however, did win the Pulitzer Prize for Drama.) As the title suggests, *Assassins*, his previous show, examines the American Dream through nine successful and attempted presidential assassins. It premiered Off-Broadway but did not transfer. Whereas the megamusical privileged spectacle over the star, Sondheim and his collaborators (Lapine for *Sunday*, *Woods*, and *Passion*; John Weidman for *Assassins*) wrote strong character studies that required skilled actors and singers. While his shows rarely profited, they did endow Broadway with a certain legitimation that it desperately sought from the cultural elite.

Therefore, many Tony Award voters saw voting for *Passion* to win Best Musical as a vote against Hollywood in general and Disney in particular. Summarizing this sentiment, David Richards mused, "Better to reward flawed Sondheim, the feeling goes, than to throw open the town to *The Little Mermaid* live in an onstage tank."[129] This logic, of course, was entirely flawed. After all, Hollywood studios had invested in, even produced, Broadway shows for decades. Recently, MCA/Universal had bankrolled *The Best Little Whorehouse Goes Public*, while Paramount had invested in *Sunset Boulevard*, Andrew Lloyd Webber's new musical, set to transfer to Broadway next season. Even *Passion* was not exempt, as one of its producers was Scott Rudin, who returned to Broadway from Hollywood because "movies are about making chicken salad out of chicken shit."[130] While some voters may have felt that they were taking a stand in supporting *Passion*, it was a fool's errand. Disney did not initiate the "Hollywoodization of Broadway";[131] it only made it visible and drew closer scrutiny to a long-standing relationship.

The 1994 Tony Awards were held on June 12 at the Gershwin Theatre, the largest house on Broadway. Disney lost two early awards to *Passion*: the first for Best Book, which went to Lapine over Woolverton, and the second to Sondheim's score over Menken, Ashman, and Rice's. Gary Beach, who played the charmingly hospitable Lumiere, soon after lost Best Featured Actor to *Damn Yankees*' Jarrod

Emick, while Nicholas Hytner won Best Director for his revival of *Carousel* over Robert Jess Roth. By the time Carol Burnett came out to award the Best Musical, the winner seemed inevitable. The only award that *Beauty and the Beast* won over *Passion* was Best Costume Design, but Ann Hould-Ward received her award in the proceedings prior to the broadcast. Coincidentally, Hould-Ward's two previous nominations had been for her work on Sondheim musicals.

Disney was hardly hurt financially by its eight losses. At the very least, the broadcast gave the company the opportunity to present its product(ion) directly to the home audience. During the ambitious five-and-a-half-minute performance, introducer Anthony Hopkins read a condensed prologue, Burke Moses performed "Me," Gary Beach led "Be Our Guest," Terrence Mann sang the Act 1 finale, "If I Can't Love Her," and then Mann and Susan Egan finished with the "End Duet" and the final reprise of "Beauty and the Beast." The sales pitch worked: the next day, Disney boasted $1.16 million in ticket sales, beating a one-day record set by *Phantom*.[132] By the end of the year, Disney would announce plans for twelve productions around the world, including London, Melbourne, Tokyo, Buenos Aires, and Hong Kong.[133] But the cold reception of *Beauty and the Beast* at the Tony Awards, especially in such a weak year, sent a clear message to Disney. Despite the expertise and experience of seasoned theatre talent, Gordon Davidson still observed, "I think they've learned a lot and may reach out to more traditional artists next time."[134] With its next show, Disney would have an opportunity to right the perceived slights of its wildly successful first foray—and a beautifully restored theater in which to do it.

CHAPTER 6

"I Don't Do Cute"

JULIE TAYMOR, *THE LION KING*, AND DISNEY, 1994–1998

To Disney's credit, it did not ignore the criticism that it received from some in the Broadway community about *Beauty and the Beast*. The perceived shortcomings, though largely unfair, were clear to the company: the show was too faithful to the film, the tightly constructed story became bloated on stage, and the production made minimal use of experienced theatre professionals. But Broadway was a profitable endeavor for Disney, and it provided the company with a new venue for its entertainment, a promising (and highly lucrative) revenue stream, and a good deal of prestige among the general public. If it were going to continue its presence on the Great White Way, Disney would have to learn how to build strong working relationships within the notoriously small and tightknit community while still maintaining its preferred level of creative and financial autonomy.

The stage version of *The Lion King* would mark an intentional departure not only from the aesthetics of its theatrical predecessor but also from the aesthetics of its animated source text. And yet Julie Taymor's use of puppetry situates *The Lion King*, both the film and stage versions, within a much longer history of animation that precedes the cinema.[1] The result was global both in its eclectic appropriation of artistic practices and traditions and in its desire for easily managed (re)productions around the world. *The Lion King* draws upon the possibilities of theatre as an artistic medium while also further exploiting an established Disney property that is standardized and widely reproduced. Critics and scholars, in turn, have treated it suspiciously for its status as a globally distributed commodity not unlike a film, thereby privileging an approach to performance culture that falsely claims to operate outside of and against capitalism.[2] But reparative readings might acknowledge the literal and metaphorical stage it gave to a female avant-garde artist and, as Brian Granger has recently contended, "the sheer visibility of black bodies and their celebrated status as the central and heroic characters within the story of the *Lion King* musical, as well as within the sensory experience an audience has in the theatre space, serves as an anti-racist affirmation of a Broadway *supportive* of racial and ethnic diversity."[3] Indeed, Taymor's sophisticated understanding of puppetry and of non-Western theatrical praxis demonstrates how craft theory allows her, like Howard Ashman years earlier, to assume a great deal of artistic and managerial control over a Disney product. But unlike Ashman, of course, the final result noticeably deviates from the integrated musicals he was writing only a few years earlier.

The time that elapsed between the premiere of *Beauty and the Beast* in April 1994 and the premiere of *The Lion King* in November 1997 proved extremely volatile for Disney. Publicly, the company experienced monumental successes at the box office and on the small screen. The corporate holdings grew considerably not through internal development but through acquisitions and landmark deregulation at the federal level. Behind the scenes, however, major turnover at the executive level shifted the power dynamics and threatened to undo the bold advances the company had made creatively, especially in animation and live-action filmmaking. What ultimately emerged, however, was the foundation of arguably the most influential entertainment conglomerate in the world today.

The year 1994 marked the tenth anniversary of Eisner, Wells, and Katzenberg's arrival at Disney, and it stands as perhaps the single most impressive year of their tenure. Disney had the top-performing film (*The Lion King*), television show (*Home Improvement*), Broadway show (*Beauty and the Beast*), album (*The Lion King* soundtrack), and theme park (Tokyo Disneyland leading the pack). For the second year in a row, filmed entertainment, not the theme parks, brought in the most revenue—evidence of a delivery on the executives' early promises. But the death of an executive and the departure of another posed new challenges for the next phase of the company's development and redirected the future of the company.

On Easter Sunday, Frank Wells was skiing with family and friends in Nevada. When others returned to lodge, Wells stayed out to ski longer. Snow accumulated in the engine of the helicopter that stayed behind to eventually return the remaining members of the party, leading to a tragic crash that killed four of the five occupants, including Wells. The death of Wells sent shockwaves through the company and across the film industry. Wells had been the level-headed peacemaker who maintained working relations among the executives, including Eisner and Katzenberg. David Geffen observed, "He was a guy who had very little need for attention—the opposite of practically everybody in Hollywood."[4] The company shut down for a memorial service, and Hollywood waited to see who would take over in Wells's absence. Katzenberg, who had long aspired to a promotion, seriously wanted the job, but he had two factors working against him. First, Wells was a lawyer keen on business decisions, whereas Katzenberg was a creative executive not unlike Eisner.[5] Second, Eisner simply did not like him. Both Eisner and Roy Disney were irritated that the media was portraying Katzenberg as the executive who had "retaken control of the movie business from the stars, the directors, and the agents, and pumped up production to nearly 60 movies a year."[6] While they maintained a professional decorum in public, it later emerged that Eisner detested

Katzenberg's ego and perceived lack of education, reportedly confiding he might even hate him.[7] Instead, Eisner boldly insisted that he would assume Wells's responsibilities, too.

In the midst of the tension between Eisner and Katzenberg, Disney continued to wrestle with the inconsistent performance of the live-action division. Whoopi Goldberg, Alec Baldwin, and Robin Williams publicly chastised the company's treatment of actors. A European recession and a series of murders near Disney World marred theme park attendance.[8] Plans for a U.S. history theme park not far from Manassas National Battlefield Park were stymied by historians and protesters, exacerbated further by one executive's notorious promise that visitors would be able to "feel what it was like to be a slave."[9] The myriad problems at Euro Disneyland continued to embarrass a company that seemed otherwise impervious to failure.

The period was not entirely gloomy. *Aladdin* surpassed *Beauty and the Beast* to become the best-selling home video of all time. Disney also moved into the direct-to-video market with *The Return of Jafar* (Toby Shelton, Tad Stones, and Alan Zaslove, 1994), which sold over nine million units to become the twelfth best-selling video to date.[10] The company continued its globalization efforts by expanding international distribution to include offices in fourteen countries.[11] Of course, the critical and commercial highlight of this period was *The Lion King*, which appealed to both young boys and young girls.[12] Unlike earlier Disney animated features, the film was not based on a fairy tale or children's book and was pitched by story department head Charlie Fink as "*Bambi* in Africa."[13] (Don Hahn described the film as "a combination Moses-Hamlet-King Arthur Meets Elton John in Africa.")[14] It also featured animals on all fours, which Katzenberg described as a "much more difficult and challenging form of animation than human beings."[15] Animators created over a thousand backgrounds, based in large part on an African safari taken by story supervisor Brenda Chapman, production designer Chris Sanders, and codirector Roger Allers.[16] Varying estimates suggest six to eight hundred artists contributed to the film over a period of three years. The cast included a number of well-known actors, including Matthew Broderick, Jeremy Irons, *Home Improvement*'s Jonathan Taylor Thomas, as well as Broadway actors Nathan Lane and Ernie Sabella fresh from the 1992 hit revival of *Guys and Dolls*. Tim Rice joined *The Lion King* after completing work on *Aladdin*. He encouraged the filmmakers to reach out to Elton John to compose the music because Alan Menken was unavailable and efforts to recruit ABBA's Benny Andersson and Björn Ulvaeus (Rice's collaborators on the Broadway musical *Chess*) had failed.[17] In fact, many of the major players at Disney Animation were working on *Pocahontas* (Mike Gabriel and Eric Goldberg, 1995), which was generally perceived to be the next prestige production out of the division. According to animation supervisor Tony Bancroft, several prominent Disney animators preferred animating humans in *Pocahontas* to animals for *The Lion King*, and Katzenberg allegedly told the team that he would be satisfied if *Lion King* grossed $50 million.[18] Elton John was an unlikely composer for an integrated musical, but Hans Zimmer helped to modify the songs for the film, and the fundamentals of the musical largely remained in place: opening number, "I want" song, love ballad.[19] The film opened in June, but it did so well that Disney actually withdrew it from theaters in late September so that it could rerelease *The Lion King* for the holiday season. One industry analyst (correctly) suggested that the film would generate over $1 billion in profits within two or three years.[20]

Within a month of *The Lion King*'s premiere, Eisner experienced chest pains and had to undergo bypass surgery. Michael Ovitz, the powerful agent behind Creative Artists Agency (CAA) and a loyal Eisner friend, stood vigil by his bedside. During this time, Katzenberg forced an ultimatum on Eisner to promote him to second in command. Eisner resisted such treatment and later claimed that Roy Disney, in particular, adamantly opposed Katzenberg's promotion.[21] Heralded as the savior of animation during the administrative changeover in 1984, Roy abhorred not only what he perceived as Katzenberg's disrespect toward him but also the credit Katzenberg received—and accepted—for animation's resurgence.[22] A 1994 *Wall Street Journal* profile proclaimed, "Prominent in the Disney formula is Mr. Katzenberg himself who, if not exactly the re-incarnation of Walt Disney, brings his own blend of passion and obsession to Disney's mission of creating animated 'classics.'"[23] Unable to secure the position and power that he truly wanted, Katzenberg announced his departure in late August 1994. David Geffen, one of Katzenberg's major allies, insisted that Katzenberg "wants to move on and run his own company" after "an extraordinary run at Disney."[24] In October, that opportunity came: Katzenberg, alongside Geffen and Steven Spielberg, launched a new studio, DreamWorks. Frank Rich slammed the men as "descendants of the egomaniacal entrepreneurs who built Hollywood, like Jack Warner and Louis B. Mayer," yet he also admitted that a struggling film industry could use the boost and creative experimentation.[25]

Despite the turmoil behind the scenes, Disney still triumphed at the box office with both *The Lion King* and the Tim Allen holiday vehicle *The Santa Clause* (John Pasquin, 1994). Warner Bros. followed once again, thanks to *Interview with the Vampire* (Neil Jordan, 1994), *Maverick* (Richard Donner, 1994), and *The Client* (Joel Schumacher, 1994), while *Forrest Gump* (Robert Zemeckis, 1994) advanced Paramount to third place. Disney became the first studio to surpass $1 billion at the box office, while Hollywood sold 1.2 billion tickets and cumulatively took in $5.25 billion.[26] At Disney, live-action family comedies, such as *Angels in the Outfield* (William Dear, 1994), *Blank Check* (Rupert Wainwright, 1994), and *D2: The Mighty Ducks* (Sam Weisman, 1994), also performed respectably but did not win the studio any critical accolades or respect. The year ahead had much of the same: action films with big stars, low-cost family comedies, and tentpole animated features, including *Pocahontas* and *Toy Story* (John Lasseter, 1995).

Years earlier, the success of *The Little Mermaid* fueled renewed industry-wide interest in feature animation. Warner Bros., Turner, and MGM pursued animated film production, but soon realized that they would have to avoid Disney's musical formula to diversify their product and avoid competing head-on with the company's sixty-year-old legacy. MGM placed its bets on *The Pebble and the Penguin*

(Don Bluth and Gary Goldman, 1995), a love story set at the South Pole, but even its animation VP, Donald Mirisch, conceded that he could not compete with Disney marketing.[27] Nevertheless, the popularity of feature animation led to a shortage of animation talent and a rise in average salaries to between $1,800 and $2,200 per week.[28] Even Katzenberg was in on the game, recruiting animators away from Disney with a backend offer for his freshman effort, *The Prince of Egypt* (Brenda Chapman, Steve Hickner, and Simon Wells, 1998), a retelling of Moses's strained relationship with his brother, Rameses.[29]

Competition for the feature animation throne spiked, but Disney remained at the top of the field. *Pocahontas* was unable to match the monumental success of *The Lion King*, but it delivered $141.6 million domestically. The leading animated film that year was the inaugural feature from Pixar, *Toy Story*. The first completely computer-animated film, the buddy comedy bested *Batman Forever* (Joel Schumacher, 1995) and *Apollo 13* (Ron Howard, 1995) for the year's top spot. Pixar was originally the Graphics Group at Lucasfilm before George Lucas sold it to Steve Jobs. John Lasseter, the company's creative genius, had become fascinated with computer animation following *Tron*.[30] When Disney fired him, he joined Pixar and the company began producing short films to showcase its technologies, winning an Oscar for the 1988 animated short *Tin Toy*. Pixar signed a contract in 1991 to produce three features for Disney, who would give Pixar 10 to 15 percent of total profits in exchange for financial backing, story guidance, marketing, and distributing the films.[31] While the deal afforded Pixar the Disney brand and access to its resources, the company worked to diversify both in its style and in its storytelling, establishing a promising new animation studio.

Toy Story required over 800,000 hours on 117 workstations to create, but it was not just a technological feat.[32] By January 1996, it was the third highest grossing animated film ever released, though *Pocahontas* outperformed *Toy Story* overseas.[33] A year later, estimates suggested that *Toy Story* had generated nearly $400 million at the box office and in related merchandise since its 1995 release.[34] The film also relaunched Steve Jobs following his ignominious departure from Apple in 1985. Reinstated and reinvigorated, Jobs helped to bring Hollywood and Silicon Valley together, as Disney and Pixar agreed to a new contract that split the profits evenly in 1997.[35] In the years that followed, he would rise to the top of Apple again and eventually help bring an end to Eisner's tenure at Disney in 2005. For now, of course, Jobs and Pixar were a source of pride and promise for Disney.

Dogged by the death of Wells and the departure of Katzenberg, Eisner needed another victory to assure shareholders he had the necessary vision to lead the company through this period of adjustment. The Financial Interest and Syndication Rules, also known as "fin-syn," had prevented networks from airing shows produced by the studios that owned them. In 1993, the Federal Communications Commission abolished these rules, making networks attractive acquisitions for studios. Jennifer Holt charts how this decision paved the way for four mergers that extensively transformed the U.S. media industries: Paramount and Viacom, UPN and the WB, ABC and Disney, and Time Warner and Turner.[36] With its own network, Disney had a guaranteed outlet for its television programming, which it could schedule at the optimal time to attract the appropriate viewership. Disney initially pursued CBS before turning to NBC, for which Disney had produced an anthology show following its fallout with ABC in 1961.[37] General Electric, which owned NBC, insisted on maintaining majority interest. Disney, however, wanted to its own network outright without answering to a partner, especially one that was in control. On July 31, 1995, Disney announced an acquisition of Capital Cities / ABC instead for $19 billion.

Programs such as *Monday Night Football*, *NYPD Blue*, *Roseanne*, and *20/20* made ABC the nation's most popular and profitable network. With Disney's *Home Improvement* and a popular youth-targeted Friday night block (*TGIF*), ABC was a perfect match for the family-friendly company. Disney also would acquire television and radio stations, newspapers, and significant portions (shared with Hearst) of ESPN, A&E, Lifetime, and the History Channel. With a film studio and a broadcast network, Disney could produce and distribute its filmed entertainment to a guaranteed audience of millions. The price tag was hefty, but the acquisition was a coup for Disney and for Eisner, who arguably became "the most powerful figure in popular culture in the world."[38] As Holt observed in 2011, the purchase "established the blueprint for most media conglomerates that were formed in its wake."[39]

Just as soon as he made the brilliant move, Eisner made perhaps his greatest mistake. Seeking to alleviate his workload, especially in light of his heart surgery a year earlier, Eisner hired Michael Ovitz to replace Frank Wells in August 1995, to begin work that October. Hollywood insiders had long speculated Ovitz would eventually want the kind of power and respect that came with running a conglomerate.[40] When he was passed over to run MCA, Ovitz was recruited by his friend Eisner. From the very beginning, Ovitz received a chilly reception from executives, who complained that he would whisper into Eisner's ear during meetings, and Disney investor Sid Bass later claimed that Eisner realized his mistake within weeks of hiring Ovitz.[41] Geffen, a vocal critic of Ovitz, opined, "He's not Michael Ovitz anymore. He's a guy who has a job working for Michael Eisner. And if you think everyone's not aware of it, you're very wrong."[42] Screenwriter Joe Eszterhas, another Ovitz adversary, admitted, "The town is not the same since he left CAA. . . . It's like the Kremlin without Stalin."[43] Eisner defended Ovitz publicly, including on a joint appearance on *Larry King Live* to give the impression all was fine, but Eisner later admitted to privately attempting to "trade" him to Sony.[44]

In the meantime, Hollywood struggled to balance the blockbuster mentality with modestly priced moviemaking. Reflecting on the 1995 box office season, United Artists president John Calley pushed for greater creative risks and stronger control over negative costs.[45] Midrange films, in particular, needed to reduce their budgets. For example, 20th Century Fox's strategy was to hire emerging directors from outside of the United States, including Danny Boyle, Alfonso Cuarón, and Baz Luhrmann. Studios also bet on young talent, such as Matthew McConaughey and Liv Tyler, to headline major releases for 1996.[46] To this end, Hollywood came around to the strategies that made Katzenberg's name during his early years at Disney.

In 1996, twelve films grossed over $100 million each, with *The Hunchback of Notre Dame* (Gary Trousdale and Kirk Wise, 1996) close behind. For the third year, Disney took the top spot, eclipsing its closer competitor, Warner Bros., by $300 million, to gross an impressive $1.2 billion.[47] Disney's strong performance was largely led by its live-action releases, including *The Rock* (Michael Bay, 1996), *Ransom* (Ron Howard, 1996), *Phenomenon* (Jon Turteltaub, 1996), and *Mr. Holland's Opus* (Stephen Herek, 1995). While the live-action *101 Dalmatians* (Stephen Herek, 1996), starring Glenn Close, outperformed *Hunchback*, the animated musical adaptation of Victor Hugo's classic novel fared well overseas.

Behind the scenes, the Ovitz drama had only intensified, fueled in part by his mishandling of *Kundun* (Martin Scorsese, 1997).[48] In December 1996, he announced he would leave his position in late January, just over a year after he started. Since Ovitz was not fired for cause, he was entitled to a sizable package totaling a staggering $140 million. Ovitz maintained a positive public face: "Michael Eisner has been my good friend for 25 years and that will not change, but it is important to recognize when something is not working."[49] Although Eisner did defend Ovitz against a lawsuit by Disney shareholders over Ovitz's compensation, he later admitted that hiring Ovitz was "a partnership that was born in hell."[50] On top of this debacle, Disney also found itself in court with Katzenberg, who successfully litigated for his share of the profits from Disney's box office successes during his tenure.

The 1997 box office marked all-time highs in both grosses ($6.24 billion) and admissions (1.31 billion).[51] The year ended with the release of *Titanic* (James Cameron, 1997), whose formidable success was fueled in part by a lack of major competition. Yet again, nearly $300 million separated the two top performing studios, but this time Sony eclipsed Disney, while Warner Bros. fell to fourth behind Paramount. Warner Bros.'s strategy of big budgets and big stars faltered, as was clear by its top performer (*Batman & Robin* [Joel Schumacher, 1997]).[52] Tom Sherak, chairman of fifth-place Fox, conceded that the best approach moving forward would be to produce fewer films annually, a move he hoped would reduce competition while improving films' box office performance.[53]

As a growing conglomerate, Disney reported record-high earnings of $22.5 billion in its annual report. The perennial historian, a proud Eisner offered shareholders his own version of Disney history in three phases in his letter opening the 1997 annual report. The first phase began with the company's founding by Walt and Roy Disney. The second phase proceeded from the establishment of Touchstone Films in 1984, months before Eisner, Wells, and Katzenberg took the reins following a Roy Disney–led coup. As Eisner explains, Touchstone brought a range of talent into the company: "The only way to replace [Walt] was to bring in many creative people, nurture them, and even pay them the way our competitors at the other film companies did."[54] (Curiously, Eisner names only on-screen talent—Tom Hanks, Bette Midler, Richard Dreyfuss, Robin Williams—before introducing the "'cool' *avant-garde* director," Julie Taymor.)[55] The acquisition of Capital Cities / ABC marked the beginning of the third phase. Curiously, this timeline ignores Katzenberg, who is minimized in favor of the talent he recruited and supervised. Eisner even decenters himself at first, though he obviously plays a key role in the last (and current) phase. Furthermore, the letter makes it clear that Eisner sees himself at the helm for years to come, the ideal leader for Disney's continuing expansion as a global entertainment conglomerate.

Although the popular perception of Disney's takeover of Times Square paints the company as a predator imposing corporate-sanctioned sanitation on a crime-ridden yet colorful area of New York City, this account is too reductive. The reality is that Broadway theater owners and nonprofit organizations, such as the 42nd Street Development Corporation, had been calling for a revitalization of Midtown Manhattan since at least the 1970s, and the major overhaul experienced in the area hardly could have taken place through the initiative of one corporation, especially considering Disney's status and wealth at the time. A more nuanced account must situate Disney within a larger plan by city and state governments as well as nonprofit groups committed to reviving the area. While it still faces the brunt of the criticism of the cleanup of Times Square, Disney's role was rather late in the game and, though impactful, not the reformative leadership demonstrated by the government and nonprofit interests.

Disney did not officially sign on to the New Amsterdam Theatre project until December 31, 1994, a day before Republican George Pataki took over the governorship of New York. Prior to committing, Disney required the city to assure them that two other nationally recognized companies would also commit to 42nd Street and that all the sex shops would be shut down.[56] New York City found Disney's partners in Madame Tussaud's Wax Museum and AMC Theatres, which would collectively take over the space currently occupied by three condemned theaters.[57] Rather than focus on historical preservation alone, the revitalization plan was decidedly commercial in nature as it cleared the way for restaurants, movie theaters, and retailers.[58] For its own part, Disney planned to meticulously restore the theater to its glory days, but now the front entrance also would allow theatergoers to enter the Disney Store next door rather than exiting back onto 42nd Street. Clearly Orlando was a closer exemplar than either London or Paris for what the new Times Square could be for Disney. The nonprofit administrators remained undeterred, with Cora Cahan boasting, "For 42nd Street, there are two kinds of times—B.D., before Disney, and A.D., after Disney."[59] For them, at least, Disney was the brand name that they had been anxiously awaiting, especially after earlier plans to develop the area into high-rise office buildings had fallen through in the late 1980s. Early estimates supported this gushing optimism, as the redevelopment efforts seemed poised to bring 49,000 jobs and $330 to $355 million in tax revenues to the city.[60]

Disney would not be the only major corporate producer on Broadway. In addition to the Really Useful Group, Livent emerged as a major player. The sumptuous "revisal"—that is, revised revival—of Jerome Kern and Oscar Hammerstein II's *Show Boat*, staged by Harold Prince, made its way to Broadway's largest house, the Gershwin Theatre, in September 1994, where weekly running costs topped $600,000—far more than most shows gross. As Garth Drabinsky later explained, "If I'm going to do something, I'm going to do it so it has implications for years."[61] In particular, he would demonstrate an ongoing interest in spectacular musical dramas address social issues as *Show Boat* had. Livent also announced plans to renovate two condemned Broadway theaters, the Lyric and the Apollo, into a single venue.[62] In *Taxi Driver* (Martin Scorsese, 1976), Travis Bickle (Robert De Niro) takes a reluctant Betsy (Cybill Shepherd) to an adult film at the Lyric. Now, some twenty years later, Drabinsky and Livent were "cleaning it up" for a new era of Broadway.

Drabinsky's lavish productions of epic proportions won him comparisons to David O. Selznick.[63] His expensive tastes, however, led to pricey tickets: $75 for the top seats. If Broadway patrons were going to pay those kinds of prices, the show would have to reward them with awe-inspiring spectacle. Disney and Livent were happy to oblige, but not all producers or shows could. One such producer was Andrew Lloyd Webber, whose disastrous *Sunset Boulevard* musical failed to recuperate its capitalization and consequently lost millions. Ironically, his production company, the Really Useful Group, admitted to following Disney's path by moving toward conglomeration, expanding into merchandising, games, records, and publishing.[64] Lloyd Webber had paved the way for corporate producers, but he struggled to keep his company at the top of the game that he had reshaped.

While Alex Bádue and Rebecca S. Schorsch recently argued that Disney stage productions "combine this legacy with technological aesthetics and commercial tactics that originated in British megamusicals,"[65] the more provocative question for film and theatre historians may be the influence of Disney in general and its animated musicals in particular on the British megamusical. My interviews suggest Disney reviewed the publicly available financial information on Mackintosh and Lloyd Webber productions, but their stagecraft owed a large debt to the theme park division and its artists' craft, much of which they honed in university theatre programs and the theatre industry. Relatedly, journalist Michael Walsh observed in 2000, "Lord Lloyd-Webber's commercial success is based not on the old Broadway model, but on the Magic Kingdom of Walt Disney."[66] Patrick McKenna, head of the Really Useful Group, similarly drew connections between Disney and Lloyd Webber as branded entertainment: "There are an awful lot of similarities between Disney and us. We have incredible copyrights. We have grown in recent years with proper management. We're a cash-rich company, and we're ready to invest in the ever-emerging world of entertainment and leisure."[67] Despite the ongoing success of *Phantom of the Opera*, the 1990s were marked by a series of brutal setbacks for Lloyd Webber: an animated film adaptation of *Cats* stalled, *Whistle Down the Wind* closed in Washington before its Broadway transfer, and a planned entertainment center at Battersea Power Station in southwest London never materialized. Coincidentally, one of Lloyd Webber's few triumphs during this period was his Academy Award for Best Original Song for "You Must Love Me," written for the film adaptation of *Evita* (Alan Parker, 1996)—produced by Disney's Hollywood Pictures. By 1997, Frank Rich drolly observed, "The man who Disneyfied the Broadway musical has been downsized by Disneyfication."[68] But as Charles R. Acland argues in his discussion of the "Disneyfication" of cinemagoing, the term "Disneyfication" is a rather lazy critical assessment that "reveals more of the intellectual and taste formation of the critic than it does of the actual phenomenon described, ultimately referring to the corporations' own branding rather than its actual operation."[69] Acland reminds us to consider the position, intellectual investments, and biases of said critic, and with Rich, his interests clearly lay in an allegiance to an understanding of Broadway theatre rendered financially infeasible by a range of political, social, economic, and industrial factors. Even Sondheim, Rich's idol, continued to develop and premiere his new work Off-Broadway.

Indeed, high production costs kept ticket prices escalating throughout the 1990s. The reality is that the easiest tickets to sell were the costliest and the cheapest. Most box offices struggled to push the midrange seats at the back of the orchestra and mezzanine.[70] Producers hesitated to release extra tickets to the TKTS booth, a discount outlet in Duffy Square, out of fear it would suggest the show's luster was fading. Producers like Cameron Mackintosh had learned long ago that even if there are no tickets available it is still the best time to increase advertisements for the show. Many shows supplemented their revenues with merchandise, which accounted for 3 to 6 percent of their weekly takes.[71] While shows like *Cats* and *Beauty and the Beast* hawked T-shirts, mugs, and souvenir programs, other productions struggled to find places to even put a merchandise booth since the decades-old theaters were not designed with such a notion in mind. The marketing strategy helped the 1994–1995 season eclipse $406 million on Broadway, with over nine million tickets sold, and another $694 million on the road.[72] The numbers marked Broadway's strongest season since 1980–1981.

Theatre may have been as strong as ever, but the art form and the industry were changing rapidly. Musicals thrived as plays continued to struggle: Tony Kushner's Tony-winning *Angels in America* closed at a loss, while producer Emanuel Azenberg lamented that theatre still was not enabling young playwrights to make a living.[73] Amplification became increasingly necessary due to the introduction of color scrollers (for changing the color of lights), moving lights, and wind machines. "If you didn't turn up the volume," sound designer T. Richard Fitzgerald explained, "it would sound like a subway was running inside the theater."[74] The stage technologies were hardly efficient, with Ben Brantley of the *New York Times* noting, "I feel like I'm watching an early silent movie" and describing the actors trying to work around the spectacular devices as "automatons."[75] His concerns did little to change the trajectory Broadway was on, and his fellow theatre critic at the *New York Times*, Vincent Canby, worried that harsh criticism may be pointless if it does nothing to support the volatile industry.[76]

Brantley's critique may have been premature, as the 1995–1996 season brought with it two fresh and innovative musicals that pushed the form forward. Opening within a week of each other, *Bring in 'da Noise, Bring in 'da Funk* and *Rent* expanded the musical idioms represented within the Broadway musical. The former was a musical revue featuring dance across decades of African American music, most notably hip-hop. The latter, a loose adaptation of the Puccini opera *La bohème*, used a pop rock score to chronicle the lives of young artists struggling with love, money, and AIDS in New York City. Both shows were developed Off-Broadway before transferring to Broadway for long runs: *Noise/Funk* played over a thousand shows, while *Rent* became a cultural phenomenon and ran for over five thousand. In fact, *Rent*'s Pulitzer Prize for Drama secured its reputation among ticket buyers, leading producer Jeffrey Seller to surmise, "It made an edgy downtown musical acceptable to an urban gold coast, Upper East Side audience."[77] Collectively, these shows earned eight Tonys, including awards for acting, direction, score, and book. A good deal of their financial success, though, came from appealing to audiences that Broadway neglected in recent years, especially African Americans and younger adults. As the megamusical stumbled, it appeared a smaller scale might be better for dramatic quality and profitability.

On April 2, 1997, Eisner assembled invited guests on a stage, pulled back the curtain, and revealed the renovated New Amsterdam Theatre following an estimated $36 million restoration.[78] From the balcony, a chorus sang "Circle of Life," the rousing opening number of the theater's upcoming production, *The Lion King*. In addition to repairing the friezes and ceiling, Disney also replaced the box seats, which had been removed while the theater exclusively showed movies. The renovations were supervised by respected architect Hugh Hardy, who observed, "There were no models to guide us because there's nothing like the New Amsterdam anywhere."[79] Even architecture critic Ada Louise Huxtable conceded, "If this is Disney magic, we need more of it."[80]

While many believe *The Lion King* opened the theater, the first show was actually *King David*, an oratorio by Alan Menken and Tim Rice. Like the flashy *Beauty* production that played up Broadway at the Palace Theatre, *King David* featured established Broadway talent, such as Marcus Lovett, Judy Kuhn, Stephen Bogardus, and Alice Ripley. Initially commissioned for the three thousandth anniversary of Jerusalem in 1996, the work eventually had its premiere during a limited engagement of nine performances at the newest venue on Broadway. "If King David were alive," director Mike Ockrent told the *New York Times*, "I'm sure he'd be delighted that Walt Disney is doing his story."[81] Despite this immodest assessment, Disney never fully staged or filmed *King David*, perhaps because its former studio chief, Katzenberg, was already producing an animated musical based on David, featuring music by Broadway veteran Stephen Schwartz, Menken's collaborator on *Pocahontas*.

King David received a mixed reception from New York theatre critics, who found it rather long and dull. One critic remarked, "Sitting in this wondrous house is more than half the fun."[82] Yet Rudy Giuliani boldly insisted the reopening of the New Amsterdam Theatre "really represents the restoration of New York City as the capital of the world."[83] The following month, Disney premiered its newest animated feature, *Hercules* (John Musker and Ron Clements, 1997), in the theater, complete with a two-mile "electrical parade" through Midtown Manhattan up to the Central Park Zoo. In addition to the film, attendees got to see a half-hour stage show beforehand. The "double bill" ran from June 15 until June 26, after which the film opened nationwide. It became the first animated Disney film to not gross $100 million domestically since *The Rescuers Down Under* seven years earlier. On Broadway, Disney's attention returned to preparing *The Lion King* for its November premiere.

But Disney was not the only corporation gearing up for a big premiere. Garth Drabinsky and Livent had their own large-scale musical coming in right behind: *Ragtime*, a sprawling epic based on E. L. Doctorow's 1975 historical novel. With music and lyrics by Lynn Ahrens and Stephen Flaherty, the new show would run over three hours and cost over $10 million. The budget was substantial, but Livent president Myron Gottlieb argued that live theatre was much more cost-effective than making blockbuster movies.[84] Like Hollywood studio owners, he closely supervised the creation of new shows, their tours around the United States and Canada, and the houses in which they played. Ahrens and Flaherty, for example, had been hired following an audition of sorts in which Drabinsky gave several composing teams a stipend to develop four demos for a *Ragtime* musical based on the novel and playwright Terrence McNally's treatment.[85] He even used focus groups to determine if the show was working, adding and removing songs based on respondents' feedback.[86]

In addition to the new show, Drabinsky was renovating a theater of his own across the street from the New Amsterdam. With over eighteen hundred seats, the newly renovated theater would rival the Gershwin for largest house on Broadway. Whereas Disney restored the New Amsterdam with government assistance, Drabinsky sought private donors, including the Ford Motor Company, which lent the theater its name: Ford Center for the Performing Arts. *Ragtime* even featured a cameo by and song about Henry Ford, lauding the virtues of assembly lines and mass production. The theater also included a VIP suite, where, by purchasing $125 tickets, audience members could have access to a private reception area, coatroom, and restroom. The cunning Drabinsky also added $1 to each ticket: half for the New 42nd Street (as required of all theaters under its aegis) and half for theater maintenance. These revenue streams, as well as a weak Canadian dollar, allowed Drabinsky to rationalize his large expenditures, which pleased directors and actors and flabbergasted his competitors. *Show Boat* director Hal Prince lauded Drabinsky as a "showman" and "theater lover," while Craig Turner of the *Los Angeles Times* described him as "brash, uncompromising, impolite, entrepreneurial and intensely competitive—the un-Canadian."[87] Regardless of one's opinion of Drabinsky or Livent, he now controlled 20 percent of the North American commercial theatre market.[88]

Beyond funding his shows through a publicly held company, Drabinsky also distinguished himself from Disney in his preference for bold, even daring productions built from the ground up. *Ragtime* explored racism, labor unions, and anti-Semitism, while his upcoming production of Jason Robert Brown and Alfred

Uhry's *Parade* dramatized the trial and murder of Leo Frank, a Jewish man kidnapped and lynched by a mob in 1915 Georgia. As Drabinsky described it, "I look for shows that can contribute constructively to an enlightened form of argument on the problems that plague society today."[89] Fusing the blockbuster musical with a timely social consciousness, he arguably tried to synthesize Broadway's two mainstays: the musical and the play. In 1995, Arthur Laurents, book writer for *West Side Story* and *Gypsy*, had decried the death of a "theater of substance,"[90] but Drabinsky tried to bring it back in a hybrid form. His business acumen seemingly made it feasible—at least for a time. Not even Drabinsky, though, could prepare for what Disney was about to unveil: an avant-garde-inspired adaptation of a blockbuster animated movie that captivated audiences and silenced Disney's critics to become a global phenomenon.

———

Disney's initial efforts on Broadway had won them few fans within the theatre industry. Broadway had long been a tightknit community, unified in its commitment to art and often against the (allegedly) crass commercialism of Hollywood—a trend that dates back to at least the 1930s.[91] Many observers perceived the arrival of Disney as an invasion that would bring with it standardization, commodification, and sanitization. Disney's blockbuster success with *Beauty and the Beast* was all the more offensive to delicate egos on Broadway. If Disney was going to maintain its presence, one that seemed promising and profitable for the company, it would have to play by at least some of Broadway's rules. Such an endeavor would require a bold move.

Disney decided in December 1995 to hire Julie Taymor as the director of its next show. Taymor's Broadway credentials were limited, but she was a well-regarded artist within avant-garde theatre. While a student at Oberlin College, she had studied under Herbert Blau, a noted theorist and leader in experimental theatre. Together with others, they had worked to create a theatre piece based on the cannibalistic Donner Party. Later, she traveled to Indonesia on a short-term fellowship, but stayed for four years and started her own theatre company, Teatr Loh. Taymor later claimed, "What grabbed me was seeing theatre in its original function, its absolutely most powerful creative state, not as entertainment but as a social mechanism, a doctor, a shaman. Theater there is sacrosanct, a daily part of life that is essential to your being."[92] Drawing from a range of traditions, including *commedia dell'arte* and *bunraku* puppetry, Taymor developed a reputation for her cross-cultural blend of time-honored practices.[93] In 1991 she won the MacArthur Fellowship, popularly known as the "Genius Grant," which provided her with five years of financial support. During that time, she staged *Juan Darién: A Carnival Mass*, a musical adaptation of a fable by Uruguayan writer Horacio Quiroga, at the Vivian Beaumont Theatre at Lincoln Center. The production was nominated for five Tonys but failed to garner any awards.

Disney's awareness of Taymor's work came through Thomas Schumacher, who worked under Peter Schneider in animation producing *The Rescuers Down Under* and *The Lion King* and then collaborated with him as producers for the stage version. Schumacher had served as associate director on the 1987 Olympic Arts Festival, an international arts exhibition that featured Peter Brook's elaborate adaptation of *The Mahabharata* and a production of *Miss Julie* directed by Ingmar Bergman. A friend had recommended Taymor to Schumacher, but he was unable to secure the funding to bring in her most recent work (cowritten with David Suehsdorf and Taymor's professional and personal partner, Elliot Goldenthal), *Liberty's Taken*, an American Revolution–era epic performed outdoors and featuring a "cast of hundreds," music, and puppetry.[94] Schumacher, who had also trained in the art of puppetry, kept Taymor in mind for possible future collaborations, which finally came in the form of *The Lion King*.

Despite Eisner's insistence, Schumacher initially resisted the idea of staging *The Lion King*. After all, the musical was not as integrated as *Beauty and the Beast* had been. As Schumacher explained in 2017, "*Lion King* is like a David Lean movie: big and epic with huge shots. It just happens to have some songs in it. . . . But for the most part, it's not really a musical. It's a film with music. And it's so cinematic. And I thought well, if we're going to try to take that and just plop it on stage, it's going to be silly."[95] Eisner persisted, so Schumacher decided to reach out to Taymor. Much to his surprise, she had not seen the film yet. Whether this fact is true or not, Taymor went to great lengths to not only maintain her avant-garde credentials but also assure interviewers and readers alike that Disney was hiring her to do what she does, not to work within its aesthetic. Yet scholars have challenged the presumption that Disney and Taymor are strange bedfellows; Rebecca-Anne Do Rozario, for example, notes that Taymor had long proved herself a skilled adapter of others artists' works, whether it be Poe or Mozart.[96] Eileen Blumenthal, a theatre scholar who coauthored a 1995 retrospective book on Taymor's career, told the *Village Voice*, "At long last, someone with an imagination as rich as Disney has taken up his mantle."[97] As Taymor saw it, their mutual fascination with myth, fairy tales, and folklore placed Disney and her in the same business, and by partnering with Taymor, Eisner saw an opportunity for the company to fulfill its ongoing efforts "to have an artistic success, to do something original."[98] It seemed a reasonable trade: Disney could provide Taymor with considerable resources, a wide audience, and greater visibility, while Taymor's outsider aesthetic could bolster Disney's artistic credibility among New York theatre professionals.

Taymor also had something—or rather, did not have something—that Disney must have found attractive: a union contract. In the preceding years, her MacArthur grant had been a major source of funding, but as that drew to a close, the Disney offer must have been appealing. As someone whose primary experience on Broadway had been in the nonprofit theatre scene, her lack of a union contract removed perceived obstacles. Disney and Taymor worked out a three-part deal where at each stage either side could exit with the work completed, bringing the terms to an end. "It means I get paid for working on the concept," Taymor explained, "but if the concept is not approved and I like it and they don't, we can part ways— and I've been paid for my time."[99] The deal gave both sides protection, allowing

Taymor to withdraw if she felt she was compromising her integrity and Disney to do so if it felt the risky adaptation was becoming too extreme or off-brand. Disney's history of antagonism toward unions, dating back to the 1941 strike that marred its namesake's reputation, meant that it often sought workarounds whenever it could in the highly regulated world of Broadway.[100] In fact, the company not only declined to join the League of American Theatres and Producers but also, like Livent, worked out its own contracts with Actors' Equity and the musicians' union.[101] Disney appeared to be neither ready nor willing to play by Broadway's rules quite yet.

Like Roth, Taymor worked to position herself as a collaborator with Disney from the very beginning: someone who had creative control and vision, uncompromised by her corporate patron. "When I took on *The Lion King*, I said, 'I'm going to make this work for me—my style, my audience. I believe if I do that with the material, children will love it, 90-year-olds will love it," she told trade publication *Back Stage*.[102] She dismissed the traditional Broadway approach as "very stale,"[103] and insisted rather bluntly, "I don't do children's theater, and I don't do cute."[104] (Similar to Walt Disney, Taymor rejected being branded a producer of children's entertainment.) Even though *Lion King* would be her second Broadway production and her first in the commercial theatre, she maintained that she had the experience and imagination to bring the show to fruition. To her credit, one of the perceived failings of the 1994 *Beauty* production was that it appealed to children but left many parents bored. Add to that the industrial ambivalence toward producing theatre for children and the show would be dead on arrival for many critics. Taymor's declaration that she would not be producing a theme park version worked to assuage those fears, but now, of course, she would have to deliver such a show. And Disney reaped the benefits of hiring this independent theatre artist.

Taymor also had a fondness for theatrical spectacle. For almost two decades, spectacle reigned on Broadway with crashing chandeliers, descending helicopters, and, for Disney's part, high-kicking cutlery celebrating hospitality. Yet the hottest ticket on Broadway at this time became the revival of Kander and Ebb's *Chicago*, a cynical antidote to the sincerity of phantoms and beasts. It offered audiences a pared-down, minimalist staging emphasizing strong performances, including the Bob Fosse–inspired choreography by his former partner and collaborator, Ann Reinking. For her own part, Taymor assured the press that her *Lion King* would not be *Cats*, even though it would also depend upon anthropomorphized felines.[105] But unlike mainstream critics, Taymor saw great potential for storytelling with spectacle.[106] The challenge remained to effectively integrate it into the narrative so that it thrilled the audience and drove the plot forward.

Before she was officially hired, Taymor had to fly to Orlando to meet with Eisner and studio executives. She brought several ideas for how the show could work, overcoming the *Cats* approach of humanlike felines to "create a bridge between the human emotions and the animal exteriors."[107] Actors would wear masks, but their faces would be visible, too, allowing the audience to see their physical reactions and, more obviously, hear their singing. The masks could adjust, though,

Figure 8. Rather than concealing the actor, Julie Taymor's *The Lion King* produces a "double event" in which the eye notes both the animal's movement and the actor's labor. Credit: Joan Marcus.

moving as the actor changed stance or posture. Taymor also brought a model of a pushcart-like structure that, when pushed forward, gave the illusion of gazelles gracefully running across the savanna. Returning to early theatrical practices, the goal was to foreground the labor of puppeteers, who would be on stage clearly manipulating the creatures. Rather than creating a pure illusion, this method underscored the making of the illusion, allowing the audience member to look back and forth between the puppet and the actor who was handling it. Taymor would call this technique "the double event" since it encouraged audiences to appreciate the effect as well as the labor producing it.[108] Indeed, this premise bears a family resemblance to what Neil Harris has called the "operational aesthetic," in which the audience understands and accepts they are being tricked by the attraction, but the attendant pleasures come from trying to figure out *how* it works.[109] To Taymor's delight, Eisner greenlit her conceptual approach, which she felt was also the riskiest, because he believed it would yield the greatest payoff.[110]

Perhaps one of Taymor's most important interventions was her feminist revision of the storyline. *The Lion King*, as a narrative of father-son relationships, patriarchal rule, and self-discovery, largely marginalizes the female characters. Sarabi, Simba's mother, must serve Scar after the death of her husband, and she becomes the subject of considerable emotional abuse. Simba's friend, Nala, rediscovers him in exile, but her role is largely a supporting one. Shenzi, the female hyena, is merely a source of comic relief in her role as henchwoman to the wry Scar. In short, the women function as simple foils to the rounder, more dynamic male characters.

Taymor addressed this issue by fleshing out Sarabi and especially Nala's character, who in the musical sings the poignant new song, "Shadowland," to express her decision to leave her homeland. Most noticeably, Taymor recast Rafiki, the wise baboon voiced by Robert Guillaume in the film, as a woman. In the film, the lead singer in the opening number, "Circle of Life," is clearly a female performer: Carmen Twillie, who performed the demo and was never replaced. (South African musician Lebo M wrote and performs the opening Zulu chant himself.) But Twillie is not singing as a character in the film itself. By giving that song to a female Rafiki, Taymor clarifies who the singer is while also establishing the show's maternal themes of birth and new life. Circular imagery permeates the costume and scenic design, from the masks to the sun that slowly rises in the opening number. The musical maintains the film's celebration of the son's ascension to the throne, yet it is a fate ensured and facilitated by the women of the pride lands.

The musical ran nearly twice as long as the film version; in fact, the first act is longer than the entire film. Yet corporate limitations prevented Taymor from filling in too many gaps. As Schumacher explained, "The point is not to reproduce the movie onstage, but the same emotional connections."[111] Taymor had early plans to explain the drought after Mufasa's death on a new villain, Papa Croc, who purchased the water for a nearby city, where Simba would encounter humans. Schumacher resisted such creative license, encouraging the director to focus on what was already within the story. She received greater leeway to develop the existing relationships, especially between Simba and Mufasa as well as Simba and Nala.

Another area in need of expansion was the show's musical component since Elton John and Tim Rice had written only five songs for the original film: the opener, "The Circle of Life"; Simba's "I want" song, "I Just Can't Wait to Be King"; Scar's chilling anthem, "Be Prepared"; Timon and Pumbaa's comical "Hakuna Matata"; and the love ballad "Can You Feel the Love Tonight?" In addition to three more songs from John and Rice, Lebo M and music supervisor Mark Mancina were called upon to expand on the original songs and Hans Zimmer's scoring. Disney has referred to Lebo M as "the voice and spirit of *The Lion King*,"[112] while for her part Taymor has insisted that his songs are the show's best. Even Elton John conceded "some of the African things work better than some of my things."[113] But Mancina publicized the central role that he, Lebo M, and Taymor played in the score, noting, "Everybody else whose name is up there was not directly involved in the creation of this show."[114] In fact, Elton John saw the show for the first time on opening night. *The Lion King* pioneered a unique phenomenon for Broadway: "a score composed by committee."[115] (Disney had used a similar tactic in *Oliver & Company*.) Broadway had long celebrated the visionary geniuses (Cole Porter, Irving Berlin, Jerry Herman, and Stephen Sondheim) and legendary partnerships (Lerner and Loewe, Rodgers and Hammerstein, Kander and Ebb), but *The Lion King*'s score was attributed to seven composers and lyricists.

Increasing the South African music in the production posed another problem for Disney on the labor front. As Taymor noted in 1997, the show is linguistically diverse: "Zulu and other languages—African languages—that everybody's fine with because again, we all understand that you don't need to understand every single word."[116] Regardless, this may make the show accessible to more audiences, but it could make (re)casting more difficult. Furthermore, Broadway actors would not be properly trained to perform Lebo M's music, so talent was recruited from South African cities, including Johannesburg and Cape Town. Disney had to appeal to Actors' Equity to keep the African singers, and a compromise was later reached to allow five performers to stay on with the production.[117] Disney also had to promise to train Equity actors in the necessary dialect to perform the roles, but to this day South African actors compose part of the company wherever the show is playing. As Taymor explained it in 2017, those cast members serve "like the spiritual foundation of *The Lion King*."[118] Furthermore, the casting of these performers helped address some of the criticism of a show set in Africa yet created by a predominantly white creative team and a corporate sponsor.

Disney opened the show out of town, but rather than returning to Houston or a prominent theatre city like Los Angeles or Chicago, *The Lion King* premiered in Minneapolis. David Hawkanson, managing director of the city's acclaimed Guthrie Theater, boldly claimed, "There isn't a theater (district) outside of New York that has this activity."[119] An eight-week tryout began at the Orpheum Theatre, a 2,600-seat house downtown where ticket sales topped $1 million on the very first day.[120] Taking a cue from Walt Disney himself, Taymor preached its appeal for all audiences: "Children will love it, but I don't think you need to play down to children."[121] Taymor was right: the appeal of the show crossed generations.

But Eisner pushed for changes, including the addition of a fight sequence with the hyenas through which Simba proves himself an able warrior and leader.[122] Taymor resisted the masculine implications of a violent rite of passage, and the show stayed largely the same as it readied itself for a November premiere in the recently reopened New Amsterdam Theatre. But at an estimated cost of $15 million, the show easily became Broadway's most expensive production to date, surpassing even Garth Drabinsky's massive expenditures. Furthermore, *Beauty and the Beast*, already in its third year on Broadway, had yet to recuperate its initial investment despite Disney's claims that it would do so by 1995.[123] *The Lion King* was a bigger gamble, but whether or not it would yield the bigger payoff Eisner desired was yet to be seen.

———

Marketing *The Lion King* entailed the creation of a striking logo: a black woodcut of an adult Simba against a golden background. Originally underlined by "the Broadway musical," it was revised to "the award-winning Best Musical" after the Tony Awards. To no surprise, the logo seems to distance the show from its status as children's entertainment—and certainly from the "cute" aesthetic developed by animator Fred Moore and long associated with Disney Animation. A commercial for *The Lion King* on Broadway later appeared among the previews for the direct-to-video sequel, *The Lion King II: Simba's Pride* (Darrell Rooney, 1998). Hosted by Disney Channel personality RuDee Lipscomb, it pitched the show directly to kids, claiming it was "so cool even your parents will love it" and highlighting its beautifully restored home, the New Amsterdam Theatre. While "Circle of Life" played over the commercial, a montage of images from the show emphasized its spectacle and awards over its score.

Following thirty-three preview performances, *The Lion King* premiered at the New Amsterdam Theatre on November 13, 1997. Considering the ornate and unusual nature of the show's signature puppets, the critics' reviews were largely positive, though few could resist the temptation to acknowledge the show's corporate origins. Patti Hartigan at the *Boston Globe* reported, "Theater mavens are murmuring about its marriage of art and commerce, its rare blend of cultural influences and styles, its craftmanship, and, of course, its potential box-office and merchandising appeal."[124] *Newsweek*'s Jack Kroll insisted the show was "sure to delight all but the stuffiest theater intellectuals, who will no doubt accuse Taymor of selling out."[125] Indeed New York's most demanding critics did not welcome the show with open arms but did offer tempered praise. Writing for the *New York Times*, Vincent Canby afforded the show excessive praise, before undercutting it with a jab at Disney: "The result is one of the most memorable, moving and original theatrical extravaganzas in years, an enterprise that can only make the profit-propelled Disney organization even richer."[126]

This trend continued among the establishment, who were apprehensive to praise the show, which critics evaluated more as an experience than as a musical. Canby's junior colleague, Ben Brantley, was a bit kinder: "Seen purely as a visual tapestry, there is simply nothing else like it."[127] John Simon started off his review with "Come to *The Lion King* with two pairs of eyes, one ear, and half a brain," but even he admitted, "This is the one such show adults will feast on, too, mostly because of the wonders wrought by Julie Taymor, who designed and directed this cornucopia of dazzlements."[128] On November 14, ticket sales eclipsed $2.7 million, undaunted by the mixed reviews published that very morning.[129]

In addition to the criticism of the show's relatively weak storyline, several critics targeted the uneven score. Fintan O'Toole of the *New York Daily News* found the Elton John and Tim Rice songs to be mundane against Taymor's puppetry and Lebo M and Mancina's new scoring.[130] Writing for the *Guardian*, Joanna Coles lambasted what she perceived as commercialism: "This is the triumph of stagecraft over musical mediocrity. . . . I have seen the future and it's manestream."[131] (Taymor herself chastised critics for focusing too much on "the scale and the money.")[132] Dismissing the show as "mostly kids' stuff," Ed Siegel of the *Boston Globe* took issue with the show's "disappointing" choreography.[133] Of course, many of these criticisms deride not so much what the show does but what it is: an adaptation of a family film, produced by a global entertainment conglomerate, for a general audience. Unsurprisingly, many critics evaluated *The Lion King* in the context of *Cats*, arguing the former improved upon the latter. Donald Lyons generally praised the show as "kid heaven! . . . This is the anti-*Cats*."[134] *The Lion King* would capitalize upon a growing family audience, as attendance for shows catering to younger audiences had doubled among children and teenagers between 1991 and 1997.[135]

The show found its greatest champion in a talk show host: Rosie O'Donnell. Since 1996, the stand-up comedian turned actress had hosted a daytime talk show, where she quickly rose in the ratings behind Oprah Winfrey and Jerry Springer. She used her platform to introduce her audience to legendary theatre talent and current productions running on the Great White Way, effectively facilitating what Kelly Kessler has called "the mainstreaming of Broadway."[136] Born and raised in New York, O'Donnell was a lifelong Broadway fan who invited current Broadway musicals to perform production numbers on her show in the time slot tradition-ally reserved for pop singers and musical groups. The show's producers even shared with the musical's producers the cost of bringing in the talent for another perfor-mance in addition to their usual show schedule. A self-proclaimed "cheerleader for theater,"[137] Rosie O'Donnell provided a national platform for the Broadway industry, effectively doing for musical theatre what Oprah Winfrey had done for books.[138]

O'Donnell featured only theatrical productions she adored,[139] and her endorse-ment was highly sought after by Broadway producers. She never criticized shows that she disliked, preferring instead to showcase those she did. But O'Donnell not just enjoyed The Lion King but exalted it as "the best show I have seen in my 35 years."[140] Peter Schneider acknowledged that O'Donnell's influence prompted sellouts amid already strong sales: "The minute Rosie went on the air, we started to sell out. The impact of her personal opinion was phenomenal."[141] By the end of 1997, The Lion King not only was grossing $800,000 a week,[142] but had over $40 million in advance ticket sales.[143] Disney beat box office records that it had set itself three years earlier with Beauty and the Beast.

Disney had another commercial success on its hands and a beautifully restored house of its own in which to present it, but it remained to be seen whether Broad-way would accept Disney Theatrical Productions. Two months after The Lion King's premiere, Ragtime arrived on Broadway with an equally ambitious scale, highly respected creative team and stage talent, and well-regarded source material. Garth Drabinsky, the show's producer, harkened back to Broadway's Golden Age when a single visionary could put together and present an original stage musical. Ragtime made its home across the street from the New Amsterdam in the newly opened Ford Center for the Performing Arts, where it too had one of the largest seating capacities on Broadway. But Ragtime did not have The Lion King's spectacle, though it was a solid integrated musical epic with a large cast. Based on E. L. Doctorow's novel, the musical had multiple plotlines and cameos by a range of historical fig-ures, including Harry Houdini, Evelyn Nesbit, and Emma Goldman. It was hardly the family-friendly musical Disney was putting on, but it garnered the prestige Disney longed for.

The Tony Award nominations pitted Drabinsky against Disney, with Ragtime taking thirteen and The Lion King receiving eleven. As one Broadway insider anon-ymously told the New York Daily News, "Ragtime is a great show, but The Lion King is a revelation."[144] There was one key difference: The Lion King hardly needed awards for commercial reasons, though Disney surely wanted the validation.

Ragtime, on the other hand, was a costly, ambitious production—and it was hemorrhaging money. At the very least, it would have to run for two to three years to even begin to seriously recuperate its initial investment. Livent also was in trouble, and as the Tony Awards neared, Drabinsky was demoted to creative control as a new major shareholder took over: Michael Ovitz. His investment in Livent not only had him facing off with his former employer but also provided him with a relatively inexpensive way to reenter the entertainment industry following his embarrassing dismissal. In addition to saving Ragtime, a Tony Award for Best Musical also would help to repair Drabinsky's tarnished reputation.

The 1998 Tony Awards were hosted by O'Donnell, whose popularity had revived interest in the ceremony and prevented CBS from dropping the broadcast altogether. As O'Donnell later explained, she understood "the next Sondheim" was out there somewhere—perhaps far from New York City—and needed access to the show.[145] A noticeable change in Broadway was already underway: it was becoming more mainstream, its two biggest shows were produced by corporate entities, and Times Square was regaining its reputation as a tourist attraction. As O'Donnell quipped during the show, "And 42d Street is back. Not the musical, the entire street. It's family-ized. It really is. Last night, I saw four hookers dressed as Teletubbies."[146] While 1998 was an unusually strong year for plays, including Martin McDonagh's The Beauty Queen of Leenane and Yasmina Reza's 'Art', the press focused on the far more dramatic showdown between The Lion King and Ragtime.

The tension persisted throughout the night. In the preshow ceremony, which aired on PBS prior to the CBS broadcast, Garth Fagan won a Tony for his choreography of The Lion King. Shortly thereafter, the songwriting team of Lynn Ahrens and Stephen Flaherty won their first Tony for the score of Ragtime. Flaherty opened his acceptance speech with a "thank you" to his beleaguered producer: "We hope that you're able to find a producer as passionate and gutsy and someone who loves musicals as much as Garth Drabinsky."[147] William David Brohn won a Tony for his orchestrations for Ragtime, then Terrence McNally took the award for his book to Ragtime. The Lion King then swept the three design categories: Taymor for costume design, Donald Holder for lighting design, and Richard Hudson for scenic design. Finally, Taymor became the first woman to win the Tony Award for directing a musical, earning a standing ovation from the audience. The honor reinforced a growing perception among theatre journalists and industry insiders that Taymor was "the woman who made Walt Disney respectable on Broadway."[148]

Oddly enough, the shows did not garner many awards during the broadcast: Audra McDonald won the Best Featured Actress in a Musical Award for her performance as Sarah in Ragtime, but neither show took another award until Best Musical, the final award of the night. The Lion King won, perhaps even to the surprise of Schneider and Schumacher, who gleefully bounded up to the stage to accept their trophies. A Disney-produced show had won the approval of the theatre community—or a majority of Tony voters, at least.

That August, Michael Ovitz announced that a review of Livent's accounting practices had revealed irregularities. While he claimed he was following the looser Canadian conventions, Drabinsky was charged with fraud and subsequently imprisoned. In 1996, Lloyd Webber had lamented that "a new show of mine cannot find a home on Broadway because some of the old shows are still running. . . . Now there aren't enough."[149] A year later, Lloyd Webber's ongoing difficulties with *Sunset Boulevard* had prompted him to significantly reduce the staff of the Really Useful Group. The future of corporate Broadway appeared to rest firmly in the hands of Disney, bringing a relationship that had begun over a decade earlier with the hiring of Ashman and Menken full circle. Of course, neither creator had found much success on Broadway in Ashman's lifetime, but the knowledge of craft that they brought to Disney enabled and energized the company's theatrical ventures.

———

The renovation of the New Amsterdam Theatre and the premiere of *The Lion King* demonstrated that Disney was doubling down on its investment in Broadway after the rocky reception of *Beauty and the Beast*. By restoring a dilapidated landmark and hiring an innovative creative force, Disney showed its commitment to both the Broadway community and the revitalization of Times Square. *The Lion King* proved to observers that Disney could transcend its profit motive to create bold, original works of art, a move reminiscent of the legitimating efforts undertaken by its namesake decades earlier. Joe Roth, who replaced Katzenberg as Disney Studios chairman, explained, "More than anything, it's the perception. This is the way you'd like the public to see the company. To take one of its classics and turn it in that form into great art."[150]

To say the gamble paid off is an understatement. By 2019, the stage version of *The Lion King* had grossed over $9 billion worldwide, superseding *Phantom of the Opera* as the most profitable stage property.[151] In fact, in its first 6,600 performances on Broadway, the house failed to meet at least 80 percent capacity fewer than a dozen times—an unconscionable feat for a show to achieve in a year, let alone across fifteen.[152] *Phantom of the Opera* remains the longest running show in Broadway history to date, but *The Lion King* easily maintains the title of most profitable, surpassing $1 billion on Broadway alone by 2013.[153] Yet as Schumacher observed in 2017, "Even though *The Lion King* has been successful, it doesn't tell us how to do the next one."[154] Indeed, Disney has been unable to replicate the same critical and commercial response in its subsequent productions, despite hiring well-regarded professionals from theatre and opera. But Disney Theatrical Group also has never had a flop, as even its less successful Broadway efforts, specifically *Tarzan* and *The Little Mermaid*, eventually recouped costs on tour and via licensing.

In the intervening years, Disney has faced a good deal of blame for what New York City has become, whether one sees it as saccharine, sanitized, or simply too expensive. While Disney was complicit, it was more accurately the public face of a series of ongoing initiatives between the city government, the governor's office, nonprofits, and even the Broadway community itself to turn around the former cornerstone of U.S. entertainment, long superseded by Hollywood. Fittingly, Hollywood (via Disney) would be perceived as the one to transform Broadway, at least in the mind of the public. In so doing, two entities that had alternately battled and collaborated found themselves more closely linked than ever as separate divisions within expanding entertainment conglomerates extending and supporting the same media franchises. What resulted has profoundly impacted not only the company but the U.S. film and theatre industries more broadly.

Conclusion

In November 2021, *Encanto* (Jared Bush, Byron Howard, and Charise Castro Smith, 2021), Disney Animation's sixtieth film, premiered to critical and commercial acclaim. Within weeks, "We Don't Talk about Bruno" topped the U.S. *Billboard* Hot 100 charts, and the film went on to win the Golden Globe and the Academy Award for Best Animated Feature. Set within a personified casita in Colombia, *Encanto* clearly draws upon Latin American history, literature, and culture—most obviously, the novels of Gabriel García Márquez—to offer a fantasy narrative that evokes the tradition of magical realism.[1] But as a film from a U.S.-based major entertainment conglomerate, it is a hybrid product that synthetizes various traditions and forms, including the integrated musical. In addition to studying Colombian music, songwriter Lin-Manuel Miranda works within and through the integrated musical tradition that Ashman and Menken reestablished at Disney. For instance, positioned right after the prologue, "The Family Madrigal" carries out the necessary expositional labor one also finds in "Belle" and *Aladdin*'s "Arabian Nights." Soon after, Mirabel sings her "I want" song, "Waiting on a Miracle," declaring her readiness for whatever life has in store for her. Similarly to "Kiss the Girl" and "Beauty and the Beast," *Encanto*'s love theme, "Dos Oruguitas," is sung not by one of the principals but by a third party—in this case, nondiegetically by Colombian pop star Sebastián Yatra. But *Encanto* also breaks away from the Renaissance-era Disney princess narratives not only in its use of Latin American rhythms and musical styles (including salsa, guajira, and reggaeton) but in its emphasis on familial over (heterosexual) romantic love. At the structural level, however, the tent-poles Ashman advocated for remain intact, holding the story together even as its creators both revise and expand Disney Animation's representational and storytelling practices.

In short, the Disney animated musical thrives over thirty years after *The Little Mermaid* premiered. It has ebbed and flowed, but if one looks at Disney more broadly, the integrated musical as a form has remained omnipresent. For

Figure 9. In *Encanto*, Lin-Manuel Miranda fuses Latin American musical styles and the Broadway-style integrated musical storytelling structure, as seen in Mirabel's "I want" song, "Waiting on a Miracle." Credit: Author's screenshot.

instance, as Pixar emerged as the dominant force in feature animation, its creative team intentionally positioned its films against the Disney aesthetic—and the princess musicals, in particular. As Andrew Stanton explains,

> We didn't have any influence [during preproduction for *Toy Story*], so we had a little secret list of rules that we kept to ourselves. And they were: No songs, no "I want" moment, no happy village, no love story. And the irony is that, in the first year, our story was not working at all and Disney was panicking. So they privately got advice from a famous lyricist, who I won't name, and he faxed them some suggestions. And we got a hold of that fax. And the fax said, there should be songs, there should be an "I want" song, there should be a happy village song, there should be a love story and there should be a villain. And thank goodness we were just too young, rebellious and contrarian at the time. That just gave us more determination to prove that you could build a better story. And a year after that, we did conquer it. And it just went to prove that storytelling has guidelines, not hard, fast rules.[2]

Despite the filmmakers' efforts to shake off the conventions of the integrated musical, one can still perceive its lingering influence on *Toy Story*. It simply replaces a romance plot with a friendship plot, but the beats remain in place: the protagonists meet, they dislike each other, they learn to like one another, they form a strong emotional bond. Furthermore, music remains paramount to the storytelling. Although Woody and Buzz do not sing any songs, Randy Newman's nondiegetic performances of his original songs, including "You've Got a Friend in Me" and "Strange Things," are essential to the film's characterization, tone, and plot development. As director John Lasseter conceded, "[Newman's] songs are touching, witty, and satirical, and he would deliver the emotional underpinning for every

‚scene."[3] Perhaps it might be understood as a form of disintegrating musical: one that both borrows and deviates from the integrated model.

While Pixar soared, 2D animation struggled throughout the late 1990s and into the early 2000s. The *New York Times* cited the poor performance of *Atlantis: The Lost Empire* (Gary Trousdale and Kirk Wise, 2001) as a reason for Peter Schneider's departure from his position as Walt Disney Studios chairman in 2001, after which he returned to independent theatrical production.[4] By the early 2000s, the writing was on the wall: digital animation, led by Pixar and DreamWorks, had superseded 2D animation among U.S. audiences. *Toy Story* (1995–) and *Shrek* (2001–) had become profitable franchises for Disney and DreamWorks, respectively, easily outperforming 2D features, including *The Iron Giant* (Brad Bird, 1999) and *The Emperor's New Groove* (Mark Dindal, 2000). The critical and commercial failure of *Titan A.E.* (Don Bluth and Gary Goldman, 2000) effectively marked the end of Fox Animation Studios and Don Bluth's career in feature animation to date.[5] By 2005, Glen Keane, the animator who had led the teams animating Ariel and the Beast, was championing digital animation at Disney, as the studio rolled out plans for its own digital projects, including *Chicken Little* (Mark Dindal, 2005), *Meet the Robinsons* (Stephen John Anderson, 2007), and *Tangled* (Nathan Greno and Byron Howard, 2010). The gradual decline of 2D feature animation happened to align with the board's waning support for Michael Eisner, eventually leading to his resignation in 2005.

His replacement was Disney president Robert Iger, who had previously served as president of ABC Television, president of Walt Disney International, and chief operating officer of Disney. He quickly proved himself a savvy executive by pitching a bold plan: buy Pixar and put its leaders, Edwin Catmull and John Lasseter, in charge of Disney animation. The relationship between Disney and Pixar had grown acrimonious because of tensions between Eisner and Jobs, but in a peacekeeping gesture, Iger realized that purchasing the company outright could restore the working relationship. Prior to his appointment, Iger had attended festivities to celebrate the new Disneyland park in Hong Kong and noticed that Pixar characters— not recent Disney characters—populated the park.[6] Acquiring Pixar would help repair the relationship with a major Disney stockholder (Jobs) and provide a wealth of established properties. Both the board and Jobs were amenable to the idea, and in 2006 Disney purchased Pixar for $7.4 billion in stock.

The Pixar acquisition was a turning point for Disney for several reasons. It established Iger's defining strategy as the head of the company: acquire major media franchises and fully exploit them. Pixar under Jobs had preferred to limit the number of sequels it produced,[7] but Iger saw the potential for several franchises in the Pixar canon. In this spirit, he also oversaw the acquisitions of Marvel Entertainment in 2009 and Lucasfilm in 2012 to provide the company with even more intellectual property to capitalize upon across various sectors, including filmed entertainment, theme parks and resorts, and consumer products. The formula has paid off handsomely, establishing a model for maintaining franchises that other entertainment conglomerates have followed—or envied. Consequently, Disney emerged as one of the world's largest entertainment conglomerates, and its leader was heralded in 2016 as the "most effective media CEO of his generation."[8]

The integrated musical also remained a successful storytelling form for the company throughout this period. It can be seen across the company's divisions, even if it was not necessarily the tentpole holiday release it had been in the past. In addition to theme park musical entertainment, Disney produced live-action adaptations of classic Broadway musicals for its Sunday night *Wonderful World of Disney* series on ABC, including the Rodgers and Hammerstein version of *Cinderella* (Robert Iscove, 1997), *Annie* (Rob Marshall, 1999), and *The Music Man* (Jeff Bleckner, 2003). Marshall would go on to direct *Chicago* (2002), distributed by Miramax, then a Disney subsidiary. The musical, still playing Broadway in its minimalist revival, became a star-studded blockbuster—and Best Picture Oscar winner. Released not long after *Moulin Rouge!* (Baz Luhrmann, 2001), *Chicago* inspired continuing optimism in the future of the film musical. Disney pursued live-action musicals further with the theatrical release of *Enchanted* (Kevin Lima, 2007), which lovingly parodied the animated Disney princess musicals, while on the Disney Channel Kenny Ortega of *Newsies* fame directed *High School Musical* (2006). It became a major global media franchise that inspired subsequent movies and related musical projects, including *Camp Rock* (Matthew Diamond, 2008), featuring pop music stars Demi Lovato and the Jonas Brothers. The Jonas Brothers had already released their second album (and their first for Disney's Hollywood Records), *Jonas Brothers* (2007), further demonstrating the company's growing interest in the music industry and its linkages to Disney's film and television efforts.[9]

With digital champions at the helm of Disney Animation, Lasseter nevertheless remained committed to hand-drawn 2D animation. The studio produced New Orleans–set *The Princess and the Frog* (John Musker and Ron Clements, 2009), starring Tony Award winner Anika Noni Rose as Tiana, the first Black Disney princess. The movie featured original songs by Randy Newman, but *Princess* was an integrated musical, so the songs were performed by the characters, except for the opening number, "Down in New Orleans," sung by New Orleans legend Dr. John, and the end titles song, "Never Knew I Needed," written and performed by R&B singer Ne-Yo. After years of delays, the animated musical adaptation of Rapunzel, *Tangled*, premiered in 2010. Although it featured songs by Alan Menken, *Tangled* represented the animated princess musical's transition to digital animation and a pop-vocal performance by its lead, voiced here by pop singer Mandy Moore. In short, musicals—and, quite often, Broadway-style integrated musicals— have been paramount for Disney across its divisions since *The Little Mermaid*. From "Under the Sea" in 1990 through 2022, composers and lyricists working on Disney films, including Stephen Sondheim and Andrew Lloyd Webber, have won the Academy Award for Best Original Song twelve times.

While the Marvel and *Star Wars* films have received the bulk of the publicity, Disney's ongoing dependence on princess musicals underscores the enduring legacy of Howard Ashman and Alan Menken as well as the integrated musical's influence at the company. In 2011, licensing of the Disney princesses led to

$1.6 billion in retail sales in North America and another $3 billion in international markets—exceeding profits generated by the Batman, *Sesame Street*, Spider-Man, and *Star Wars* franchises.[10] Two years later, the studio released another computer-animated musical, *Frozen*, based on Hans Christian Andersen's "The Snow Queen." The film featured new songs from Kristen Anderson-Lopez and Robert López, the latter of whom had won Tonys for his scores for *Avenue Q* and *The Book of Mormon*. The film's vocal talent included experienced Broadway talents Jonathan Groff, Santino Fontana, Josh Gad, and Idina Menzel, who sang the showstopping "Let It Go." *Frozen* became the highest grossing animated film to date, and Disney capitalized on its success by licensing *Frozen* toys, converting the Norway exhibit in EPCOT to a *Frozen* ride, and developing a mobile game that prompted 105 million downloads.[11] The company soon announced plans for a film sequel and a Broadway show.

After a tryout in Denver, *Frozen* opened in New York in March 2018, five months after the twentieth anniversary of *The Lion King*. The show found quite a different Broadway than its sister production had witnessed in 1997. The Disney Store next to the New Amsterdam had moved to Times Square, now teeming with supersigns, street performers, bistro tables, and tourists from around the world. Chain restaurants and national retailers, including Sephora, Olive Garden, Forever 21, TGI Friday's, and Starbucks, could be found within the theatre district. Many Broadway shows were based on movies—some blockbuster hits, other lesser-known indie films—like *A Bronx Tale* (Robert De Niro, 1993), *Anastasia* (Don Bluth and Gary Goldman, 1997), *Kinky Boots* (Julian Jarrold, 2005), and *Waitress* (Adrienne Shelly, 2007). Some critics have dismissed these shows as evidence of "creative bankruptcy,"[12] but show creators have noted that films provide solid plots on which they can add original music, choreography, and staging.[13] In addition to the so-called "movical,"[14] other popular shows have adopted the "jukebox musical" formula, in which a plot pieces together the musical catalog of an established pop star, including Carole King (*Beautiful*), Donna Summer (*Summer*), Tina Turner (*Tina*), and Jimmy Buffett (*Escape to Margaritaville*). Despite concerns that these shows dominate Broadway, only about one-third of Broadway theaters are big enough to make elaborate musicals financially viable. In fact, the 2017–2018 Broadway season also included musical revivals (*Once on This Island*, *Carousel*), small-scale musicals (*The Band's Visit*, *Chicago*), new plays (*Farinelli and the King*, *Latin History for Morons*, *Meteor Shower*), and revivals of plays with prominent actors (*Angels in America* with Andrew Garfield, *The Iceman Cometh* with Denzel Washington, *Three Tall Women* with Glenda Jackson). Broadway actually offers a wealth of options for theatergoers, from plays to Disney musicals. But the costs of production, often blamed on city taxes, compensation agreements, and union fees, lead Broadway producers to seek new ways of minimizing risk. Disney did not bring in an era of dumbed-down entertainment so much as continued an era of theatrical experiences, even stunts. To justify the ticket prices, Broadway producers must deliver more than a good story. The enticements vary from show to show but may include Hollywood stars (Uma Thurman,

Amy Schumer), celebrated Broadway veterans (Bernadette Peters, Nathan Lane), familiar characters or plots (*Mean Girls*, *SpongeBob SquarePants*), or pure spectacle (the stage "wizardry" developed for *Harry Potter and the Cursed Child*). The sheer variety demonstrates the desire to target diverse audiences while betraying the truth behind many critiques of Broadway: it's becoming too accessible—not in ticket prices, of course, but in its storytelling and subject matter.

Buoyed by *Harry Potter*, *Hamilton*, Bruce Springsteen, and *Frozen*, the 2017–2018 Broadway season was the most profitable and well-attended in the industry's history to that point, with ticket sales of $1.7 billion and attendance at nearly 13.8 million.[15] Unsurprisingly, trade groups often neglect to mention that the best tickets for *Hamilton* or *Springsteen on Broadway* went as high as $850 each. While 11 percent of Americans have household incomes over $150,000, the Broadway League found in 2016 that 41 percent of Broadway theatergoers came from such households.[16] Furthermore, 67 percent of attendees are female, 63 percent are tourists, and 77 percent are white.[17] Broadway, like Hollywood, attempts to appeal to the widest possible audience, but not everybody can afford the experience. While many shows attempt to counter accusations of price gouging through digital lotteries, rush tickets, and school programs, Broadway remains an exclusive opportunity. Ironically, seasoned drama critics still have dismissed Broadway as "our east coast Las Vegas"[18]—glitzy, gimmicky, even philistine.

In 2018, *New York Times* theatre critic Jesse Green echoed a common sentiment among such commentators when he stated, "If Broadway is our national theater, we're in trouble."[19] His comment reveals less a concern about access for the masses than the perceived lack of intellectual rigor and artistic experimentation behind recent productions. But Green's concern also demonstrates a reality of Broadway today: it no longer presents the most cutting-edge dramatic work—at least, not at first. In the 1940s and 1950s, new works by major playwrights Lillian Hellman, Arthur Miller, and Tennessee Williams premiered on Broadway. During the 2016–2017 season, Lynn Nottage and Paula Vogel had their work produced on Broadway for the first time, even though both were accomplished dramatists who had already (respectively) won Pulitzer Prizes for Drama. When a challenging new drama actually makes it to Broadway, it usually does so after a successful run elsewhere. Of course, this significant change predates Disney, but nonetheless the company has become the mascot (and scapegoat) for a revitalized Broadway where popular entertainment allegedly prevents the staging of what critics believe to be inventive drama. Instead, Broadway has more and more often drawn the attention of Hollywood producers and major entertainment conglomerates. In 2018, Broadway offered shows produced by J. J. Abrams, Ryan Murphy, Nickelodeon, and Universal, but Disney clearly dominates Broadway theatrical production by the entertainment conglomerates. Prior to the COVID-19 pandemic, Disney had three productions running—*The Lion King*, *Aladdin*, and *Frozen*—and planned to stage *The Jungle Book* and *Hercules* in the near future. Disney has a wealth of properties (musical or otherwise), of course, but as Schumacher notes, not all of them are stage-worthy: "I always look for what about it would be enhanced by being told in the theatre, what about it is classical enough that calls for what the theatre wants to do, and also which ones utilize their music in a way that is most theatrical."[20]

Amy S. Osatinski has identified a remarkable consistency across Disney Theatrical's productions that has bolstered its success, including its investment in promoting the company brand, facility in utilizing Disney resources, awareness of the shows' role in larger media franchises, and dedication to high production values.[21] Disney theatre provides an opportunity to commercially reinvigorate a creative property while artistically reinventing it for a new medium, boosting that story's extensions in various corporate investments in the process. Although *Frozen* received a mixed reception when it premiered, its association with Broadway reinforces its cultural legitimacy and value, helping to bolster the franchise's public visibility until *Frozen 2* (Chris Buck and Jennifer Lee, 2019) premiered. It also positions the show for a profitable afterlife from stage productions beyond Broadway. Disney does not report how much each Broadway show nets for the company, but any returns these shows generate for their respective franchises are merely icing on the cake when one considers the sheer number of videos, books, toys, and merchandise they help to sell.

In 2005, Jed Bernstein of the League of American Theaters and Producers remarked, "The two-way traffic between New York and Hollywood has been a fact of life since Hollywood was invented."[22] Amid the developments mentioned above, film and theatre—as media and as industries—remain closer than ever. Indeed, the COVID-19 pandemic shut Broadway down, but sent many theatremakers online to share their craft with audiences around the world. And yet as early as the 1930s, Broadway had voiced concern about the corrupting, corrosive nature of the film industry for poaching its talent and shifting its production practices and storytelling techniques. What we see with the emergence of globalized entertainment conglomerates is the ongoing convergence not only of two media but of mediated and unmediated forms. It is not just about the cinematization of theatre, but the theatricalization of cinema. As theatre becomes more standardized, replicable, and consistent, cinema displays the reflexivity, spontaneity, and intimacy of theatre. While entertainment conglomerates produce musical adaptation of their film properties, streaming services seek prestige and unique content for their platforms by producing proshot recordings of Broadway musicals.[23] Of course, this is not new. In Disney animated musicals, we see theatre talent staging integrated musicals while animators lean into the musical's defining artifice to demonstrate the flourishes and excesses that animation thrives upon. Much like a video cassette, a Disney theatrical production could offer—or at least attempt to offer—the very same experience on Broadway as on tour. The goal was not to see a major talent offer their take or to be challenged by innovative new work but to indulge in the combination of a beloved Disney story and surprising, spectacular stagecraft. It is the negotiated pleasure of contemporary commercial theatergoing: as ticket prices rise, ticket buyers, many of whom are tourists, want the safe surprises Disney theatrical entertainment can provide in combining the comfort of a recognizable storyline and the delight of stylization that enhances without deviating beyond what is familiar and acceptable for the presold audience.

It would be an obvious overstatement to claim that Broadway saved Disney. The company's theme parks and live-action filmmaking would have easily kept Disney solvent throughout this period. But theatrical talent, led by Ashman and Menken, provided the narrative techniques that allowed Disney to produce animated features that strengthened the brand and gave the division a competitive edge. To a certain degree, Ashman, Menken, Rice, Schneider, Schumacher, and Woolverton simply returned Disney to its roots through a renewed emphasis on storytelling, musical integration, and high production values. What was less clear at the time is how Disney's recruitment of theatre professionals created links between its films and Broadway musicals. Their labor helped enact industrial convergence that, in turn, helped expand Disney's investments while securing the company's finances and brands through diversification and synergy. Close attention to the efforts of creators who moved between entertainment industries uncovers how convergence operates in terms of not only technology, industry, and economics but also craft, labor, and individual media workers.

During his visit to Indiana University in 1987, Ashman was asked about the future of the theatre. He soberly observed that "the commercial musical theatre is evolving toward Disneyland—is evolving toward the $10 million dollar, highly mechanized, strictly Las Vegas–style production."[24] Ironically, the spectacular, heavily marketed, and widely reproduced musicals that Disney now produces on Broadway and the big screen could not be further from the intimate, small-scale musicals that Ashman and Menken started out writing in the 1970s. Ashman's careful attention to complex characterization, clever and thematically revealing lyrics, and tight, structured plots endures throughout Disney culture, be it in its animated films, theme park entertainment, or Broadway theatrical productions. In reviving Disney's historical investment in musical storytelling, Ashman and Menken, much like Team Disney, played a significant role in reviving the company itself. While *The Great Mouse Detective*, *Who Framed Roger Rabbit*, and *Oliver & Company* laid important groundwork, one can clearly see how *The Little Mermaid*, *Beauty and the Beast*, and *Aladdin* supplied invaluable franchise fodder, as those films' characters and music, in particular, have energized the company's efforts in film, television, theme park, music, and merchandising.

As Schumacher, president of the Disney Theatrical Group, has noted, the songs of Disney musicals now represent "the new American songbook. . . . We are this new era of Broadway."[25] Broadway abounds with franchised musicals, following Disney's lead to extend movie properties into theatrical productions that can begin on Broadway, tour the country and the world, and generate revenue in regional and amateur productions for years to come. In 2007, after 5,462 performances, *Beauty and the Beast* played its last performance at the Lunt-Fontanne Theatre—the same Broadway house where *Smile* had flopped twenty-one years earlier. Since then, Disney has produced a "live-action remake" of the 1991 film, which employed extensive digital animation, directed by Bill Condon and starring

Figure 10. The restored New Amsterdam Theatre, currently home to Disney Theatrical's production of *Aladdin*, is the crown jewel of a revitalized 42nd Street. Credit: Author's photograph.

Emma Watson. *Playbill* reports that *Beauty and the Beast* has been staged more often around the country than the top four musicals on Broadway combined.[26] Disney licenses condensed stage versions of its musicals for elementary and middle schools via its Disney JR. brand. In 2019, twenty-five years after *Beauty and the Beast* premiered at the Palace Theatre, Schumacher announced that he was preparing a Broadway revival, revised and reimagined for contemporary audiences.

No studio has done more for the film musical over the past forty years than Disney has, yet too often it has been omitted or downplayed in histories of the film and the stage musical.[27] And it only seems to be escalating its interest and investment in musical theatre storytelling. In 2019, Disney produced a live television adaptation of *The Little Mermaid*, starring *Moana* star Auli'i Cravalho as Ariel and Queen Latifah as Ursula.[28] With the launch of its own streaming service, Disney very much followed a trend it helped fuel in the first place. It acquired the live capture of *Hamilton* (Thomas Kail, 2020), produced *Better Nate Than Ever* (Tim Federle, 2022), and revived an ABC reality television series, *Encore!*, featuring the casts of high school musicals reuniting years later for a special encore performance. The stage adaptation of *Hercules* premiered in the Public Theater's Shakespeare in the Park series in 2019, and in 2022 plans were announced for it to be restaged during the 2022–2023 season at the Paper Mill Playhouse, the same theatre where the stage adaptation of *Newsies* got started a decade earlier.

In their attempts at diversification and brand saturation, media companies have more accurately become entertainment conglomerates, with investments in theme parks, cruise lines, real estate, retail stores, sports, and theatre. Sony, Time Warner, Fox, and Universal all have theatrical production units that have developed and produced shows with varying degrees of success. Sony, for example, coproduced Julie Taymor's disastrous 2010 musical *Spider-Man: Turn Off the Dark*, which ran for over two years and still lost $60 million for investors.[29] Yet when musicals succeed, the profit potential for the primary members of the creative team can also be quite high. As Schumacher observed, "A hit Broadway show, if you're a director, is vastly more lucrative than a hit Hollywood movie."[30] Consequently, it should come as no surprise that directors—Thomas Kail, Phyllida Lloyd, Sam Mendes, and George C. Wolfe, for example—move back and forth between industries.

Derek Johnson has called upon media industry scholars to note connections between media and "industries outside of the media sphere."[31] We also might consider how these "unmediated" forms and industries, of course, have long been mediated themselves.[32] Indeed, studying Disney theatre reveals a seeming contradiction: the role of "unmediated" culture in entertainment conglomerates so often associated with media as well as the mediated nature of live entertainment through amplification, the use of video and recorded sound elements, even the "mediation" of one's memory and familiarity. This (re)convergence happens not organically but through the work of creative laborers who ease these often rocky intersections. As such, media scholars must understand convergence as an economic, technological, and medial phenomenon that is inherently labor-driven. After all, in 2022, when Bob Iger took over Disney again in a stunning return, he issued a memo to employees that reaffirmed the centrality of creativity to the company's long-term stability: "I fundamentally believe that storytelling is what fuels this company, and it belongs at the center of how we organize our businesses."[33] How Disney tells stories is not just a creative decision, but an economic one as well. Therefore, the storytellers themselves and their craft are central to Disney's market value and financial viability.

Craft theory, in particular, provides a way of identifying, understanding, and appreciating the creative labor of film workers and, in this instance, tracing how such labor enables industrial convergence. As this study demonstrates, Ashman's knowledge of the integrated musical tradition afforded him creative and managerial authority at Disney animation while also emboldening and catalyzing the company's eventual turn to Broadway theatrical production on the global scale. Understanding his indebtedness to craft also encourages us to ground and temper popular evaluations of Ashman as a singular creative genius, focusing instead on how he worked within and through an established tradition. This reframing does not diminish his creative contribution but rather contextualizes it with consideration for the everyday realities of feature animation production. Ashman provides a node for examining Disney animation as a production culture and how authorship therein is negotiated, networked, and hierarchal. As such, *Staging a Comeback* has explained the operations of, changes to, and continuities within production cultures as these forms (musical, animation), crafts (theatremaking and animating), and industries (theatre and film) converged in the late 1980s and early 1990s—a period whose influence and importance continue to resonate today.

Revisiting an earlier turning point in the Disney's history also affords scholars the opportunity to examine the logics and decisions that fuel changes within conglomerates and the culture that they produce. Future research will hopefully consider the complex cultural politics behind the policies and practices, especially in terms of race, gender, class, and sexuality, that I have alluded to but have been unable to unpack here in depth. Scholars must continue to explore the role of site-specific entertainment (e.g., theme parks, theatre, concerts, cruises, sports) in Disney's corporate endeavors as well as the broader contextualization of the value of live entertainment for conglomerates generally perceived as media-oriented. An in-depth history surveying Broadway and Hollywood since 1970, when Robert McLaughlin's study concludes, would also help to complicate and enrich perceptions of media convergence, entertainment industries, and media itself. Additional studies in networked authorship, especially in animation, are required to challenge the long-standing investment in auteur-centered approaches. At the same time, examining individual contributions to conglomerate-produced culture focuses necessary attention on individual agency in a corporate structure that erases creative labor through branding. It also contextualizes how culture is defined, produced, and exploited throughout media history.

While this study tries to push media studies research forward by challenging certain assumptions about convergence, historiography, and even media ontology, it also has returned to some of the foundational concerns of our field. It has deliberately engaged in traditional analyses of authorship, genre, and adaptation to underscore its ongoing relevance to the field and to media industry studies in particular. Some may regard Broadway as a minor, niche industry, but its historical and continuing significance to the film and television industries remains undeniable. The recent trend of live musicals on broadcast television networks as well as the live casting of theatre to movie theaters bring the event logic of Broadway to screens across the country and around the world. In an age characterized by portability, increasing isolation, and on-demand culture, this underexamined return to real-time communal experiences underscores the importance of live entertainment for media conglomerates and for contemporary popular culture. In examining transitional moments in industrial history similar to this period, we can better position ourselves to understand and assess the status and future(s) of media culture and the industries that produce and distribute it.

Acknowledgments

This book has had a long, twisted journey, and I probably owe gratitude to more people than I could ever name here. I'll buy a drink for those beloved folks I've forgotten. I wanted to highlight some of the real champions who understood and supported this project from the very beginning. First and foremost, this project came out of the good fortune I had to work with Tom Schatz at the University of Texas at Austin. His guidance, questions (interrogations?), and strong editorial hand can be found in nearly every sentence herein. Alisa Perren has challenged me to think deeper, to explore wider, and to write more clearly. Her mentorship has been invaluable as well, dating back to a brief aside at the end of a 2015 meeting, where she said, "Why not write about Broadway?" I am grateful for the kindness and support of my other committee members, including Donna Kornhaber and Madhavi Mallapragada. And I must single out Donald Crafton for praise. Don responded to my random email asking him to come aboard, and he did so with generosity, insight, and good humor. I am grateful to be among the many film historians who have benefited from his kindness and erudition.

Graduate school is nothing without the support of good friends with a good sense of humor and a good appetite. Selena Dickey, Aubrey Plourde, and Tim Piper have become family; I owe them more than I can say here, but it's all love, admiration, and irritation. Ceci Moffett, you're the little sister I never wanted but always needed. Ramna Walia, Gejun Huang, Hogeun Seo, Laura Felschow, Kyle Wrather, Swapnil Rai, and Lesley Willard have been generous supporters with a snarky word and a sympathetic ear. I also have to thank those dear friends whom I haven't shaken in all these years since our Florida State days, especially Kilby Allen, Samantha Levy Arnold, Kimberly Bowers, Regina N. Bradley, Rose Bunch, Jack Canter, Martha McKay Canter, Rich Canter, Jared Champion, Matt Davis, Olivia Johnson Kelly, April McCray, Brooke Adams, D McKean, Taylor Murphy, Jacob Newberry, Scott Ortolano, Ashley Harris Paul, Lindsey Phillips, Mireille Rebeiz, Jillian Koopman Smith, Katrina Smith, V Wetlaufer, and Amanda Wicks.

And to Andrew Epstein, who directed my master's and first doctorate and has remained the mentor we should all aim to be now for almost twenty years.

This project is shamelessly promiscuous in its interests: adaptation, animation, children's culture, comedy, Disney, media history, media industry studies, and musical theatre. In the process of completing it, I have benefited from the brilliance, kindness, and generosity of a range of colleagues: Michelle Anya Anjirbag-Reeve, Sheri Chinen Biesen, Trevor Boffone, Gina Boldman, Noel Brown, Ryan Bunch, Kate Capshaw, Renee Camus, Llana Carroll, Wenhong Chen, Karen Coats, Olivia Cosentino, William V. Costanzo, Sarah Park Dahlen, Leigh Edwards, Rebekah Fitzsimmons, Tanya Goldman, Paige Gray, Viveca Greene, Julie Grossman, Marah Gubar, Heather Holian, Madeleine Hunter, Kelly Kessler, Jenny Kokai, Beck Krefting, Judith Yaross Lee, Stefania Marghitu, Marton Marko, Beth Marshall, Kyle Meikle, Michael Meindl, Mike Miley, Sabrina Mittermeier, Tracey Mollet, Danielle Fuentes Morgan, Golan Moskowitz, Robyn Muir, Susan Ohmer, Raúl Pérez, Leah Phillips, Allen Redmon, Tom Robson, Rebecca Rowe, Phil Scepanski, Matt Boyd Smith, Victoria Ford Smith, Joseph Michael Sommers, Gwen Athene Tarbox, Ebony Elizabeth Thomas, Yannis Tzioumakis, Alexandra Valint, Timothy J. Viator, Annette Wannamaker, Elizabeth L. Wollman, and Tracy Wuster. In particular, I must acknowledge my dear friends and favorite Facebook backchannelers, Naomi Hamer, Derritt Mason, Angel Daniel Matos, and Kate Slater. Coming up with you guys has been a blessing.

Special thanks must also be extended to folks who trudged through writing groups with me over the years, including Anna Reynolds Cooper, Selena Dickey, Britta Hanson, Joy Hayes, Amanda Konkle, Kirsten Leng, Colleen Montgomery, Erica Moulton, Timothy Piper, R. Colin Tait, Lesley Willard, Pamela Robertson Wojcik, and Kyle Wrather. I am especially grateful to Al Martin and Nora Patterson, whose friendship and support was invaluable through the final stages. And, of course, to Nathan Andersen and Christina Petersen, then Ana M. López, who gave me not only encouragement, but a job when the pandemic made my professional future seem uncertain. Furthermore, to my people at Tulane, especially Ava L'Herisse, thank you all for keeping me (mostly) sane. I feel so fortunate to call you my friends and colleagues.

Thank you to my correspondents, including Jeremy Gerard, Ann Hould-Ward, Doug Long, Rosie O'Donnell, Stephen Sondheim, and Maury Yeston. I especially appreciate the incredible opportunity to talk at length with Maureen Donley, Charlie Fink, Kathleen Gavin, Sarah Ashman Gillespie, Don Hahn, Bill Lauch, Bob McTyre, Alan Menken, Stan Meyer, Nancy Parent, Robert Jess Roth, George Scribner, Tom Sito, Gary Trousdale, Edith Vonnegut, and Linda Woolverton. Additional thanks to Sarah Ashman Gillespie, Sarah L. Douglas, and Rick Kunis for facilitating conversations. I also benefitted from the kindness and generosity of librarians, archivists, and assistants at the Beinecke Library, Billy Rose Theatre Division (New York Public Library), Harry Ransom Center (University of Texas at Austin), Howard Gotlieb Archival Research Center (Boston University), Jen Library (Savannah College of Art and Design), Library of Congress, Nabb Research

Center (Salisbury University), Rare Book & Manuscript Library (Columbia University), Theatre on Film and Tape Archive (New York Public Library), Writers Guild of America West, and Charles E. Young Research Library (University of California, Los Angeles). Primary research shouldn't be this much fun.

There are also people who obstructed, discouraged, and dismissed this project. I'll save their names for anyone who wants to buy me a drink at a conference. But I am grateful for the team at Rutgers University Press, especially Nicole Solano, who recognized the value of such a project and shepherded it to publication with good cheer. Additional thanks to Catherine Denning, Sarah Fitts, Jeremy Grainger, Brice Hammack, Kiely Schuck, and Michelle Witkowski. Joseph Dahm, the copy editor of this book, was incredibly helpful in rendering 300 pages of writing into a clear and comprehensible volume.

This was book was heavily revised and completed without course releases or a sabbatical. I say this to those who read this and are facing similar obstacles: Please persist. Your readers are waiting. And feel free to drop me a line at peter.c.kunze@gmail.com or @petecanttweet.

And, of course, I must thank my family and friends. My mom, my fiercest cheerleader from the beginning, and my brothers, who might be impressed if they cared what I do for a living. Much love to the Kunzes, Aiellos, Bakers, Blacks, Brenners, Bulickis, DiCamillos, and Magees. And for my new family, the Feldmans, including Robert, Diane, Daniel, and Betty. Kimberly Feldman came into my life right before the COVID-19 pandemic and saw me not only through that shitshow but through this one. I could not have finished this book without her love, her patience, and her sense of humor. She deserves pages and pages of gratitude. Instead, she'll have to settle for some measly sentences. Much love, of course, for my Deptford friends, including Eric and Kaila Giusini, Jennifer Rafter, Ron Ruddy, Lauren and Cody Silva, Kevan and Jessica Will, and Carlie and Jasmin Worden. Finally, my Rowan friends, including Elizabeth Lanahan, Christina Barbato Lukaszewicz, and Anthony and Diana Magaraci.

This book was in development hell for some time, and I lost two people who meant so much to me during it. One of them was Pauline Jonas, who introduced me to the best culture Philadelphia had to offer: theatre, fine arts, folk art, the symphony. Every child deserves a generous and loving guide to and through the arts. The other was my dad—my champion, my hero. I wish he were here to see this, even though he'd just use the book as a coaster or a doorstop. So it goes.

Notes

INTRODUCTION

1. I use "theatre" to refer to the art form and "theater" to refer to presentation/exhibition spaces.

2. Card Walker, quoted in Wayne Warga, "Disney Films: Chasing the Changing Times," *Los Angeles Times*, October 26, 1980, O36.

3. Lin-Manuel Miranda, quoted in Rebecca Rubin, "*Hamilton* Movie with Original Broadway Cast Coming to Theaters," *Variety*, February 3, 2020, https://variety.com/2020/film/news/hamilton-movie-lin-manuel-miranda-2-1203490645/.

4. Benj Pasek, quoted in Crystal Bell, "Songwriting Duo Pasek and Paul Say Disney Was Their 'Gateway Drug' to Musical Theater," *MTV News*, December 19, 2017, http://www.mtv.com/news/3054075/pasek-and-paul-live-action-aladdin-new-songs-alan-menken/.

5. Ashman also contributed lyrics to the opening song of *Oliver & Company*, while Tim Rice was brought on to *Aladdin* following Ashman's death to assist with additional songs, including "A Whole New World."

6. Disney Princess as a media franchise was not formalized until 2005.

7. *1993 Annual Report* (Burbank, CA: Walt Disney Company, 1993), 18.

8. Thomas Schatz, "Film Industry Studies and Hollywood History," in *Media Industries: History, Theory, and Method*, ed. Jennifer Holt and Alisa Perren (Malden, MA: Wiley-Blackwell, 2009), 45.

9. Charlie Fink, personal interview, March 1, 2022.

10. The major exceptions have been Don Hahn's documentaries, *Waking Sleeping Beauty* (2009) and *Howard* (2018). The former was a major inspiration for this study.

11. Michael Eisner, "Letter to Owners and Fellow Disney Employees," December 15, 1986, in *1986 Annual Report* (Burbank, CA: Walt Disney Company, 1986), 1.

12. David Landis and Jay McCormick, "Lotus Chief Leads in Pay; Top Execs' Pay Jumps 48% to $1.8M," *USA Today*, April 22, 1988.

13. James B. Stewart, *DisneyWar* (New York: Simon & Schuster, 2005), 105–106.

14. Michael D. Eisner, "To Our Owners and Fellow Employees," December 4, 1991, in *1991 Annual Report* (Burbank, CA: Walt Disney Company, 1991), 1.

15. Jason Sperb, "How (Not) to Teach Disney," *Journal of Film and Video* 70, no. 1 (Spring 2018): 50.

16. Christopher Anderson, *Hollywood TV: The Studio System in the Fifties* (Austin: University of Texas Press, 1994), 133–155.

17. Janet Wasko, *Understanding Disney: The Manufacture of Disney*, 2nd ed. (Malden, MA: Polity, 2020), 10.

18. John Taylor, *Storming the Magic Kingdom: Wall Street, the Raiders and the Battle for Disney* (New York: Knopf, 1987), 240.

19. Joe Flower, *Prince of the Magic Kingdom: Michael Eisner and the Re-making of Disney* (New York: John Wiley, 1991), 298.

20. In media scholarship on Disney, Sean Griffin and John Wills have credited Eisner as the leader, whereas Douglas Gomery favors Eisner and Wells (but acknowledges Katzenberg), Thomas Schatz focuses on Eisner, Wells, and Katzenberg, and Janet Wasko points to "Team Disney" more broadly. And Eric Smoodin notes a renaissance in animation taking place across the film industry including but also beyond Disney. See John Willis, *Disney Culture* (New Brunswick, NJ: Rutgers University Press, 2017), 20; Sean Griffin, *Tinker Belles and Evil Queens: The Walt Disney Company from the Inside Out* (New York: New York University Press, 2000), xv; Douglas Gomery, "Disney's Business History: A Reinterpretation," in *Disney Discourse: Producing the Magic Kingdom*, ed. Eric Smoodin (New York: Routledge, 1994), 79–84; Thomas Schatz, "The Studio System and Conglomerate Hollywood," in *The Contemporary Hollywood Film Industry*, ed. Paul McDonald and Janet Wasko (Malden, MA: Wiley-Blackwell, 2008), 23; Wasko, *Understanding Disney*, 34–37; and Eric Smoodin, *Animating Culture: Hollywood Cartoons from the Sound Era* (New Brunswick, NJ: Rutgers University Press, 1993), 188.

21. For example, Janet Wasko allots Disney's theatre operations two paragraphs in her book-length study of the company. See Wasko, *Understanding Disney*, 54–55.

22. Janet Staiger and Sabine Hake, "Preface," in *Convergence Media History*, ed. Janet Staiger and Sabine Hake (New York: Routledge, 2009), ix.

23. Mark Williams, "Rewiring Media History: Intermedia Borders," in Staiger and Hake, *Convergence Media History*, 46.

24. Cari McDonnell, "Genre Theory and the Film Musical," in *The Oxford Handbook of Film Music Studies*, ed. David Neumeyer (New York: Oxford University Press, 2014), 264.

25. David Savran, "Toward a Historiography of the Popular," *Theatre Survey* 45, no. 2 (November 2004): 213.

26. Michele Hilmes, "Nailing Mercury: The Problem of Media Industry Historiography," in Holt and Perren, *Media Industries*, 27.

27. Jennifer Holt, *Empires of Entertainment: Media Industries and the Politics of Deregulation, 1980–1996* (New Brunswick, NJ: Rutgers University Press, 2011), 7.

28. Philip Auslander, *Liveness: Performance in a Mediatized Culture*, 2nd ed. (New York: Routledge, 2008), 34.

29. Jonathan Burston, "Spectacle, Synergy, and Megamusicals: The Global-Industrialisation of Live-Theatrical Production," in *Media Organisations in Society*, ed. James Curran (London: Arnold, 2000), 77.

30. David Saltz, "Media, Technology, and Performance," *Theatre Journal* 65, no. 3 (January 2013): 421–432, and Gary Giesekam, *Staging the Screen: The Use of Film and Video in Theatre* (New York: Palgrave Macmillan, 2007).

31. Sarah Bay-Cheng, "Theater Is Media: Some Principles for a Digital Historiography of Performance," *Theater* 42, no. 2 (2012): 27–41; Martin Harries, "Theater and Media before 'New Media': Beckett's *Film* and *Play*," *Theater* 42, no. 2 (2012): 7–25; and Christopher Balme, "Surrogate Stages: Theatre, Performance, and the Challenge of New Media," *Performance Research* 13, no. 2 (2008): 80–91.

32. Vsevolod Pudovkin, *Film Technique and Film Acting: The Cinema Writings of V. I. Pudovkin*, trans. Ivor Montagu (London: Vision, 1954); Erwin Panofsky, "Style and Medium in the Motion Pictures," in *Three Essays on Style*, by Erwin Panofsky, ed. Irving Lavin (Cambridge, MA: MIT Press, 1997); André Bazin, "Theater and Cinema," in *What Is Cinema?*, vol. 1, by André Bazin, trans. Hugh Gray (Berkeley: University of California Press, 1967), 76–124; Susan Sontag, "Film and Theatre," *Tulane Drama Review* 11, no. 1 (Autumn 1966): 24–37.

33. See, for example, Ben Brewster and Lea Jacobs, *Theatre to Cinema: Stage Pictorialism and the Early Feature Film* (New York: Oxford University Press, 1998).

34. See, for example, Vincent Longo, "Multimedia Magic in *Around the World*: Orson Welles's Film-and-Theater Hybrid," in *Orson Welles in Focus: Texts and Contexts*, ed. James N. Gilmore and Sidney Gottlieb (Bloomington: Indiana University Press, 2018), 150–175, and Peter C. Kunze, "Belles Are Singing: Broadway, Hollywood, and the Failed *Gone with the Wind* Musical," *Historical Journal of Film, Radio and Television* 38, no. 4 (2018): 787–807.

35. Robert McLaughlin, *Broadway and Hollywood: A History of Economic Interaction* (New York: Arno, 1974).

36. Burston, "Spectacle, Synergy, and Megamusicals"; Laura E. Felschow, "Broadway Is a Two-Way Street: Integrating Hollywood Distribution and Exhibition," *Media Industries* 6, no. 1 (2019): 21–42; Kelly Kessler, *Broadway in the Box: Television's Lasting Love Affair with the Musical* (New York: Oxford University Press, 2020).

37. In September 2019, I requested permission to visit the Disney Archives in Burbank to research the influence of Broadway on the company. In March 2020, I received a letter from a Disney legal representative declining my request "because of our increasing internal demands."

38. See, for example, Amy S. Osatinski, *Disney Theatrical Productions: Producing Broadway Musicals the Disney Way* (New York: Routledge, 2019). It is done, in part, in Alex Bádue and Rebecca S. Schorsch, "Animated Broadway: Disney and Musical Theater in the 1990s and Early 2000s," *American Music* 39, no. 2 (2021): 212–225.

39. For more on Disney's theatrical adaptations for child performers, see Stacy E. Wolf, "Not Only on Broadway: Disney JR. and Disney KIDS Across the USA," in *The Disney Musical on Stage and Screen: Critical Approaches from "Snow White" to "Frozen,"* ed. George Rodosthenous (New York: Bloomsbury, 2017), 133–154.

40. Eric Smoodin, "Introduction: How to Read Walt Disney," in Smoodin, *Disney Discourse*, 19.

41. Donald Crafton, personal communication, November 4, 2016.

42. Peter Schneider, in Laura Muşat, "Interview with Peter Schneider, First CEO of Disney Animation," *Films in Frame*, September 15, 2019, https://www.filmsinframe.com/en/interviews/interview-with-peter-schneider-first-ceo-of-disney-animation/. Note: Schneider was president, not CEO, of Disney Animation.

43. Gary Trousdale, personal correspondence, September 18, 2022.

44. John Thornton Caldwell, *Production Culture: Industrial Reflexivity and Critical Practice in Film and Television* (Durham, NC: Duke University Press, 2008), 199.

45. Peter Schneider, in "Studio Approaches to Story: A Conversation among John Canemaker, Bill Pete, Joe Ranft, Jerry Rees and Peter Schneider," in *Storytelling in Animation*, ed. John Canemaker (Los Angeles: American Film Institute, 1988), 75.

46. Kathleen Gavin, personal interview, April 14, 2022.

47. Donald Crafton, *Shadow of a Mouse: Performance, Belief, and World-Making in Animation* (Berkeley: University of California Press, 2013), 22, emphasis in original.

48. Thomas Schumacher, quoted in Richard Turner, "Jungle Fever: Disney, Using Cash and Claw, Stays King of Animated Movies," *Wall Street Journal*, May 16, 1994, A8.

49. Maureen Donley, personal interview, February 18, 2022.

50. Douglas Gomery warns against such historiographical approaches in "Disney's Business History."

51. Cynthia Erb, "Another World or the World of an Other? The Space of Romance in Recent Versions of *Beauty and the Beast*," *Cinema Journal* 34, no. 4 (Summer 1995): 50–70; Griffin, *Tinker Belles and Evil Queens*, 143–152; and Sam Baltimore, "Ashman's *Aladdin* Archive: Queer Orientalism in the Disney Renaissance," in Rodosthenous, *Disney Musical on Stage and Screen*, 205–220.

52. Hilmes, "Nailing Mercury," 26.

53. Hilmes, "Nailing Mercury," 22.

54. Schatz, "Film Industry Studies and Hollywood History," 50.

55. Schatz, "Film Industry Studies and Hollywood History," 46.

56. Although there are a number of studies of Disney music during the Walt years, including Daniel Goldmark's *Tunes for 'Toons: Music and the Hollywood Cartoon* (Berkeley: University of California Press, 2005) and James Bohn's *Music in Disney's Animated Features: Snow White and the Seven Dwarfs to The Jungle Book* (Jackson: University Press of Mississippi, 2018), there are few musicological works examining Disney music during and after the Renaissance. Consult, for instance, Rebecca Coyle and Jon Fitzgerald, "Disney Does Broadway: Musical Storytelling in *The Little Mermaid* and *The Lion King*," in *Drawn to Sound: Animation Film Music and Sonicity*, ed. Rebecca Coyle (London: Equinox, 2010), 191–208, and several of the chapters in Rodosthenous, *Disney Musical on Stage and Screen*.

57. See, for example, Michele Hilmes, *Hollywood and Broadcasting: From Radio to Cable* (Urbana: University of Illinois Press, 1990), and Thomas Schatz, *The Genius of the System: Hollywood Filmmaking in the Studio Era* (New York: Pantheon, 1989).

58. Alisa Perren, *Indie, Inc: Miramax and the Transformation of Hollywood in the 1990s* (Austin: University of Texas Press, 2012), 5.

59. There is a thorny distinction to be made between arts and crafts, as explored by Howard S. Becker in *Art Worlds*, 25th anniversary ed. (Berkeley: University of California Press, 2008).

60. John Thornton Caldwell, "Screen Studies and Industrial 'Theorizing,'" *Screen* 50, no. 1 (Spring 2009): 167–168.

61. Caldwell, *Production Culture*, 5. What I mean by "craft theory" may be similar to what Caldwell calls "industrial aesthetic theory" (6); unfortunately, he does not go on to theorize it thereafter.

62. Lehman Engel, *The American Musical Theater*, rev. ed. (New York: Collier, 1975), 37.

63. Lehman Engel, *Words with Music* (New York: Macmillan, 1972), 1.

64. Engel, *Words with Music*, 13.

65. Engel, *Words with Music*, 19.

66. Engel, *Words with Music*, 81.

67. Engel, *Words with Music*, 61.

68. Engel, *Words with Music*, 75, 152.

69. Engel, *Words with Music*, 116.

70. Alan Menken in "A Friend Like Me: Alan Menken on Howard Ashman and the Rebirth of the Film Musical," in *Knowing the Score: Film Composers Talk about the Art, Craft, Blood, Sweat, and Tears of Writing for Cinema*, by David Morgan (New York: Harper-Collins, 2000), 114.

71. For more on this lecture, see *Waking Sleeping Beauty*, DVD, directed by Don Hahn (2009; Burbank, CA: Walt Disney Studios Home Entertainment, 2010).

72. Andrew Stanton, "The Clues to a Great Story," *TED* video, 19:10, February 2012, https://www.ted.com/talks/andrew_stanton_the_clues_to_a_great_story.

73. Richard Wagner, "The Art-Work of the Future," in *The Art-Work of the Future and Other Works*, trans. William Ashton Ellis (Lincoln: University of Nebraska Press, 1993), 184; emphasis in original.

74. Theodor Adorno, "Music Drama," in *In Search of Wagner*, trans. Rodney Livingstone (New York: Verso, 2009), 86–102.

75. Bradley Rogers, "The Interpellations of Interpolation; or, The Disintegrating Female Musical Body," *Camera Obscura* 23, no. 1 (2009): 98.

76. Matthew Wilson Smith, *The Total Work of Art from Bayreuth to Cyberspace* (New York: Routledge 2007): 10.

77. Andrea Most, *Making Americans: Jews and the Broadway Musical* (Cambridge, MA: Harvard University Press, 2004), 9–11. We also must note Wagner's anti-Semitism and how it connects to *Gesamtkunstwerk*; see Smith, *The Total Work of Art*, 18.

78. While the point about commodification is my own, the overall contention about the musical in this sentence comes from Anne Anlin Cheng, *The Melancholy of Race: Psychoanalysis, Assimilation, and Hidden Grief* (New York: Oxford University Press, 2001), 42.

79. Steven Watts, *The Magic Kingdom: Walt Disney and the American Way of Life* (Columbia: University of Missouri Press, 1997), 108.

80. Anderson, *Hollywood TV*, 155, and Smith, *The Total Work of Art from Bayreuth to Cyberspace*, 114–133.

81. Wilfred Jackson, quoted in Neal Gabler, *Walt Disney: The Triumph of the American Imagination* (New York: Vintage, 2006), 127.

82. Jerome Kern, quoted in John Culhane, "*Snow White* at 50: Undimmed Magic," *New York Times*, July 12, 1987, H31.

83. For recent attempts to situate *Snow White* within the film and stage musical, consult Sadeen Elyas, "With a Smile and a Song: *Snow White and the Seven Dwarfs* as the First Integrated Musical," in *Snow White and the Seven Dwarfs: New Perspectives on Production, Reception, and Legacy*, ed. Chris Pallant and Christopher Holliday (New York: Bloomsbury, 2021), 117–132, and Daniel Batchelder, "*Snow White* and the Seventh Art: Sound, Song, and Respectability in Disney's First Feature," *American Music* 39, no. 2 (2021): 138–153.

84. See, for example, Susan Smith, "The Animated Film Musical," in *The Oxford Handbook of the American Musical*, ed. Raymond Knapp, Mitchell Morris, and Stacy Wolf (New York: Oxford University Press, 2011), 167–178, as well as Rodosthenous, *Disney Musical on Stage and Screen*.

85. John Mueller, "Fred Astaire and the Integrated Musical," *Cinema Journal* 24, no. 1 (Autumn 1984): 30.

86. Geoffrey Block, "Integration," in Knapp, Morris, and Wolf, *Oxford Handbook of the American Musical*, 98–99.

87. Lehman Engel, *The Making of a Musical: Creating Songs for the Stage* (New York: Macmillan, 1977), 1.

88. Alan Menken, personal interview, March 29, 2022.

89. Mueller, "Fred Astaire and the Integrated Musical."

90. Stacy Wolf, *Changed for Good: A Feminist History of the Broadway Musical* (New York: Oxford University Press, 2011), 9.

91. For example, see Alisa Roost, "Before *Oklahoma!* A Reappraisal of Musical Theatre during the 1930s," *Journal of American Drama and Theatre* 16, no. 1 (Winter 2004): 1–35, and Savran, "Toward a Historiography of the Popular," 211–217.

92. Richard Rodgers, quoted in Block, "Integration," 103.

93. Block, "Integration," 101.

94. Engel, *Making of a Musical*, xii.

95. Margaret M. Knapp, "Integration of Elements as a Viable Standard for Judging Musical Theatre," *Journal of American Culture* 1, no. 1 (Spring 1978): 114–115.

96. Millie Taylor, *Musical Theatre, Realism and Entertainment* (New York: Routledge, 2016), 4.

97. Scott McMillin, *The Musical as Drama* (Princeton, NJ: Princeton University Press, 2006), 2.

98. McMillin, *Musical as Drama*, 6.

99. Rick Altman, *The American Film Musical* (Bloomington: Indiana University Press, 1987), 115.

100. Alan Menken, quoted in Harry Haun, "Songwriting Duo Makes Big Splash with Latest Dip into Film, *Mermaid*," *New York Daily News*, December 15, 1989, Factiva.

101. For more on school productions of Disney musicals, see Stacy Wolf, *Beyond Broadway: The Pleasure and Promise of Musical Theatre across America* (New York: Oxford University Press, 2020), 249–277.

102. Logan Culwell-Block, "The 10 Most-Produced High School Plays and Musicals of 2021–2022," *Playbill*, June 7, 2022, https://playbill.com/article/the-10-most-produced-high-school-plays-and-musicals-of-2021-2022.

103. Alan Menken, in 92nd Street Y, "Disney+'s *Howard*: Don Hahn, Alan Menken, Paige O'Hara, Jodi Benson, Bill Lauch, and Sarah Gillespie," YouTube video, 1:00:56, August 19, 2020, https://www.youtube.com/watch?v=PIDOoKpMNrM.

104. Tim Donahue and Jim Patterson, *Stage Money: The Business of the Professional Theater* (Columbia: University of South Carolina, 2010), 4.

105. Thomas Schumacher, quoted in Steven Adler, *On Broadway: Art and Commerce on the Great White Way* (Carbondale: Southern Illinois University Press, 2004), 75.

106. Anderson, *Hollywood TV*, 134.

CHAPTER 1 — "JUST WAITING FOR THE PRINCE TO ARRIVE"

1. Chris Pallant, *Demystifying Disney: A History of Disney Feature Animation* (New York: Continuum, 2011), 89.

2. Maureen Furniss, *A New History of Animation* (New York: Thames & Hudson, 2016), 338–351.

3. Sam Baltimore, "Ashman's *Aladdin* Archive: Queer Orientalism in the Disney Renaissance," in *The Disney Musical on Stage and Screen: Critical Approaches from "Snow White" to "Frozen*," ed. George Rodothenous (New York: Bloomsbury Metheun Drama, 2017), 205.

4. Jessica Sternfeld clearly defines the "megamusical" in the introduction to her monograph, *The Megamusical* (Bloomington: Indiana University Press, 2006), 1–7.

5. Frank Rich, "A Detour in the Theater That No One Predicted," *New York Times*, October 18, 1998, AR7.

6. David Savran, "The Do-Re-Mi of Musical Theatre Historiography," in *Changing the Subject: Marvin Carlson and Theatre Studies 1959–2009*, ed. Joseph Roach (Ann Arbor: University of Michigan Press, 2009), 224.

7. Leonard Sloane, "What Makes the Broadway Angels Take the Plunge?," *New York Times*, September 18, 1977, D9.

8. Timothy R. White, *Blue-Collar Broadway: The Craft and Industry of Broadway* (Philadelphia: University of Pennsylvania Press, 2015), 3–5.

9. William J. Baumol and Hilda Baumol, "The Impact of Broadway Theatre on the Economy of New York City," in *Baumol's Cost Disease: The Arts and Other Victims*, by William J. Baumol, ed. Ruth Towse (Cheltenham, UK: Edward Elgar, 1997), 338–339.

10. Stacy Wolf, *Changed for Good: A Feminist History of the Broadway Musical* (New York: Oxford University Press, 2011), 92.

11. Elizabeth L. Wollman, *The Theater Will Rock: A History of the Rock Musical, from Hair to Hedwig* (Ann Arbor: University of Michigan Press, 2006), 100.

12. Harold C. Schonberg, "The Surrender of Broadway to Amplified Sound," *New York Times*, March 15, 1981, D1.

13. David Mamet, "Against Amplification," in *Writing in Restaurants* (New York: Penguin, 1987), 135.

14. See Jonathan Burston, "Theatre Space as Virtual Place: Audio Technology, the Reconfigured Singing Body, and the Megamusical," *Popular Music* 17, no. 2 (May 1998): 205–218.

15. Philip Auslander, *Liveness: Performance in a Mediatized Culture*, 2nd ed. (New York: Routledge, 2008), 56.

16. Mel Gussow, "Broadway Will Be Booming with Drama," *New York Times*, August 29, 1976, 61.

17. Geoffrey Holder and Bernard Jacobs, quoted in Leticia Kent, "On Broadway, the Spectacle's the Thing," *New York Times*, March 12, 1978, D1.

18. This sentiment is commonly echoed in articles of the time, though Milton Friedman argued that the quality of the entertainment had a greater impact than the state of economic affairs. See Leonard Sloane, "What Keeps Broadway: Behind the Theater Boom," *New York Times*, May 11, 1980, D8.

19. John Houseman, quoted in Sloane, "What Keeps Broadway," D8.

20. Edith Vonnegut, personal interview, August 5, 2022.

21. Sandra Salmans, "Broadway Lures the Corporate Angel," *New York Times*, October 31, 1982.

22. Tom Wilhite, quoted in Aljean Harmetz, "Disney Backs Second Stage Production," *New York Times*, April 1, 1983, C8.

23. Barry Diller, quoted in Aljean Harmetz, "Hollywood Shivers in a Crisis of Confidence," *New York Times*, December 20, 1981, D1.

24. Harmetz, "Hollywood Shivers," D1.

25. Michael Eisner, quoted in Aljean Harmetz, "Hollywood Shaken by *Heaven's Gate*," *New York Times*, November 22, 1980, 12.

26. "Business Bulletin," *Wall Street Journal*, February 7, 1980, 1.

27. Eddie Kalish, quoted in Dale Pollock, "Hollywood Hoping for a Biggie in Santa's Bag," *Los Angeles Times*, December 18, 1981, J6.

28. Nick Galluccio, "The Last Great Dream," *Forbes*, May 11, 1981, 87.

29. Tom Wilhite, quoted in Wayne Warga, "Disney Films: Chasing the Changing Times," *Los Angeles Times*, October 26, 1980, O37.

30. William R. Yates, quoted in Jerry Buck, "Disney Studios: Back to the Drawing Board," *Sun*, February 24, 1980, TV4.

31. Leslie Wayne, "Hollywood Sequels Are Just the Ticket," *New York Times*, July 18, 1982, F1.

32. Ron W. Miller, quoted in John Culhane, "The Old Disney Magic," *New York Times*, August 1, 1976, 32.

33. Sara Terry, "Disney School for Animators—Keeping Legendary Skills Alive," *Christian Science Monitor*, July 31, 1981, 6.

34. Aljean Harmetz, "Disney Incubating New Artists," *New York Times*, July 27, 1978, C13.

35. Charles Champlin, "Smoke, But No Fire in *Dragon*," *Los Angeles Times*, December 16, 1977, J22–J23.

36. Eric Larson, quoted in Wayne Warga, "Disney's Endangered Species," *Los Angeles Times*, July 2, 1978, N25.

37. Clay Kaytis, "John Musker (b, 1953) and Ron Clements (b, 1953)," in *Walt's People*, vol. 5, ed. Didier Ghez (Bloomington, IN: Xlibris, 2008), 403.

38. Ron Miller, quoted in Aljean Harmetz, "11 Animators Quit Disney, Form Studio," *New York Times*, September 20, 1979, C14.

39. Ron Miller, quoted in "The Rebel Nibbling at Disney's World," *Fortune*, October 4, 1982, 68.

40. Eric Larson, quoted in Harmetz, "11 Animators Quit Disney," C14.

41. Ed Hansen, quoted in Andrew J. Neff, "Two Disney Animators Ankle for Bluth," *Daily Variety*, November 16, 1979, 16.

42. Ed Hansen, quoted in Aljean Harmetz, "Animation Again a Priority at Disney," *New York Times*, August 27, 1984, C11.

43. Bill Mechanic, quoted in Don Bluth, *Somewhere Out There: My Animated Life* (Dallas, TX: BenBella Books, 2022), 214.

44. Pamela G. Hollie, "Animators' Loss Shakes Disney," *New York Times*, October 10, 1979, D1.

45. Hollie, "Animators' Loss Shakes Disney," D1.

46. Ron W. Miller, quoted in Sally Ogle Davis, "Wishing Upon a Falling Star at Disney," *New York Times*, November 16, 1980, 148.

47. David Ehrman, quoted in Warga, "Disney Films," O37.

48. Tom Wilhite, quoted in Charles Solomon, "Will the Real Walt Disney Please Stand Up?," *Film Comment*, July/August 1982, 51.

49. Solomon, "Will the Real Walt Disney Please Stand Up?," 53.

50. *The Secret of NIMH* Press Kit, James Welsh Collection, Nabb Research Center, Salisbury University, Salisbury, MD.

51. *Secret of NIMH* Press Kit.

52. "Bluth Completes Cartoon Feature," *Variety*, May 19, 1982, 34.

53. Don Bluth, quoted in Howard Reich, "Don Bluth Quit Disney—to Make Disney-Style Films," *Chicago Tribune*, July 11, 1982, D8.

54. Reich, "Don Bluth Quit Disney."

55. Richard Irvine, quoted in Aljean Harmetz, "Ex-Disney Animators Try to Outdo Their Mentor," *New York Times*, July 14, 1982, C17.

56. Sheila Benson, "*NIMH*: A Mixture of Genres," *Los Angeles Times*, July 2, 1982, H1.

57. Benson, "*NIMH*," H14.

58. Roger Ebert, review of *The Secret of NIMH*, January 1, 1982, https://www.rogerebert.com/reviews/the-secret-of-nimh-1982.

59. Vincent Canby, "*N.I.M.H.*, Shades of Disney's Golden Era," *New York Times*, July 30, 1982, C12.

60. Gerald Duchovnay, "Don Bluth," in *Film Voices: Interviews from Post Script*, ed. Gerald Duchovnay (Albany: State University of New York Press, 2004), 150.

61. Animation historians tend to focus almost exclusively on features, but Tom Sito includes chapters on gaming and special effects in *Moving Innovation: A History of Computer Animation* (Cambridge, MA: MIT Press, 2013).

62. "WCI Completes Atari Stock and Debt Acquisition," *Daily Variety*, October 5, 1976, 6.

63. Stephanie Chavez, "Movie Studios Enter Video Game Battles," *Los Angeles Times*, June 8, 1982, E1.

64. Aljean Harmetz, "Video Games Go to Hollywood," *New York Times*, July 1, 1982, D1.

65. Harmetz, "Video Games Go to Hollywood," D4.

66. Kathryn Harris, "Video Games: Is It Too Late to Play?," *Los Angeles Times*, November 21, 1982, F16.

67. Carly Kocurek, *Coin-Operated Americans: Rebooting Boyhood at the Video Game Arcade* (Minneapolis: University of Minnesota Press, 2015), 117.

68. Of course, Disney—specifically Walt Disney—had been a pioneer in television, producing *Disneyland* for ABC so as to gain the necessary funding for Disneyland. See Christopher Anderson's *Hollywood TV* (Austin: University of Texas Press, 1994).

69. Warga, "Disney Films," 37.

70. Sito, *Moving Innovation*, 160. Wilhite was particularly referring to films like *20,000 Leagues Under the Sea* (Richard Fleischer, 1954) and *Mary Poppins*, both successful fantasy films for the company under Walt Disney.

71. Marsha Kinder, *Playing with Power in Movies, Television, and Video Games: From Muppet Babies to Teenage Mutant Ninja Turtles* (Berkeley: University of California Press, 1991), 129.

72. Steven Lisberger, quoted in Lawrence O'Toole, "'Prince' Lisberger Waking Disney Up," *Globe and Mail*, July 16, 1982, E1.

73. Bill Kroyer, quoted in Peter Sørensen, "Tronic Imagery," *Cinefex* 8 (1982): 35.

74. Bruce Boxleitner, quoted in Glenn Lovell, "Programmers Are Heroes in Disney Computer Caper," *Sun*, July 19, 1981, D12.

75. "Stock Decline after Screening of *TRON* Irks Disney Studio," *New York Times*, July 9, 1982, C8.

76. David Sterritt, "Walt Disney's *Tron*, the Ultimate Computer Movie," *Christian Science Monitor*, July 15, 1982, 18.

77. Sheila Benson, "High-Tech *TRON*: All the Lines," *Los Angeles Times*, July 9, 1982, G1.

78. "Stock Decline," C8.

79. James B. Stewart, *DisneyWar* (New York: Simon & Schuster, 2005), 45.

80. Harmetz, "Video Games Go to Hollywood," D4.

81. Beth Ann Krier, "Whither the Video-Game Industry?" *Los Angeles Times*, March 11, 1983, I8.

82. Mark J. P. Wolf, "The Video Game Industry Crash," in *The Video Game Explosion: A History from Pong to Playstation and Beyond*, ed. Mark J. P. Wolf (Westport, CT: Greenwood, 2008), 105.

83. Martin Picard, "Video Games and Their Relationship with Other Media," in *The Video Game Explosion*, 294.

84. Mel Gussow, "Musical: A Cactus Owns *Little Shop of Horrors*," *New York Times*, May 30, 1982, 47.

85. Thank you to Dominic Broomfield-McHugh for this example.

86. Dan Scapperotti, "The Off-Broadway Hit," *Cinefantastique*, January 1987, 23.

87. Bill Lauch, personal interview, February 28, 2022.

88. Howard Ashman, quoted by Alan Menken, in Zina Goldrich, "Alan Menken: On His Lyricists," *Dramatist* 7, no. 6 (July/August 2005): 36.

89. Adam Abraham, *Attack of the Monster Musical: A Cultural History of Little Shop of Horrors* (New York: Methuen Drama, 2022), 23–26.

90. Howard Ashman and Ira Weitzman, *Anything Goes*, WBAI, New York, n.d., Howard Ashman Papers, Music Division, Library of Congress, Washington, DC.

91. Bill Lauch, personal interview, February 28, 2022.

92. Howard Ashman, quoted in Janice Arkatov, "Man-Eating Plant Hopes to Capture Los Angeles," *Los Angeles Times*, April 25, 1983, G3.

93. Walter Kerr, "*Little Shop of Horrors* and the Terror of Special Effects," *New York Times*, August 22, 1982, H3.

94. Kerr, "*Little Shop of Horrors*," H15.

95. Kerr, "*Little Shop of Horrors*," H15.

96. Gussow, "Musical," 47.

97. Burt A. Folkart, "Howard Ashman; Oscar-Winning Lyricist," *Los Angeles Times*, March 15, 1991, VCA32.

98. Valerie Eliot, quoted in "What's a Jellicle Cat? The Making of *Cats: The Video*," in *Cats*, dir. David Mallet (PolyGram Video, 1998), DVD (Universal, 2000).

99. "What's a Jellicle Cat?"

100. Ironically, "Memory" is the most popular song in the show but is not based on a poem in *Practical Cats*. The lyrics were largely written by *Cats* director Trevor Nunn, inspired by Eliot's poem "Rhapsody on a Windy Night."

101. Valerie Eliot, quoted in "What's a Jellicle Cat?"

102. Robert Brustein, "This 'Money-Got, Mechanic Age,'" *New Republic*, November 15, 1982, 23.

103. Stephen Sondheim, quoted in Stephen Citron, *Sondheim and Lloyd-Webber: The New Musical* (New York: Oxford University Press, 2001), 277.

104. Justin Wyatt, *High Concept: Movies and Marketing in Hollywood* (Austin: University of Texas Press, 1994), 13.

105. Gillian Lynne, quoted in Jack Kroll with Constance Guthrie, "The *Cats* Meow on Broadway," *Newsweek*, October 11, 1982, 80.

106. Lorin Maazel, quoted in John Rockwell, "Andrew Lloyd Webber: Superstar," *New York Times Magazine*, December 20, 1987, 71.

107. Steven Adler, *On Broadway: Art and Commerce on the Great White Way* (Carbondale: Southern Illinois University Press, 2004), 12.

108. Frank Rich, "Theater: Lloyd Webber's *Cats*," *New York Times*, October 8, 1982, C3.

109. Rich, "Theater."

110. *New York Times* drama critic Frank Rich linked the success of *Cats* to the later success of Julie Taymor's *The Lion King* in *Hot Seat: Theater Criticism for the New York Times, 1980–1993* (New York: Random House, 1998), 179.

111. Maureen Donley, personal interview, February 28, 2022.

112. Consult Jonathan Burston, "Spectacle, Synergy, and Megamusicals: The Global-Industrialisation of Live-Theatrical Production," in *Media Organisations in Society*, ed. James Curran (London: Arnold, 2000).

CHAPTER 2 — "SORT OF LIKE THE SOPRANOS TOOK OVER THE STUDIO"

1. Thomas C. Hayes, "Steinberg Sells Stake to Disney," *New York Times*, June 12, 1984, D1.

2. Aljean Harmetz, "Disney Hopes Eisner Can Wake Sleeping Beauty," *New York Times*, October 17, 1984, C20.

3. Michael Eisner, quoted in Thomas C. Hayes, "New Disney Team's Strategy: Emphasis Put on Film Unit," *New York Times*, September 24, 1984, D5.

4. Michael Eisner, quoted in Harmetz, "Disney Hopes," C20.

5. See, for example, Chris Pallant, *Demystifying Disney: A History of Disney Feature Animation* (New York: Continuum, 2011), 80.

6. Michael D. Eisner, "To Our Owners and Fellow Disney Employees," December 4, 1989, in *1989 Annual Report* (Burbank, CA: Walt Disney Company, 1989), 4.

7. Ron W. Miller, quoted in Thomas C. Hayes, "Fanfare as Disney Opens Park: But Company Has Troubles," *New York Times*, October 2, 1982, 34.

8. Richard Berger, quoted in Dale Pollock, "New Disney Productions Team Gets Off the Fence," *Los Angeles Times*, April 25, 1983, G2.

9. Lisa Belkin, "Life On and Off Ice at *Disney's Magic Kingdom*," *New York Times*, August 19, 1983, C13.

10. Stephen Godfrey, "Playboy and Disney Successes Discussed at Trade Forum TV Sale of Bunny and Mouse," *Globe and Mail*, September 14, 1983, P18.

11. Peter C. Kunze, "Stay Tuned: A Political History of Saturday Morning Cartoons," in *A Companion to Children's Literature*, ed. Karen Coats, Deborah Stevenson, and Vivian Yenika-Agbaw (Hoboken, NJ: John Wiley, 2022), 105–117.

12. Bob Keeshan, quoted in Ernest Holsendolph, "Are Children No Longer in the Programming Picture?," *New York Times*, July 25, 1982, H21.

13. Steve Knoll, "The Disney Channel Has an Expensive First Year," *New York Times*, April 29, 1984, H28.

14. Thomas C. Hayes, "The Troubled World of Walt Disney Productions," *New York Times*, September 25, 1983, F1.

15. Ray Loynd, "Wilhite Quits as Prod'n V.P. of Disney Pix," *Daily Variety*, November 7, 1983, 11.

16. "Introducing Touchstone Films," *Daily Variety*, February 24, 1984, 9.

17. Gary Putka, "Disney's Recent Buoyancy Tied to Assets Value by Some Who See a Ripeness for Takeover Bids," *Wall Street Journal*, January 4, 1984, 57.

18. Stanley Gold, quoted in David Kline, "New Magic in the Magic Kingdom," *Globe and Mail*, September 27, 1985, P87.

19. N. R. Kleinfield, "Reliance Units Buy 6.3% of Disney," *New York Times*, March 30, 1984, D3.

20. Ron W. Miller, quoted in Kathryn Harris, "Takeover Talk Adds Pressure as Disney Tries to Snap Back," *Los Angeles Times*, April 1, 1984, E9.

21. Roy E. Disney, quoted in Bill Johnson, "Disney Productions Holder Roy Disney Calls Move to Acquire Arvida Wasteful," *Wall Street Journal*, May 21, 1984, 10.

22. Roy J. Harris Jr., "Disney to Buy Gibson Greetings for $310 Million," *Wall Street Journal*, June 7, 1984, 3.

23. Lee Isgur, quoted in Thomas C. Hayes, "Disney Still Appears Turbulent," *New York Times*, August 20, 1984, D1.

24. Michael Eisner, quoted in Hayes, "New Disney Team's Strategy," D1.

25. Carol Lawson, "Broadway Is in Worst Slump in a Decade," *New York Times*, January 3, 1983, A1.

26. Joseph Papp, quoted in Samuel G. Freedman, "As Off Broadway Thrives, Its Problems Mount," *New York Times*, October 9, 1983, H5.

27. Peter C. Kunze, "Belles Are Singing: Broadway, Hollywood, and the Failed *Gone with the Wind* Musical," *Historical Journal of Film, Radio and Television* 38, no. 4 (2018): 790–792.

28. Robert Brustein, "The Siren Song of Broadway Is a Warning," *New York Times*, May 22, 1988, 5.

29. Howard Ashman, quoted in J. Wynn Rousuck, "Howard Ashman's Greenery Knocks 'em Dead on Stage," *Sun*, April 8, 1984, D1.

30. Frank Rich, "What Ails Today's Broadway Musical?," *New York Times*, November 14, 1982, A25.

31. Stephen Sondheim, quoted in Linda Winer, "Sondheim in His Own Words," *American Theatre* 2, no. 2 (May 1985): 42.

32. Alan Menken, quoted in Alvin Klein, "Composer Finds His Niche in Life," *New York Times*, June 27, 1986, WC24.

33. Howard Ashman, quoted in Stephen Holden, "Composer and Lyricist: The New Chemistry," *New York Times*, July 27, 1986, H14.

34. Howard Ashman, quoted in Don Shewey, "On the Go with David Geffen," *New York Times*, July 21, 1985, SM30.

35. "Directors for LITTLE SHOP OF HORRORS—THE MOVIE," box 13, folder 8, Ashman Papers, Music Division, Library of Congress, Washington, DC.

36. Letter from John Landis to Howard Ashman, June 29, 1984, box 13, folder 8, Ashman Papers.

37. Frank Oz, quoted in Anne Thompson, "Muppeteer Oz Manipulates *Little Shop of Horrors* Miss Piggy Supplanted by Audrey," *Globe and Mail*, December 17, 1986, D6.

38. Rita Kempley, "*Little Shop*, Big Smile," *Washington Post*, December 19, 1986, WK35.

39. Janet Maslin, "The Screen: *Little Shop of Horrors*," *New York Times*, December 19, 1986, C5.

40. Julie Salamon, "*Little Shop of Horrors* Tops the Holiday Fare," *Wall Street Journal*, December 23, 1986, 18.

41. Ashman, quoted in Rousuck, "Howard Ashman's Greenery," D1.

42. Pauline Kael, "Little Shocks, Big Shocks," *New Yorker*, January 12, 1987, 92, 94.

43. Mark Potts, "New Team in Charge at Disney," *Washington Post*, October 28, 1984, G6.

44. "Disney Theme Parks Plan to Use Attraction Based on *Star Wars*," *Wall Street Journal* February 7, 1985, 6.

45. Eisner, quoted in Hayes, "New Disney Team's Strategy," D5.

46. Aljean Harmetz, "The Man Re-animating Disney," *New York Times*, December 29, 1985.

47. Harmetz, "Man Re-animating Disney."

48. Bette Midler, quoted in Aljean Harmetz, "Who Makes Disney Run?," *New York Times*, February 7, 1988, 30.

49. Harmetz, "Who Makes Disney Run?"

50. Roy Disney, quoted in Raymond Snoody, "Nine Months of Turmoil End Happily for Disney," *Financial Times*, February 6, 1985, 28.

51. Jeffrey Katzenberg, quoted in Aljean Harmetz, "Raising the Odds," *New York Times*, September 11, 1988, SMA76.

52. Kaytis, "John Musker (b. 1953) and Ron Clements (b. 1953)," 415.

53. Roger Allers, in "Roger Allers Interview," in *On Animation: The Director's Perspective*, vol. 1, by Bill Kroyer, ed. Ron Diamond (New York: CRC Press, 2020), 265–266. Also see Chris Pallant and Steven Price, *Storyboarding: A Critical History* (New York: Palgrave Macmillan, 2015).

54. John Thornton Caldwell, *Production Culture: Industrial Reflexivity and Critical Practice in Film and Television* (Durham, NC: Duke University Press, 2008), 232.

55. Joe Hale, quoted in Didier Ghez, "Joe Hale (b. 1925)," in *Walt's People*, vol. 11, ed. Didier Ghez (Bloomington, IN: Xlibris, 2011), 546.

56. Steve Hulett, *Mouse in Transition: An Insider's Look at Disney Feature Animation* (Winter Garden, FL: Theme Park Press, 2014), 101–102.

57. Andrew Gabor and Steven L. Hawkins, "A New Management Rouses Disney from a Long Sleep," *U.S. News & World Report*, December 22, 1986, 44.

58. Don Hahn, personal interview, March 3, 2022.

59. Frederick Wasser, *Veni, Vidi, Video: The Hollywood Empire and the VCR* (Austin: University of Texas Press, 2001), 165.

60. Patrick C. Fleming, "Dickens, Disney, Oliver, and Company: Adaptation in a Corporate Media Age," *Children's Literature Association Quarterly* 41 (2016): 190.

61. Michael Eisner with Tony Schwartz, *Work in Progress: Risking Failure, Surviving Success* (New York: Hyperion, 1999), 179.

62. Kathleen Gavin, personal interview, April 14, 2022.

63. Justin Wyatt, *High Concept: Movies and Marketing in Hollywood* (Austin: University of Texas Press, 1994), 8.

64. Wyatt, *High Concept*, 8.

65. Stephen Prince, "Introduction: Movies and the 1980s," in *American Cinema of the 1980s*, ed. Stephen Prince (New Brunswick, NJ: Rutgers University Press, 2007), 8–9.

66. David Ansen with Peter McAlevey, "The Producer Is King Again," *Newsweek*, May 20, 1985, 84.

67. Peter Bogdanovich, quoted in Ansen with McAlevey, "Producer Is King Again," 84.

68. Jeffrey Katzenberg, quoted in Harmetz, "Who Makes Disney Run?," SM30.

69. Eisner with Schwartz, *Work in Progress*, 178.

70. Didier Ghez, "Steve Hulett (b. 1948)," in *Walt's People*, vol. 6, ed. Didier Ghez (Bloomington, IN: Xlibris, 2008), 345.

71. Hulett, *Mouse in Transition*, 91.

72. Fleming, "Dickens, Disney, Oliver, and Company," 195, 190.

73. During an interview, director George Scribner confirmed the film is not trying to be a musical so much as a film with musical numbers. Scribner, personal interview, February 15, 2022.

74. Kathleen Gavin, personal interview, April 14, 2022.

75. David Geffen, quoted in David T. Friendly, "Seeking the Groove in Movie Sound Tracks," *Los Angeles Times*, October 2, 1986, 6.

76. Marc Napolitano, "Disneyfying Dickens: *Oliver & Company* and *The Muppet Christmas Carol* as Dickensian Musicals," *Studies in Popular Culture* 32, no. 1 (Fall 2009): 85.

77. Napolitano, "Disneyfying Dickens," 83.

78. See Warren Littlefield, in FoundationINTERVIEWS, "Warren Littlefield Discusses Developing 'The Golden Girls'—EMMYTVLEGENDS.ORG," YouTube video, 9:04, August 24, 2015, https://www.youtube.com/watch?v=zBlJ--kq9GE, and Tony Thomas, in FoundationINTERVIEWS, "Producer Tony Thomas on Creating 'The Golden Girls'—EMMYTVLEGENDS.ORG," YouTube video, 5:08, December 7, 2016, https://www.youtube.com/watch?v=5u9FJkElQOk.

79. Ron Grover, *The Disney Touch: How a Daring Management Team Revived an Entertainment Empire* (Homewood, IL: Business One Irwin: 1991), 155–156.

80. Don Bluth, quoted in Nina Darnton, "Steven Spielberg Ventures into Animation," *New York Times*, November 10, 1986, C8.

81. Gary Goldman, quoted in *An American Tail* [Press Kit], Archives and Special Collections, Salisbury University, Salisbury, MD.

82. Eleanor Ringel, "Beat Path Out Door to Better Mouse Tale," *Atlanta Journal and Constitution*, November 21, 1986, 1.

83. Vincent Canby, "*An American Tail*," *New York Times*, November 21, 1986, C8.

84. Charles Solomon, "*American Tail* Lavishly Disappoints," *Los Angeles Times*, November 22, 1986, H8.

85. Harry McCracken, "Don Bluth Is Good, But He's No Walt Disney," *Cinefantastique* 17, no. 3/4 (1987): 110.

86. Charles Champlin, "*Mouse Detective* Good News for Animation," *Los Angeles Times*, July 12, 1986, D1.

87. Roger Ebert, "*The Great Mouse Detective*," RogerEbert.com, July 2, 1986, https://www.rogerebert.com/reviews/the-great-mouse-detective-1986.

88. Hulett, *Mouse in Transition*, 79.

89. Leslie Wayne, "An Annual Report on 1984," *New York Times*, December 23, 1984, F4.

90. Kline, "New Magic in the Magic Kingdom," 87.

91. Aljean Harmetz, "Disney Hires Another Paramount Aide," *New York Times*, March 12, 1985, C18.

92. Stephen Holden, "To Its Creators, *Smile* Was Always a Beauty," *New York Times*, November 23, 1986, H3.

93. Alan Jones, "*Little Shop of Horrors*," *Cinefantastique* 17, no. 1 (January 1987): 18.

94. Marvin Hamlisch, quoted in Michael Kuchwara, "Broadway Music Man Laments Latest Trend to Playing Money Man," *Globe and Mail*, November 24, 1986, D11.

95. Letter from Gerald Schoenfeld and Bernard Jacobs to Howard Ashman, September 15, 1986, box 31, folder 9, Ashman Papers.

96. Howard Ashman, quoted in Holden, "To Its Creators," H3.

97. Clive Barnes, "The British Are Singing a Requiem for Broadway," *Sunday Times*, June 14, 1987, 49.

98. Howard Ashman, quoted in Michael Coveney, "Broadway Malady," *Financial Times*, December 27, 1986, xiii.

99. Frank Rich, "*Smile*, a Musical Comedy," *New York Times*, November 25, 1986, C20.

100. Linda Sherbert, "The New and Old; The Hot and Cold Broadway," *Atlanta Journal and Constitution*, December 7, 1986, J1.

101. Richard Hummler, "*Smile*," *Variety*, November 26, 1986, 144.

102. Letter from Jeffrey Katzenberg to Howard Ashman, April 8, 1986, box 20, letter 9, Ashman Papers.

103. Andrew Lloyd Webber, *Unmasked: A Memoir* (New York: Harper, 2018), 451–452.

104. Don Hahn, personal interview, March 3, 2022.

105. Ron Clements and John Musker, notes on meeting with Howard Ashman, 6/11/86, box 8, folder 6, Ashman Papers.

106. Clements and Musker, notes on meeting.

107. John Musker, "John Musker Question Countdown #1," in *Howard Ashman: Part of His World*, n.d., https://www.howardashman.com/blog/john-musker-question-countdown-1.

108. Clements and Musker, notes on meeting.

CHAPTER 3 — "MAKE THE AUDIENCE FALL IN LOVE WITH ARIEL"

1. Bill Lauch, personal interview, February 28, 2022.

2. Alan Menken, in Zina Goldrich, "In Conversation with Alan Menken," *Dramatist* 7, no. 3 (January/February 2005): 26.

3. Jane Feuer, *The Hollywood Musical*, 2nd ed. (Bloomington: Indiana University Press, 1993), 126.

4. Jack Mathew, "Has Hollywood Decided It's Time to Grow Up?," *Los Angeles Times*, January 5, 1988, G1.

5. Ronald Clarke, "Hollywood Has a Boom Year without Teenage Sex Romps," *Reuters News*, January 26, 1988, Factiva.

6. Peter Biskind, "Low Concept," *Premiere*, February 1988, 76.

7. Alan Bunce, "At the Center of Home and Hearth Is the VCR," *Christian Science Monitor*, October 24, 1988, 1.

8. Will Tusher, "Brisk Biz in '87 May Lead to Peril, Promise in '88," *Daily Variety*, January 4, 1988, 45.

9. Will Leigh, "Disney Swims into Underwater Animation," *Animation Magazine*, Fall 1989, 31.

10. Michael D. Eisner, "To Our Owners and Fellow Disney Employees," December 8, 1987, in *1987 Annual Report* (Burbank, CA: Walt Disney Company, 1987), 1.

11. Eisner, "To Our Owners and Fellow Disney Employees" (1987), 1–2.

12. Sabrina Mittermeier, *A Cultural History of the Disneyland Theme Parks: Middle Class Kingdoms* (Chicago: Intellect, 2020), 107.

13. *1987 Annual Report*, 16.

14. Douglas Gomery, "The New Hollywood, 1981–1999," in *Producing*, ed. Jon Lewis (New Brunswick, NJ: Rutgers University Press, 2016), 115.

15. Jeffrey Katzenberg, quoted in Nat Segaloff, "Planning Disney's Future," *Animation Magazine*, December 1987, 3.

16. Katzenberg, quoted in Segaloff, "Planning Disney's Future," 5.

17. *Video*, quoted in *1987 Annual Report*, 20.

18. Steve Pond, "For '88, Staying the Course," *Washington Post*, January 1, 1988, C7.

19. Stephen Prince, *A New Pot of Gold: Hollywood under the Electronic Rainbow, 1980–1989* (New York: Charles Scribner's Sons, 2000), 221.

20. Robert Zemeckis, quoted in Kim Masters, "*Roger Rabbit*—Disney's Bold Gamble in Animation," *Washington Post*, June 19, 1988, G4.

21. Michael D. Eisner, "To Our Owners and Fellow Disney Employees," December 5, 1988, in *1988 Annual Report* (Burbank, CA: Walt Disney Company, 1988), 2.

22. *1988 Annual Report*, 17.

23. Eileen R. Meehan, "'Holy Commodity Fetish, Batman!' The Political Economy of a Commercial Intertext," in *The Many Lives of the Batman: Critical Approaches to a Superhero and His Media*, ed. Roberta E. Pearson and William Uricchio (New York: Routledge, 1991), 55–56.

24. Thomas Schatz, "The New Hollywood," in *Film Theory Goes to the Movies*, ed. Jim Collins, Hilary Radner, and Ava Preacher Collins (New York: Routledge, 1993), 29.

25. Tom Sito, personal interview, March 1, 2022.

26. Eisner, "To Our Owners and Fellow Disney Employees," December 4, 1989, in *1989 Annual Report* (Burbank, CA: Walt Disney Company, 1989), 2.

27. Eisner, "To Our Owners and Fellow Disney Employees," 2.

28. David Richards, "*Starlight*: On the Flash Track," *Washington Post*, March 16, 1987, B1, and Stephen Holden, "*Starlight Express* Rolls to Market with a Rock Beat," *New York Times*, March 1, 1987, H3.

29. Trevor Nunn, quoted in Meg Cox, "Skating Fast toward Broadway: *Starlight Express*," *Wall Street Journal*, February 3, 1987, 30.

30. Robert Lenzner, "Economics Is Dimming the Lights of Broadway," *Boston Globe*, February 1, 1987, 77.

31. Des McAnuff, "The Reproduced Actor," *American Theatre* 4, no. 7 (October 1987): 86.

32. Frank Rich, "Broadway: The Empire Strikes Back," *New York Times*, March 29, 1987, H36; Clive Barnes, "The British Are Singing a Requiem for Broadway," *Sunday Times*, June 14, 1987, 49.

33. Cameron Mackintosh, quoted in Mervyn Rothstein, "On Broadway, Spectacles Raise the Stakes," *New York Times*, January 8, 1989, H11.

34. Porter Anderson, "Insurers Nix Arts Coverage," *American Theatre* 6, no. 10 (January 1990): 42.

35. Bob Mondello, "Rewriting the Script: From Broadway to Hollywood," *Washington Post Health*, December 29, 1987, 10.

36. Vito Russo, quoted in Sean Mitchell, "AIDS and the Arts: Behind the Scenes of a Tragedy," *Los Angeles Times*, December 26, 1989, F5.

37. Carole Shorestein Hays, quoted in Lenzner, "Economics Is Dimming the Lights," 79.

38. Robert Brustein, "The Siren Song of Broadway Is a Warning," *New York Times*, May 22, 1988, 58.

39. Mervyn Rothstein, "Record Regards for Broadway," *New York Times*, June 2, 1988, C21.

40. Stephen Sondheim, *Look, I Made a Hat: Collected Lyrics (1981–2011) with Attendant Comments, Amplifications, Dogmas, Harangues, Digressions, Anecdotes and Miscellany* (New York: Knopf, 2011), 89.

41. Sondheim, *Look, I Made a Hat*, 58.

42. Mimi Kramer, "The Phantom of Broadway," *New Yorker*, February 8, 1988, 97.

43. Frank Rich, "Stage: *Phantom of the Opera*," *New York Times*, January 27, 1988, C19.

44. Foster Hirsch, "The Prince Difference," *American Theatre* 6, no. 1 (April 1989): 20.

45. David Richards, "The Seductive Spell of *Phantom*," *Washington Post*, January 27, 1988, D1.

46. Elizabeth I. McCann, "Not That Dumb," *New York Times*, December 24, 1989, H2.

47. Rothstein, "On Broadway," H12.

48. Mimi Kramer, "Without Words," *New Yorker*, May 15, 1989, 96.

49. Ron Clements, in Animation Guild, "TAGInterview RonClements 1," YouTube video, 1:15:03, April 12, 2012, https://www.youtube.com/watch?v=TTQJniQ8mSo.

50. Although she was not credited as executive producer, Kathleen Gavin served in that capacity on *Oliver & Company*. But technically, Ashman is the first person not from the animation division credited as executive producer on a Disney animated feature.

51. Sarah Ashman Gillespie, personal interview, August 16, 2022.

52. Ashman, "Notes on Music for Theatre & Film," Ashman Papers, Music Division, Library of Congress, Washington, DC.

53. Ashman, "Notes on Music for Theatre & Film."

54. Amy M. Davis, *Good Girls and Wicked Witches: Women in Disney's Feature Animation* (New Barnet, UK: John Libbey, 2006), 178.

55. Roberta Trites, "Disney's Sub/version of Andersen's *The Little Mermaid*," *Journal of Popular Film & Television* 18, no. 4 (Winter 1991): 145.

56. Laura Sells, "'Where Do the Mermaids Stand?': Voice and Body in *The Little Mermaid*," in *From Mouse to Mermaid: The Politics of Film, Gender, and Culture*, ed. Elizabeth Bell, Lynda Haas, and Laura Sells (Bloomington: Indiana University Press, 1995), 175–192.

57. Howard Ashman, quoted in "John Musker Question Countdown #9," in *Howard Ashman: Part of His World*, n.d., https://www.howardashman.com/blog/john-musker-question-countdown-number-9.

58. Howard Ashman, quoted in *Waking Sleeping Beauty*, DVD, directed by Don Hahn (2009; Burbank, CA: Walt Disney Studios Home Entertainment, 2010).

59. *Waking Sleeping Beauty*.

60. Meeting 1/26/88, Ron Clements's room, box 8, folder 7, Ashman papers.

61. Meeting 1/26/88.

62. Meeting 1/26/88.

63. Animation reels screened for Jeffrey Katzenberg 2/11/88, Ashman Papers.

64. John Musker, "John Musker Question Countdown #7," in *Howard Ashman: Part of His World*, n.d., https://www.howardashman.com/blog/john-musker-question-countdown-7.

65. Elaine Stritch shares this anecdote in *Elaine Stritch at Liberty*, DVD, directed by Andy Picheta, Chris Hegedus, D. A. Pennebaker, Nick Doob, and Rick McKay (Los Angeles: Image Entertainment, 2003).

66. Pat Carroll, quoted in Kate Brandt, "From Squid to Nun to Man," *Advocate*, January 2, 1990, 31.

67. Pat Carroll, quoted in Cynthia Sanz, "Those Faces! Those Voices!," *People*, December 11, 1989, 125.

68. 9/16 Little Mermaid Meeting with Animators and Jeffrey Katzenberg, box 8, folder 6, Ashman Papers.

69. Jennifer Fleeger, *Mismatched Women: The Siren's Song through the Machine* (New York: Oxford University Press, 2014), 118.

70. Kyle Counts, "*The Little Mermaid*," *Cinefantastique*, January 1990, 31.

71. Samuel E. Wright, quoted in Sanz, "Those Faces!" 124.

72. 9/16 Little Mermaid Meeting.

73. 9/16 Little Mermaid Meeting.

74. Ron Clements and John Musker, The Little Mermaid Story Notes, 2/26/88, box 8, folder 7, Ashman Papers.

75. Clements and Musker, Little Mermaid Story Notes.

76. Clements and Musker, Little Mermaid Story Notes.

77. Story Meeting 4/7/88, 4/8/88, box 8, folder 7, Ashman Papers.

78. Sean Griffin, *Tinker Belles and Evil Queens: The Walt Disney Company from the Inside Out* (New York: New York University Press, 2000), 146.

79. Story Meeting Sunday, 5/1, 5/2/88, box 8, folder 7, Ashman Papers.

80. Story Meeting Sunday, 5/1, 5/2/88.

81. Story Meeting Sunday, 5/1, 5/2/88.

82. Jeffrey Katzenberg Sweatbox Notes, 5/13/88, box 8, folder 7, Ashman Papers.

83. Jeffrey Katzenberg Sweatbox Notes, 5/13/88.

84. Jeffrey Katzenberg Sweatbox Notes, 6/17/88, box 8, folder 7, Ashman Papers.

85. 9/16 Little Mermaid Meeting.

86. 9/16 Little Mermaid Meeting.

87. 9/16 Little Mermaid Meeting.

88. Story Meeting—12/7/88—Jeffrey K's notes, 12/8/88, box 8, folder 6, Ashman Papers.

89. 9/16 Little Mermaid Meeting.

90. Gary Trousdale, personal interview, March 1, 2022.

91. Clay Kaytis, "John Musker (b, 1953) and Ron Clements (b, 1953)," in *Walt's People*, vol. 5, ed. Didier Ghez (Bloomington, IN: Xlibris, 2008), 420.

92. Ron Clements, in "239: Director Ron Clements Chats 'Mermaid' Memories, 'Treasure Planet' Woes, and More," *Mad Chatters Podcast*, March 4, 2020, https://directory.libsyn.com/episode/index/id/13417538.

93. Didier Ghez, "Andreas Deja (b, 1957)," in *Walt's People: Talking Disney with the Artists Who Knew Him*, vol. 3, ed. Didier Ghez (Winter Garden, FL: Theme Park Press, 2015), 238.

94. Nina Darnton, "At the Movies," *New York Times*, November 28, 1986, C8.

95. Stacy Jenel Smith, "Marketing *Dogs* and a *Mermaid*," *Los Angeles Times*, November 12, 1989, U19.

96. Duncan Marjoribanks, "Animation Guild | Duncan Marjoribanks," Animation Guild, May 23, 2012, https://animationguild.org/oral_history/duncan-marjoribanks/.

97. Dave Kehr, "*All Dogs, Little Mermaid* a Winning Animated Pair," *Chicago Tribune*, November 17, 1989, 7M.

98. Roger Ebert, review of *The Little Mermaid*, November 17, 1989, http://www.rogerebert.com/reviews/the-little-mermaid-1989.

99. Janet Maslin, "Out of the Sandbox, Right to the Box Office," *New York Times*, November 19, 1989, H17.

100. Bernice Cohen, letter to Howard Ashman, 11/18/89, box 8, folder 9, Ashman Papers.

101. Michael Wilmington, "*Little Mermaid* Makes Big Splash," *Los Angeles Times*, November 15, 1989, F1, F8.

102. Jay Carr, "Disney Animators Back in Form with *Mermaid*," *Boston Globe*, November 17, 1989, Factiva.

103. Hal Hinson, "*Mermaid* with a Plan," *Washington Post*, November 17, 1989, D7.

104. Roy Edward Disney to Howard Ashman, November 10, 1989, box 8, folder 9, Ashman Papers.

105. Jeffrey Katzenberg to Academy Members, March 7, 1990, box 8, folder 9, Ashman Papers.

106. Michael D. Eisner to Howard Ashman, November 17, 1989, box 8, folder 9, Ashman Papers.

107. Michael Eisner with Tony Schwartz, *Work in Progress: Risking Failure, Surviving Success* (New York: Hyperion, 1999), 183.

108. Claudia Eller, "*Mermaid* Swims to Animation Record," *Daily Variety*, January 9, 1990, 1.

109. Cynthia Weil Mann to Howard Ashman, February 3, 1991, box 8, folder 9, Ashman Papers.

110. Jack Viertel to Howard Ashman, November 20, 1989, box 8, folder 9, Ashman Papers.

CHAPTER 4 — "A CELEBRATION OF CERTAIN SENSIBILITIES"

1. Alan Menken, quoted in David J. Fox, "Looking at *Beauty* as Tribute to Lyricist Who Gave 'Beast His Soul,'" *Los Angeles Times*, November 15, 1991, F1.

2. The James Lapine Papers at Yale University reveal Disney considered a Broadway musical adaptation of *Dick Tracy* in 1996. After all, the film contained songs by Stephen Sondheim, Lapine's occasional collaborator.

3. Cynthia Erb, "Another World or the World of an Other? The Space of Romance in Recent Versions of *Beauty and the Beast*," *Cinema Journal* 34, no. 4 (Summer 1995): 50–70, and Sean Griffin, *Tinker Belles and Evil Queens: The Walt Disney Company from the Inside Out* (New York: New York University Press, 2000).

4. Notebook, n.d., box 3, folder 7, Ashman Papers, Music Division, Library of Congress, Washington, DC.

5. Linda Woolverton, personal interview, October 7, 2016.

6. Michael D. Eisner, "To Our Owners and Fellow Disney Employees," December 4, 1992, in *1992 Annual Report* (Burbank, CA: Walt Disney Company, 1992), 1.

7. Jennifer Holt, *Empires of Entertainment: Media Industries and the Politics of Deregulation, 1980–1996* (New Brunswick, NJ: Rutgers University Press, 2011), 122.

8. Richard Turner, "Disney's Venture in Record Business Has Hit Sour Note," *Wall Street Journal*, November 27, 1991, B1.

9. Michael D. Eisner, "To Our Owners and Fellow Disney Employees," November 25, 1990, in *1990 Annual Report* (Burbank, CA: Walt Disney Company, 1990), 2.

10. Roger Ebert, *"Dick Tracy,"* *Chicago Sun-Times*, June 15, 1990, https://www.rogerebert.com/reviews/dick-tracy-1990.

11. Likely Beatty—not Disney—recruited Sondheim, who had also written music for *Reds* (1981).

12. Bill Givens, *"The Rescuers Down Under*: Directors Butoy and Gabriel Give This Sequel Its Own Identity," *Animation Magazine*, Fall 1990, 24–25.

13. Hendel Butoy, quoted in Givens, *"The Rescuers Down Under,"* 25.

14. See Janet Maslin, "Mickey Places the Palace, and Rescuers Go Walkabout," *New York Times*, November 16, 1990, C10, and Charles Solomon, "Fantasy, Animation Soar in *Rescuers Down Under,"* *Los Angeles Times*, November 16, 1990, F15.

15. James B. Stewart, *DisneyWar* (New York: Simon & Schuster, 2005), 24.

16. Jeffrey Katzenberg, "Katzenberg's Bottom Line Strategy for Disney," *Daily Variety*, January 31, 1991, 18.

17. Katzenberg, "Katzenberg's Bottom Line Strategy for Disney," 19–20.

18. Katzenberg, "Katzenberg's Bottom Line Strategy for Disney," 20.

19. Katzenberg, "Katzenberg's Bottom Line Strategy for Disney," 22. Also see Walt Disney, "The Cartoon's Contribution to Children," *Overland Monthly*, October 1933, 138.

20. Michael Eisner, quoted in Bernard Weinraub, "Though a Year Old, Disney Memo Still Provokes Gossip," *New York Times*, February 11, 1992, C11.

21. Shawna Kidman, *Comic Books Incorporated: How the Business of Comics Became the Business of Hollywood* (Oakland: University of California Press, 2019), 195.

22. Jeffrey Katzenberg, quoted in Jack Mathews, "Leaked Memo a Stark Look at Industry," *Los Angeles Times*, January 31, 1991, OCF4.

23. Anita Elberse, *Blockbusters: Hit-Making, Risk-Taking, and the Big Business of Entertainment* (New York: Henry Holt, 2013), 1–14.

24. Mark Canton, quoted in Amy Dawes, "Warner Bros.," *Daily Variety*, January 4, 1991, 31.

25. Joseph McBride, "'91: Welcome to Reality, Hollywood," *Daily Variety*, January 8, 1992, 1.

26. Eisner, "To Our Owners and Fellow Disney Employees," December 4, 1991, in *1991 Annual Report* (Burbank, CA: Walt Disney Company, 1991), 1.

27. Alfred Borcover, "Bring Money—Lots and Lots of It," *Chicago Tribune*, March 3, 1991, K11.

28. Eisner, "To Our Owners and Fellow Disney Employees" (1991), 1.

29. Anonymous, quoted in Marcia B. Siegel, "What They Did for Michael," *American Theatre* 6, no. 12 (March 1990): 35.

30. Frank Rich, "Lloyd Webber's *Aspects of Love*," *New York Times*, April 9, 1990, C11.

31. David Richards, *"Aspects of Love*, Palpitations on a Theme," *Washington Post*, April 9, 1990, C1.

32. Jeremy Gerard, "Broadway's Bloody Nose," *Variety*, March 14–20, 1994, 1.

33. Frank Rich, "The Musical Returns to America," *New York Times*, January 25, 1991, C16.

34. B. D. Wong, quoted in Michael Paulson, "The Battle of *Miss Saigon*," *New York Times*, March 19, 2017, AR9.

35. Cameron Mackintosh, quoted in Linda Joffee, "The Man Behind Musical Hits," *Christian Science Monitor*, April 22, 1991, 10.

36. Jennie Williams, *"Miss Saigon* Gets Raves, Protesters," *USA Today*, April 12, 1991, 2D.

37. Consult Paul Wells, "The Animation Auteur," in *Animation: Genre and Authorship* (New York: Wallflower, 2002), 72–111.

38. During our correspondence, Linda Woolverton could not recall ever working on the film with Ashman in California. She was based in the Los Angeles area, exchanging

memos and drafts via fax machine, but she occasionally traveled to New York to collaborate with Ashman.

39. *Beauty and the Beast* Meeting Notes, 11/6/89, box 24, folder 1, Bob Thomas Papers (Collection PASC 299), Library Special Collections, Charles E. Young Research Library, University of California, Los Angeles.

40. Linda Woolverton, personal interview, October 7, 2016.

41. Charlie Fink, personal interview, March 1, 2022.

42. Wendy Denise Gunkel, "Linda Woolverton: A Personal Look at the Beauty Behind the Beast" (MA thesis, California State University, Fullerton, 1993), 17.

43. Don Hahn, quoted in Steve Daly, "An Oral History of the Animated *Beauty and the Beast*," *Entertainment Weekly*, March 14, 2017, https://ew.com/movies/2017/03/14/beauty-and-the-beast-oral-history/.

44. Linda Woolverton, personal interview, October 7, 2016.

45. The Disney princesses have prompted a good deal of research by scholars in women's and gender studies, feminist media studies, and related fields. A good starting point into this important body of work is Amy M. Davis's *Good Girls and Wicked Witches: Women in Disney's Feature Animation* (New Barnet, UK: John Libbey, 2006).

46. For more on page and stage adaptations of Anna Leonowens's travels in Siam, consult Sharon Aronofsky Weltman, *Victorians on Broadway: Literature, Adaptation, and the Modern American Musical* (Charlottesville: University of Virginia Press, 2020), 55–78.

47. Lehman Engel, *The American Musical Theater*, rev. ed. (New York: Collier, 1975), 49.

48. Rick Altman, *The American Film Musical* (Bloomington: Indiana University Press, 1987), 167.

49. Laura Donalson, "*The King and I* in Uncle Tom's Cabin, or On the Border of the Women's Room," *Cinema Journal* 29, no. 3 (Spring 1990): 53.

50. Caren Kaplan, "'Getting to Know You': Travel, Gender, and the Politics of Representation in *Anna and the King of Siam* and *The King and I*," in *Late Imperial Culture*, ed. Román de la Campa, E. Ann Kaplan, and Michael Sprinker (New York: Verso, 1995), 36.

51. Alan Menken, personal interview, March 29, 2022.

52. Jeffrey Katzenberg, quoted in "*Beauty* Is a Classic, and So Is Disney PR Drive," *Atlanta Journal and Constitution*, November 17, 1991.

53. Raymond Knapp, *The American Musical and the Formation of National Identity* (Princeton, NJ: Princeton University Press, 2005), 266.

54. Lehman Engel, *The Making of a Musical: Creating Songs for the Stage* (New York: Macmillan, 1977), xv.

55. Don Hahn to Richard Purdum, November 13, 1989, box 3, folder 6, Ashman Papers.

56. Charles Hix, "Paige O'Hara: Her Future Looks Beauteous," *Show Music* 8, no. 2 (Summer 1992): 20.

57. 12/12 Meeting Notes, Ashman Papers.

58. Alan Menken, quoted in Stephen Holden, "For Alan Menken, A Partnership Ends but the Song Plays On," *New York Times*, March 15, 1992, H17.

59. Alan Menken, personal interview, March 29, 2022.

60. 3/9/90 Meeting Notes, Ashman Papers.

61. Storyreel Meeting Notes, April 13, 1990, box 24, folder 1, Thomas Papers.

62. Storyreel Meeting Notes, April 13, 1990.

63. Storyreel Meeting Notes, April 13, 1990.

64. Andreas Deja, in *Beauty and the Beast* Press Information (Burbank, CA: Walt Disney Pictures, 1991), 10.

65. *Beauty and the Beast* Meeting with Jeffrey Katzenberg [recording], August 23, 1990, Ashman Papers.

66. For more discussion of this interpretation, consult Griffin, *Tinker Belles and Evil Queens*, 134–136.

67. *Beauty and the Beast* Meeting with Jeffrey Katzenberg [recording].

68. "030-ASHMAN & MENKEN: Interview on WBAI Radio" (audio recording), Ashman Papers. This recording includes Ira Weitzman's undated interview with Howard Ashman for the WBAI radio program *Anything Goes*.

69. "030-ASHMAN & MENKEN: Interview on WBAI Radio."

70. Linda Woolverton to Jeffrey Katzenberg, Peter Schneider, and Don Hahn, August 27, 1990, Linda Woolverton Papers, Writers Guild of America, West, Los Angeles.

71. Woolverton to Katzenberg, Schneider, and Hahn.

72. Woolverton to Katzenberg, Schneider, and Hahn.

73. Jeffrey Meeting Condensed Notes, November 1, 1990, box 24, folder 1, Thomas Papers.

74. Michael Eisner / Jeffrey Katzenberg Sceening [*sic*] Condensed Notes, November 8, 1990, box 24, folder 1, Thomas Papers.

75. Michael Eisner / Jeffrey Katzenberg Sceening [*sic*] Condensed Notes.

76. Linda Woolverton to All Concerned, Re: The Character Arc of the Beast, November 12, 1990, Woolverton Papers.

77. Jeffrey Katzenberg Story Meeting Condensed Notes, November 13, 1990, box 24, folder 1, Thomas Papers.

78. John Thornton Caldwell, *Production Culture: Industrial Reflexivity and Critical Practice in Film and Television* (Durham, NC: Duke University Press, 2008), 216–223.

79. Jeffrey Katzenberg Story Meeting Condensed Notes.

80. Jeffrey Katzenberg Story Meeting Condensed Notes.

81. Considering what he wanted the scene to do, it is likely Allers actually meant the "Quintet," not "Tonight."

82. Jeffrey Katzenberg Story Meeting, November 16, 1990, box 24, folder 1, Thomas Papers.

83. Jeffrey Katzenberg / Animators Story Meeting, n.d., Thomas Papers.

84. Jeffrey Katzenberg with 20–20 Video Screening & Discussion with Animators, December 18, 1990, box 24, folder 1, Thomas Papers.

85. Jeffrey Katzenberg Meeting Condensed Notes, January 5, 1991, box 24, folder 1, Thomas Papers.

86. Jeffrey Katzenberg, quoted in Kim Masters, "The Mermaid and the Mandrill," *Premiere*, November 1991, 82.

87. Lin-Manuel Miranda, quoted in Jessica Derschowitz, in "A Tale as Old as 25," *Entertainment Weekly*, September 9, 2016, 46–47.

88. William H. Honan, "At the New York Film Festival, Works on Art," *New York Times*, August 19, 1991, C11.

89. Gary Trousdale, personal interview, March 1, 2022.

90. Don Hahn, quoted in Honan, "At the New York Film Festival, Works on Art."

91. Although Walt Disney won more Oscars than any person in Hollywood history, only one of his films—*Mary Poppins*—was ever nominated for the Academy Award for Best Picture. It lost to another musical, *My Fair Lady*.

92. Eleanor Ringel, "Film Review: *Beauty and the Beast*," *Atlanta Journal and Constitution*, November 22, 1991, D1, and Roger Ebert, "*Beauty and the Beast*," *Chicago Sun-Times*, November 22, 1991, https://www.rogerebert.com/reviews/beauty-and-the-beast-1991.

93. Richard Corliss, "Keep an Eye on the Furniture," *Time*, November 25, 1991, 96.

94. Hal Hinson, "Beautiful *Beast*: Disney's Fairest Fairy Tale," *Washington Post*, November 22, 1991, B1.

95. Jeff Strickler, "*Beauty and the Beast* Brings Out the Best in Disney Studio," *Minneapolis–St. Paul Star-Tribune*, November 22, 1991, E1.

96. Janet Maslin, "Disney's *Beauty and the Beast* Updated in Form and Content," *New York Times*, November 13, 1991, C17.

97. Jay Carr, "Triple Threat: Films That Children Will Enjoy—and Bring the Parents," *Boston Globe*, November 22, 1991, 33.

98. Terry Orme, "*Beast* Is a Beauty to Behold," *Salt Lake Tribune*, November 22, 1991, C8.

99. See, for example, June Cummins, "Romancing the Plot: The Real Beast of Disney's *Beauty and the Beast*," *Children's Literature Association Quarterly* 20, no. 1 (Spring 1995): 22–28.

100. Ellen Futterman, "Disney Does Spielberg One Better," *St. Louis Post-Dispatch*, November 22, 1991, 3G.

101. Thomas O'Connor, "*Beast*'s Vibrant, Witty Tunes Put Broadway to Shame," *Orange County Register*, November 22, 1991, P4.

102. Ringel, "Film Review," D1.

103. Jesse White, "The Brain Drain," *TheaterWeek*, December 30, 1991–January 6, 1992, 15. Of course, Ashman had passed away by the time this article was published.

104. Alan Menken, quoted in White, "Brain Drain," 15.

105. Frank Rich, "Theater/1991," *New York Times*, December 29, 1991, H5.

106. Michael Eisner with Tony Schwartz, *Work in Progress: Risking Failure, Surviving Success* (New York: Hyperion, 1999), 254.

CHAPTER 5 — "LIKE THE OLD-FASHIONED MUSICALS DID"

1. Michael Eisner with Tony Schwartz, *Work in Progress: Risking Failure, Surviving Success* (New York: Hyperion, 1999), 254.

2. Bob McTyre, quoted in Jan Breslauer, "Disney's Newest Franchise?," *Los Angeles Times*, April 9, 1995, F4.

3. Bob McTyre, personal interview, March 9, 2022.

4. Matthew Wilson Smith, *The Total Work of Art from Bayreuth to Cyberspace* (New York: Routledge 2007): 120, and Jennifer A. Kokai and Tom Robson, eds., *Performance and the Disney Theme Park Experience: The Tourist as Actor* (Cham, CH: Palgrave Macmillan, 2019).

5. Sheryl Kahn, "The Brains Behind *Beauty and the Beast*," *TheaterWeek*, April 4–10, 1994, 18.

6. Bob McTyre, personal interview, May 19, 2022.

7. Robert Jess Roth, personal interview, April 19, 2022.

8. American Theatre Wing, "Playwright, Director and Choreographer (*Working In The Theatre* #213)," filmed April 1994, YouTube video, 1:25:52, posted November 19, 2013, http://www.youtube.com/watch?v=oyeelioXomE.

9. Robert Jess Roth, personal interview, April 19, 2022.

10. As of April 2022, it is the tenth longest running Broadway show of all time.

11. Sumner Redstone, quoted in Laura Landro, "For Many Studios, Holidays Are Failing to Bring about a Happy Ending to 1991," *Wall Street Journal*, December 17, 1991, B1.

12. Thomas R. King, "Another Sequel for Hollywood: Box Office Blues," *Wall Street Journal*, January 6, 1992, B1.

13. Thomas R. King, "Hollywood Studios Focus on Trimming Spending to Market Their New Releases," *Wall Street Journal*, May 1, 1992, B1.

14. Eisner, "To Our Owners and Fellow Disney Employees," in *1992 Annual Report* (Burbank, CA: Walt Disney Company, 1992), 1.

15. Bill Lauch in Oscars, *"Beauty And The Beast* Wins Original Song: 1992 Oscars," YouTube video, 5:48, March 24, 2015, https://www.youtube.com/watch?v=Bntiz357OjM.

16. A. D. Murphy, "Domestic Film Box Office Market Shares: 1990–1992," *Daily Variety,* January 6, 1993, 1.

17. *1993 Annual Report* (Burbank, CA: Walt Disney Company, 1993), 18.

18. Michael Saunders, "Aladdin Goes on Magic Video Ride," *Boston Globe*, September 28, 1993, 61.

19. Charles Fleming and Judy Brennan, "The Party's Not Over," *Variety*, January 4, 1993, 83.

20. Alisa Perren, *Indie, Inc: Miramax and the Transformation of Hollywood in the 1990s* (Austin: University of Texas Press, 2012), 71.

21. *1992 Annual Report*, 28.

22. Steven Greenhouse, "Playing Disney in the Parisian Fields," *New York Times*, February 17, 1991, F1.

23. Anonymous, quoted in Greenhouse, "Playing Disney in the Parisian Fields." Greenhouse anonymously credits Mnouchkine as a "French intellectual," but she took credit for the phrase in 2003. See Ariane Mnouchkine, "Disneyland Resort Paris, France: 1992," *Time*, August 10, 2003.

24. Sabrina Mittermeier, *A Cultural History of the Disneyland Theme Parks: Middle Class Kingdoms* (Chicago: Intellect, 2020), 126–133.

25. *1993 Annual Report*, 18.

26. Gordon Davidson, quoted in S. L. Mintz, "A Marriage of Convenience," *American Theatre* 11, no. 9 (November 1994): 27.

27. Frank Rich, *Hot Seat: Theater Criticism for the New York Times, 1980–1993* (New York: Random House, 1998), 66.

28. Alex Witchel, "As Others Fold, One Show Just Keeps Tapping Along," *New York Times*, August 29, 1990, C16.

29. Rich, *Hot Seat*, 66.

30. Witchel, "As Others Fold," C13, C16.

31. "Broadway Ticket Sales Hit Record $292 Million in '92," *Wall Street Journal*, June 4, 1992, B6.

32. Frank Rich, "A Fresh Chorus of Gershwin on Broadway," *New York Times*, February 20, 1992, C15.

33. Matt Wolf, "Do I Hear a Musical?," *American Theatre* 9, no. 10 (February 1993): 46.

34. Jeffrey Katzenberg, quoted in David Patrick Stearns, "Disney Sets Up Shop on the Great White Way," *USA Today*, February 22, 1994, 3D.

35. John Lahr, "The High Roller," *New Yorker*, June 2, 1997, 70.

36. Kenneth Feld, quoted in Kenneth N. Gilpin, "The Circus Is Just One of His Acts," *New York Times*, March 24, 1993, D1.

37. Paula Crouch Thrasher, "Tour of Disney's *Beauty and the Beast* Glides into the Omni," *Atlanta Constitution*, November 6, 1993, L6.

38. Suzan Bibisi, *"Beauty* on Ice with $6 Million and 46 Skaters, Disney's Tale Glides to L.A.," *Los Angeles Daily News*, January 10, 1994, Factiva.

39. Lawrence Van Gelder, "The World of Disney Transferred to Ice," *New York Times*, February 18, 1993, C24.

40. Lynn Underwood, *"Beauty and the Beast* on Skates," *Star-Tribune*, March 27, 1994, 4F.

41. Kara Swisher, "Ringling to Roll Out Circus Store," *Washington Post*, September 11, 1990, C1.

42. Swisher, "Ringling to Roll Out Circus Store."

43. Eisner with Schwartz, *Work in Progress*, 256.

44. Michael Eisner, quoted in Anthony Bianco, *Ghosts of 42nd Street: A History of America's Most Infamous Block* (New York: William Morrow, 2004), 278.

45. Deliberations began under Dinkins, but it was ultimately Giuliani who would benefit from the deal.

46. Paul Goldberger, "The New Times Square: Magic That Surprised the Magicians," *New York Times*, October 15, 1996, C12.

47. Mary C. Henderson, *The City and the Theater* (New York: Back Stage Books, 2004), 221.

48. Ward Morehouse III, "A 'Little White Way' Planned for Tawdry 42nd St.," *Christian Science Monitor*, November 9, 1977, 9.

49. Stephen Godfrey, "Changing Times," *Globe and Mail*, March 12, 1993, 19.

50. B. Ruby Rich, *New Queer Cinema: The Director's Cut* (Durham, NC: Duke University Press, 2013), xviii.

51. Samuel R. Delany, *Times Square Red, Times Square Blue* (New York: New York University Press, 1999), 193–194.

52. Rudy Giuliani, quoted in Frank Lynn, "Giuliani Tries to Offer a Softer Image," *New York Times*, September 9, 1989, 27.

53. Rudy Giuliani, quoted in Frank Lynn, "Giuliani Sheds Frown for Candidate's Smile," *New York Times*, July 6, 1989, B1.

54. John Taylor, "Rudy's Shot: Are New Yorkers Ready for Giuliani's Tough Love?," *New York*, October 11, 1993, 45.

55. Norman Podhoretz and William F. Buckley Jr., qtd. in "How to Save New York," *New York*, November 26, 1990, 39, 41.

56. Rudy Giuliani, quoted in Taylor, "Rudy's Shot."

57. "How to Save New York."

58. Mario Cuomo, quoted in William A. Schambra, "Cuomo's Sense of Community Is a Political Hand-Me-Down," *Wall Street Journal*, July 24, 1984, 34.

59. Jeremy Gerard, "Disney's New Dream: 42nd Street Fantasia," *Variety*, February 7–13, 1994, 59.

60. Mario Cuomo, quoted in "Disney May Restore 42nd Street Theater," *PR Newswire*, February 2, 1994, Factiva.

61. Michael Eisner, quoted in Gerard, "Disney's New Dream," 59.

62. Alan Mirabella, "Broadway Fears a Mouse That Will Roar," *Crain's New York Business*, February 28, 1994, 1.

63. Stewart Lane, quoted in Simi Horwitz, "The New 42nd Street," *TheaterWeek*, January 29–February 5, 1996, 36.

64. Bob McTyre, quoted in Breslauer, "Disney's Newest Franchise?," F4.

65. Rebecca Robertson, quoted in Bruce Weber, "In Times Square, Keepers of the Glitz," *New York Times*, June 25, 1996, B6.

66. Elizabeth L. Wollman, "The Economic Development of the 'New' Times Square and Its Impact on the Broadway Musical," *American Music* 20, no. 4 (Winter 2002): 450–451.

67. Tom Viertel, quoted in Wollman, "Economic Development," 450–451.

68. Wollman, "Economic Development," 449–450.

69. Steve Nelson, "Broadway and the Beast: Disney Comes to Times Square," *Drama Review* 39, no. 2 (Summer 1995): 78.

70. In my earlier work, I explore how differences in production cultures have hindered earlier Broadway/Hollywood collaborations. See Peter C. Kunze, "Belles Are Singing: Broadway, Hollywood, and the Failed *Gone with the Wind* Musical," *Historical Journal of Film, Radio and Television* 38, no. 4 (2018): 790–792 and "Herding *Cats*; or, The Possibilities of Unproduction Studies," *Velvet Light Trap* 80 (Fall 2017): 18–31.

71. Michael Eisner, quoted in Eisner and Schwartz, *Work in Progress*, 254.

72. Stan Meyer, personal interview, March 30, 2022.

73. Interview with Michael Eisner [videorecording], directed by Michael Kantor, probably April 18, 2003, Theatre on Film and Tape Archive, New York Public Library.

74. Jeffrey Katzenberg, quoted in Stearns, "Disney Sets Up Shop," 3D.

75. Eisner and Schwartz, *Work in Progress*, 255.

76. Robert Jess Roth, personal interview, April 19, 2022.

77. Bob McTyre, quoted in Michael Goldstein, "Broadway's New Beast," *New York*, March 14, 1994, 42.

78. Robert Jess Roth, quoted in Goldstein, "Broadway's New Beast," 43.

79. Robert Jess Roth, personal interview, April 19, 2022.

80. Alan Menken, quoted in Kahn, "Brains Behind *Beauty and the Beast*," 20.

81. Anonymous, quoted in Alex Witchel, "Is Disney the Newest Broadway Baby?," *New York Times*, April 17, 1994, H10.

82. David Richards, "Disney Does Broadway, Dancing Spoons and All," *New York Times*, April 19, 1994, C19.

83. Greg Evans, "Booty and *The Beast*," *Variety*, April 11–17, 1994, 170.

84. Ann Hould-Ward, personal correspondence, April 12, 2022.

85. Stan Meyer, quoted in David Patrick Stearns, "*Beast* on Broadway: Will Disney Way Play in New York?," *USA Today*, April 8, 1994, 1D.

86. Goldstein, "Broadway's New Beast," 43.

87. Tim Rice, quoted in Donald Frantz, *Disney's Beauty and the Beast: A Celebration of the Broadway Musical* (New York: Hyperion, 1995), 139.

88. Linda Woolverton, quoted in Goldstein, "Broadway's New Beast," 42.

89. Linda Woolverton, personal interview, October 7, 2016.

90. Robert Jess Roth, personal interview, April 19, 2022.

91. Alan Menken, quoted in Kahn, "Brains Behind *Beauty and the Beast*," 19.

92. Robert Jess Roth, quoted in Frantz, *Disney's Beauty and the Beast*, 92.

93. Rebecca-Anne Do Rozario, "Reanimating the Animated: Disney's Theatrical Productions," *Drama Review* 48, no. 1 (Spring 2004): 166.

94. Goldstein, "Broadway's New Beast," 44.

95. Ann Hould-Ward, quoted in Frantz, *Disney's Beauty and the Beast*, 101.

96. Frantz, *Disney's Beauty and the Beast*, 90.

97. "Staged *Beauty and the Beast* Too Tame," *Austin American-Statesman*, December 11, 1993, 4.

98. "Staged *Beauty and the Beast* Too Tame," 4.

99. Jerome Weeks, "*Disney's Beauty and the Beast*," *Daily Variety*, December 10, 1993, 18.

100. Jerry Tallmer, "Linda Woolverton Pens a Fairy Tale for the Palace: B'Way's *Beauty and the Beast*," *Back Stage*, April 22, 1994, 23.

101. For more on the "critic-proof" musical, see Paul R. Laird, "'It Couldn't Happen Here in Oz': *Wicked* and the Creation of a 'Critic-Proof' Musical," *Studies in Musical Theatre* 5, no. 1 (2011): 35–47.

102. Michael David, quoted in Witchel, "Is Disney the Newest Broadway Baby?," H1.

103. Interview with Michael Eisner [videorecording], directed by Michael Kantor, probably April 18, 2003, Theater on Film and Tape Archive, New York Public Library.

104. Michael Eisner, quoted in Marc Peyser, "Beauty and the Bucks," *Newsweek*, April 25, 1994, 65.

105. "Amex, Dis Promo *Beauty*," *Hollywood Reporter*, March 7, 1994, 14.

106. "Amex, Dis Promo *Beauty*."

107. McTyre, quoted in Breslauer, "Disney's Newest Franchise?," F4.

108. Jane Alexander, quoted in Ed Lange, "Who Needs Kids' Theatre?," *American Theatre* 11, no. 8 (October 1994): 9.

109. Robert Jess Roth, quoted in Lou Lumenick, "Suburban Families Broadway-Bound," *Record*, May 1, 1994, Factiva.

110. Jeffrey Seller, quoted in Thomas R. King, "Disney Bets Broadway Beast Is Golden Boy," *Wall Street Journal*, February 24, 1994, B8.

111. Edwin Wilson, "A Bit of Disneyland Comes to Broadway," *Wall Street Journal*, April 19, 1994, A18.

112. Thomas R. King, "Critics See the Beast in Disney's *Beauty*—But Will It Matter?," *Wall Street Journal*, April 20, 1994, B8.

113. Stearns, "*Beast* on Broadway," 1D.

114. Richards, "Disney Does Broadway," C15.

115. John Simon, "Hairy Fairy Tale," *New York*, May 2, 1994, 72.

116. See, for example, Lahr, "The Shock of the Neutral," *New Yorker*, May 2, 1994, 102–104, and Frank Scheck, "Girl Meets Beast, Lives Happily Ever After Shagginess Is No Obstacle to Romance in Disney's Broadway Musical," *Christian Science Monitor*, April 20, 1994, 15.

117. King, "Critics See the Beast," B8.

118. King, "Critics See the Beast," D8.

119. Jeremy Gerard, "Disney's *Beauty and the Beast*," *Daily Variety*, April 19, 1994, 2, 15.

120. Lahr, "Shock of the Neutral," 103.

121. See Scheck, "Girl Meets Beast," and Robert Feldberg, "Disney's Beaut," *Record*, April 19, 1994, Factiva.

122. Janet Maslin, "A Beauty or a Beast? Contrasting Film and Musical," *New York Times*, April 23, 1994, 16.

123. Charles Marowitz, "Do We Want a Disney World?," *TheaterWeek*, August 8–14, 1994, 26.

124. Since Broadway shows rarely open over the summer, the Tony Awards in June might be seen as the unofficial end of the season.

125. "*Beast* Best: 708g," *Variety*, June 6–12, 1994, 48.

126. Bruce Weber, "*Passion* and *Beast* Square Off in Tonys; *Angels* Cited Again," *New York Times*, May 17, 1994, C17.

127. James Kaplan, "The Cult of Saint Stephen Sondheim," *New York*, April 4, 1994, 50.

128. David Kaufman, "Theater," *The Nation*, June 13, 1994, 845.

129. David Richards, "On Stage, Survival of the Fizziest," *New York Times*, June 12, 1994, H32.

130. Scott Rudin, quoted in Kaplan, "Cult of Saint Stephen Sondheim," 54.

131. Evans, "Booty and *The Beast*," 1.

132. Jeremy Gerard, "*Beauty* Is the Best in Single Day," *Daily Variety*, June 14, 1994, 1.

133. Kathleen O'Steen, "Disney Plans Global *Beauty* Blitz," *Variety*, November 21–27, 1994, 40.

134. Gordon Davidson, quoted in Patrick Pacheco, "Slipping Tony a Mickey?," *Los Angeles Times*, June 12, 1994, F80.

CHAPTER 6 — "I DON'T DO CUTE"

1. See, for example, Lev Manovich, *The Language of New Media* (Cambridge, MA: MIT Press, 2001), 298–300, as well as Giannalberto Bendazzi's three-volume *Animation: A World History* (New York: Routledge, 2016).

2. See, for example, Maurya Wickstrom, *Performing Consumers: Global Capital and Its Theatrical Seductions* (New York: Routledge, 2006).

3. Brian Granger, "Disney's *The Lion King on Broadway* (1997) as a Vital Sign for Understanding Civic and Racialized Presence in the Early Twenty-First Century," in *Reframing the Musical: Race, Culture and Identity*, ed. Sarah Whitfield (London: Red Globe Press, 2019), 42.

4. David Geffen, quoted in E. Scott Reckard, "Wells Is Remembered as Stability Behind Disney," *Sun*, April 5, 1994, 13C.

5. Richard Turner, "Disney Studio Chief Jeffrey Katzenberg Isn't Given the Edge to Become President," *Wall Street Journal*, July 20, 1994, A3.

6. Corie Brown, "The Third Man," *Premiere*, November 1994, 112.

7. Michael Eisner, quoted in Kim Masters, "The Epic Disney Blow-Up of 1994: Eisner, Katzenberg and Ovitz 20 Years Later," *Hollywood Reporter*, April 9, 2014, https://www.hollywoodreporter.com/features/epic-disney-blow-up-1994-694476.

8. Terry Williams, "Major Investors Still Buying Disney Stock," *Pensions & Investments*, September 5, 1994.

9. Bob Weis, quoted in William Styron, "Slavery's Pain, Disney's Gain," *New York Times*, August 4, 1994, A23.

10. *1994 Annual Report* (Burbank, CA: Walt Disney Company, 1994), 11.

11. *1994 Annual Report*, 12, 23.

12. Sallie Hofmeister, "In the Realm of Marketing, *The Lion King* Rules," *New York Times*, July 12, 1994, D17.

13. David Chandler, "Creating *The Lion King*: Story Development, Authorship, and Accreditation in the Disney Renaissance," *Journal of Screenwriting* 9, no. 3 (September 2018): 329–345.

14. Ari Posner, "The Mane Event," *Premiere*, July 1994, 82.

15. Jeffrey Katzenberg, quoted in Yardena Arar, "Disney Studios Roar into Action for *Lion King*," *Austin American-Statesman*, June 15, 1994, F7.

16. Posner, "Mane Event," 82.

17. Don Hahn, personal interview, March 3, 2022.

18. Posner, "Mane Event," 84.

19. Don Hahn, personal interview, March 3, 2022.

20. Hofmeister, "In the Realm of Marketing, *The Lion King* Rules," D1.

21. "Michael Eisner on Former Disney Colleagues, Rivals and Bob Iger's Successor," *Hollywood Reporter*, July 27, 2016, https://www.hollywoodreporter.com/news/michael-eisner-disney-colleagues-rivals-914841.

22. Robert Marich, "Disney's New Duopoly Reflects Hollywood Trend," *Hollywood Reporter*, August 26, 1994, 1.

23. Richard Turner, "Jungle Fever: Disney, Using Cash and Claw, Stays King of Animated Movies," *Wall Street Journal*, May 16, 1994, A1.

24. David Geffen, quoted in "Disney Executive Unexpectedly Resigns," *Charleston Daily Mail*, August 25, 1994, P5B.

25. Frank Rich, "The Last Tycoons," *New York Times*, October 20, 1994, A27.

26. Leonard Klady, "Bountiful B.O. Makes BV Boss," *Daily Variety*, January 3, 1995, 1.

27. John Brodie, "Disney Wannabes Play Copycat-and Mouse," *Variety*, January 2–8, 1995, 87.

28. Sallie Hofmeister, "Hollywood Falls Hard for Animation," *New York Times*, October 17, 1994, D5.

29. Peter Biskind, "Win, Lose—but Draw," *Premiere*, July 1995, 85.

30. Ellen Wolff, "Lasseter: Kid in Candy Store," *Daily Variety*, October 30, 1996, 14.

31. Steve Lohr, "Woody and Buzz, The Untold Story," *New York Times*, February 24, 1997, D11.

32. Ty Ahmad-Taylor, "Beyond the California Raisins," *New York Times*, November 27, 1995, D7.

33. According to *Box Office Mojo*, *Pocahontas* grossed $204 million in international release compared to *Toy Story*'s $181 million.

34. Steve Lohr, "Woody and Buzz," D11.

35. Steve Lohr, "Disney in 10-Year, 5-Film Deal with Pixar," *New York Times*, February 25, 1997, D8.

36. Jennifer Holt, *Empires of Entertainment: Media Industries and the Politics of Deregulation, 1980–1996* (New Brunswick, NJ: Rutgers University Press, 2011), 148–163.

37. J. P. Telotte, *Disney TV* (Detroit: Wayne State University Press, 2004), 16–17.

38. "This Man Is Twice as Big as Murdoch," *Independent*, August 3, 1995, 2–3.

39. Holt, *Empires of Entertainment*, 158.

40. Kim Masters, "What's Ovitz Got to Do with It?," *Vanity Fair*, April 1995, https://www.vanityfair.com/news/1995/04/ovitz-199504.

41. Dominick Dunne, "The Sorcerer's Apprentice," *Vanity Fair*, February 2005, https://www.vanityfair.com/news/2005/02/ovitz-200502.

42. David Geffen, quoted in Kim Masters, "The Mouse Trap," *Vanity Fair*, December 1996, 270.

43. Joe Eszterhas, quoted in Army Archerd, "Just for Variety," *Daily Variety*, December 13, 1996, 4.

44. Bruce Orwall, "In Court Case, a Vivid Portrayal of Eisner's Boardroom Tactics," *Wall Street Journal*, November 23, 2004, A9.

45. John Brodie, "H'wood Morphs Its Marquees," *Variety*, January 1–7, 1996, 94.

46. Brodie, "H'wood Morphs Its Marquees."

47. Leonard Klady, "Wrapping '96 on a Bang," *Daily Variety*, January 3, 1997, 1.

48. Hongmei Yu, "From *Kundun* to *Mulan*: A Political Economic Case Study of Disney and China," *AsiaNetworkExchange* 22, no. 1 (Fall 2014): 13–22.

49. Michael Ovitz, quoted in Anita M. Busch, "Mouse House Loses Big Cheese," *Daily Variety*, December 13, 1996, 73.

50. Michael Eisner, quoted in "Michael Eisner on Former Disney Colleagues, Rivals, and Bob Iger's Successor," *Hollywood Reporter*, July 27, 2016, https://www.hollywoodreporter.com/news/general-news/michael-eisner-disney-colleagues-rivals-914841/.

51. Leonard Klady, "'97 B.O. Hits New Record," *Daily Variety*, January 5, 1998, 1.

52. Klady, "'97 B.O. Hits New Record," 40.

53. Klady, "'97 B.O. Hits New Record."

54. Michael Eisner, Letter to Shareholders, n.d., in *1997 Annual Report* (Burbank, CA: Walt Disney Company, 1997), 3.

55. Eisner, Letter to Shareholders.

56. Ilana Wernick, "Disney Starts Work on New Amsterdam," *Back Stage*, December 1, 1995, 2.

57. Simi Horwitz, "The New 42nd Street," *TheaterWeek*, January 29–February 5, 1996, 29–30.

58. James Traub, *The Devil's Playground: A Century of Pleasure and Profit in Times Square* (New York: Random House, 2004), 173.

59. Cora Cahan, quoted in Kristin Downey Grimsley, "The *Beast* That Ate Broadway: Disney's Play and Preservation Score in N.Y.," *Washington Post*, September 7, 1994, F2.

60. Eric Gerard, "A Triple-Play for Times Square!," *Real Estate Weekly*, July 26, 1995, 1.

61. Garth Drabinsky, quoted in Bruce Weber, "Canadian Showman Takes on Broadway with a Swagger," *New York Times*, November 1, 1994, C13.

62. Dana Flavelle, "Musicals Still Sing: Drabinsky Livent Boss Angry at Reports of Big Shows' Demise," *Toronto Star*, January 6, 1996, C1.

63. Ben Brantley, "*Ragtime*: A Diorama with Nostalgia Rampant," *New York Times*, January 19, 1998, E1.

64. Alan Riding, "A Tune That Carries beyond Broadway," *New York Times*, June 10, 1996, D1.

65. Alex Bádue and Rebecca S. Schorsch, "Animated Broadway: Disney and Musical Theater in the 1990s and Early 2000s," *American Music* 39, no. 2 (2021): 213.

66. Michael Walsh, "Lloyd Webber: Now, but Forever?," *New York Times*, April 9, 2000, AR9.

67. Patrick McKenna, quoted in Riding, "Tune That Carries beyond Broadway," D1.

68. Frank Rich, "*Cats* and Mouse," *New York Times*, June 19, 1997, A23.

69. Charles R. Acland, *Screen Traffic: Movies, Multiplexes, and Global Culture* (Durham, NC: Duke University Press, 2003), 203.

70. Bruce Weber, "The Broadway Ticket Game: Bargain-Hunters *Can* Play," *New York Times*, March 18, 1994, C7.

71. Peter Marks, "Saw the Show? Buy the Trinket," *New York Times*, December 4, 1994, H35.

72. Greg Evans, "Great White Way in Green," *Variety*, June 2, 1995, 1, 41.

73. Donald G. McNeil Jr., "The Balance Sheet: A Broadway Villain," *New York Times*, November 21, 1994, C13.

74. T. Richard Fitzgerald, quoted in Lawrence O'Toole, "Musical Theater Is Discovering a New Voice," *New York Times*, January 22, 1995, H7.

75. Ben Brantley, quoted in Terry Allen, "On Broadway and Off, a Seesaw Season," *New York Times*, June 2, 1996, H1.

76. Vincent Canby, quoted in Allen, "On Broadway and Off," H4.

77. Jeffrey Seller, quoted in William Grimes, "On Stage, and Off," *New York Times*, April 25, 1997, C2.

78. Carol Diuguid, "A New House for Mouse," *Daily Variety*, April 3, 1997, 23.

79. Hugh Hardy, quoted in Dan Hulbert, "Disney Rescues a Faded Broadway Jewel," *Atlanta Journal-Constitution*, May 25, 1997, K4.

80. Ada Louise Huxtable, "Miracle on 42nd Street," *Wall Street Journal*, April 3, 1997, A16.

81. Mike Ockrent, quoted in Ralph Blumenthal, "Disney Takes on Broadway and Bible," *New York Times*, August 20, 1996, C13.

82. Michael Kuchwara, "*King David* Opens Disney's New Amsterdam Theatre," *Associated Press*, May 19, 1997, Factiva.

83. Rudy Giuliani, quoted in Rick Lyman, "With Its Glory Restored, Theater Is Itself a Star," *New York Times*, May 20, 1997, C12.

84. "A Series of Firsts, Like the $75 Seat," *New York Times*, February 19, 1998, B10.

85. "Lynn Ahrens and Stephen Flaherty," in *The Art of the American Musical: Conversations with the Creators*, ed. Jackson R. Bryer and Richard A. Davison (New Brunswick, NJ: Rutgers University Press, 2005), 15–16.

86. Elizabeth L. Wollman, "The Economic Development of the 'New' Times Square and Its Impact on the Broadway Musical," *American Music* 20, no. 4 (Winter 2002): 453.

87. Hal Prince, quoted in Craig Turner, "He Just Keeps Rolling Along," *Los Angeles Times*, November 10, 1996, 9.

88. Turner, "He Just Keeps Rolling Along,"8.

89. Garth Drabinsky, quoted in Turner, "He Just Keeps Rolling Along," 89.

90. Arthur Laurents, "Entertainment Is Killing Broadway," *New York Times*, December 17, 1995, H4.

91. For more on this antagonism, see Peter C. Kunze, "Belles Are Singing: Broadway, Hollywood, and the Failed *Gone with the Wind* Musical," *Historical Journal of Film, Radio and Television* 38, no. 4 (2018): 790–792.

92. Julie Taymor, quoted in Patti Hartigan, "Leaps of Faith," *Boston Globe*, December 8, 1996, N1.

93. Eileen Blumenthal, "West Meets East Meets West," *American Theatre* 3, no. 10 (January 1987): 15.

94. Eileen Blumenthal and Julie Taymor, *Julie Taymor, Playing with Fire: Theater, Opera, Film* (New York: Harry N. Abrams, 1995), 95, 98.

95. Thomas Schumacher, in BUILD Series, "Thomas Schumacher Chats about the 20th Anniversary of *The Lion King*," YouTube video, 1:09:02, November 15, 2017, https://www.youtube.com/watch?v=FfaxyYKxoW8&t=434s.

96. Rebecca-Anne Do Rozario, "Reanimating the Animated: Disney's Theatrical Productions," *Drama Review* 48, no. 1 (Spring 2004): 169.

97. Eileen Blumenthal, quoted in Randy Gener, "Nasty Girl," *Village Voice*, January 2, 1996, 69.

98. Michael Eisner, quoted in Patrick Pacheco, "Disney's Great Leap," *Los Angeles Times*, November 3, 1997, F8.

99. Julie Taymor, quoted in Michael Kuchwara, "The Young Performers Who Are the Heart and Humanity of *The Lion King*," Associated Press, November 3, 1997, Factiva.

100. See Tom Sito, "The Great Disney Studio Strike," in *Drawing the Line: The Untold Story of the Animation Unions from Bosko to Bart Simpson* (Lexington: University Press of Kentucky, 2006), 101–152, and Jake S. Friedman, *The Disney Revolt: The Great Labor War of Animation's Golden Age* (Chicago: Chicago Review Press, 2022).

101. Robert Simonson, "*Lion* Director Taymor on Non-union Deal," *Back Stage*, November 28, 1997, 1.

102. Julie Taymor, quoted in T. M. Hartmann, "A Wealth of Invention, A Passion for Integrity: Julie Is the *Lion* Taymor," *Back Stage*, November 14, 1997, 18.

103. Julie Taymor, quoted in David Patrick Stearns, "*Lion King* Leaps to Theater's Cutting Edge," *USA Today*, July 28, 1997, 1D.

104. Julie Taymor, quoted in "The Mouse That Roars on Broadway," *Boston Globe*, April 27, 1997, D1.

105. Mike Steele, "*The Lion King* to Make Stage Debut at Orpheum," *Minneapolis Star-Tribune*, November 7, 1996, 1A.

106. Sylviane Gold, "The Possession of Julie Taymor," *American Theatre* 15, no. 7 (September 1998): 25.

107. Julie Taymor, quoted in William Grimes, "Disney *King* for 42d Street: No Lion Suits," *New York Times*, November 7, 1996, C17.

108. Julie Taymor, interview by Richard Schechner, "Julie Taymor: From Jacques Lecoq to *The Lion King*," *Drama Review* 43, no. 3 (Fall 1999): 43.

109. Neil Harris, *Humbug: The Art of P. T. Barnum* (Chicago: University of Chicago Press, 1973), 57.

110. Elysa Gardner, "*The Lion King*'s Julie Taymor Opens Up about Her Success, Her Mistakes, and Being a Woman in Theater," *Town & Country*, October 20, 2017, https://www .townandcountrymag.com/leisure/arts-and-culture/a13036213/julie-taymor-interview-lion -king/.

111. Thomas Schumacher, quoted in Grimes, "Disney *King* for 42d Street," C21.

112. Quoted in Mike Steele, "Here's the Lionup," *Star-Tribune*, July 27, 1997, 1F.

113. Elton John, quoted in Barry Singer, "On an Assembly Line of Hits," *New York Times*, December 21, 1997, AR34.

114. Mark Mancina, quoted in Singer, "On an Assembly Line of Hits," AR34.

115. Singer, "On an Assembly Line of Hits," AR34.

116. Julie Taymor, interview with Alexis Green, *SDCF Masters of the Stage*, podcast audio, March 12, 1997 (January 16, 2009), https://podcasts.apple.com/us/podcast/julie -taymor/id380227754?i=1000410587650/.

117. Robert Simonson, "African *Lion* Performers Allowed to Stay," *Back Stage*, October 31, 1997, 1.

118. Julie Taymor, quoted in Michael Paulson, "The *Lion King* Effect: How a Broadway Smash Changed South African Lives," *New York Times*, November 15, 2017, https://www .nytimes.com/2017/11/15/theater/the-lion-king-south-africa.html.

119. David Hawkanson, quoted in Jeff Baenen, "A Burgeoning Business for Broadway Shows in America's Heartland," *Salt Lake Tribune*, August 12, 1997, D6.

120. David Patrick Stearns, "*Lion King* Leaps to Theater's Cutting Edge: Disney Show Will Be a Different Broadway Animal," *USA Today*, July 28, 1997, 1D.

121. Julie Taymor, quoted in "*Lion King*, the Stage Show, Makes World Premiere in Minneapolis," Associated Press, July 6, 1997. Refusing to pigeonhole as a children's entertainer, Disney himself claimed his work appealed to the child within. See also Walt Disney, "The Cartoon's Contribution to Children," *Overland Monthly*, October 1933, 138.

122. Pacheco, "Disney's Great Leap," *Los Angeles Times*, November 3, 1997, F9.

123. Dan Cox and Greg Evans, "B'way Rules Rewritten to Heed *Lion*'s Roar," *Variety*, December 22, 1997–January 4, 1998, 78.

124. Patti Hartigan, "Broadway's New *King*," *Boston Globe*, November 9, 1997, K1.

125. Jack Kroll, "*The Lion King* (New Amsterdam Theatre, New York, NY)," *Newsweek*, November 24, 1997, 70.

126. Vincent Canby, "*The Lion King* Earns Its Roars of Approval," *New York Times*, November 23, 1997, AR5.

127. Ben Brantley, "Cub Comes of Age: A Twice-Told Cosmic Tale," *New York Times*, November 14, 1997, B35.

128. John Simon, review of *The Lion King*, in *John Simon on Theater: Criticism, 1974–2003* (New York: Applause, 2005), 687–688.

129. Rick Lyman, "Disney's Thanks: Deed and Word," *New York Times*, November 21, 1997, E2.

130. Fintan O'Toole, "Mane Event Is Spectacular," *New York Daily News*, November 14, 1997, Factiva.

131. Joanna Coles, "Great Packaging, Pity There's Nothing Inside," *Guardian*, November 24, 1997, 2.

132. Julie Taymor, quoted in David Richards, "The Pride of Broadway," *New York Times*, December 28, 1997, G4.

133. Ed Siegel, "*The Lion King* Rules Broadway," *Boston Globe*, November 14, 1997, D4.

134. Donald Lyons, "Jungle King; Camelot Queen," *Wall Street Journal*, November 14, 1997, A16.

135. Cynthia Tournquist, quoted in Donald Van De Mark and Beverly Schuch, "Younger Broadway Audience," *CNNfn: Biz Buzz*, April 8, 1998, Factiva.

136. Kelly Kessler, *Broadway in the Box: Television's Lasting Love Affair with the Musical* (New York: Oxford University Press, 2020), 176.

137. Michael Kuchwara, "A Tony Battle of Big, Corporate-Produced Musicals," Associated Press, June 7, 1998.

138. Janny Scott, "Rosie Speaks, and Broadway Ticket Sellers Cheer," *New York Times*, May 3, 1998, 1.

139. Rosie O'Donnell, personal correspondence, May 17, 2018.

140. Rosie O'Donnell, quoted in Janny Scott, "Rosie Speaks, and Broadway Ticket Sellers Cheer," *New York Times*, May 3, 1998, 1.

141. Peter Schneider, quoted in Janny Scott, "Rosie Speaks, and Broadway Ticket Sellers Cheer," *New York Times*, May 3, 1998, 1.

142. Richards, "Pride of Broadway," G4.

143. "Disney Has That Midas Touch," *Record*, December 7, 1997, Factiva.

144. Anonymous, quoted in Michael Riedel, "The Early *Lion* on Tony Race," *New York Daily News*, January 14, 1998, Factiva.

145. Rosie O'Donnell, personal correspondence, May 17, 2018.

146. Rosie O'Donnell, quoted in Rick Lyman, "'Art' Wins Best Play in Tonys; *Lion King* Gets Best Musical," *New York Times*, June 8, 1998, B11.

147. Stephen Flaherty, quoted in Kathleen Kenna, "Disney Beats *Ragtime* for Top Award," *Toronto Star*, June 8, 1988, A1.

148. Richards, "Pride of Broadway," G1.

149. Andrew Lloyd Webber, quoted in Riding, "Tune That Carries beyond Broadway," D8.

150. Joe Roth, quoted in Dan Cox and Greg Evans, "B'way Rules Rewritten to Heed *Lion*'s Roar," *Variety*, December 22, 1997–January 4, 1998, 78.

151. Mark Beech, "Disney's Lion King Tops $11.6 Billion on Anniversary, Most Successful Franchise Ever," *Forbes*, October 30, 2019, https://www.forbes.com/sites/markbeech/2019/10/30/lion-king-tops-116-billion-on-anniversary-most-successful-franchise-ever/?sh=67f71b1d1c0a.

152. Rebecca Sun, "*Lion King* First Show to Hit $1B on Broadway," *Hollywood Reporter*, October 25, 2013, https://www.hollywoodreporter.com/news/general-news/lion-king-is-broadways-first-648455/.

153. Sun, "*Lion King* First Show to Hit $1B."

154. Thomas Schumacher, quoted in Ruthie Fierberg, "How Broadway's *The Lion King* Launched Disney Theatrical Productions," *Playbill*, November 1, 2017, https://www.playbill.com/article/how-broadways-the-lion-king-launched-disney-theatrical-productions.

CONCLUSION

1. I appreciate Cristina Rhodes for drawing my attention to García Márquez's influence.

2. Andrew Stanton, "The Clues to a Great Story," *TED* video, 19:10, February 2012, https://www.ted.com/talks/andrew_stanton_the_clues_to_a_great_story.

3. John Lasseter, quoted in Anne Thompson, "'Toy' Wonder," *Entertainment Weekly*, December 8, 1995, 32.

4. Rick Lyman, "Chairman of Disney's Studios Resigns to Return to Broadway," *New York Times*, June 21, 2001, C3.

5. Plans have been announced for an adaptation of the *Dragon's Lair* video game, starring Ryan Reynolds and directed by Bluth and Goldman.

6. Daniel Miller, "How Robert Iger's 'Fearless' Deal-Making Transformed Disney," *Los Angeles Times*, June 6, 2015, https://www.latimes.com/entertainment/envelope/cotown/la-et-ct-disney-iger-20150607-story.html.

7. David A. Price, *The Pixar Touch: The Making of a Company* (New York: Knopf, 2008), 237.

8. Matthew Belloni, "In Depth with Disney CEO Bob Iger on China Growth, *Star Wars* Reshoots, and Political Plans: 'A Lot of People Have Urged Me to [Run],'" *Hollywood Reporter*, June 22, 2016, https://www.hollywoodreporter.com/movies/movie-features/bob-iger-interview-star-wars-905320/.

9. For more on the "tween moment" in children's media, see Tyler Bickford, *Tween Pop* (Durham, NC: Duke University Press, 2020).

10. Jenna Goudreau, "Disney Princess Tops List of the 20 Best-Selling Entertainment Products," *Forbes*, September 17, 2012, https://www.forbes.com/sites/jennagoudreau/2012/09/17/disney-princess-tops-list-of-the-20-best-selling-entertainment-products/?sh=2afad6d8ab06.

11. Ben Fritz, "How Disney Milks It Hits for Profits Ever After," *Wall Street Journal*, June 8, 2015, https://www.wsj.com/articles/how-disney-milks-its-hits-for-profits-ever-after-1433813239.

12. Jesse McKinley, "Fast Lane to Broadway Begins in Hollywood," *New York Times*, September 11, 2005, A10.

13. Margo Lion, "From Screen to Stage (and Back Again): Hollywood's Impact on Broadway," *Columbia Journal of Law & the Arts* 29, no. 4 (2006): 467.

14. McKinley, "Fast Lane to Broadway," A13.

15. Ryan McPhee, "Broadway Sees Highest-Grossing and Best Attended Season in History," *Playbill*, May 29, 2018, https://www.playbill.com/article/broadway-sees-highest-grossing-and-best-attended-season-in-history.

16. *The Demographics of the Broadway Audience 2015–2016* (New York: Broadway League, 2016), 27.

17. *Demographics of the Broadway Audience 2015–2016*, 5.

18. Ben Brantley, in Ben Brantley, Jesse Green, and Scott Heller, "Loving and Hating the Broadway Season: Our Critics Could Have Argued All Night," *New York Times*, May 9, 2018, https://www.nytimes.com/2018/05/09/theater/tony-awards-2018-critics-conversation.html.

19. Green, in Brantley, Green, and Heller, "Loving and Hating the Broadway Season."

20. Thomas Schumacher, interview with Ken Davenport, *Producer's Perspective Podcast*, podcast audio, February 23, 2020, https://kendavenport.com/episode-206-the-president-of-disney-theatrical-group-thomas-schumacher/.

21. Amy S. Osatinski, *Disney Theatrical Productions: Producing Broadway Musicals the Disney Way* (New York: Routledge, 2019), 14.

22. Jed Bernstein, quoted in Jesse McKinley, "Fast Lane to Broadway Begins in Hollywood," *New York Times*, September 11, 2005, A10.

23. Peter C. Kunze, "Stream Heat: Netflix, Broadway, and Industrial Convergence," *Flow*, April 27, 2019, https://www.flowjournal.org/2019/04/stream-heat/.

24. Howard Ashman, "Howard Ashman Interview with R. Keith Michael," Indiana University Media Collections Online video, 22:38, [1987] 2014, https://media.dlib.indiana.edu/media_objects/9s161p314?fbclid=IwAR0OEWPhWKCC3bgSQWh63aeUffCzM1zcEIH2AomddEfWF3fLCZ-1fzzC2no.

25. Thomas Schumacher, quoted in Stacy Wolf, *Beyond Broadway: The Pleasure and Promise of Musical Theatre across America* (New York: Oxford University Press, 2020), 27.

26. Ruthie Fierberg, "How Disney Shows Are Changing the Landscape of the American Musical Theatre," *Playbill*, August 10, 2018, https://www.playbill.com/article/how-disney-shows-are-changing-the-landscape-of-the-american-musical-theatre.

27. See, for example, Jeanine Basinger, *The Movie Musical!* (New York: Knopf, 2019).

28. For more on the live musical television events of the 2010s, see Kessler, *Broadway in the Box*, 225–260.

29. Nicholas Barber, "How a Spider-Man Musical Became a Theatrical Disaster," *BBC*, November 25, 2020, https://www.bbc.com/culture/article/20201125-how-a-spider-man-musical-became-a-theatrical-disaster.

30. Schumacher, interview with Davenport, *Producer's Perspective Podcast*.

31. Derek Johnson, "Culture Industries," in *Reimagining Communication: Action*, ed. Michael Filimowicz and Veronika Tzankova (New York: Routledge, 2020), 254.

32. For a thoughtful discussion of theatre as media(ted), consult Philip Auslander, *Liveness: Performance in a Mediatized Culture*, 2nd ed. (New York: Routledge, 2008), and Sarah Bay-Cheng, "Theater Is Media: Some Principles for a Digital Historiography of Performance," *Theater* 42, no. 2 (2012): 27–41.

33. Bob Iger, quoted in Joe Otterson, "Bob Iger Announces Restructuring After Taking Disney Reins, Kareem Daniel to Exit," *Variety*, November 21, 2022, https://variety.com/2022/biz/news/bob-iger-restructuring-disney-kareem-daniel-exit-1235439263/.

Index

101 Dalmatians: 1961 film, 57, 61; 1997
  film, 142
1776, 130
20/20, 141
20th Century Fox, 29, 30, 36, 45, 46, 49, 69,
  71, 73, 90, 93, 117, 141, 142, 168
42nd Street, 39
60 Minutes, 30
8½, 27

A&E, 141
ABBA, 138
ABC, 59, 62, 140, 141, 143, 161, 162, 168,
  183n68
Abraham, Adam, 39
Abrahams, Jim, 5, 29, 63
Abrams, J. J., 164
Absent-Minded Professor, The, 54
Abyss, The, 73
Academy Awards, 6, 52, 61, 63, 89, 92, 93,
  110, 111, 116, 140, 144, 159, 162, 195n91
Acland, Charles R., 145
Actors' Equity, 99, 129, 150, 153
Addams Family, The, 111
Adler, Steven, 43
Adorno, Theodor, 15
Adventures in Babysitting, 86
Adventures of the Gummi Bears, The, 59
Agnes of God, 27
Ahrens, Lynn, 99, 147, 156
AIDS, 15, 74, 75, 106, 110, 116, 146
Aladdin: film, 1, 3, 20, 90, 93, 116, 117, 118,
  138, 159, 166, 175n5; show, 164, 167
Alexander, Jane, 131–132
Alexander, Lloyd, 31
Algar, James, 16
Alice in Wonderland, 56

All Dogs Go to Heaven, 87, 88
Allen, Tim, 118
Allers, Roger, 1, 55, 109, 138, 195n81
All in the Family, 60
Altman, Rick, 18, 102
Amadeus, 28
Amblin, 69, 72, 90
AMC Theatres, 143
American Repertory Theatre, 75
American Tail, An, 52, 60, 61, 62, 87
American Tail: Fievel Goes West, An, 111
amplification, 26, 74, 145, 168
Anastasia, 163
Andersen, Hans Christian, 68, 99, 163
Anderson, Christopher, 16, 183n68
Anderson, Stephen John, 161
Anderson-Lopez, Kristen, 21, 163
Andersson, Benny, 138
Angels in America, 145, 163
Angels in America: Perestroika, 133
Angels in the Outfield, 139
Animalympics, 36
Annapurna Theatre, 10
Annie: show, 130; 1982 film, 30, 65; 1999
  film, 162
Anything Goes, 77
Apocalypse Now, 110
Apollo 13, 140
Apollo Theatre, 144
Aquino, Ruben, 84
Ardolino, Emile, 58, 117
Aristocats, The, 30
Armstrong, Samuel, 16
'*Art,*' 156
"Art and Revolution" ("Die Kunst und die
  Revolution"), 15
Arthur, Bea, 60, 81

"Art-Work of the Future, The" ("Das
  Kunstwerk der Zukunft"), 15
Arvida Corporation, 48, 49, 70
ASCAP, 89
Ashman, Howard, *Aladdin*, 116, 175n5;
  Beauty and the Beast (film), 92–93,
  100–113; *Beauty and the Beast* (show), 128,
  133; early life, 39; influence on Disney,
  2–6, 9, 12–15, 17–21, 24, 28, 56, 58, 97, 116,
  127, 133, 137, 157, 159, 162, 166, 169; *Little
  Mermaid*, 66–67, 68, 77–91; *Little Shop*,
  38–41, 50–52, 63–65; *Smile*, 51, 63–65, 68
As Is, 75
Aspects of Love, 98, 100, 120
Assassins, 134
Atari, 28, 35, 36
Atlantis: The Lost Empire, 161
Atlas, Larry, 28
"At the Ballet," 65
At the Movies, 59
audience anxiety, 43
Aurora Productions, 24, 32, 34
Auslander, Philip, 8, 27
Avildsen, John G., 54
Azenberg, Emanuel, 145

Bacall, Lauren, 28, 119
Back to the Future, 56, 72
Badham, John, 36, 70
Bádue, Alex, 144, 177n38
Bakshi, Ralph, 90
Balanchine, George, 17
Baldwin, Alec, 138
Ballard, Carroll, 48
Baltimore, Sam, 12, 23, 178n51
Bambi, 31, 33, 56, 60, 71, 80, 138
Bancroft, Tony, 138
Band's Visit, The, 163
Barnes, Clive, 64, 74
Barrymore, John, 98
Barrymore, Lionel, 98
Barton, Charles, 54
Basil of Baker Street, 55
Bass, Sid, 45, 141
Batman, 69, 72, 73, 94, 96
Batman & Robin, 142
Batman Forever, 140
Batman Returns, 117
Battersea Power Station, 144
Baum, Vicki, 98
Baumol, Hilda, 26
Baumol, William J., 26
Bay, Michael, 142
Bazin, André, 8
Beach, Gary, 130, 134, 135
Beaches, 72
Beatty, Warren, 33, 73, 95, 193n11

Beaumont, Jeann-Marie Leprince de, 93
Beauty and the Beast (film), 1, 3, 4, 25, 126,
  127, 128; musical numbers, 11, 149;
  production of, 90–93, 100–110; reception,
  111–113, 116; significance for Disney, 6, 19,
  24, 97, 113, 115–117, 138, 166
Beauty and the Beast (show), 20, 145, 149,
  153, 155; influence on Broadway, 12, 77, 122,
  125, 167; production, 114–115, 126–130;
  reception, 130–137, 148, 157
"Beauty and the Beast," 103, 104, 108, 116,
  131, 135, 159
Beauty Queen of Leenane, The, 156
Bébé's Kids, 90
Becker, Howard S., 178n59
Beebe, Ford, Jr., 16
Beetlejuice, 71
Beggar's Opera, The, 71
"Belle," 104, 105, 108, 110, 111, 159
Belle et la Bête, La, 93
Bells Are Ringing, 39, 51
Bennett, Michael, 26, 40, 75
Benson, 60
Benson, Jodi, 65, 82, 83, 119
Benson, Robby, 107, 110, 112, 120
Benson, Sheila, 34, 37
"Be Our Guest," 11, 103, 104, 108, 109, 110,
  111, 129, 131, 132, 135
Berger, Richard, 46, 47, 49
Bergman, Ingmar, 39, 149
Berkeley, Busby, 17, 129, 132
Berman, Ted, 31
Bernstein, Jed, 165
Bernstein, Leonard, 109, 112
Best Little Whorehouse Goes Public, The, 134
Best Little Whorehouse in Texas, The; film,
  30; show, 27
Better Nate Than Ever, 168
Beverly Hills Cop, 94; *Beverly Hills Cop II*, 69
Big, 71
Billboard, 61, 159
Birch, Patricia, 30
Bird, 82
Bird, Brad, 161
Black and Blue, 119
Black Cauldron, The, 31, 38, 55, 95
Blake, Eubie, 18
Blank Check, 139
Blau, Herbert, 148
Bleckner, Jeff, 162
Block, Geoffrey, 16, 17
Bloomberg, Michael, 122
Bluth, Don, 6, 9, 59, 83, 140, 161, 163, 206n5;
  An American Tail, 52, 60–62; career at
  Disney, 31–32; departure from Disney, 2,
  32; *Land Before Time*, 72, 87; *Secret of
  NIMH*, 19, 24, 33–35

Bock, Jerry, 104
Bogardus, Stephen, 146
Bogdanovich, Peter, 57
Bohn, James, 178n56
Bonkers!, 118
Boorman, John, 98
Bosley, Tom, 130
Boublil, Alain, 99
Boudu Saved from Drowning, 50
Boxleitner, Bruce, 37
Boyle, Danny, 141
Bradley, Alan, 37
Brantley, Ben, 145, 154
Braxton, Toni, 130
Brest, Martin, 94
Brewster, Ben, 177n33
Brickman, Paul, 85
Bring in 'da Noise, Bring in 'da Funk, 145, 146
Broadway League, 10, 164
Broderick, Matthew, 138
Brohn, William David, 156
Bronx Tale, A, 163
Brook, Peter, 149
Brown, Jason Robert, 147–148
Bruckheimer, Jerry, 94
Brustein, Robert, 42, 75, 119
Brynner, Yul, 93, 105
Buck, Chris, 1, 5, 165
Buckley, William F., Jr., 116, 123
Buena Vista, 88, 117
Buffett, Jimmy, 163
bunraku, 148
Burnett, Frances Hodgson, 99
Burston, Jonathan, 8, 184n112
Burton, Tim, 69, 71, 72, 117
Bush, Jared, 159
Butoy, Hendel, 94, 95

CAA (Creative Artists Agency), 139, 141
Cahan, Cora, 122, 143
CalArts (California Institute of the Arts), 12, 30, 31
Caldwell, John Thornton, 12, 14
California Institute of the Arts (CalArts), 12, 30, 31
Calley, John, 141
Cameron, James, 73, 142
Camp Rock, 162
Canby, Vincent, 34, 35, 61, 145, 154
Cannon Films, 69
Canton, Mark, 96
"Can You Feel the Love Tonight?," 152
Capital Cities / ABC, 141, 143
CAPS, 94, 95
Captain Kangaroo, 47
Care Bears Movie, The, 56
Carnival of the Animals, The, 104

Carousel, 5, 133, 135, 163
Carr, Jay, 89, 112
Carroll, Pat, 81, 82, 85, 89
Castle Rock, 90
Catmull, Edwin, 161
Cats, 40, 51, 68, 74, 75, 129, 132, 150, 154; film version, 144; influence, 43–44, 64, 76–77, 112, 119, 125, 145; production, 24–25, 40–43, 76, 184n98; reception, 19, 39, 43, 50, 64
CBS, 30, 71, 141, 156
Central Park Zoo, 147
Champion, Marge, 82
Chapman, Brenda, 105, 138, 140
Charisse, Cyd, 98
Chase, Chevy, 57
Cheers, 60
Cheng, Anne Anlin, 179n78
Chesley, Robert, 75
Chess, 76, 127, 138
Chicago: film, 162; show, 26, 150, 163
Chicken Little, 161
"Chim Chim Cher-ee," 89
Chip 'n Dale: Rescue Rangers, 94
Chorus Line, A, 26, 27, 64, 65
Chronicles of Prydain, The, 31
Cimino, Michael, 28
Cinderella: (1950 film), 56, 60, 80, 85, 102
Cinderella (1997 TV movie), 162
Cinecom, 69
Cineplex Odeon, 69, 120
"Circle of Life," 146, 152, 154
City of Angels, 77, 98
Clark, Greydon, 36
Clayton, Jack, 47
Clements, Ron, 1, 4, 146, 162; *The Little Mermaid*, 58, 66–67, 77, 80, 81, 84–86
Client, The, 139
Close, Glenn, 142
Close Encounters of the Third Kind, 36
Cocktail, 80
Coco, 15
Cocteau, Jean, 93, 100, 101, 102
Cohen, Bernice, 89
Coleman, Cy, 98, 99
Collins, Joan, 81, 82
Collins, Pauline, 74
Color of Money, The, 80
Columbia Live Stage, 9, 10
Columbia Pictures, 27, 29, 49, 73, 94, 117
Columbia TriStar, 96
Columbus, Chris, 86
Comden, Betty, 99
Coming to America, 71
commedia dell'arte, 148
Company, 26
Computer Assisted Production System (CAPS), 94, 95

Conan the Barbarian, 30
Condon, Bill, 166
consumer products, 3, 4, 87, 118, 161
Convergence Culture, 7
Cool World, 90
Coppola, Francis Ford, 110
Corliss, Richard, 111
Corman, Roger, 19, 39
Cornell, John, 71
Cosby Show, The, 60
Cosmatos, George P., 56
Covent Garden, 79
COVID-19 pandemic, 164, 165
Cox, James Douglas, 100, 101
Coyle, Rebecca, 178n56
Crafton, Donald, 11, 12
craft theory, 14, 17, 78, 87, 93, 106, 137, 169,
    178n61
Cravalho, Auli'i, 168
Crawford, Joan, 98
Crazy for You, 119
Creative Artists Agency (CAA), 139, 141
Crimes of the Heart, 28
Cristofer, Michael, 77
critical industrial practices, 14
Crocodile Dundee II, 71
Cruise, Tom, 80, 85
Cuarón, Alfonso, 141
Cukor, George, 83
Cunningham, Sean S., 29
Cuomo, Mario, 124
Cyrano, 133
Cyrano de Bergerac, 134

D2: The Mighty Ducks, 139
Dailey, Peter, 49
Daly, Robert, 57
Daly, Tyne, 77
Damn Yankees, 39, 133, 134
Danny Thomas Show, The, 81
Dante, Joe, 69
Darkwing Duck, 97, 118
Das Kunstwerk der Zukunft" ("The
    Art-Work of the Future"), 15
David, Michael, 131
Davidson, Gordon, 119, 135
Davis, Amy M., 79, 194n45
Davis, Luther, 98
Dead Poets Society, 73, 90, 116
Dear, William, 69, 139
Dear Evan Hansen, 2
Deja, Andreas, 87, 106
Delany, Samuel R., 123
de Mille, Agnes, 17
Demme, Jonathan, 52
De Niro, Robert, 144, 163
De Palma, Brian, 69

Diamond, Matthew, 162
Diamond, Selma, 59
Dickens, Charles, 57
Dick Tracy, 73, 92, 94, 95, 126, 192n2
Die Hard, 71
Die Kunst und die Revolution" ("Art and
    Revolution"), 15
Diller, Barry, 28, 45, 57, 107
Dindal, Mark, 161
Dinkins, David, 123, 198n45
Dirty Dancing, 58
Discover, 97
Disney, Roy E., 62, 137, 139; animation, 50,
    54, 55, 58, 65, 71, 73, 117; *Beauty and the
    Beast*, 105; Disney board, 2, 45, 49–50, 54,
    142; *The Little Mermaid*, 80, 85, 89
Disney, Roy O., 142
Disney, Walt, 2, 11, 12, 48, 139, 156; executive
    leadership, 6, 13, 29, 30, 54, 57, 62, 91, 114,
    125; influence, 32–35, 142, 144; storyteller,
    16, 41, 96–97, 110, 111, 150, 153
Disney Archives, 9, 177n37
Disney Channel, 6, 46, 47, 48, 53, 56, 65, 118,
    131, 153, 162
Disney Decade, 94
Disneyfication, 145
Disney JR., 20, 167
Disneyland, 6, 16
Disneyland, 11, 16, 40, 54, 74, 122, 126, 127,
    128, 133
"Disneyland," 65, 82
Disney-MGM Studios, 72, 90, 100
Disney on Ice, 74
Disney+, 1
Disney Stores, 70, 143, 163
Disney Sunday Movie, The, 62
Disney Theatrical Group, 1, 21, 126, 155, 157,
    165, 166, 167
Disney Vacation Club, 97
Disney Vault, 6, 56
Disney's Hollywood Studios, 72
Disney's Symphonic Fantasy, 114
Disney's Wonderful World, 30, 162
DisneyWar, 46
Doctorow, E. L., 147, 155
Doctor Zhivago, 110
Dodger Productions, 131
Donaldson, Roger, 80
Donalson, Laura, 102
Donley, Maureen, 2, 12, 43
Donner, Richard, 73, 117, 139
Donner Party, 148
Donoghue, Mary Agnes, 70
Do Rozario, Rebecca-Anne, 128, 149
"Dos Oruguitas," 159
double event, 151
Down and Out in Beverly Hills, 5, 50, 63, 70

"Down in New Orleans," 162
Drabinsky, Garth, 9, 20, 69, 120, 125, 144, 147, 148, 153, 155–157
Dragon's Lair, 35, 206n5
Drama Desk, 99
Dramatists Guild, 27
Dreamgirls, 40, 51
DreamWorks, 20, 139, 161
Dresser, The, 28
Dreyfuss, Richard, 28, 54, 63, 142
"Drinking Song, The," 104
Dr. John, 162
DuckTales, 59, 71
Dumbo, 56, 111
Dynasty, 60, 66

Eastwood, Clint, 57, 82
Ebb, Fred, 26, 28, 120, 150, 152
Ebert, Roger, 34, 59, 61, 88, 94, 111
Egan, Susan, 129, 130, 135
Ehrman, David, 33
Eisner, Michael, 25, 63, 71–72, 84, 96, 137–143, 161, 176n20; attitude toward animation, 19, 54–58, 90; *Beauty and the Beast*, 6, 97, 104–109, 115–116; hiring, 2, 45–46, 49–50, 53; influence, 6–7, 18; *The Lion King*, 149–151, 153; *Little Mermaid*, 89; music, 94; New York City, 121–122, 124; at Paramount, 28–29, 36; Renaissance discourse, 5, 93, 117; television, 50, 59, 62; theatre, 114–117, 126, 131–132, 146; theme parks, 70, 118
Elephant, Man, The, 28, 108
Eliot, T. S., 25, 41, 42, 184n100
Eliot, Valerie, 41, 42
Elyas, Sadeen, 179n83
embodied acting, 12
Emick, Jarrod, 134, 135
Emperor's New Groove, The, 161
Empire of the Sun, 69
Encanto, 159, 160
Enchanted, 162
Encino Man, 117
Encore!, 168
"End Duet," 135
Engel, Lehman, 14, 15, 17, 18, 19, 38, 76, 102, 103, 127
EPCOT, 6, 29, 36, 46, 47, 48
Ephron, Nora, 65
Erb, Cynthia, 12, 178n51
Escape to Margaritaville, 163
ESPN, 141
Eszterhas, Joe, 141
E.T. the Extra-Terrestrial, 24, 30, 36, 38
Euro Disneyland, 90, 118, 121, 138
Evita: film, 145; show, 27, 64, 76, 104, 116, 127
Eyen, Tom, 51

Fabulous Invalid, The, 25
Fagan, Garth, 156
"Family Madrigal, The," 159
Fantasia, 16, 56, 97, 117
Fantasmic!, 114
Farinelli and the King, 163
Fatal Attraction, 69, 75
Father of the Bride, 117
Federal Communications Commission (FCC), 47, 71
Federal Trade Commission (FTC), 71
Federle, Tim, 168
Feld, Kenneth, 77, 120
Feldberg, Robert, 133
Feld Productions, 47, 120, 121, 125
Fellini, Federico, 27
Felschow, Laura E., 8
Fences, 74, 75
Ferguson, Norman, 16
FernGully: The Last Rainforest, 90
Feuer, Jane, 68
Few Good Men, A, 99
Fiddler on the Roof, 81
Fierstein, Harvey, 60, 75
Financial Interest and Syndication Rules, 140
Fink, Charlie, 4, 101, 138
Finn, Will, 35, 82
Finn, William, 112
fin-syn, 140
Fiorello!, 130
Fisher King, The, 116
Fitzgerald, Jon, 178n56
Fitzgerald, T. Richard, 127, 145
Flaherty, Stephen, 99, 147, 156
Flashdance, 52, 58
Fleming, Patrick C., 58
flop hit, 119
Flower, Joe, 7
Fontana, Santino, 163
Footloose, 52, 58
Ford, Henry, 147
Ford Center for the Performing Arts, 147, 155
Ford Foundation, 118
Ford Motor Company, 147
Forrest, George, 98
Forrest Gump, 139
Fosse, Bob, 26, 150
For the Boys, 90
Fowler, Beth, 130
Fowler, Mark, 47, 71
Fox (20th Century Fox), 29, 30, 36, 45, 46, 49, 69, 71, 73, 90, 93, 117, 141, 142, 168
Fox and the Hound, The, 31, 32, 33
Frank, Leo, 148
Friday the 13th, 29

Frozen: film, 1, 15, 29, 68, 163; franchise, 1, 3, 163; *Frozen 2*, 165; show, 20, 163, 164, 165
Funny Thing Happened on the Way to the Forum, A, 105
Furniss, Maureen, 23

Gabor, Eva, 31
Gabriel, Mike, 94, 138
Gad, Josh, 163
Gallagher, Peter, 130
Garbo, Greta, 98
García Márquez, Gabriel, 159
Gardenia, Vincent, 52
Gardner, Ava, 82
Garfield, Andrew, 163
Garnett, David, 98
"Gaston," 101, 104, 131
Gavin, Kathleen, 2, 12, 58, 190n50
Gay, John, 17
Geffen, David, 19, 24, 40, 51, 52, 58, 64, 65, 110, 137, 139, 141
Geffen Company, 51, 52
Gelbart, Larry, 98
General Electric, 141
Gerard, Jeremy, 133
Geronimi, Clyde, 31, 56, 67, 85, 97, 105
Gershwin, George, 27, 119
Gershwin, Ira, 27, 119
Gershwin Theatre, 134, 144, 147
Gesamtkunstwerk, 15, 16, 179n77
"Getting to Know You," 103
Getty, Estelle, 60
Gibson, Brian, 90
Gibson, Debbie, 130
Gibson Greetings, 49
Giesekam, Greg, 8
Gillespie, Dizzy, 82
Gillespie, Sarah Ashman, 78
Gilliam, Terry, 116
Giuliani, Rudy, 121, 122, 123, 124, 146
Gleason, Jackie, 105
God Bless You, Mr. Rosewater: novel, 28; show, 28, 39
Godspell, 26
Gold, Stanley, 2, 48, 49
Goldberg, Eric, 138
Goldberg, Whoopi, 138
Golden Girls, The, 5, 50, 59, 60, 72, 73, 81, 90, 118
Golden Globes, 117, 159
Goldenthal, Elliot, 149
Goldman, Emma, 155
Goldman, Gary, 31, 32, 35, 60, 140, 161, 163, 206n5
Goldmark, Daniel, 178
Gombert, Ed, 55
Gomery, Douglas, 71, 176n20, 178n50

Gong Show, 57
Good Fairy, The, 39
"Good Morning, Good Day," 104
Good Morning, Vietnam, 71, 72
Goof Troop, 118
Gordon, Lawrence, 89
Gottlieb, Myron, 147
Graduate, The, 30
Grand Hotel, 98
Grand Night for Singing, A, 134
Granger, Brian, 136
Graphics Group (Lucasfilm), 38, 140
Grease, 39; *Grease 2*, 30
Greatest Showman, The, 2
Great Mouse Detective, The, 4, 35, 55, 61, 62, 63, 79, 80, 87, 166
Green, Adolph, 99
Green, Jesse, 164
Greene, Ellen, 52, 53
Greenwald, Robert, 33
Greno, Nathan, 161
Griffin, Sean, 12, 176n20, 178n51
Groff, Jonathan, 163
Groundlings, The, 82
guajira, 159
Guare, John, 99
Guber, Peter, 73
Guillaume, Robert, 152
Gun Shy, 30
Guns N' Roses, 94
Gussow, Mel, 40
Gutierrez, Gerald, 126
Guys and Dolls, 103, 119, 130, 138
Gypsy, 77, 148

Hackett, Buddy, 83
Hackford, Taylor, 30
Hahn, Don, 56, 65, 79, 97, 100, 101, 104, 111, 138
Hair, 26, 27
"Hakuna Matata," 152
Hale, Joe, 55
Hall, Peter, 75
Hamilton: show, 132, 164; film, 1, 2, 168
Hamlisch, Marvin, 26, 51, 63, 64, 65
Hammerstein, Oscar, II, 5, 16, 17, 40, 76, 92, 93, 102, 120, 134, 144, 152, 162
Hampton, Christopher, 74
Hand, David, 16, 31
Handley, Jim, 16
Hand That Rocks the Cradle, The, 117
Hanks, Tom, 73, 142
Hannah, Daryl, 80
Hansen, Ed, 32, 34
Hanson, Curtis, 117
Happy Days, 50, 130
Hardy, Hugh, 146
Harlem Nights, 73, 88

Harmetz, Aljean, 45, 62
Harnick, Sheldon, 104
Harries, Martin, 176n31
Harris, Neil, 151
Harris, Robin, 90
Harris, Susan, 50, 60, 81
Harrison, Rex, 83
Harry and the Hendersons, 69
Harry Potter and the Cursed Child, 164
Hart, Moss, 25
Hartigan, Patti, 154
Hawkanson, David, 153
Hawn, Goldie, 57
Hayes, Thomas C., 45
Hays, Carole Shorenstein, 75
Hearst, 141
Heaven's Gate, 28
Hee, T., 16
Heidi Chronicles, The, 74
Heiskell, Marian Sulzberger, 121
Hellman, Lillian, 164
Hello, Dolly!, 105
Henning, Doug, 28
Henson, Jim, 52
Hercules: film, 146, 164; show, 168
Herek, Stephen, 142
Herman, Jerry, 105, 112, 152
Herman, Pee-wee, 104
Hickner, Steve, 140
Higgins, Colin, 30, 36
high concept, 25, 29, 42, 52, 57, 58, 59, 61, 69,
     70, 73, 74, 77, 96, 117
High School Musical, 162; franchise, 1, 162
Hill, George Roy, 63
Hiller, Arthur, 70
Hilmes, Michele, 8, 13
Hinson, Hal, 89, 111
hip hop, 77, 146
Hirsch, Foster, 76
Hirschfield, Alan J., 49
History Channel, 141
Hoffman, Dustin, 111
Hoffman, William M., 75
Hofsiss, Jack, 126
Holder, Donald, 156
Holder, Geoffrey, 27, 67, 82
Holliday, Judy, 39
Hollie, Pamela G., 32
Hollywood Pictures, 2, 94, 117, 145
Hollywood Records, 94, 162
Holt, Jennifer, 8, 140, 141
"Home," 128
Home Improvement, 97
home video, 6, 7, 53, 54, 56, 59, 63, 70, 71, 72,
     73, 80
Honey, I Shrunk the Kids, 73, 90
Honeymooners, The, 90, 105

Hooper, Tobe, 30
Hopkins, Anthony, 135
Hoskins, Bob, 72
Hot Gossip, 42
Houdini, Harry, 155
Hould-Ward, Ann, 126, 127, 129, 130, 135
Houseman, John, 27
Howard, Byron, 159, 161
Howard, Ron, 5, 52, 140, 142
Hudson, Richard, 156
Hughes, John, 52
Hugo, Victor, 142
"Human Again," 109, 128
Hummler, Richard, 65
Hunchback of Notre Dame, The, 142
Huston, John, 30
Huston, Walter, 122
Huxtable, Ada Louise, 146
Hwang, David Henry, 74
Hyperion Books, 94

I, Tina, 90
Iceman Cometh, The, 163
"If I Can't Love Her," 128, 135
Iger, Robert, 161, 168
"I Just Can't Wait to Be King," 152
Indiana Jones and the Last Crusade, 73
Ingram, James, 61
Innerspace, 69
Intellivision, 35
Interview with the Vampire, 139
Into the Woods, 76, 127, 134
Iron Giant, The, 161
Irons, Jeremy, 138
Irwin, Bill, 77
Iscove, Robert, 162
"I want" song, 53, 66, 69, 79, 86, 105, 139, 152,
     159, 160
Iwerks, Ub, 16

Jackson, Glenda, 74, 163
Jackson, Wilfred, 16, 56, 71, 85, 105
Jacobs, Bernard, 27
Jacobs, Irwin, 49
Jacobs, Lea, 177n33
Jarrold, Julian, 163
Jaws, 25
Jelly's Last Jam, 119
Jenkins, Henry, 7
Jerker, 75
Jerome Robbins' Broadway, 77, 119
Jesus Christ Superstar, 26, 64, 116, 127
Jeter, Michael, 98
Jobs, Steve, 140, 161
Joel, Billy, 59
John, Elton, 138, 152, 154
Johnson, Derek, 168

Johnson, Patrick Read, 95
Johnston, Joe, 73
Johnston, Ollie, 83, 84
Jonas Brothers, 162
Jones, Reed, 75
Jordan, Neil, 139
Joysticks, 36
Juan Darién: A Carnival Mass, 148
Jujamcyn Theaters, 89–90, 122
Jungle Book, The, 30, 164

Kael, Pauline, 53
Kail, Thomas, 168
Kalish, Eddie, 29
Kander, John, 26, 28, 120, 150, 152
Kaplan, Caren, 102
Katzenberg, Jeffrey, 5, 6, 25, 62, 71, 97;
    attitude toward animation, 19, 50, 54–58;
    Beauty and the Beast, 100–103, 105–110;
    departure from Disney, 136–139, 142–143,
    157; DreamWorks, 139–140, 146; hiring, 2,
    45–46, 49, 176n20; the Katzenberg memo,
    92, 95–96, 117; *The Little Mermaid*, 80–81,
    83–86, 91; managerial strategy and style,
    2, 13, 18, 50, 54, 57, 59, 112, 117, 142;
    relationship with Ashman, 65, 89,
    106–107; and theatre, 114, 120, 126
Kaufman, George S., 25
Kay, Alan, 36
Kaye, Stubby, 72
KCAL, 71
Keane, Glen, 82, 86, 161
Keeshan, Bob, 47
Kehr, Dave, 88
Kellman, Barnet, 65
Kempley, Rita, 52
Kentucky Cycle, The, 133
Kern, Jerome, 16, 120, 144
Kerr, Walter, 40
Kessler, Kelly, 8, 155
KHJ-TV, 71
Kicks, 51
Kidman, Shawna, 96
King, Carole, 163
King, Thomas R., 132
King and I, The, 15, 92, 93, 102, 103, 104, 108
King David, 146
Kinky Boots, 163
Kiss of the Spider Woman, 120
"Kiss the Girl," 79, 82, 159
Kleban, Edward, 26
Knapp, Margaret M., 18
Knickerbocker, 28
Koch, Ed, 123
Kocurek, Carly, 36
Kramer, Larry, 75
Kramer, Mimi, 76, 77

Kroll, Jack, 154
Kroyer, Bill, 37, 90
Kuhn, Judy, 146
Kundun, 142
Kushner, Tony, 133, 145

La bohème, 146
La Cage aux Folles, 134
Lady and the Tramp, 71
Lahr, John, 120, 133
Lamberts, Heath, 130
Land Before Time, The, 62, 72, 87
Landis, John, 52, 71
Landon, Margaret, 102
Lane, Nathan, 138, 163–164
Lang, Walter, 93
Lansbury, Angela, 112, 120
Lapine, James, 51, 126, 134, 192n2
Largely New York, 77
Larry King Live, 141
Larson, Eric, 31, 32, 34
Lasseter, John, 23, 139, 140, 160, 161, 162
Latifah, Queen, 168
Latin History for Morons, 163
Lauch, Bill, 40, 68, 116
Laurents, Arthur, 148
Laverne & Shirley, 50
Lawrence of Arabia, 94
League of American Theatres and
    Producers, 150, 165
Lean, David, 94, 110, 149
Lee, Jennifer, 1, 165
Leigh, Carolyn, 63, 64
Leonowens, Anna, 102, 194n46
Lerner, Alan Jay, 5, 152
Les Misérables, 73, 75, 77, 112, 115, 129, 133
"Les Poissons," 86
Lethal Weapon: Lethal Weapon 2, 73; *Lethal
    Weapon 3*, 117
Lettice and Lovage, 99
Levinson, Barry, 55, 71, 95
Liberty's Taken, 149
Lifetime, 141
Lima, Kevin, 5, 162
Lincoln Center, 148
Lion King, The: film, 1, 4, 93, 117; show, 1, 8,
    20, 136–158, 163, 164
Lion King II: Simba's Pride, The, 153
Lipscomb, RuDee, 153
Lisberger, Steven, 19, 36, 37, 53
Littlefield, Warren, 59, 60
Little Me, 68
"Little Mermaid, The," 99
Little Mermaid, The (film), 2, 6, 20, 92,
    105–106, 111–112, 117, 119, 134, 166, 168;
    musical numbers, 65–67, 101, 104;
    production, 15, 19, 35, 58, 65–70, 77–87;

reception, 87–90, 93–94; significance for
  Disney, 3, 4, 5, 23, 25, 72, 73, 90–91, 95–96,
  103, 139, 162
Little Mermaid, The (show), 20, 157
Little Night Music, A, 39, 130
Little Shop of Horrors, The (film), 19, 24
Little Shop of Horrors (film), 51, 52, 53, 63,
  64, 65
Little Shop of Horrors (show), 15, 55, 65, 78,
  79; Off-Broadway production, 38–40,
  43–44, 50–51, 81; Off-Off-Broadway
  production, 19, 24–25, 64; legacy, 20, 127
Livent, 9, 120, 143, 144, 147, 150, 156, 157
Lloyd, Christopher, 72
Lloyd, Phyllida, 168
Lloyd Webber, Andrew, 64, 65, 127, 162;
  Aspects of Love, 98, 120; as brand, 20, 74,
  100, 116, 125, 129, 130, 144; *Cats*, 19, 40–43,
  50; *Evita*, 27; *Jesus Christ Superstar*, 26;
  Phantom of the Opera, 76; Really Useful
  Group, 9, 24, 120, 157; reputation, 39, 43,
  98; *Sunset Boulevard*, 100, 134, 144, 157
Loewe, Frederick, 5, 112, 152
Longo, Vincent, 177n34
Lopez, Robert, 21, 163
Lost in Yonkers, 99
Lounsbery, John, 31
Lovato, Demi, 162
Lovett, Marcus, 146
low-concept, 69
Lucas, Craig, 99
Lucas, George, 57, 71, 60, 62, 69, 95, 140
Lucasfilm, 36, 38, 140, 161
Luhrmann, Baz, 141, 162
LuPone, Patti, 77
Luske, Hamilton, 16, 31, 56, 67, 71, 85
Lyles, Aubrey, 18
Lynch, David, 108
Lyne, Adrian, 52, 69
Lynne, Gillian, 42
Lyons, Donald, 154

M, Lebo, 152, 153, 154
Maazel, Lorin, 43
M. Butterfly, 74, 99
MacArthur Fellowship, 148, 149
Mackintosh, Cameron, 9, 74, 100, 120, 125,
  144, 145; *Cats*, 43; *Little Shop*, 19, 20, 24,
  40; *Miss Saigon*, 99
MacMurray, Fred, 54
Madama Butterfly, 99
Madame Tussaud's Wax Museum, 143
Madonna, 77
Mahabharata, The, 143
"Maison Des Lunes," 128
Make a Wish, 39
Mame, 81

Mamet, David, 77
Manassas National Battlefield Park, 138
Mancina, Mark, 152, 154
Mancuso, Frank, 57, 58
Mann, Terrence, 129, 135
Marjoribanks, Duncan, 88
Marowitz, Charles, 133
Marsden, Pam, 12
Marshall, Garry, 72, 92, 95
Marshall, Penny, 71
Marshall, Rob, 1, 162
Martin, Hugh, 39
Martin, Steve, 52, 77
Marvel, 161, 162
Marx, Groucho, 116
Mary Poppins, 65, 89, 92, 115, 195n91
Mary Poppins Return, 1
Maslin, Janet, 52, 88, 112, 133
Masteroff, Joe, 104
Matsushita, 96
Matthau, Walter, 83
Mattinson, Burny, 4
Maude, 60, 81
"Maude's Dilemma," 60
Maverick, 139
Mayer, Louis B., 139
Mayfield, Les, 117
Mazursky, Paul, 5, 50, 54, 63
McAnuff, Des, 74
McCann, Elizabeth I., 1, 28, 77
McClanahan, Rue, 60
McConaughey, Matthew, 141
McCracken, Harry, 61
McDonagh, Martin, 156
McDonald, Audra, 156
McDonald's, 62, 70, 87
McDonnell, Cari, 7
McKenna, Patrick, 144
McLaughlin, Robert, 8, 169
McMillin, Scott, 18
McNally, Terrence, 147, 156
McTiernan, John, 71
McTyre, Bob, 114, 124, 126, 131
"Me," 128, 135
Meadow, Lynne, 89
Me and My Girl, 76, 77
Mean Girls, 164
"Mean Green Mother from Outer Space," 52
media convergence, 7, 22, 169
medium anxiety, 26, 40
Meehan, Eileen, 72
Meet the Robinsons, 161
megamusical, British dominance, 5, 68–69,
  73–75, 99–100, 128, 133, 144; as mode of
  production, 20, 25, 77, 92, 98, 112, 115, 125,
  127, 130–131, 134, 146
Méliès, Georges, 40

"Memory," 42, 64, 184n100
Mendes, Sam, 168
Menken, Alan, 2, 13; *Aladdin*, 116; *Beauty and the Beast* (film), 92, 93, 97, 101, 103–105, 109, 112–114; *Beauty and the Beast* (show), 126–128, 134, 138; *King David*, 146; *Little Shop*, 24, 38–40, 52; *God Bless You, Mr. Rosewater*, 28; *Little Mermaid*, 67–68, 75, 79, 80, 88, 89, 90; partnership with Ashman, 2–6, 12, 15, 17–21, 51, 157, 159, 162, 166; *Tangled*, 162
Menzel, Idina, 163
merchandising, *Aladdin*, 3, 117; on Broadway, 140, 144–145, 154, 165; children's television, 47, 59; *The Great Mouse Detective*, 55; *The Little Mermaid*, 87; merchandising interests, 7, 70, 87, 89, 97; *Secret of NIMH*, 34; total merchandising, 22; *Toy Story*, 140; *Tron*, 38
Merlin, 27
Merrick, Joseph, 108
Metallica, 94
Meteor Shower, 163
Metro-Goldwyn-Mayer (MGM), 28, 29, 34, 49, 69, 72, 90, 93, 96, 98, 100
Meyer, Nicholas, 30
Meyer, Stan, 115, 126, 127, 130
MGM (Metro-Goldwyn-Mayer), 28, 29, 34, 49, 69, 72, 90, 93, 96, 98, 100
Miami Vice, 59
Michener, Dave, 4
microphones, 8, 26
Midler, Bette, 54, 59, 63, 65, 72, 142
Milius, John, 30
Miller, Ann, 27
Miller, Arthur, 164
Miller, F. E., 18
Miller, Ron, 2, 6, 29, 30, 32, 33, 34, 45, 46, 48, 49, 53, 54, 55, 56, 59, 63
Minkoff, Rob, 1
Miramax, 2, 13, 118, 162
Miranda, Lin-Manuel, 1, 2, 21, 110, 159, 160
Mirisch, Donald, 140
Miss Julie, 149
Miss Saigon, 99, 100, 133
Mittermeier, Sabrina, 118
Mixed Nuts, 65
Miyazaki, Hayao, 100
Mnouchkine, Ariane, 118
Moana, 168
Molina, Adrian, 15
Monday Night Football, 141
Moore, Fred, 85, 153
Moore, Mandy, 162
Moranis, Rick, 52
Morton, Jelly Roll, 119
Moses, Burke, 129, 130, 133, 135

Most, Andrea, 16
Most Happy Fella, The, 119
Moulin Rouge!, 162
Mozart, Wolfgang Amadeus, 149
Mr. Destiny, 95
Mr. Holland's Opus, 142
Mrs. Frisby and the Rats of NIMH, 33
MTV Networks, 73
Mueller, John, 16, 17
Muppets, The, 39
Murdoch, Rupert, 93
Murphy, Eddie, 73, 88
Murphy, Ryan, 164
Music Man, The, 162
Musker, John, 1, 4, 31, 79, 146, 162; *The Little Mermaid*, 58, 66–67, 77, 80, 81, 84–86
My Fair Lady: film, 83, 93; show, 5, 15, 79, 108, 163
My One and Only, 27

National Amusements, 115
National Endowment for the Arts, 119, 131
National Theatre, 75
NBC, 30, 59, 60, 141
Nederlander Organization, 122
Nelson, Steve, 125
Nesbit, Evelyn, 155
Never Cry Wolf, 48
"Never Knew I Needed," 162
New 42nd Street, 121, 122, 147
New Amsterdam Theatre, 20, 122, 124, 131, 143, 146, 147, 153, 154, 155, 157, 163, 167
Newhart, Bob, 31
New History of Animation, A, 23
Newman, Randy, 160
Newsies, 91, 162, 168
New York Film Festival, 110
Ne-Yo, 162
Nibbelink, Phil, 111
Nichols, Mike, 30
Nicholson, William, 99
Nichtern, Claire, 28, 72
Nickelodeon, 47, 164
Nimoy, Leonard, 70
Nine, 27, 38
Nine Old Men, 30, 31, 83
"No Matter What," 128
Normal Heart, The, 75
Norman, Marsha, 99
Nottage, Lynn, 164
Nugent, Nelle, 1, 28
Nunn, Trevor, 42, 74, 75, 184n100
Nuts, 27
NYPD Blue, 141

O'Brien, Robert C., 33
Ockrent, Mike, 146

O'Connor, Thomas, 112
O'Donnell, Rosie, 155, 156
Odyssey, 35
Off-Broadway theatre, 50, 51, 64, 118, 145, 146; *Assassins*, 134; *God Bless You, Mr. Rosewater*, 28, 39; *Little Shop of Horrors*, 19, 24, 40, 43, 81, 127
Off-Off-Broadway theater, 21, 39, 118
O'Hara, Maureen, 54
O'Hara, Paige, 104, 120
Oklahoma!, 5, 17
Old Possum's Book of Practical Cats, 25, 41
Oliver & Company, 73; as a musical, 66, 79, 80, 152, 175n5; production, 56–58, 190n50; reception, 61, 72, 86–87; significance, 117, 166
Oliver Twist, 57
Olympic Arts Festival, 55, 149
Once on This Island, 99, 163
"Once Upon a Time in New York City," 56
operational aesthetic, 151
Orbach, Jerry, 112, 120
Ordinary People, 29
Oriental Land Company, 29
Orr, James, 95
Ortega, Kenny, 91, 162
Osatinski, Amy S., 165, 177n38
Othello, 122
O'Toole, Fintan, 154
Outrageous Fortune, 70
Ovitz, Michael, 139, 141, 142, 156, 157
Oz, Frank, 52

Pajama Game, The, 51
Pallant, Chris, 23
Panofsky, Erwin, 8
Papp, Joseph, 50
Parade, 148
Paradise, 70
Paramount, 2, 27, 28, 29, 30, 36, 45, 46, 49, 54, 55, 57, 58, 69, 70, 71, 73, 90, 94, 96, 108, 111, 134, 139, 140, 142
Parent Trap, The, 54
Parker, Alan, 145
Partridge Family, The, 60
"Part of Your World," 78, 79, 86, 87
Pasek, Benj, 2, 21
Pasquin, John, 139
Passion, 134
Passione d'amore, 134, 135
Pataki, George, 143
Paterno, Peter, 94
Pathé, 96
Patinkin, Mandy, 104
Paul, Justin, 21
PBS, 47, 156
Pebble and the Penguin, The, 139

performative branding, 11
Perren, Alisa, 13, 118
Personal Best, 51
Peter Pan: film, 85, 105; show, 63
Peters, Bernadette, 164
Peters, Jon, 73
Pete's Dragon, 2, 31
Phantom of the Opera, 65, 76, 77, 112, 115, 133, 134, 135, 144, 157
Phenomenon, 168
Piano Lesson, The, 99
"Piano Man," 58
Picard, Martin, 38
Pielmeier, John, 27
Pinewood Studios, 52
Pinocchio, 31, 56, 80, 82, 109, 111
Pixar, 15, 20, 38, 94, 140, 160, 161
Playwrights Horizons, 51, 126, 127
Pleasure Island, 72, 90
Pocahontas, 138, 139, 140, 146, 202n33
Podhoretz, Norman, 123
Poe, Edgar Allan, 149
Pollack, Sydney, 63
Poltergeist, 30, 38
Polygram, 119
Pong, 36
"Poor Unfortunate Souls," 79, 81, 85
Porter, Cole, 17, 39, 152
Prelude to a Kiss, 99
Pretty Woman, 92, 95
Price, Frank, 57
Prince, Harold, 27, 39, 76, 144
Prince, Stephen, 57, 71
Prince of Egypt, The, 140
Prince of the Magic Kingdom, 6
Princess and the Frog, The, 162
Princess Bride, The, 104
Pryce, Jonathan, 99
Pryor, Richard, 88
Public Theater, 50, 168
Puccini, Giacomo, 99, 146
Pudovkin, Vsevolod, 8
Pulitzer Prize, 77, 99, 134, 146, 164
Purdum, Jill, 100, 101
Purdum, Richard, 100, 101, 104

Quiroga, Horacio, 148

Rae, Charlotte, 81
Ragtime: book, 147, 155; show, 147, 155, 156
Rambo: First Blood Part II, 56
Ransom, 142
Raskin, Kenny, 130
Reagan, Ronald, 46, 63, 71
Really Useful Group, 9, 24, 120, 143, 144, 157
Redford, Robert, 29
Reds, 33, 193n11

Redstone, Sumner, 115
reggaeton, 159
Reiner, Rob, 104
Reinking, Ann, 150
Reitherman, Wolfgang, 2, 30, 31, 56, 67
Reliance Financial Services, 48
Rent, 132, 145, 146
Rescuers, The, 31, 56, 58
Rescuers Down Under, The, 94, 95, 96, 117, 147, 148
Return of Jafar, The, 138
Reubens, Paul, 104
Reynolds, Kevin, 96
Reza, Yasmina, 156
Rice, Tim, 26, 27, 41, 64, 116, 127, 138, 146, 152, 154, 175n5
Rich, B. Ruby, 122
Rich, Frank, 43, 51, 64, 74, 76, 77, 98, 112, 114, 119, 139, 145
Rich, Richard, 31
Richards, David, 76, 98, 127, 132, 133, 134
Ringel, Eleanor, 61, 112
Ringling Brothers and Barnum & Bailey, 120
Ripley, Alice, 146
Risky Business, 85
Ritchie, Michael, 63
Roberts, Bill, 16
Roberts, Doris, 59
Roberts, Julia, 95
Robertson, Rebecca, 125
Robin Hood, 2, 30, 31, 56; Robin Hood: Prince of Thieves, 96
Robinson, Martin P., 40, 52
Rock, The, 142
Rockettes, 51
Rocky: Rocky III, 30; Rocky IV, 56
Rodgers, Richard, 5, 17, 40, 92, 93, 102, 134, 152, 162
Rogers, Bradley, 15
Romberg, Sigmund, 104
Ronstadt, Linda, 61
Rooney, Darrell, 153
Rooney, Mickey, 27
Rose, Anika Noni, 162
Rose, Billy, 74, 152
Roseanne, 141
Ross, Herbert, 52
Rostand, Edmond, 134
Roth, Joe, 73, 93, 157
Roth, Robert Jess, 114, 115, 126, 127, 128, 129, 131, 135, 150
Roundabout Theatre Company, 125
Royal Shakespeare Company, 75
Rudin, Scott, 134
Russell, Willy, 74
Ruthless People, 5, 63
Rydell, Mark, 91

Sabella, Ernie, 138
Safe Sex, 75
Sagansky, Jeff, 57
Saint-Saëns, Camille, 104
Salamon, Julie, 52
Salonga, Lea, 99
salsa, 159
Saltz, David, 8
Sanders, Chris, 138
Santa Clause, The, 139
Satterfield, Paul, 16
Savran, David, 7, 25
Schatz, Thomas, 13, 73, 176n20
Scheck, Frank, 133
Schenkkan, Robert, 133
Schneider, Peter, 2, 11, 12, 166; Beauty and the Beast, 110; departure, 161; hiring, 55, 67; The Lion King (show), 148, 155, 156; The Little Mermaid, 83–84
Schönberg, Claude-Michel, 99
Schonberg, Harold C., 26
Schorsch, Rebecca S., 144
Schumacher, Joel, 139, 140, 142
Schumacher, Thomas, 2, 12, 21, 148, 149, 152, 156, 157, 164, 166, 167, 168
Schumer, Amy, 163
Schwartz, Stephen, 143
Schwarzenegger, Arnold, 104
Scola, Ettore, 134
Scorsese, Martin, 52, 80, 109, 142, 144
Scott, Ridley, 75
Scott, Tim, 75
Scott, Tony, 52, 69
Scribner, George, 56, 187n73
SEC (Securities and Exchange Commission), 49
Secret Garden, The, 99
Secret of NIMH, The, 19, 24, 34, 43, 61, 87
Securities and Exchange Commission (SEC), 49
Seller, Jeffrey, 132
Selznick, Arna, 56
Selznick, David O., 13, 57, 144
Sesame Street, 65, 163
"Shadowland," 152
Shadowlands, 99
Shaffer, Peter, 99
Shaggy Dog, The, 54
"Shall We Dance," 103, 104, 108
Sharpsteen, Ben, 16, 31, 56
Shatner, William, 73
She Loves Me, 104
Shelly, Adrienne, 163
Shelton, Toby, 138
Shepherd, Cybill, 144
Sherak, Tom, 142
Sherbert, Linda, 65

Show Boat, 16, 104, 120, 144, 147
Shrek (franchise), 161
Shubert Organization, The, 24, 27, 40, 64, 122
Shue, Elisabeth, 86
Shuffle Along, 18
Shuffle Along, or, the Making of the Musical Sensation of 1921 and All That Followed, 18
Shyer, Charles, 117
Siegel, Ed, 154
Silver Screen Partners, 62, 63, 94
Simon, John, 132, 154
Simon, Neil, 99
Simpson, Don, 94
Simpsons, The, 6
Siskel, Gene, 59, 88
Sissle, Noble, 18
Sister Act, 117
Sito, Tom, 73
Six Degrees of Separation, 99
Skase, Christopher, 93
Sleeping Beauty, 31
Small & Frye, 30
Smalls, Charlie, 26
Smile, 51, 63, 64, 65, 68, 73, 81, 82, 89, 166
Smiles of a Summer's Night, 39
Smith, Anna Deavere, 133
Smith, Bruce W., 90
Smith, Charise Castro, 159
Smith, Matthew Wilson, 16, 114, 179nn76, 77, 79
Smith, Susan, 179n84
Smoodin, Eric, 11, 176n20
"Snow Queen, The," 68, 163
Snow White and the Seven Dwarfs, 16, 30, 31, 53, 56, 61, 67, 71, 80, 97, 179n83
Soap, 50, 60
Solomon, Charles, 61
Someone to Watch Over Me, 75
"Something There," 104, 109, 110, 111
Something Wicked This Way Comes, 47, 56
"Somewhere Out There," 52, 61
"Somewhere That's Green," 52, 53, 78
Sondheim, Stephen, 40, 98, 112, 145, 152, 156, 162; criticism of Broadway, 42, 51; *Dick Tracy*, 94, 126, 192n2, 193n11; *Into the Woods*, 76; *A Little Night Music*, 39; *Passion*, 134–135; *Sunday in the Park with George*, 126; *Sweeney Todd*, 27; *West Side Story*, 109
Song of the Sea, 99
Sonnenfeld, Barry, 111
Sontag, Susan, 8
Sony, 9, 71, 73, 96, 141, 142, 168
Sorkin, Aaron, 99
Sound of Music, The: film, 111; show, 17
South Pacific, 5
Spaced Invaders, 95

Spector, Phil, 39
Speed-the-Plow, 77
Spelling, Aaron, 81
Spider-Man: Turn Off the Dark, 168
Spielberg, Steven, 24, 33, 35, 36, 55, 57, 60, 62, 69, 72, 73, 87, 95, 139
Splash, 5, 48, 80
Splash Mountain, 90
SpongeBob SquarePants, 164
Spottiswoode, Roger, 73
Springer, Jerry, 155
Springsteen, Bruce, 164
Stakeout, 70
Stalin, Josef, 141
Stallone, Sylvester, 30, 56
Stanfill, Dennis, 49
Stanton, Andrew, 160
Starlight Express, 68, 73, 74, 75, 76, 98
Star Trek II: The Wrath of Khan, 30, 38
Star Trek IV, 57
Star Trek V: The Final Frontier, 73
Star Wars, 31, 36, 115, 162, 163
Steamboat Willie, 16
Stearns, David Patrick, 132
Steel, Dawn, 94
Steinberg, Saul, 45, 48, 49, 53, 55
Stern, Robert A. M., 121, 122
Sternfeld, Jessica, 180n4
Sterritt, David, 37
Stevens, Art, 31
Stevens, George, 28
Stevenson, Robert, 54
Stewart, James B., 6, 46
Stewart, James L., 32
Stiers, David Ogden, 120
Sting, The, 63
St. Nicholas Theatre Company, 12
Stone, Lucy, 99
Stoner, Sherri, 82
Stones, Tad, 138
Storaro, Vittorio, 110
Straight Talk, 65
"Strange Things," 160
Streisand, Barbra, 27
Strickler, Jeff, 112
Stritch, Elaine, 81, 191n65
Stubbs, Levi, 52
Student Prince, The, 104
Sturges, Preston, 39
Suehsdorf, David, 149
Sugar Babies, 27, 39
Sullivan, Ed, 116
Summer, Donna, 163
Sunday in the Park with George, 51, 104, 126, 134
Sunset Boulevard, 100, 119, 134, 144, 157
Sweeney Todd, 27, 39, 130

Swift, David, 54
Sword in the Stone, The, 56

"Take My Breath Away," 52
TaleSpin, 94
Tangled, 161, 162
Tap Dance Kid, The, 82
Tarzan, 5, 23
Tatum, Donn, 49
Taxi Driver, 144
Taylor, John, 6
Taylor, Ron, 40
Taymor, Julie, development and directing,
    148–154; The Lion King, 8, 20, 136, 143,
    184n110; Spider-Man: Turn Off the Dark,
    168; Tony Awards, 156
Teatr Loh, 148
Teletubbies, 156
TGIF, 141
Thalberg, Irving, 13, 57
"There Are No Cats in America," 61
Thomas, Bob, 9
Thomas, Danny, 81
Thomas, Frank, 83
Thomas, Jonathan Taylor, 138
Thomas, Tony, 50, 60
Three Fugitives, 70
Three Men and a Baby, 70, 71
Three Tall Women, 163
Thurman, Uma, 163
Times Square, 25, 26, 122, 123, 125, 132, 143,
    156, 157, 163
Times Square Redevelopment Project, 125
Time Warner, 93, 140, 168
Tina, 163
Tin Toy, 140
Titan A.E., 161
Titanic, 142
TKTS booth, 145
Tokyo Disneyland, 29, 46, 137
Tony Awards, 81, 82, 85, 129, 130, 133, 145,
    162, 163; Beauty and the Beast, 133–135;
    Cats, 42; A Chorus Line, 64; Grand Hotel,
    98; Jerome Robbins' Broadway, 119; Juan
    Darién: A Carnival Mass, 148; Les
    Misérables, 74; Lost in Yonkers, 99; M.
    Butterfly, 99; Phantom of the Opera, 76;
    Rent, 146; The Lion King, 153, 155–156
Top Gun, 52, 58, 94
Topor, Tom, 27
Torch Song Trilogy, 60
Total Abandon, 28
Touchstone Films (Pictures), 86; founding,
    5, 6, 29, 47–48, 50, 142; success, 2, 4, 63,
    70, 73, 80, 89, 94, 96
Touchstone Television, 2, 50, 59, 60, 81, 89
Touchwood Pacific Partners I, 94

Towne, Robert, 51
Toys R Us, 61
Toy Story, 139, 140, 160, 161, 202n33
Toy Story franchise, 161
Toy Story 2, 23
Tri-Star (TriStar), 57, 65, 96
Trites, Roberta, 79
Tron, 19, 24, 33, 35, 36, 37, 38, 43, 47, 87, 140
Trousdale, Gary, 1, 86, 97, 142, 161
Tune, Tommy, 27, 98, 99
Turner, Craig, 147
Turner, Tina, 90, 163
Turner & Hooch, 73
Turteltaub, Jon, 142
Twiggy, 27
Twilight: Los Angeles, 1992, 133
Tyler, Liv, 141
Typhoon Lagoon, 72, 90

Uhry, Alfred, 148
Ulvaeus, Björn, 138
"Under the Sea," 67, 79, 82, 88, 89, 162
United Artists, 141
Universal, 9, 10, 24, 27, 29, 56, 57, 62, 71, 90,
    96, 111, 117, 118, 164, 168
Universal Theatre Group, 9
Unkrich, Lee, 15
Untouchables, The, 69
UPN, 140

Van Gelder, Lawrence, 121
VCR, 36, 56
Veber, Francis, 70
Vestron, 69
Viacom, 140
Victor/Victoria, 119
Viertel, Jack, 89–90
Viertel, Tom, 125
Vogel, Paula, 164
Vonnegut, Kurt, 28

Wagner, Richard, 15, 16
Wainwright, Rupert, 139
Waiting for Godot, 77
"Waiting on a Miracle," 159, 160
Waitress, 163
Waking Sleeping Beauty, 79
Walker, Card, 2, 6, 29, 38, 46, 49
Walsh, Michael, 144
Walsh, Thommie, 126
Walt Disney Records, 94
Walt Disney's Magic Kingdom on Ice, 47
WarGames, 36
Warner, Jack, 139
Warner Bros., 2, 28, 45, 46, 49, 51, 54, 57, 69,
    70, 71, 72, 73, 93, 96, 97, 117, 139, 142
Warner Communications, 28

Warner Theatrical Productions, 9, 28
Washington, Denzel, 163
Wasko, Janet, 6, 176n20
Wasser, Frederick, 56
Wasserstein, Wendy, 74
Waters, John, 82
Watson, Emma, 167
Watson, Ray, 48
Way We Were, The, 63
WB, The, 140
"We Don't Talk About Bruno," 159
Weidman, John, 134
Weil, Cynthia, 89
Weill, Kurt, 79
Weir, Peter, 73
Weisman, Sam, 139
Weitzman, Ira, 39, 106, 126, 195n68
Wells, Frank, 84, 137, 142; contributions to
    Disney, 5, 6, 25, 62–63; death, 137–138,
    140–141; hiring, 2, 45, 49, 53, 54, 176n20
Wells, Simon, 111, 140
West, Matt, 115
West End, 19, 24, 69, 76, 93, 99, 127
West Side Story, 15, 85, 103, 109, 148
What's Love Got to Do with It?, 90
Wheeler, Hugh, 27, 39
Where the Heart Is, 95
Whistle Down the Wind, 144
White, Betty, 60, 104
White, Jesse, 112
Who Censored Roger Rabbit?, 72
Who Framed Roger Rabbit, 4, 71, 72, 100,
    111, 117, 166
"Whole New World, A," 116, 175n5
Who's Tommy, The, 132
Wilder, Billy, 100
Wilhite, Tom, 28, 29, 30, 33, 36, 38, 46, 47,
    48, 54, 183n70
Williams, Esther, 105
Williams, Mark, 7
Williams, Richard, 72, 100
Williams, Robin, 77, 104, 116, 138, 142
Williams, Tennessee, 164
Will Rogers Follies, The, 99, 119
Wills, John, 176n20
Wilmington, Michael, 89
Wilson, August, 74, 99
Wilson, Edwin, 132

Winfrey, Oprah, 155
Winnie the Pooh and Tigger Too, 31
Wise, Kirk, 1, 97, 105, 142, 161
Wise, Robert, 111
Witchel, Alex, 119
Witt, Paul Junger, 50, 60
Wiz, The, 26
Wizard of Oz, The, 26, 80
Wolf, Gary K., 72
Wolf, Matt, 120
Wolf, Stacy, 26
Wolfe, George C., 17–18, 168
Woman of the Year: film, 28; show, 28, 119
Wonderful World of Disney, 162
Wong, B. D., 99
Woodside, Bruce, 11
Woolverton, Linda, 9, 166; *Beauty and the
    Beast* (film), 97, 101, 102, 104, 106–109;
    Beauty and the Beast (show), 127–128, 130,
    134; hiring, 92–93
Words with Music, 14
Work in Progress, 46, 89
WPA Theatre, 19, 24, 27, 28, 38, 39
Wright, Robert, 98
Wright, Samuel E., 82, 83, 89
Wuzzles, The, 59
Wyatt, Justin, 42, 57
Wyler, William, 39

Xanadu, 33
Xerox, 36

Yates, William R., 30
Yatra, Sebastián, 159
Yeston, Maury, 27, 38, 98
"You Must Love Me," 144
Young, Pete, 57, 58
Young Sherlock Holmes, 55
"You've Got a Friend in Me," 160

Zaslove, Alan, 138
Zemeckis, Robert, 4, 56, 72, 139
Ziegfeld, Florenz, 74, 125
Ziegfeld Follies, 99, 105, 122, 132
Zimmer, Hans, 138, 152
Zippel, David, 98
Zucker, David, 5, 29, 63
Zucker, Jerry, 5, 29, 63

About the Author

Peter C. Kunze is an assistant professor of communication at Tulane University. He holds a PhD in English from Florida State University as well as a PhD in media studies from the University of Texas at Austin. His research has appeared in *Feminist Media Studies*, *Black Camera*, *The Velvet Light Trap*, *Creative Industries*, and the *Historical Journal of Film, Radio, and Television*.